MySpace Dark Horse Presents™

FEATURING WORK BY

John Arcudi ★ Gabriel Bá ★ Peter Bagge ★ Matt Bernier ★ Haden Blackman
Frans Boukas ★ Brodie H. Brockie ★ Brian Churilla ★ Katie Cook ★ Ezra Claytan Daniels
Kieron Dwyer ★ Guy Davis ★ The Fillbäch Brothers ★ Bob Fingerman
Adam Gallardo ★ Rick Geary ★ Chris Grine ★ Ron Marz ★ Mike Mignola
Tony Millionaire ★ Fábio Moon ★ Steve Niles ★ Cary Nord ★ Núria Peris
Rick Remender ★ Luke Ross ★ Sergio Sandoval ★ Dave Stewart ★ Rebecca Sugar
Herb Trimpe ★ Adam Warren ★ Gerard Way ★ Joss Whedon

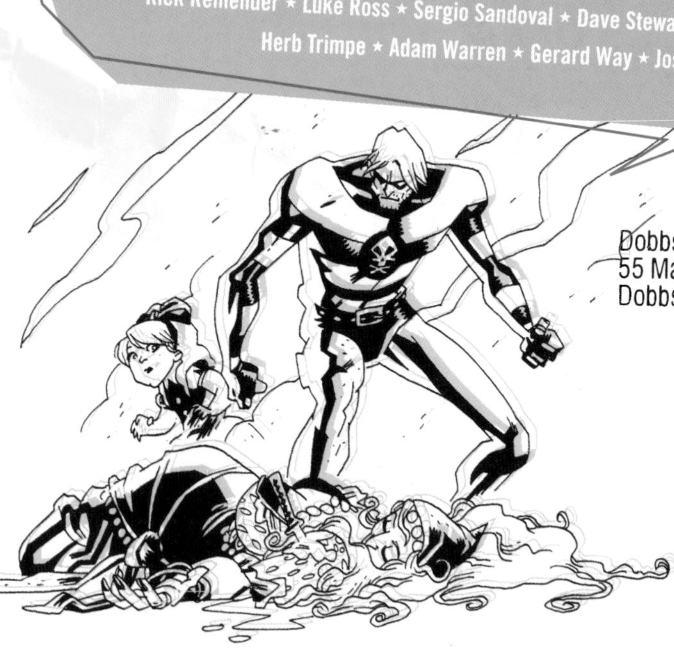

DARK HORSE BOOKS®

Publisher
MIKE RICHARDSON

Editors
SCOTT ALLIE & SIERRA HAHN

Collection Designer
SCOTT COOK

Sock Monkey: "In the Deep, Deep Woods"; *Founding Fathers Funnies Presents* Martha Washington in "A Widow's Worries" and George Washington in "Sticks and Stones"; *Gear School; Samurai: Heaven and Earth:* "The Forest"; and *Fear Agent:* "Nothing to Fear" edited by DAVE LAND.

"Eat the Walls" edited by KATIE MOODY.

Empowered: "Who da Übermensch?" edited by CHRIS WARNER with SAMANTHA ROBERTSON.

Chickenhare: "Random Bones" edited by SHAWNA GORE with JEMIAH JEFFERSON.

Special thanks to Ryan Jorgensen and Jeremy Atkins. Special thanks also to Sam Humphries and Jessica Chanen at MySpace. Thanks also to Tom Sniegoski and Micah Smith.

MYSPACE DARK HORSE PRESENTS™ VOLUME ONE

This volume prints the online comic-book anthology *MySpace Dark Horse Presents* #1–6.

Published by
Dark Horse Books
A division of
Dark Horse Comics, Inc.
10956 SE Main Street
Milwaukie, OR 97222

darkhorse.com

To find a comics shop in your area, call the Comic Shop Locator Service toll-free at (888) 266-4226.

First edition: September 2008
ISBN 978-1-59307-998-7

10 9 8 7 6 5 4 3 2 1
Printed in China

OUR STORY SO FAR . . .

MySpace Dark Horse Presents was conceived over a breakfast table in the best vegan restaurant in New York's East Village. It was after the 2007 New York Comic Con, which is fast becoming my favorite show, not least of all because it's given me the book you hold in your hands. Although the *book* was never the point . . .

Our publicist, Jeremy Atkins, and Sam Humphries, the marketing director at MySpace, had both made a lot of things happen for our company on that website. Breakfast seemed a great way to wrap up the New York trip. Our shared love of comics— way beyond the love workaholics usually have for their jobs—made it easy to spend a morning talking about books we love, the ones we missed, and things that hadn't been done before. Which sums up *MySpace Dark Horse Presents*.

In 1986, Dark Horse Comics was born with the release of the black-and-white anthology *Dark Horse Presents* #1, featuring the first appearance of Paul Chadwick's *Concrete*. The first *Sin City* series ran in *DHP* in 1991 to 1992. *DHP* not only featured the big names; the book also debuted a lot of new talent. But it's *widely known* (i.e., not entirely true) that anthologies don't sell, and *DHP* had its ups and downs. In 2000, the final issue was published, with the first Dark Horse appearance of *The Goon*.

Part of me wants to make an analogy between the meatless sausage we were eating that morning in New York and a comics industry bereft of great anthologies, but I'll just say we saw a hole that needed filling.

We also talked about the challenge of selling comics online. It's easy to get comics to people digitally, but no one's come up with a good way to bring money in.

Sometimes it takes you a minute to realize you're the one who can fix a problem. The lack of great anthologies and the trick of selling comics online led us to *MySpace Dark Horse Presents*: a full-color, monthly anthology, featuring heavy hitters like Mignola, Whedon, and Niles, as well as new talent—Ezra Claytan Daniels, Katie Cook, Brian Churilla, Matt Bernier, Rebecca Sugar, and Frans Boukas—discovered on the world's top networking site. And the best part, the way we solved the riddle of making money online, was to give the damn thing away. Rather than solving the revenue-stream riddle, we made the bold move to abandon income, to write it off as a marketing expense, and make up for it in volume. I obviously never went to business school.

Of course, we appreciate you buying this book . . .

Mike Richardson, Dark Horse's progenitor, went for the idea immediately. Sam's bosses did too. Randy Stradley, the original editor on *DHP*, who'd steered it back from some dark times before putting it to rest in 2000, agreed to let me edit the new incarnation, while pitching in occasionally for a story.

All we needed were some stories.

It came together with "Sugarshock." I asked Joss Whedon if he'd take time from *Buffy*, which was just starting up. I thought he'd say no, but he said he'd think about it. I wasn't counting on it for the first issue, until one night he e-mailed to say he was stuck on *Buffy* because all he could think about was this thing he wanted to do for *DHP*. Eight pages arrived the next day, and I laughed my ass off reading it. Brand-new characters from Joss helped make the live launch of *MDHP* one of the biggest events of San Diego 2007.

Thanks to all the creators, and Sam, Jeremy, Randy, and Mike, for making this possible. Also Jessica Chanen and everybody at MySpace, and Lia Ribacchi and the Dark Horse designers who set the look for *MDHP* online and in print. Thanks to *MDHP*'s main production man, Dan Jackson, Dark Horse's marketing folks, and the other editors who pitched in—in particular Dave Land, who delivers a story every issue. And thanks to my coeditor, Sierra Hahn, who takes over the book as we head into the second year. Two heads have definitely proven better than one.

Scott Allie

Athens, Ohio
May 7, 2008

INCLUDED AT NO EXTRA COST

5 SUGARSHOCK
Story – Joss Whedon
Art – Fábio Moon
Colors – Dave Stewart
Letters – Nate Piekos of Blambot®

29 SOCK MONKEY
Story and Art – Tony Millionaire
Colors – Jim Campbell

31 A CIRCUIT CLOSED
Story and Art – Ezra Claytan Daniels
Colors – Richard Lee

41 THE COMIC CON MURDER CASE
Story and Art – Rick Geary

43 THE UMBRELLA ACADEMY
Story – Gerard Way
Art – Gabriel Bá
Colors – Dave Stewart
Letters – Nate Piekos of Blambot®

51 FOUNDING FATHERS FUNNIES
Story and Art – Peter Bagge

53 GEAR SCHOOL
Story – Adam Gallardo
Art and Colors –
Núria Peris and Sergio Sandoval

61 SAMURAI
Story – Ron Marz
Art – Luke Ross
Colors – Dan Jackson
Letters – Dave Lanphear

69 EMPOWERED
Story and Art – Adam Warren
Colors – Guru eFX

77 CHICKENHARE
Story and Art – Chris Grine

79 THE NOCTURNAL ADVENTURES OF SCRATCH AND SUCK
Story – Steve Niles
Art – Brian Churilla
Colors – Jeremy Shepherd
Letters – Nate Piekos of Blambot®

87 TRICKS OF THE TRADE
Story – Brodie H. Brockie
Art – Katie Cook
Letters – Nate Piekos of Blambot®

95 THE AXEMAN
Story – Haden Blackman
Art – Cary Nord
Colors – Dave Stewart
Letters – Nate Piekos of Blambot®

111 THE CHRISTMAS SPIRIT
Story – Mike Mignola
Art – Guy Davis
Colors – Dave Stewart
Letters – Clem Robins

119 EAT THE WALLS
Story and Art – Matt Bernier

121 FEAR AGENT
Story – Rick Remender
Pencils – Kieron Dwyer
Inks – Hilary Barta
Colors – John Rauch & Michelle Madsen
Letters – Rus Wooten

137 THE GOON
CHAPTER ONE:
"THE BIG BLUE NOTE"
Story and Art – The Fillbäch Brothers
Colors – Wil Glass

CHAPTER TWO:
"BOGGED DOWN AT BUSH STREET"
Story and Colors – Rebecca Sugar
Art – Frans Boukas
Letters – Nates Piekos of Blambot®

CHAPTER THREE:
"A REASONABLE AMOUNT OF TROUBLE"
Story – John Arcudi
Pencils – Herb Trimpe
Inks – Al Milgrom
Colors – Dan Jackson
Letters – Nates Piekos of Blambot®

CHAPTER FOUR:
"ENTER THE PECKER"
Story and Art – Bob Fingerman

163 MYSPACE DARK HORSE PRESENTS MISCELLANY

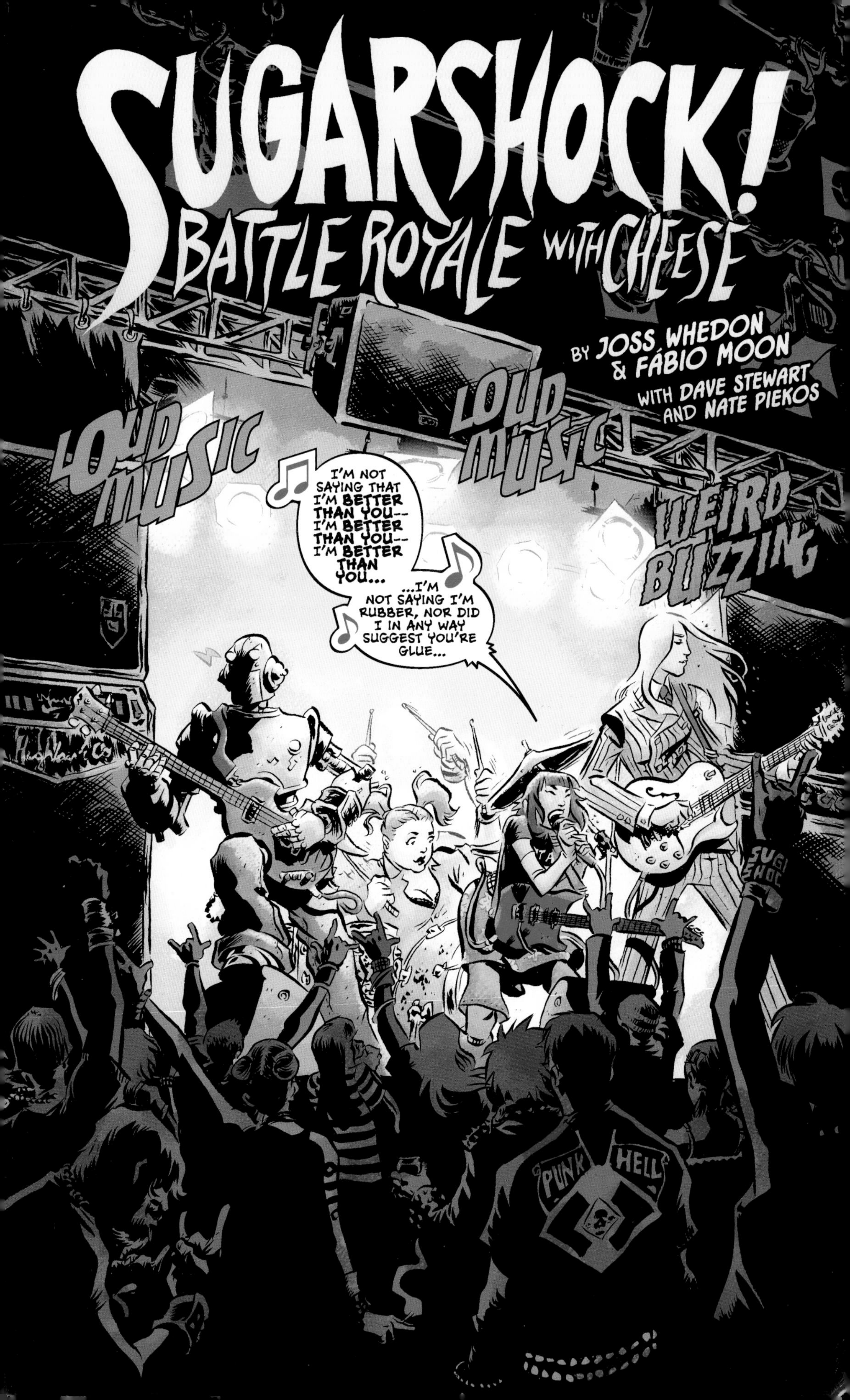

SUGARSHOCK!
BATTLE ROYALE WITH CHEESE
BY JOSS WHEDON & FÁBIO MOON
WITH DAVE STEWART AND NATE PIEKOS
LOUD MUSIC
LOUD MUSIC
WEIRD BUZZING
I'M NOT SAYING THAT I'M BETTER THAN YOU-- I'M BETTER THAN YOU-- I'M BETTER THAN YOU...
...I'M NOT SAYING I'M RUBBER, NOR DID I IN ANY WAY SUGGEST YOU'RE GLUE...
PUNK
HELL

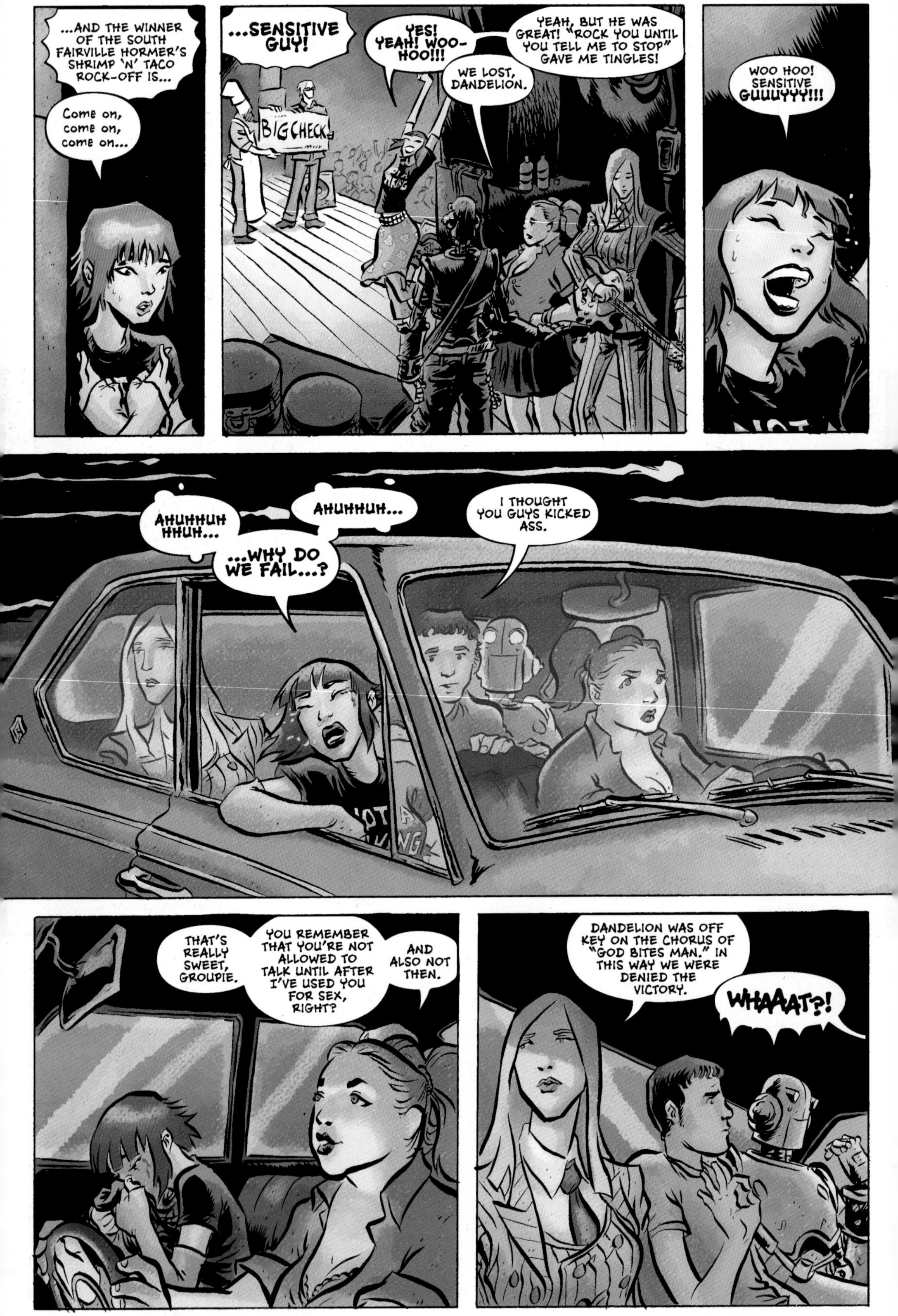
...AND THE WINNER OF THE SOUTH FAIRVILLE HORMER'S SHRIMP 'N' TACO ROCK-OFF IS...
Come on, come on, come on...
...SENSITIVE GUY!
BIG CHECK
YES! YEAH! WOO-HOO!!!
WE LOST, DANDELION.
YEAH, BUT HE WAS GREAT! "ROCK YOU UNTIL YOU TELL ME TO STOP" GAVE ME TINGLES!
WOO HOO! SENSITIVE GUUUYYY!!!
AHUHHUH HHUH...
AHUHHUH...
...WHY DO WE FAIL...?
I THOUGHT YOU GUYS KICKED ASS.
THAT'S REALLY SWEET, GROUPIE.
YOU REMEMBER THAT YOU'RE NOT ALLOWED TO TALK UNTIL AFTER I'VE USED YOU FOR SEX, RIGHT?
AND ALSO NOT THEN.
DANDELION WAS OFF KEY ON THE CHORUS OF "GOD BITES MAN." IN THIS WAY WE WERE DENIED THE VICTORY.
WHAAAT?!

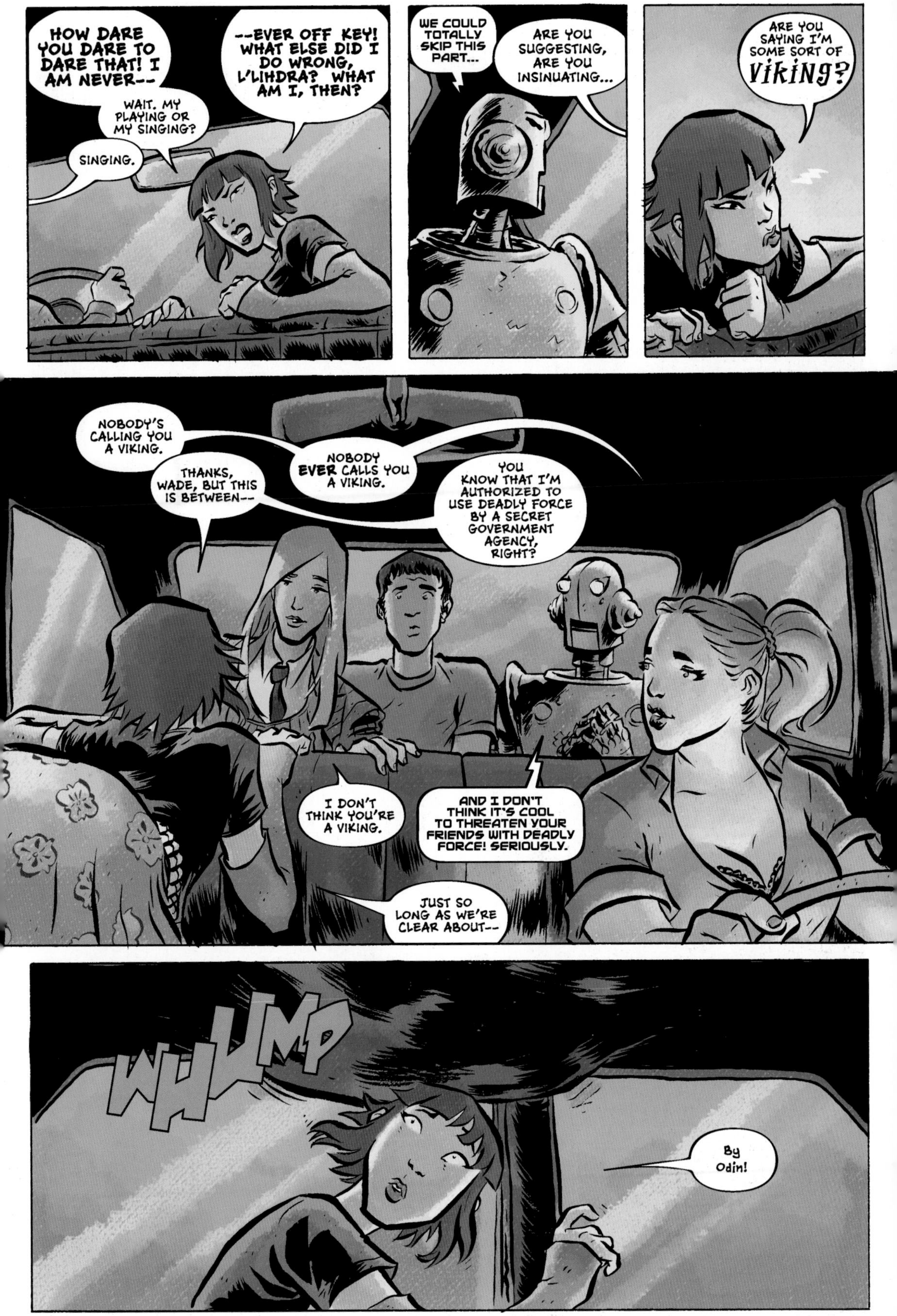
HOW DARE YOU DARE TO DARE THAT! I AM NEVER--
WAIT. MY PLAYING OR MY SINGING?
SINGING.
--EVER OFF KEY! WHAT ELSE DID I DO WRONG, L'LIHDRA? WHAT AM I, THEN?
WE COULD TOTALLY SKIP THIS PART...
ARE YOU SUGGESTING, ARE YOU INSINUATING...
ARE YOU SAYING I'M SOME SORT OF VIKING?
NOBODY'S CALLING YOU A VIKING.
NOBODY EVER CALLS YOU A VIKING.
THANKS, WADE, BUT THIS IS BETWEEN--
YOU KNOW THAT I'M AUTHORIZED TO USE DEADLY FORCE BY A SECRET GOVERNMENT AGENCY, RIGHT?
I DON'T THINK YOU'RE A VIKING.
AND I DON'T THINK IT'S COOL TO THREATEN YOUR FRIENDS WITH DEADLY FORCE! SERIOUSLY.
JUST SO LONG AS WE'RE CLEAR ABOUT--
WHUMP
By Odin!

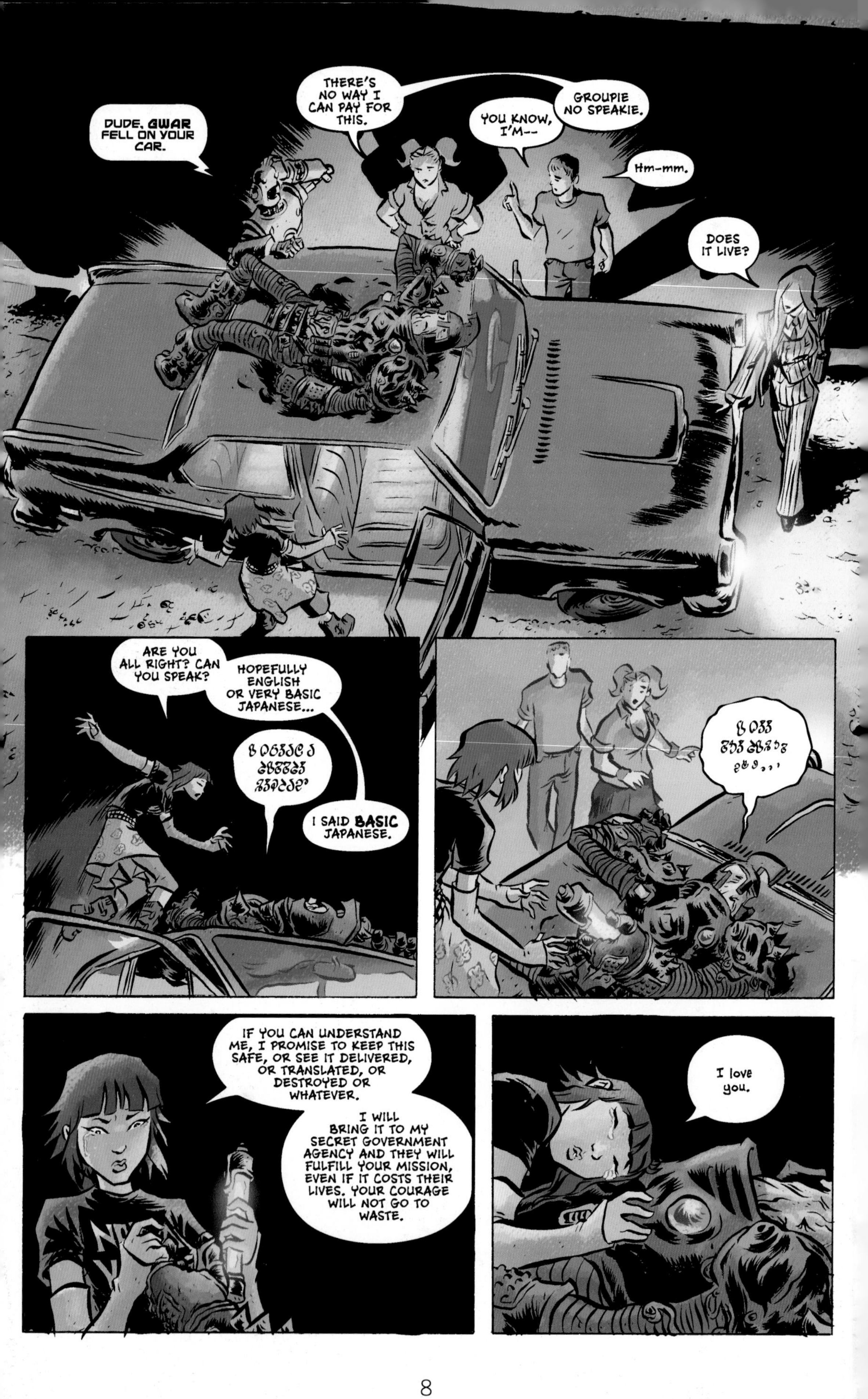
DUDE. GWAR FELL ON YOUR CAR.
THERE'S NO WAY I CAN PAY FOR THIS.
YOU KNOW, I'M--
GROUPIE NO SPEAKIE.
Hm-mm.
DOES IT LIVE?
ARE YOU ALL RIGHT? CAN YOU SPEAK?
HOPEFULLY ENGLISH OR VERY BASIC JAPANESE...
I SAID BASIC JAPANESE.
IF YOU CAN UNDERSTAND ME, I PROMISE TO KEEP THIS SAFE, OR SEE IT DELIVERED, OR TRANSLATED, OR DESTROYED OR WHATEVER.
I WILL BRING IT TO MY SECRET GOVERNMENT AGENCY AND THEY WILL FULFILL YOUR MISSION, EVEN IF IT COSTS THEIR LIVES. YOUR COURAGE WILL NOT GO TO WASTE.
I love you.

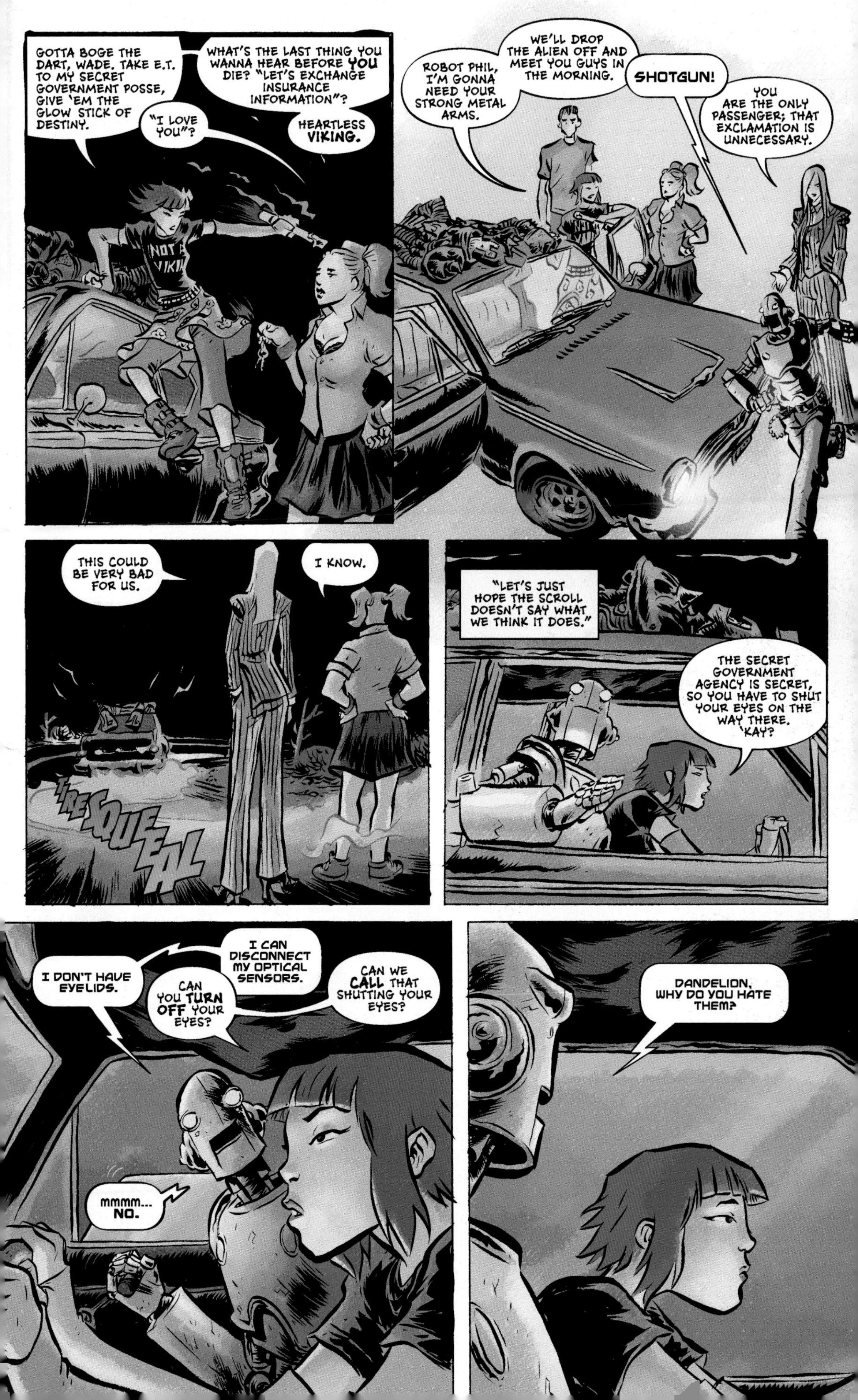
GOTTA BOGE THE DART, WADE. TAKE E.T. TO MY SECRET GOVERNMENT POSSE, GIVE 'EM THE GLOW STICK OF DESTINY.
WHAT'S THE LAST THING YOU WANNA HEAR BEFORE YOU DIE? "LET'S EXCHANGE INSURANCE INFORMATION"?
"I LOVE YOU"?
HEARTLESS VIKING.
ROBOT PHIL, I'M GONNA NEED YOUR STRONG METAL ARMS.
WE'LL DROP THE ALIEN OFF AND MEET YOU GUYS IN THE MORNING.
SHOTGUN!
YOU ARE THE ONLY PASSENGER; THAT EXCLAMATION IS UNNECESSARY.
THIS COULD BE VERY BAD FOR US.
I KNOW.
TIRE SQUEEAL
"LET'S JUST HOPE THE SCROLL DOESN'T SAY WHAT WE THINK IT DOES."
THE SECRET GOVERNMENT AGENCY IS SECRET, SO YOU HAVE TO SHUT YOUR EYES ON THE WAY THERE. 'KAY?
I DON'T HAVE EYELIDS.
I CAN DISCONNECT MY OPTICAL SENSORS.
CAN YOU TURN OFF YOUR EYES?
CAN WE CALL THAT SHUTTING YOUR EYES?
MMMM... NO.
DANDELION, WHY DO YOU HATE THEM?

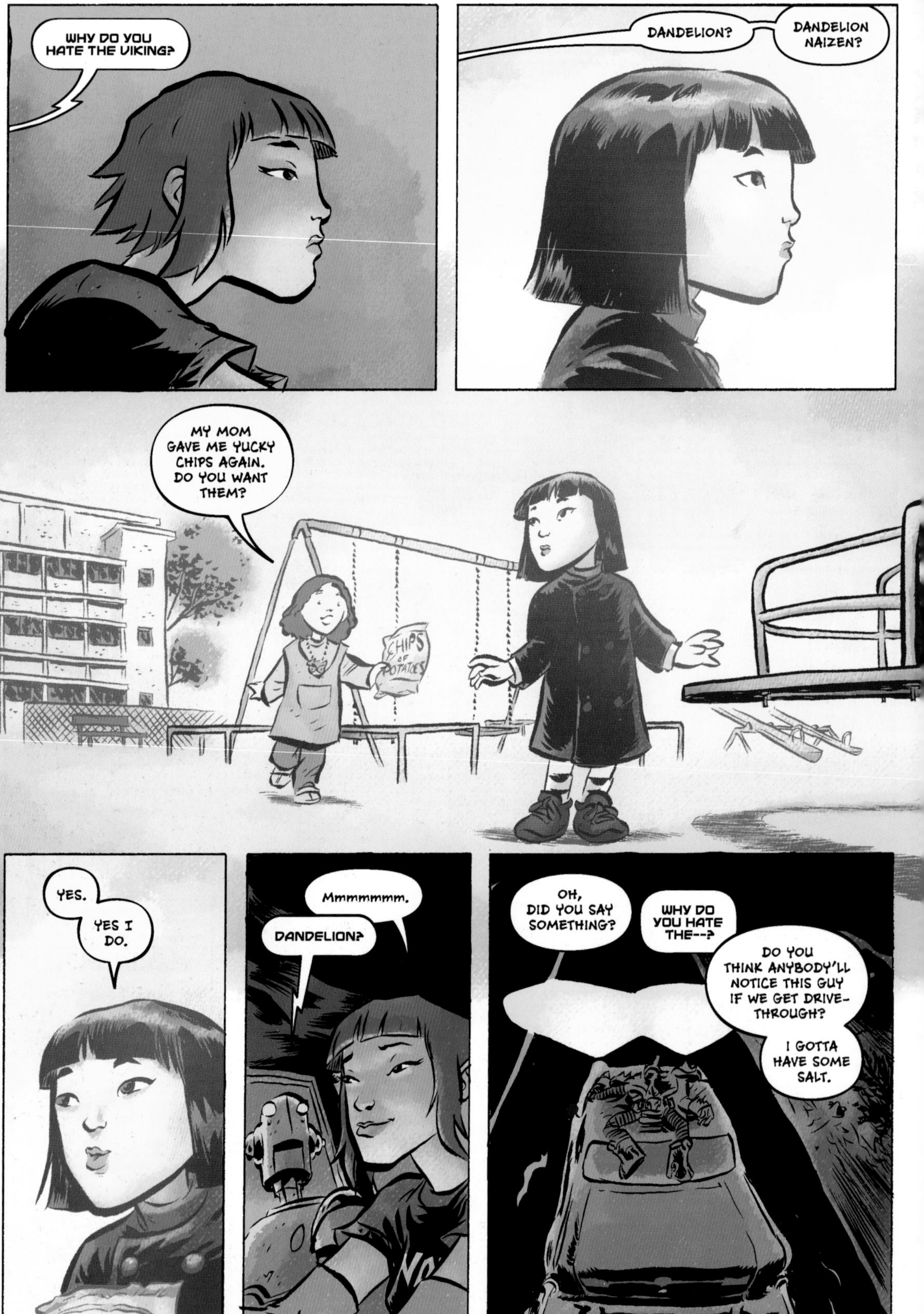
WHY DO YOU HATE THE VIKING?
DANDELION?
DANDELION NAIZEN?
MY MOM GAVE ME YUCKY CHIPS AGAIN. DO YOU WANT THEM?
CHIPS OF POTATOES
YES.
YES I DO.
CHIPS OF
Mmmmmmm.
DANDELION?
OH, DID YOU SAY SOMETHING?
WHY DO YOU HATE THE--?
DO YOU THINK ANYBODY'LL NOTICE THIS GUY IF WE GET DRIVE-THROUGH?
I GOTTA HAVE SOME SALT.

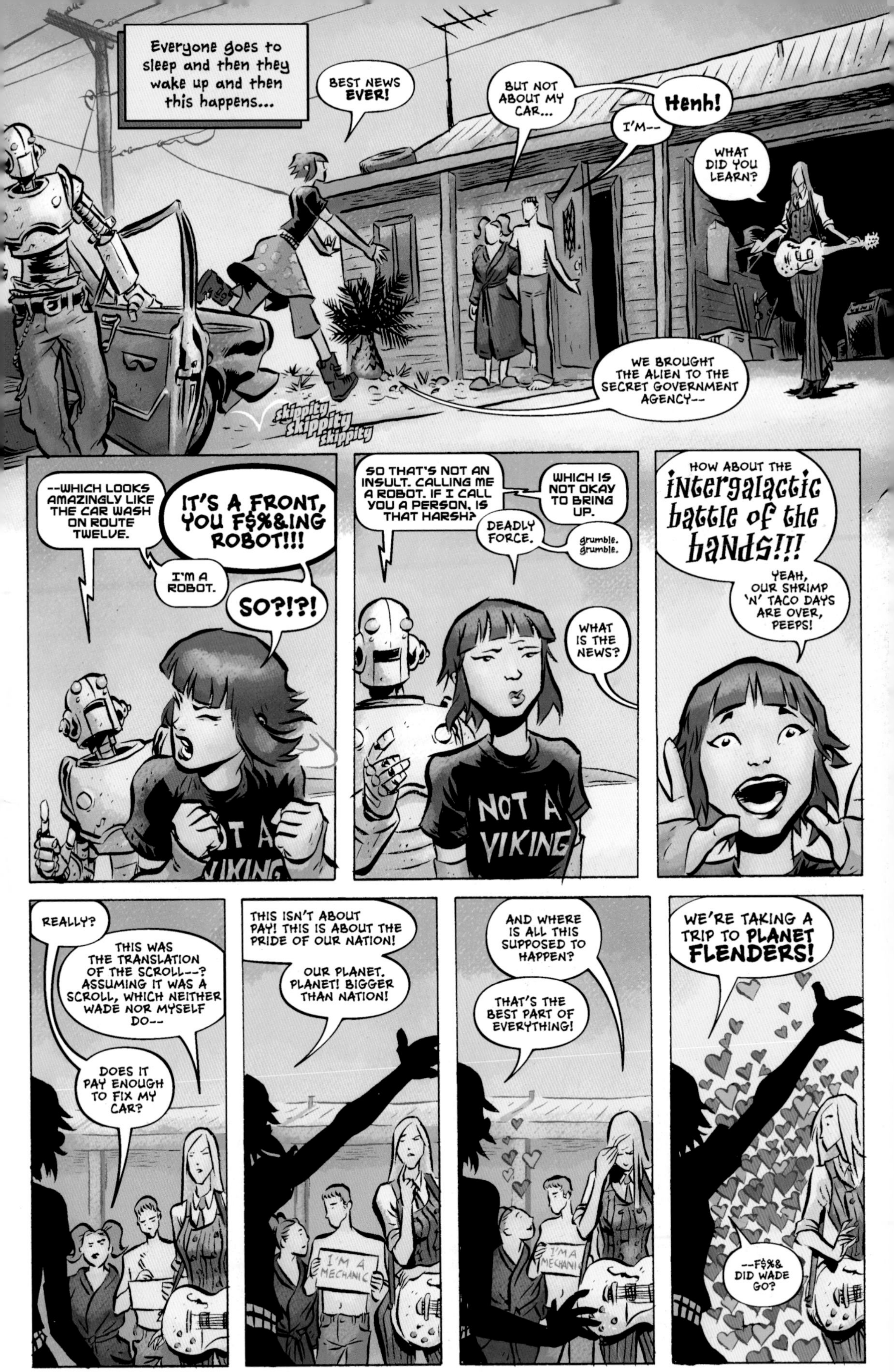
Everyone goes to sleep and then they wake up and then this happens...
BEST NEWS EVER!
BUT NOT ABOUT MY CAR...
Henh!
I'M--
WHAT DID YOU LEARN?
WE BROUGHT THE ALIEN TO THE SECRET GOVERNMENT AGENCY--
skippity skippity skippity
--WHICH LOOKS AMAZINGLY LIKE THE CAR WASH ON ROUTE TWELVE.
IT'S A FRONT, YOU F$%&ING ROBOT!!!
I'M A ROBOT.
SO?!?!
SO THAT'S NOT AN INSULT. CALLING ME A ROBOT. IF I CALL YOU A PERSON, IS THAT HARSH?
WHICH IS NOT OKAY TO BRING UP.
DEADLY FORCE.
grumble. grumble.
WHAT IS THE NEWS?
NOT A VIKING
HOW ABOUT THE intergalactic battle of the bands!!!
YEAH, OUR SHRIMP 'N' TACO DAYS ARE OVER, PEEPS!
REALLY?
THIS WAS THE TRANSLATION OF THE SCROLL--? ASSUMING IT WAS A SCROLL, WHICH NEITHER WADE NOR MYSELF DO--
DOES IT PAY ENOUGH TO FIX MY CAR?
THIS ISN'T ABOUT PAY! THIS IS ABOUT THE PRIDE OF OUR NATION!
OUR PLANET. PLANET! BIGGER THAN NATION!
I'M A MECHANIC
AND WHERE IS ALL THIS SUPPOSED TO HAPPEN?
THAT'S THE BEST PART OF EVERYTHING!
WE'RE TAKING A TRIP TO PLANET FLENDERS!
--F$%& DID WADE GO?

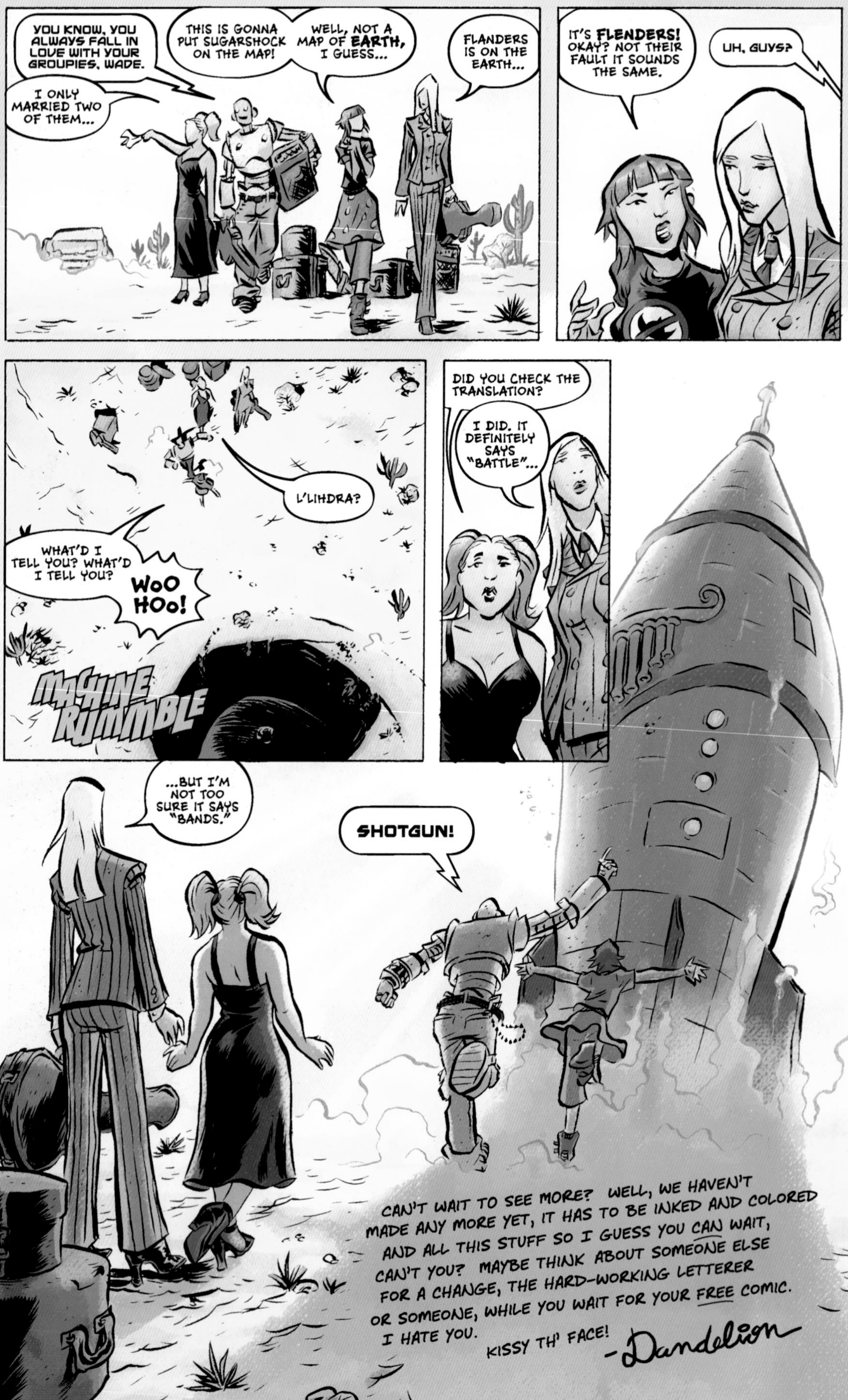

YOU KNOW, YOU ALWAYS FALL IN LOVE WITH YOUR GROUPIES, WADE.
I ONLY MARRIED TWO OF THEM...
THIS IS GONNA PUT SUGARSHOCK ON THE MAP!
WELL, NOT A MAP OF EARTH, I GUESS...
FLANDERS IS ON THE EARTH...
IT'S FLENDERS! OKAY? NOT THEIR FAULT IT SOUNDS THE SAME.
UH, GUYS?
L'LIHDRA?
WHAT'D I TELL YOU? WHAT'D I TELL YOU?
WOO HOO!
MACHINE RUMMBLE
DID YOU CHECK THE TRANSLATION?
I DID. IT DEFINITELY SAYS "BATTLE"...
...BUT I'M NOT TOO SURE IT SAYS "BANDS."
SHOTGUN!
CAN'T WAIT TO SEE MORE? WELL, WE HAVEN'T MADE ANY MORE YET, IT HAS TO BE INKED AND COLORED AND ALL THIS STUFF SO I GUESS YOU CAN WAIT, CAN'T YOU? MAYBE THINK ABOUT SOMEONE ELSE FOR A CHANGE, THE HARD-WORKING LETTERER OR SOMEONE, WHILE YOU WAIT FOR YOUR FREE COMIC. I HATE YOU.
KISSY TH' FACE!
-Dandelion

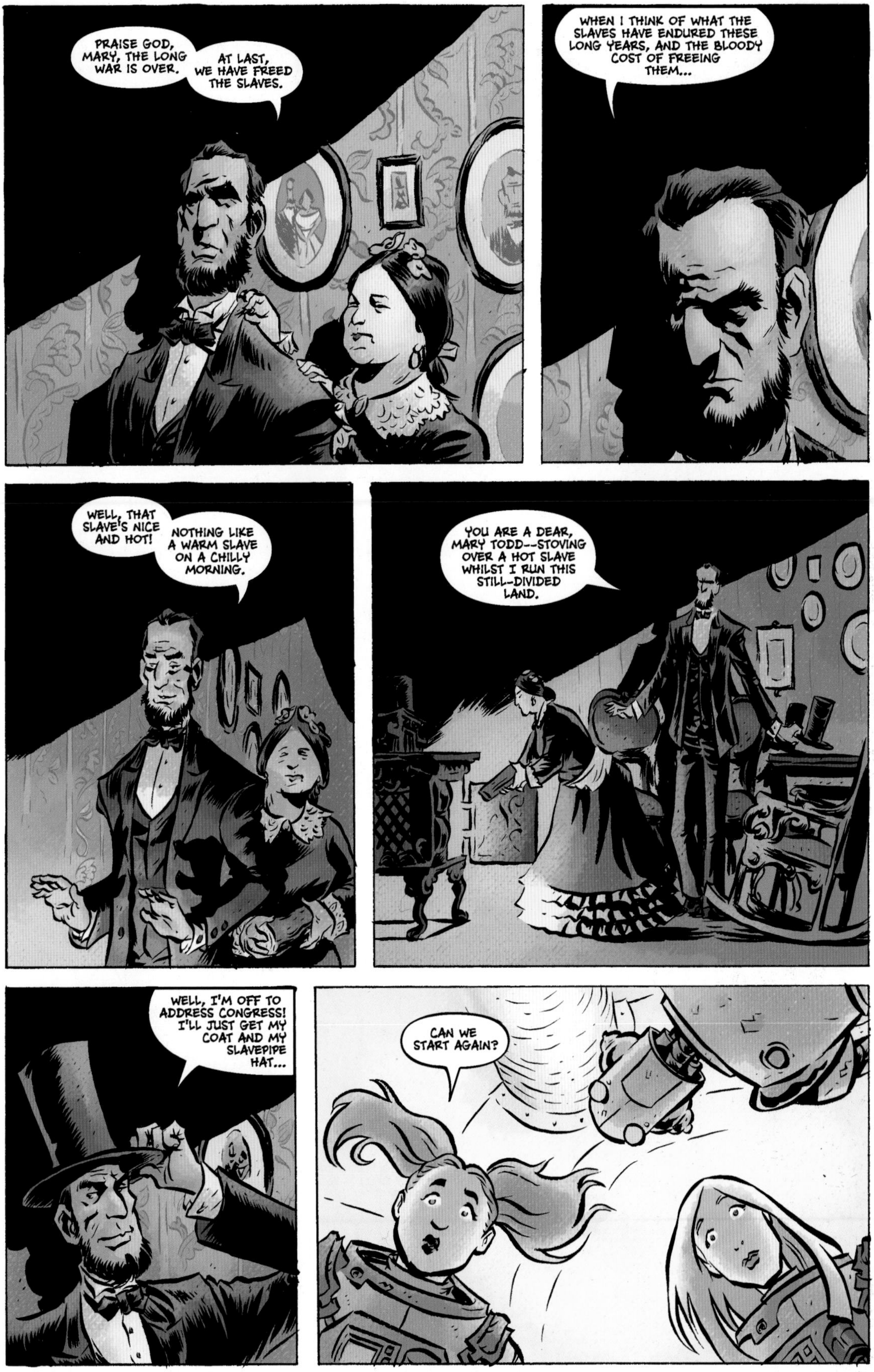
PRAISE GOD, MARY, THE LONG WAR IS OVER.
AT LAST, WE HAVE FREED THE SLAVES.
WHEN I THINK OF WHAT THE SLAVES HAVE ENDURED THESE LONG YEARS, AND THE BLOODY COST OF FREEING THEM...
WELL, THAT SLAVE'S NICE AND HOT!
NOTHING LIKE A WARM SLAVE ON A CHILLY MORNING.
YOU ARE A DEAR, MARY TODD--STOVING OVER A HOT SLAVE WHILST I RUN THIS STILL-DIVIDED LAND.
WELL, I'M OFF TO ADDRESS CONGRESS! I'LL JUST GET MY COAT AND MY SLAVEPIPE HAT...
CAN WE START AGAIN?

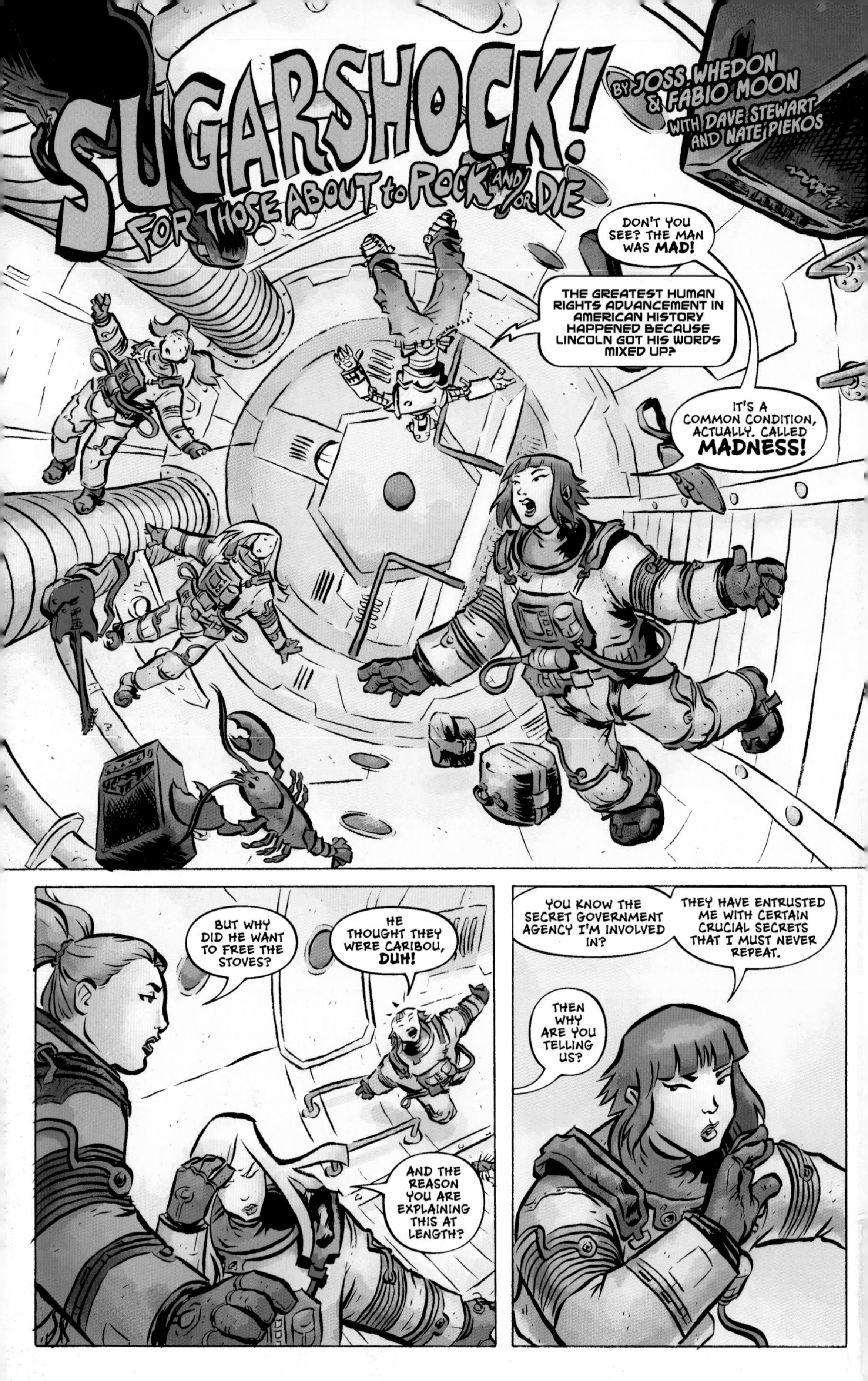
SUGARSHOCK!
FOR THOSE ABOUT TO ROCK AND/OR DIE
BY JOSS WHEDON & FABIO MOON
WITH DAVE STEWART AND NATE PIEKOS
DON'T YOU SEE? THE MAN WAS MAD!
THE GREATEST HUMAN RIGHTS ADVANCEMENT IN AMERICAN HISTORY HAPPENED BECAUSE LINCOLN GOT HIS WORDS MIXED UP?
IT'S A COMMON CONDITION, ACTUALLY. CALLED MADNESS!
BUT WHY DID HE WANT TO FREE THE STOVES?
HE THOUGHT THEY WERE CARIBOU, DUH!
AND THE REASON YOU ARE EXPLAINING THIS AT LENGTH?
YOU KNOW THE SECRET GOVERNMENT AGENCY I'M INVOLVED IN?
THEY HAVE ENTRUSTED ME WITH CERTAIN CRUCIAL SECRETS THAT I MUST NEVER REPEAT.
THEN WHY ARE YOU TELLING US?

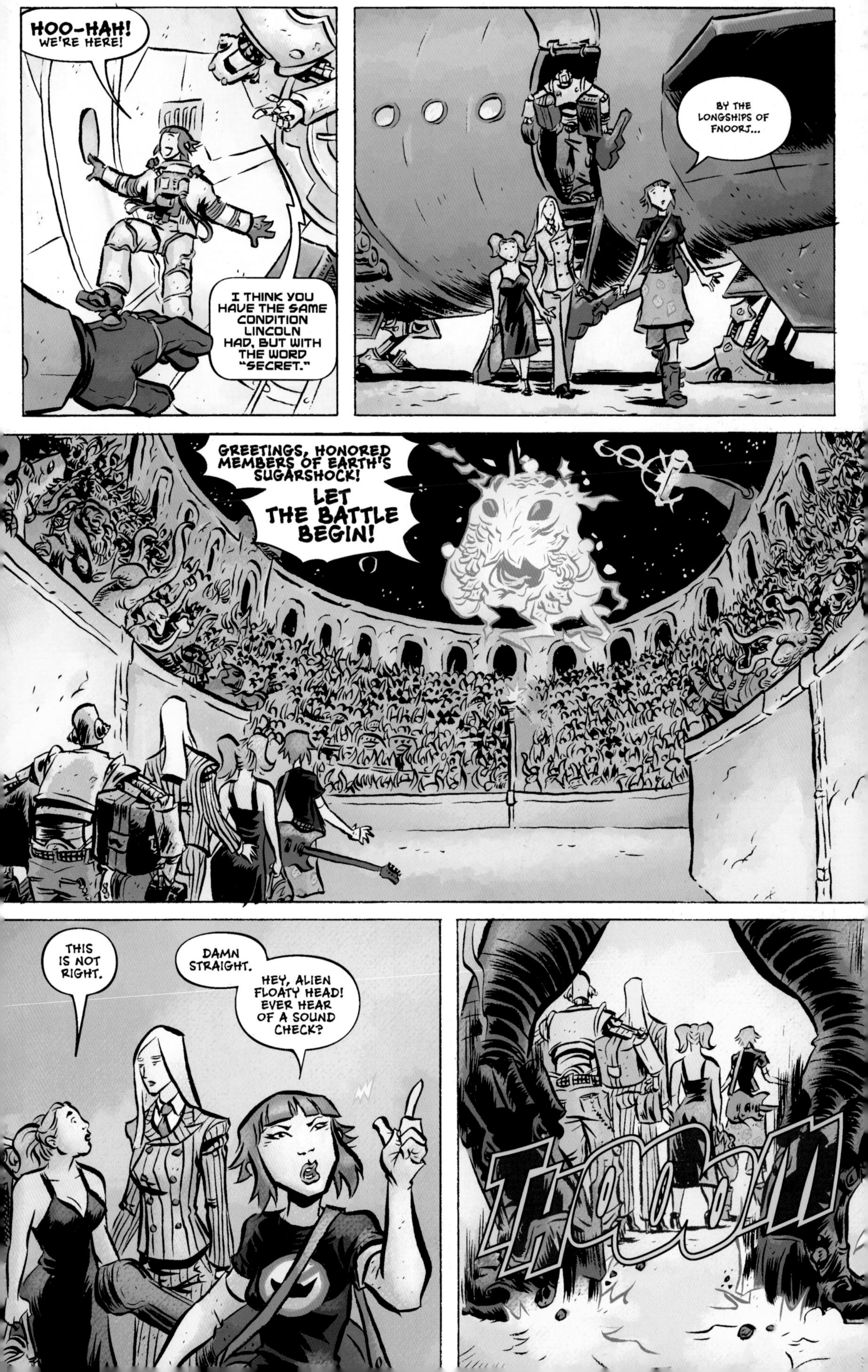
HOO-HAH! WE'RE HERE!
I THINK YOU HAVE THE SAME CONDITION LINCOLN HAD, BUT WITH THE WORD "SECRET."
BY THE LONGSHIPS OF FNOORJ...
GREETINGS, HONORED MEMBERS OF EARTH'S SUGARSHOCK!
LET THE BATTLE BEGIN!
THIS IS NOT RIGHT.
DAMN STRAIGHT.
HEY, ALIEN FLOATY HEAD! EVER HEAR OF A SOUND CHECK?

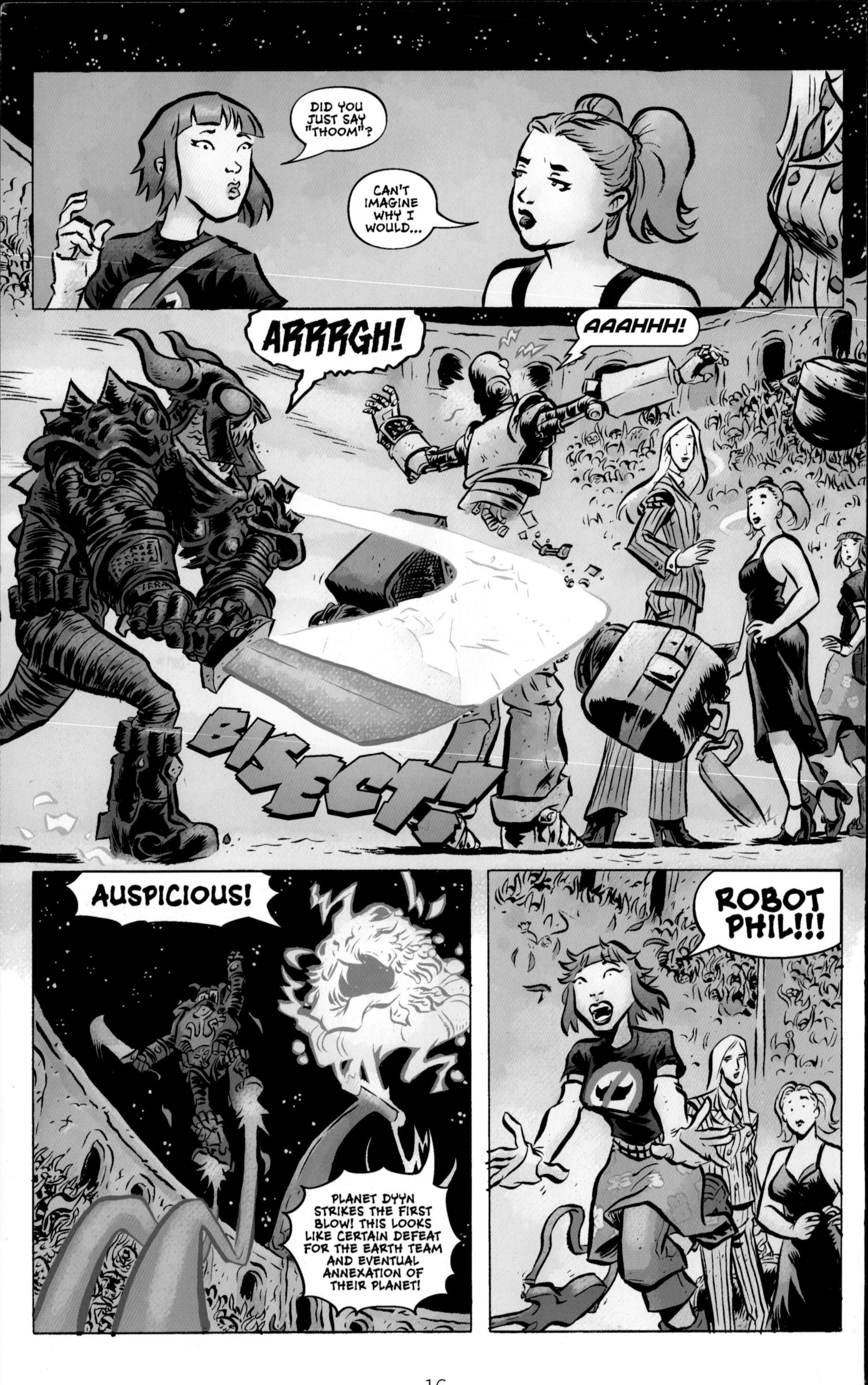

DID YOU JUST SAY "THOOM"?
CAN'T IMAGINE WHY I WOULD...
ARRRGH!
AAAHHH!
BISECT!
AUSPICIOUS!
PLANET DYYN STRIKES THE FIRST BLOW! THIS LOOKS LIKE CERTAIN DEFEAT FOR THE EARTH TEAM AND EVENTUAL ANNEXATION OF THEIR PLANET!
ROBOT PHIL!!!

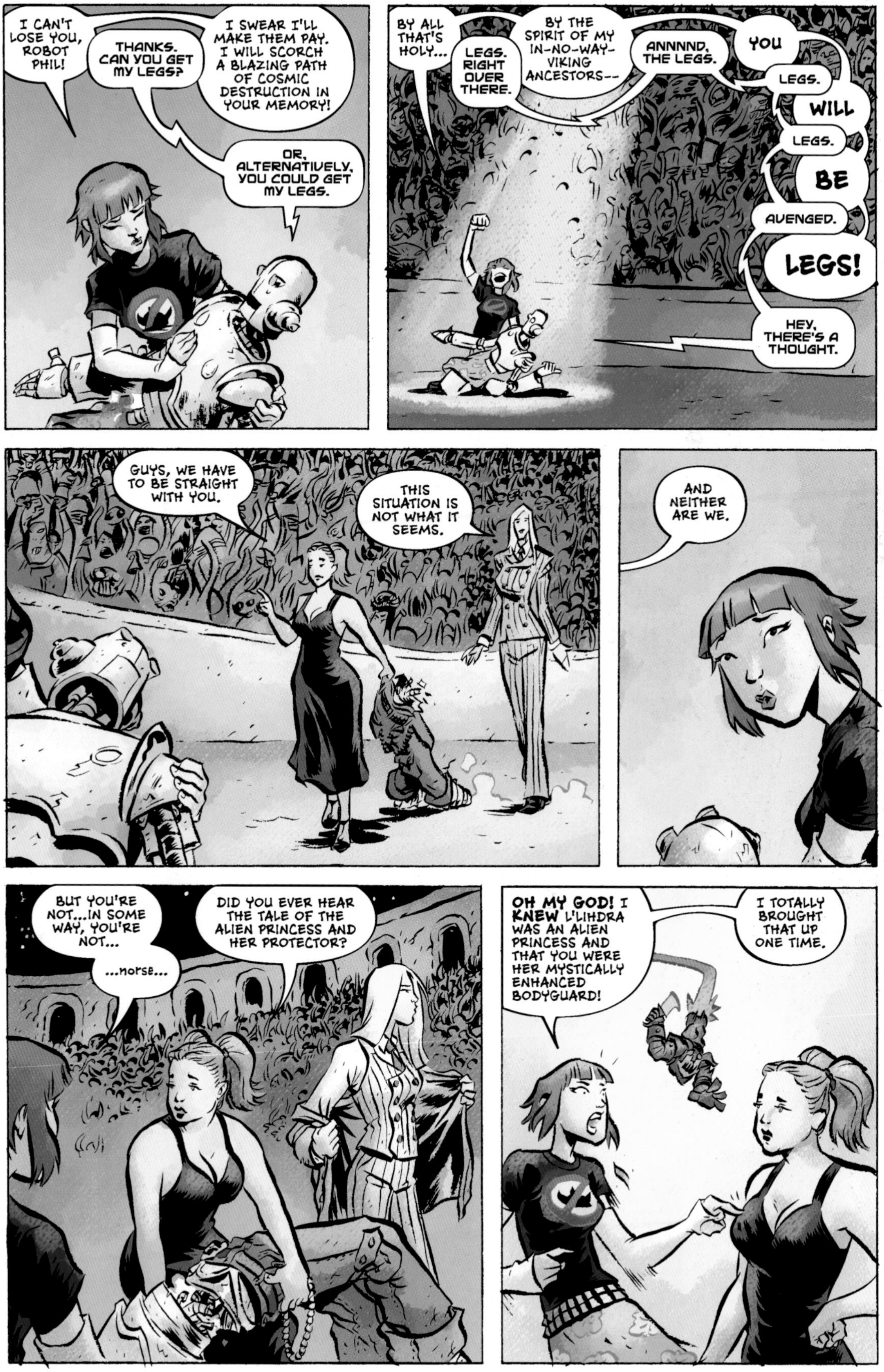
I CAN'T LOSE YOU, ROBOT PHIL!
I SWEAR I'LL MAKE THEM PAY. I WILL SCORCH A BLAZING PATH OF COSMIC DESTRUCTION IN YOUR MEMORY!
THANKS. CAN YOU GET MY LEGS?
OR, ALTERNATIVELY, YOU COULD GET MY LEGS.
BY ALL THAT'S HOLY...
BY THE SPIRIT OF MY IN-NO-WAY-VIKING ANCESTORS--
LEGS. RIGHT OVER THERE.
ANNNND, THE LEGS.
YOU
LEGS.
WILL
LEGS.
BE
AVENGED.
LEGS!
HEY, THERE'S A THOUGHT.
GUYS, WE HAVE TO BE STRAIGHT WITH YOU.
THIS SITUATION IS NOT WHAT IT SEEMS.
AND NEITHER ARE WE.
BUT YOU'RE NOT...IN SOME WAY, YOU'RE NOT...
...norse...
DID YOU EVER HEAR THE TALE OF THE ALIEN PRINCESS AND HER PROTECTOR?
OH MY GOD! I KNEW L'LIHDRA WAS AN ALIEN PRINCESS AND THAT YOU WERE HER MYSTICALLY ENHANCED BODYGUARD!
I TOTALLY BROUGHT THAT UP ONE TIME.

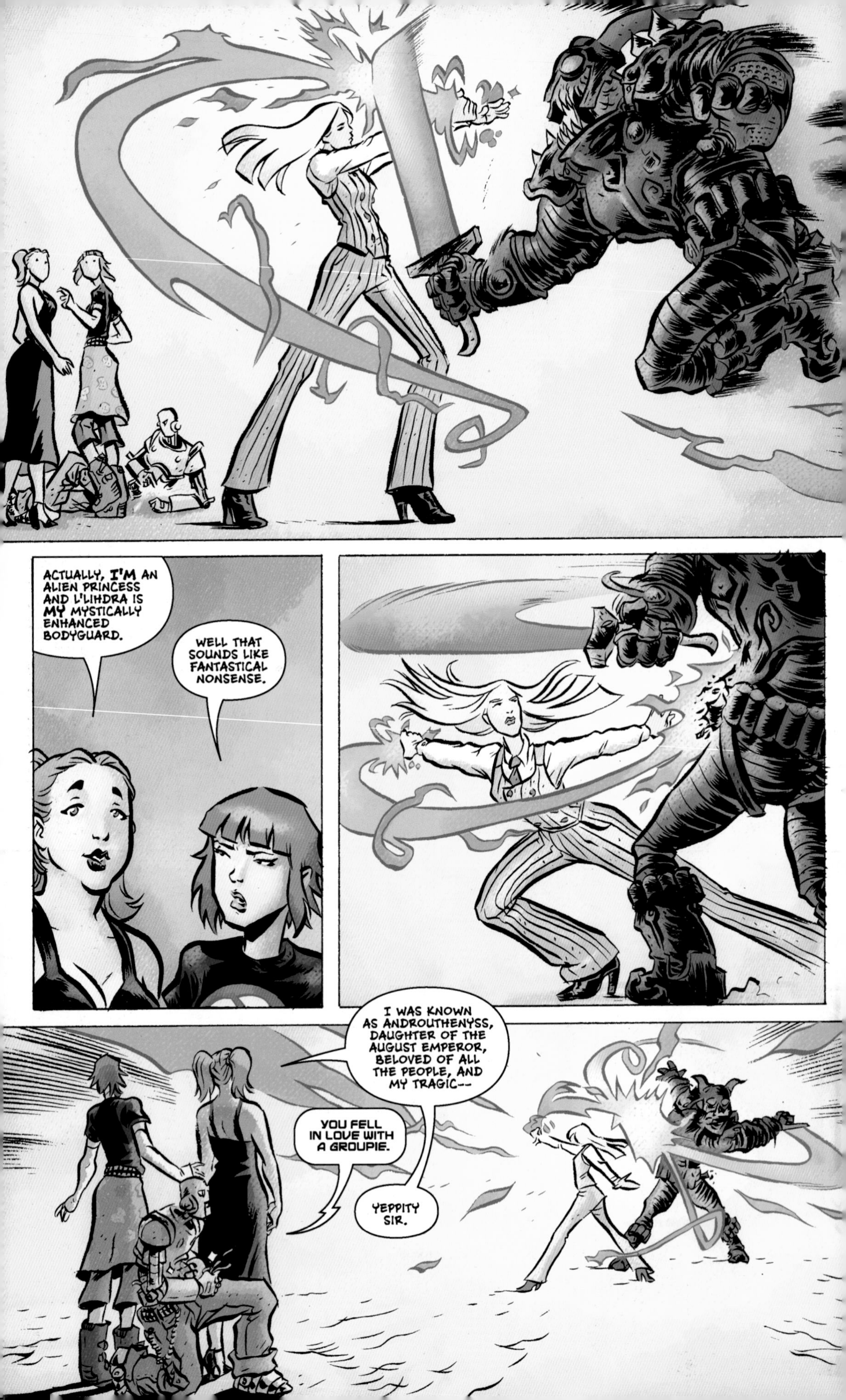
ACTUALLY, I'M AN ALIEN PRINCESS AND L'LIHDRA IS MY MYSTICALLY ENHANCED BODYGUARD.
WELL THAT SOUNDS LIKE FANTASTICAL NONSENSE.
I WAS KNOWN AS ANDROUTHENYSS, DAUGHTER OF THE AUGUST EMPEROR, BELOVED OF ALL THE PEOPLE, AND MY TRAGIC--
YOU FELL IN LOVE WITH A GROUPIE.
YEPPITY SIR.

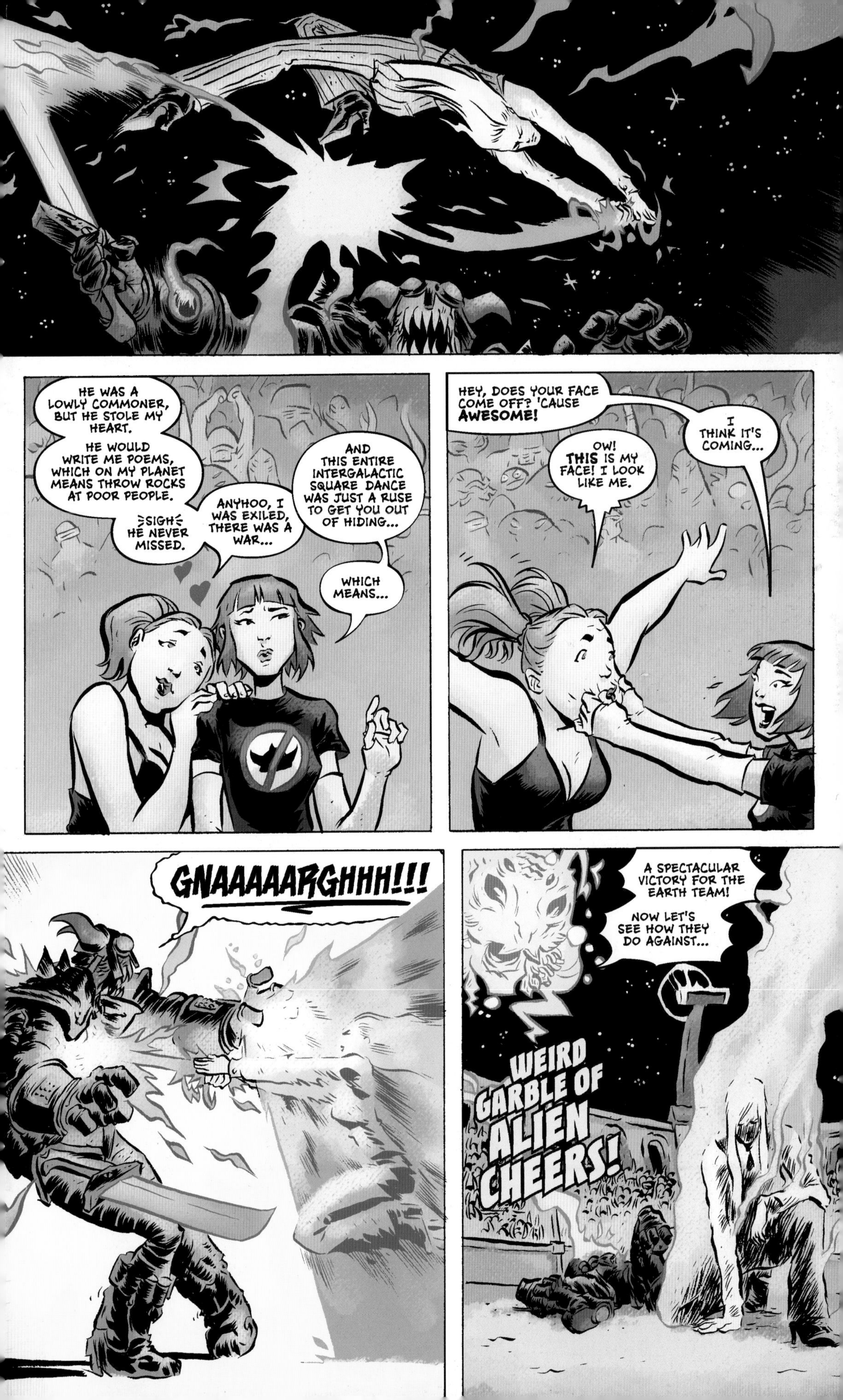
HE WAS A LOWLY COMMONER, BUT HE STOLE MY HEART.
HE WOULD WRITE ME POEMS, WHICH ON MY PLANET MEANS THROW ROCKS AT POOR PEOPLE.
SIGH HE NEVER MISSED.
ANYHOO, I WAS EXILED, THERE WAS A WAR...
AND THIS ENTIRE INTERGALACTIC SQUARE DANCE WAS JUST A RUSE TO GET YOU OUT OF HIDING...
WHICH MEANS...
HEY, DOES YOUR FACE COME OFF? 'CAUSE **AWESOME!**
OW! **THIS** IS MY FACE! I LOOK LIKE ME.
I THINK IT'S COMING...
GNAAAAARGHHH!!!
A SPECTACULAR VICTORY FOR THE EARTH TEAM!
NOW LET'S SEE HOW THEY DO AGAINST...
WEIRD GARBLE OF ALIEN CHEERS!

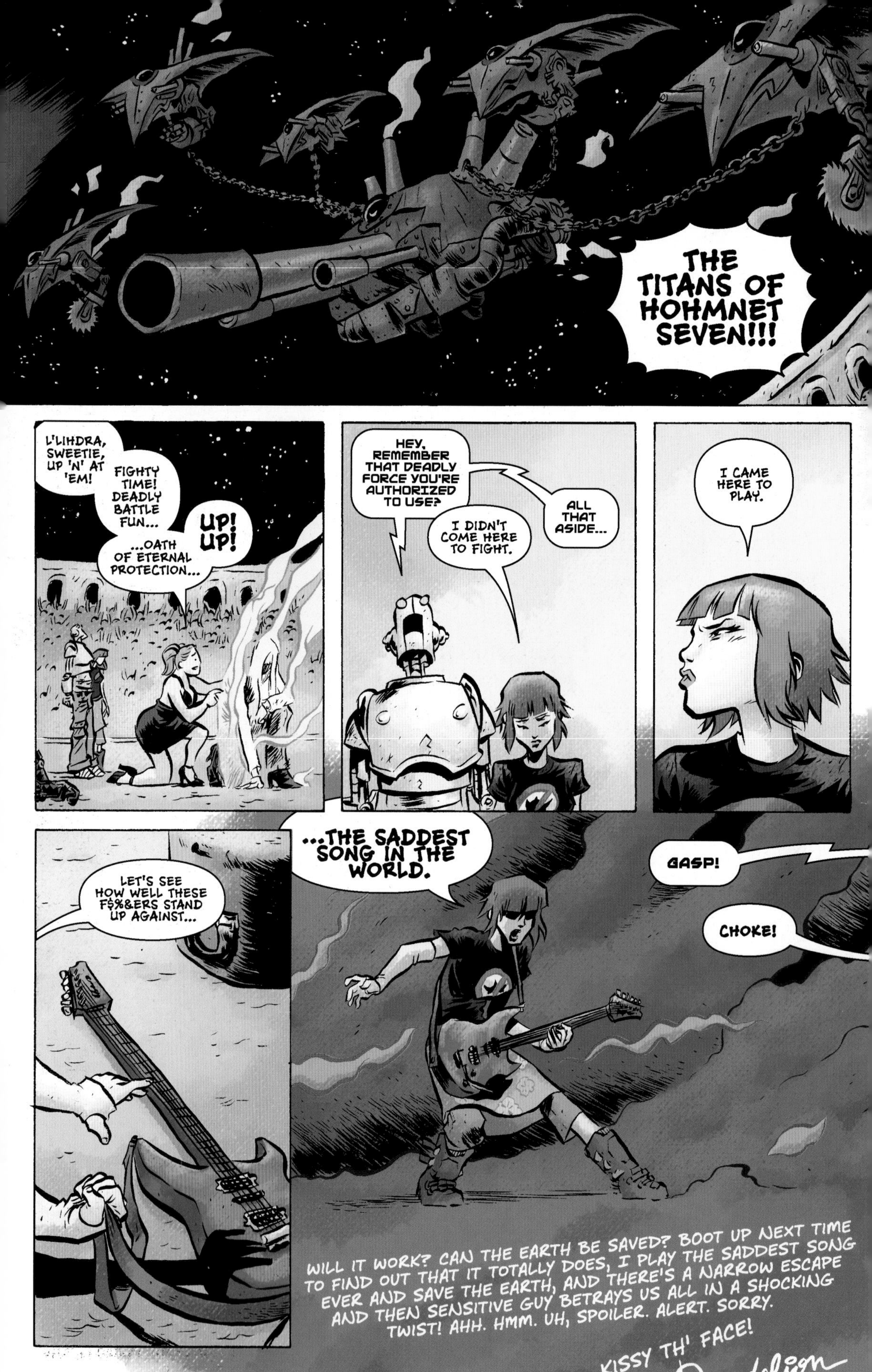
THE TITANS OF HOHMNET SEVEN!!!
L'LIHDRA, SWEETIE, UP 'N' AT 'EM!
FIGHTY TIME! DEADLY BATTLE FUN...
UP! UP!
...OATH OF ETERNAL PROTECTION...
HEY, REMEMBER THAT DEADLY FORCE YOU'RE AUTHORIZED TO USE?
ALL THAT ASIDE...
I DIDN'T COME HERE TO FIGHT.
I CAME HERE TO PLAY.
LET'S SEE HOW WELL THESE F$%&ERS STAND UP AGAINST...
...THE SADDEST SONG IN THE WORLD.
GASP!
CHOKE!
WILL IT WORK? CAN THE EARTH BE SAVED? BOOT UP NEXT TIME TO FIND OUT THAT IT TOTALLY DOES, I PLAY THE SADDEST SONG EVER AND SAVE THE EARTH, AND THERE'S A NARROW ESCAPE AND THEN SENSITIVE GUY BETRAYS US ALL IN A SHOCKING TWIST! AHH. HMM. UH, SPOILER. ALERT. SORRY.
KISSY TH' FACE!
-Dandelion

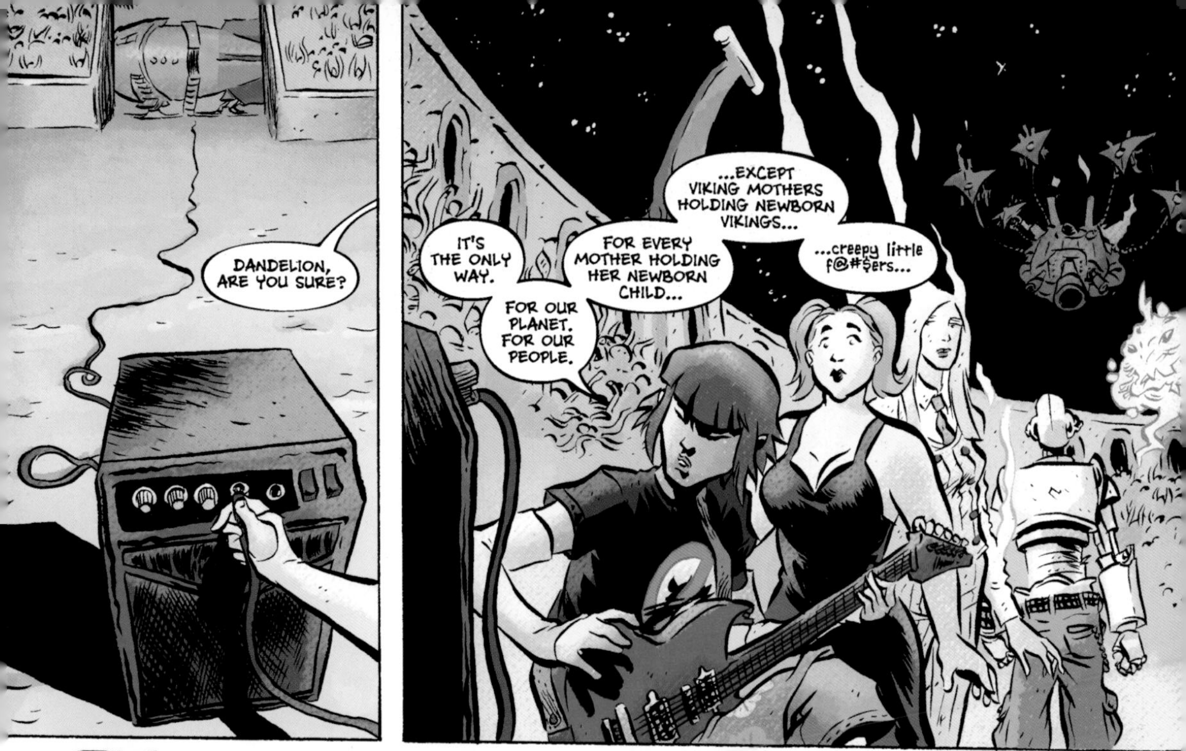
DANDELION, ARE YOU SURE?
IT'S THE ONLY WAY.
FOR OUR PLANET. FOR OUR PEOPLE.
FOR EVERY MOTHER HOLDING HER NEWBORN CHILD...
...EXCEPT VIKING MOTHERS HOLDING NEWBORN VIKINGS...
...creepy little f@#$ers...

SUGARSHOCK!

THE GREATEST STORY EVER BLOGGED

BY JOSS WHEDON & FÁBIO MOON
WITH DAVE STEWART AND NATE PIEKOS

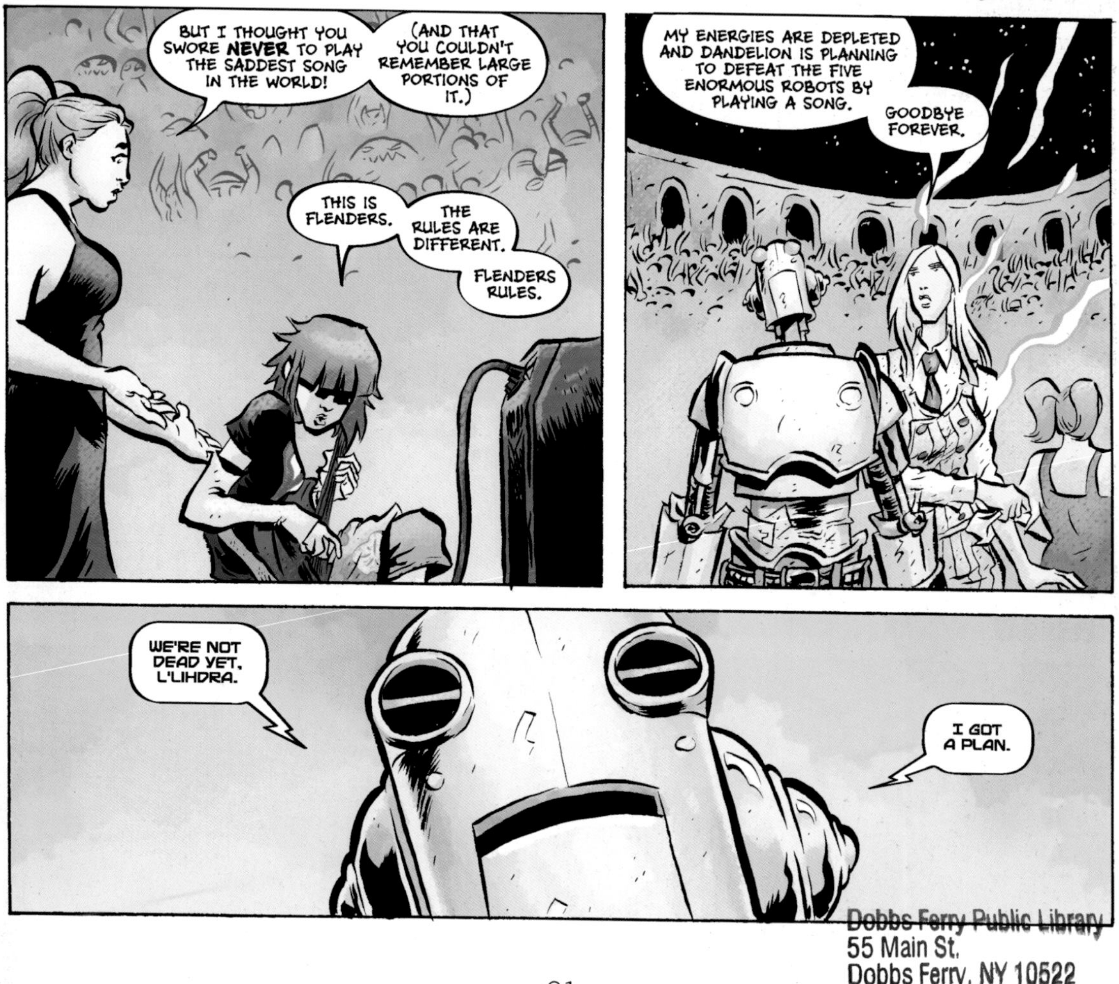
BUT I THOUGHT YOU SWORE **NEVER** TO PLAY THE SADDEST SONG IN THE WORLD!
(AND THAT YOU COULDN'T REMEMBER LARGE PORTIONS OF IT.)
THIS IS FLENDERS.
THE RULES ARE DIFFERENT.
FLENDERS RULES.
MY ENERGIES ARE DEPLETED AND DANDELION IS PLANNING TO DEFEAT THE FIVE ENORMOUS ROBOTS BY PLAYING A SONG.
GOODBYE FOREVER.
WE'RE NOT DEAD YET, L'LIHDRA.
I GOT A PLAN.

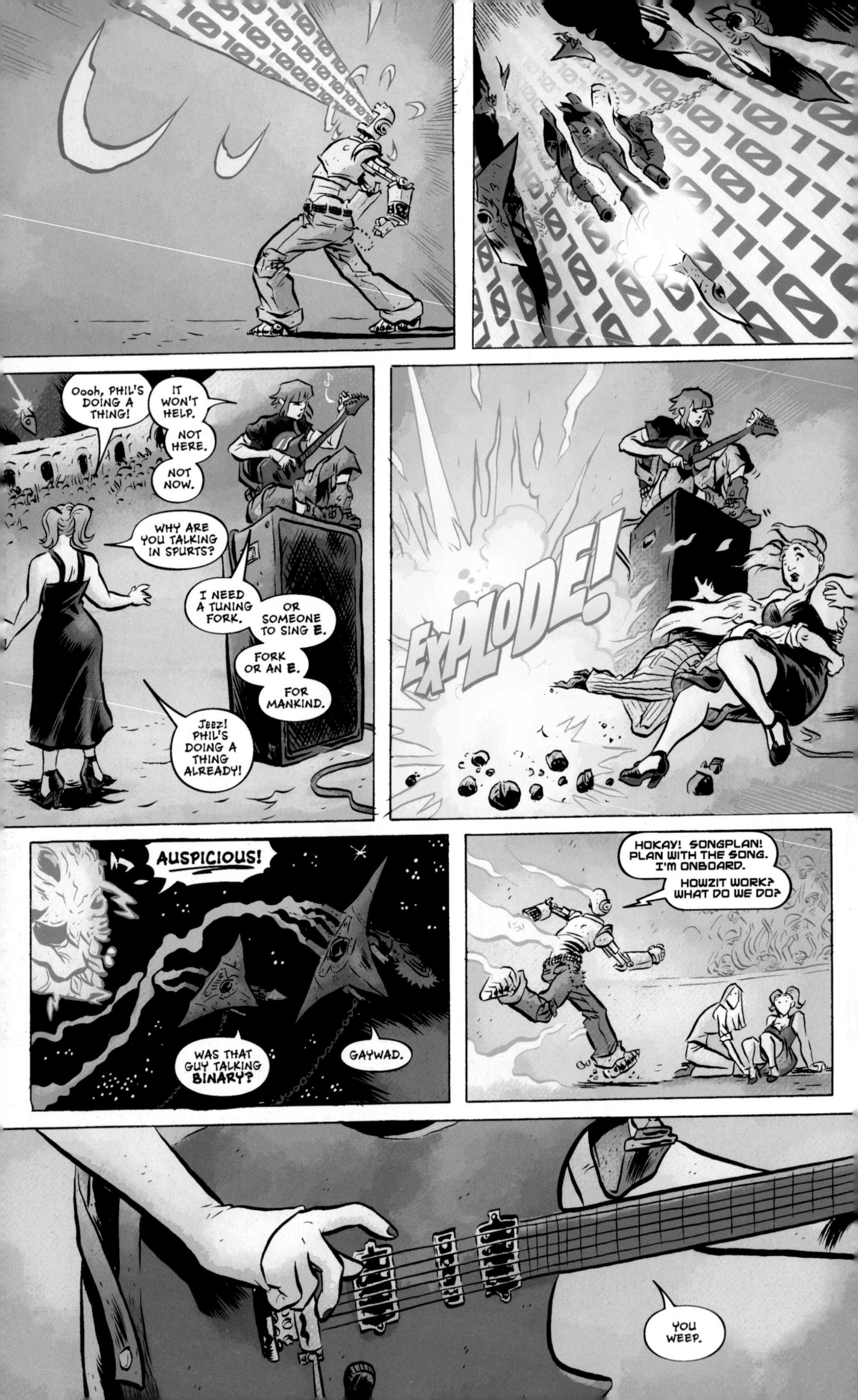

Oooh, PHIL'S DOING A THING!
IT WON'T HELP.
NOT HERE.
NOT NOW.
WHY ARE YOU TALKING IN SPURTS?
I NEED A TUNING FORK.
OR SOMEONE TO SING E.
FORK OR AN E.
FOR MANKIND.
Jeez! PHIL'S DOING A THING ALREADY!
EXPLODE!
AUSPICIOUS!
WAS THAT GUY TALKING BINARY?
GAYWAD.
HOKAY! SONGPLAN! PLAN WITH THE SONG. I'M ONBOARD.
HOWZIT WORK? WHAT DO WE DO?
YOU WEEP.

And they do.

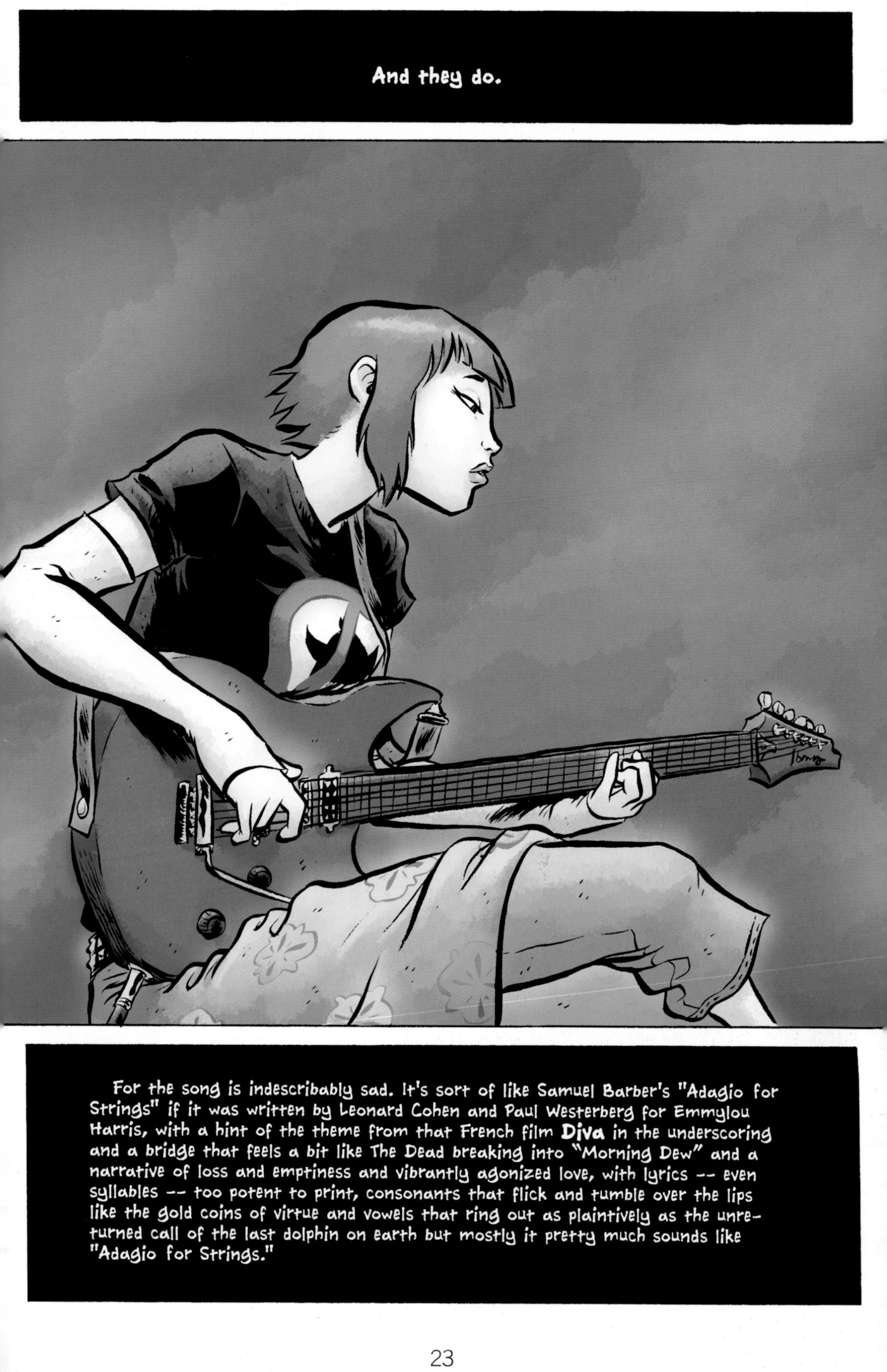

For the song is indescribably sad. It's sort of like Samuel Barber's "Adagio for Strings" if it was written by Leonard Cohen and Paul Westerberg for Emmylou Harris, with a hint of the theme from that French film **Diva** in the underscoring and a bridge that feels a bit like The Dead breaking into "Morning Dew" and a narrative of loss and emptiness and vibrantly agonized love, with lyrics -- even syllables -- too potent to print, consonants that flick and tumble over the lips like the gold coins of virtue and vowels that ring out as plaintively as the unreturned call of the last dolphin on earth but mostly it pretty much sounds like "Adagio for Strings."

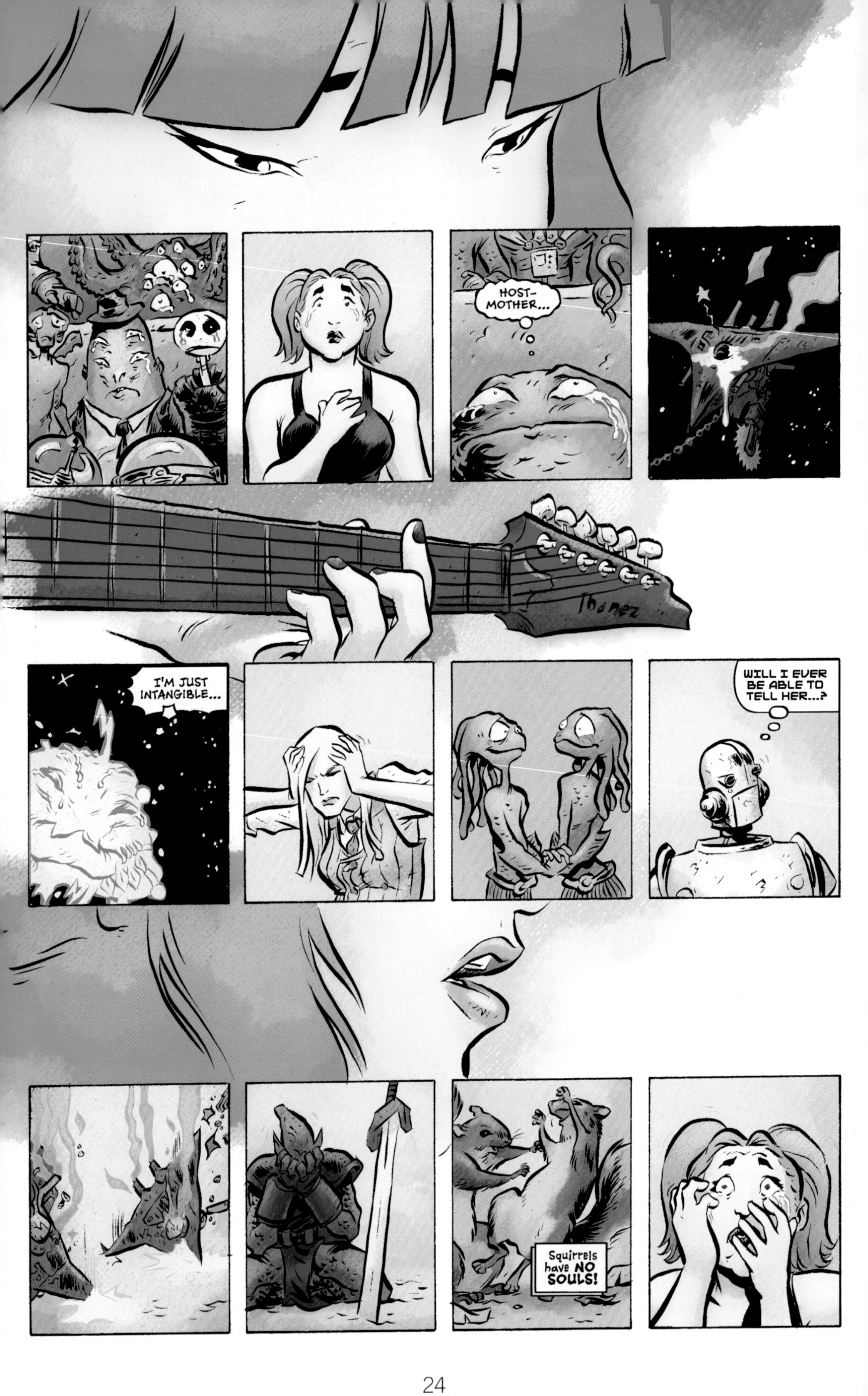
HOST-MOTHER...
I'M JUST INTANGIBLE...
WILL I EVER BE ABLE TO TELL HER...?
Squirrels have NO SOULS!

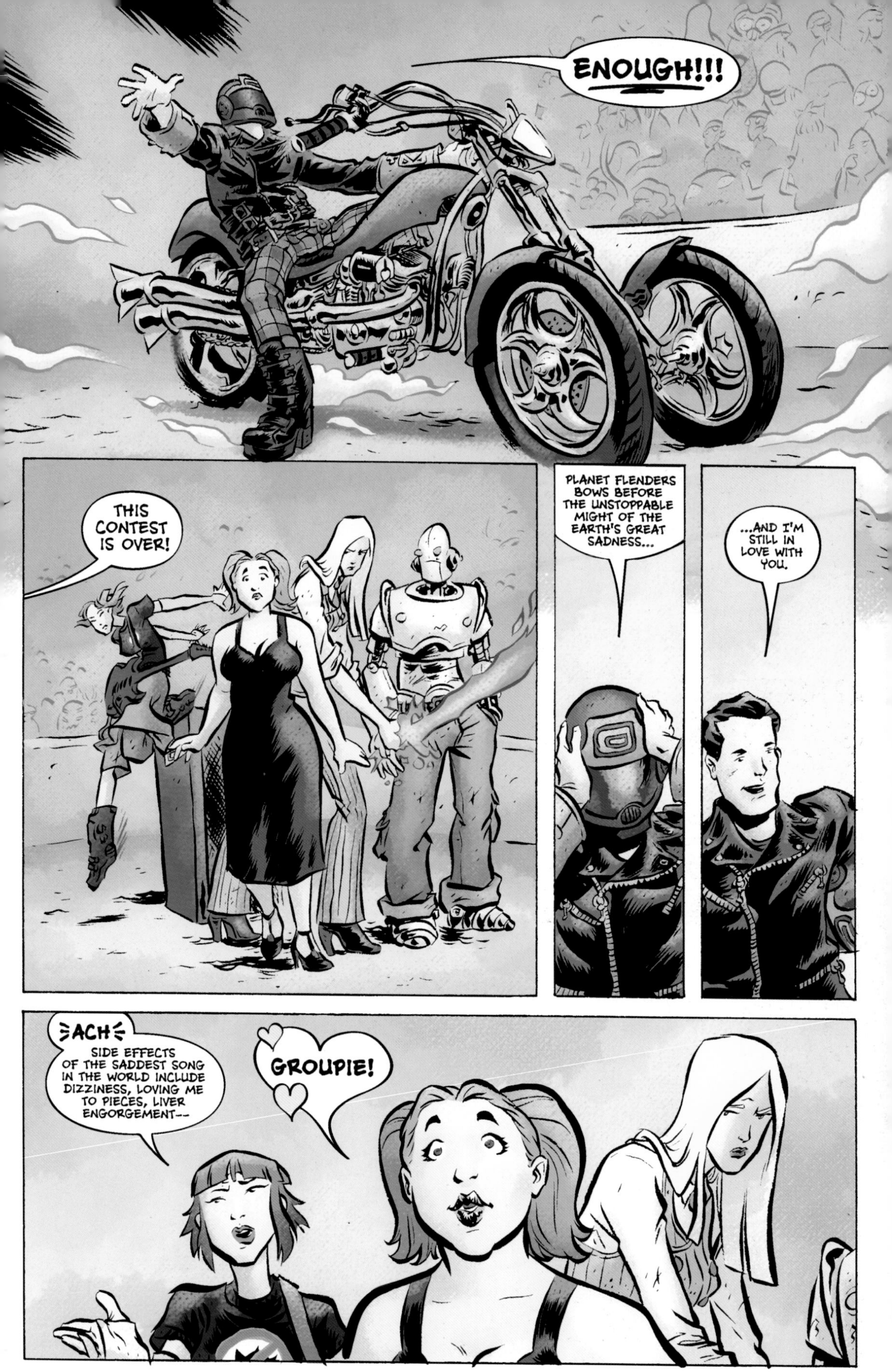
ENOUGH!!!
THIS CONTEST IS OVER!
PLANET FLENDERS BOWS BEFORE THE UNSTOPPABLE MIGHT OF THE EARTH'S GREAT SADNESS...
...AND I'M STILL IN LOVE WITH YOU.
ACH
SIDE EFFECTS OF THE SADDEST SONG IN THE WORLD INCLUDE DIZZINESS, LOVING ME TO PIECES, LIVER ENGORGEMENT--
GROUPIE!

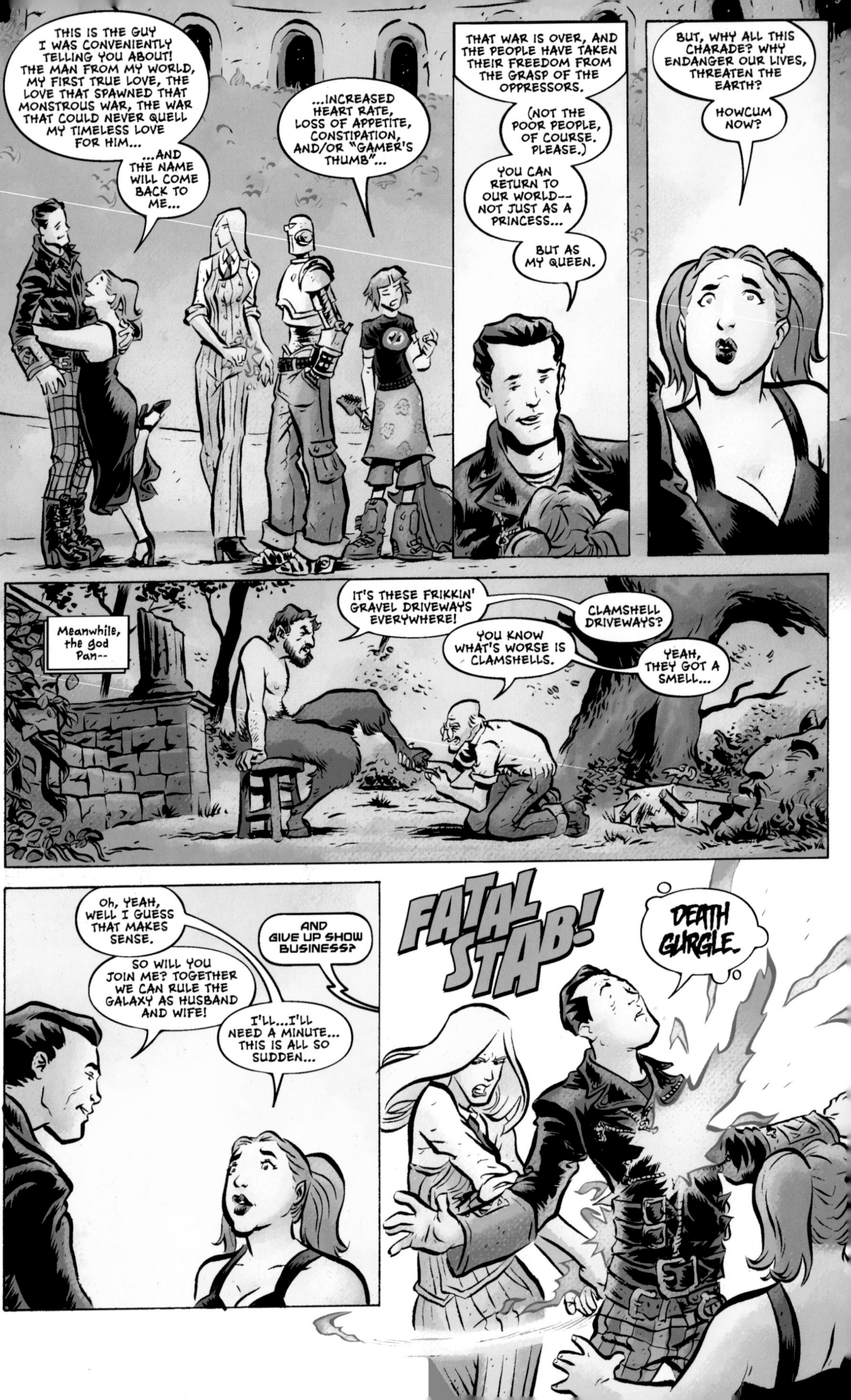
THIS IS THE GUY I WAS CONVENIENTLY TELLING YOU ABOUT! THE MAN FROM MY WORLD, MY FIRST TRUE LOVE, THE LOVE THAT SPAWNED THAT MONSTROUS WAR, THE WAR THAT COULD NEVER QUELL MY TIMELESS LOVE FOR HIM...
...AND THE NAME WILL COME BACK TO ME...
...INCREASED HEART RATE, LOSS OF APPETITE, CONSTIPATION, AND/OR "GAMER'S THUMB"...
THAT WAR IS OVER, AND THE PEOPLE HAVE TAKEN THEIR FREEDOM FROM THE GRASP OF THE OPPRESSORS.
(NOT THE POOR PEOPLE, OF COURSE. PLEASE.)
YOU CAN RETURN TO OUR WORLD-- NOT JUST AS A PRINCESS...
BUT AS MY QUEEN.
BUT, WHY ALL THIS CHARADE? WHY ENDANGER OUR LIVES, THREATEN THE EARTH?
HOWCUM NOW?
Meanwhile, the god Pan--
IT'S THESE FRIKKIN' GRAVEL DRIVEWAYS EVERYWHERE!
YOU KNOW WHAT'S WORSE IS CLAMSHELLS.
CLAMSHELL DRIVEWAYS?
YEAH, THEY GOT A SMELL...
Oh, YEAH, WELL I GUESS THAT MAKES SENSE.
SO WILL YOU JOIN ME? TOGETHER WE CAN RULE THE GALAXY AS HUSBAND AND WIFE!
AND GIVE UP SHOW BUSINESS?
I'LL...I'LL NEED A MINUTE... THIS IS ALL SO SUDDEN...
FATAL STAB!
DEATH GURGLE.

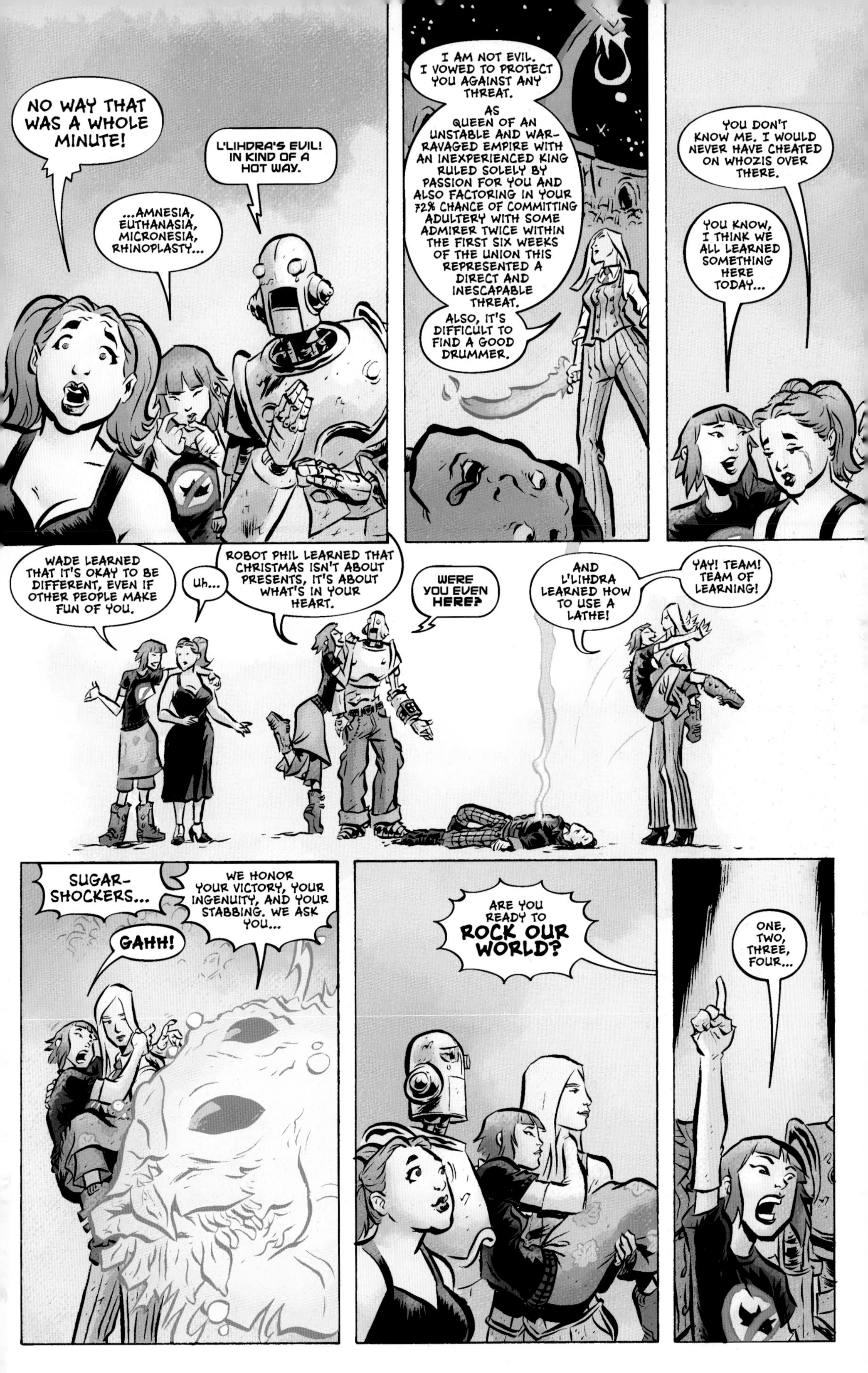
NO WAY THAT WAS A WHOLE MINUTE!
...AMNESIA, EUTHANASIA, MICRONESIA, RHINOPLASTY...
L'LIHDRA'S EVIL! IN KIND OF A HOT WAY.
I AM NOT EVIL. I VOWED TO PROTECT YOU AGAINST ANY THREAT.
AS QUEEN OF AN UNSTABLE AND WAR-RAVAGED EMPIRE WITH AN INEXPERIENCED KING RULED SOLELY BY PASSION FOR YOU AND ALSO FACTORING IN YOUR 72% CHANCE OF COMMITTING ADULTERY WITH SOME ADMIRER TWICE WITHIN THE FIRST SIX WEEKS OF THE UNION THIS REPRESENTED A DIRECT AND INESCAPABLE THREAT.
ALSO, IT'S DIFFICULT TO FIND A GOOD DRUMMER.
YOU DON'T KNOW ME. I WOULD NEVER HAVE CHEATED ON WHOZIS OVER THERE.
YOU KNOW, I THINK WE ALL LEARNED SOMETHING HERE TODAY...
WADE LEARNED THAT IT'S OKAY TO BE DIFFERENT, EVEN IF OTHER PEOPLE MAKE FUN OF YOU.
Uh...
ROBOT PHIL LEARNED THAT CHRISTMAS ISN'T ABOUT PRESENTS, IT'S ABOUT WHAT'S IN YOUR HEART.
WERE YOU EVEN HERE?
AND L'LIHDRA LEARNED HOW TO USE A LATHE!
YAY! TEAM! TEAM OF LEARNING!
SUGAR-SHOCKERS...
WE HONOR YOUR VICTORY, YOUR INGENUITY, AND YOUR STABBING. WE ASK YOU...
GAHH!
ARE YOU READY TO ROCK OUR WORLD?
ONE, TWO, THREE, FOUR...

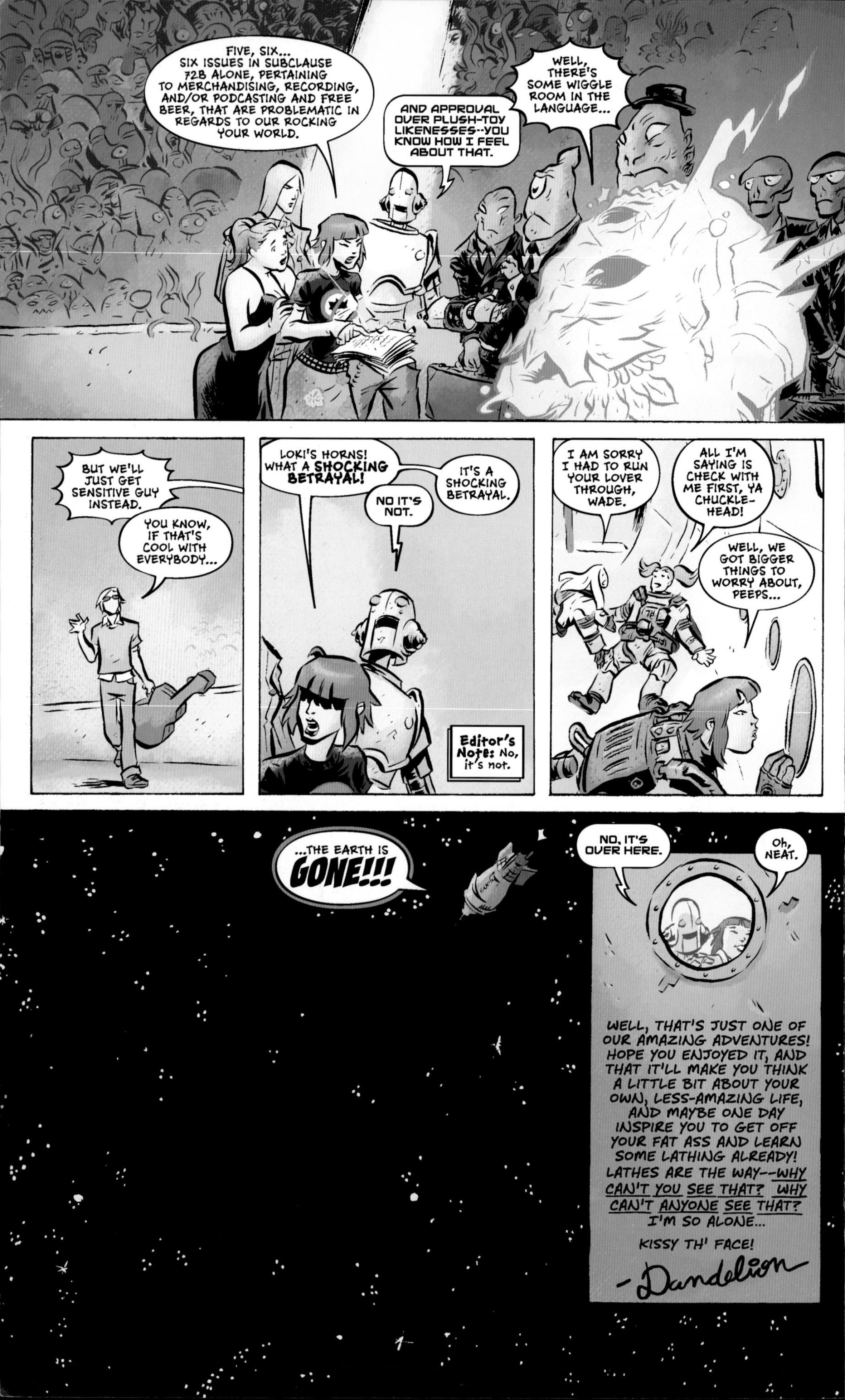
FIVE, SIX... SIX ISSUES IN SUBCLAUSE 72B ALONE, PERTAINING TO MERCHANDISING, RECORDING, AND/OR PODCASTING AND FREE BEER, THAT ARE PROBLEMATIC IN REGARDS TO OUR ROCKING YOUR WORLD.
AND APPROVAL OVER PLUSH-TOY LIKENESSES--YOU KNOW HOW I FEEL ABOUT THAT.
WELL, THERE'S SOME WIGGLE ROOM IN THE LANGUAGE...
BUT WE'LL JUST GET SENSITIVE GUY INSTEAD.
YOU KNOW, IF THAT'S COOL WITH EVERYBODY...
LOKI'S HORNS! WHAT A SHOCKING BETRAYAL!
IT'S A SHOCKING BETRAYAL.
NO IT'S NOT.
Editor's Note: No, it's not.
I AM SORRY I HAD TO RUN YOUR LOVER THROUGH, WADE.
ALL I'M SAYING IS CHECK WITH ME FIRST, YA CHUCKLE-HEAD!
WELL, WE GOT BIGGER THINGS TO WORRY ABOUT, PEEPS...
...THE EARTH IS GONE!!!
NO, IT'S OVER HERE.
Oh, NEAT.
WELL, THAT'S JUST ONE OF OUR AMAZING ADVENTURES! HOPE YOU ENJOYED IT, AND THAT IT'LL MAKE YOU THINK A LITTLE BIT ABOUT YOUR OWN, LESS-AMAZING LIFE, AND MAYBE ONE DAY INSPIRE YOU TO GET OFF YOUR FAT ASS AND LEARN SOME LATHING ALREADY! LATHES ARE THE WAY--WHY CAN'T YOU SEE THAT? WHY CAN'T ANYONE SEE THAT? I'M SO ALONE...
KISSY TH' FACE!
-Dandelion

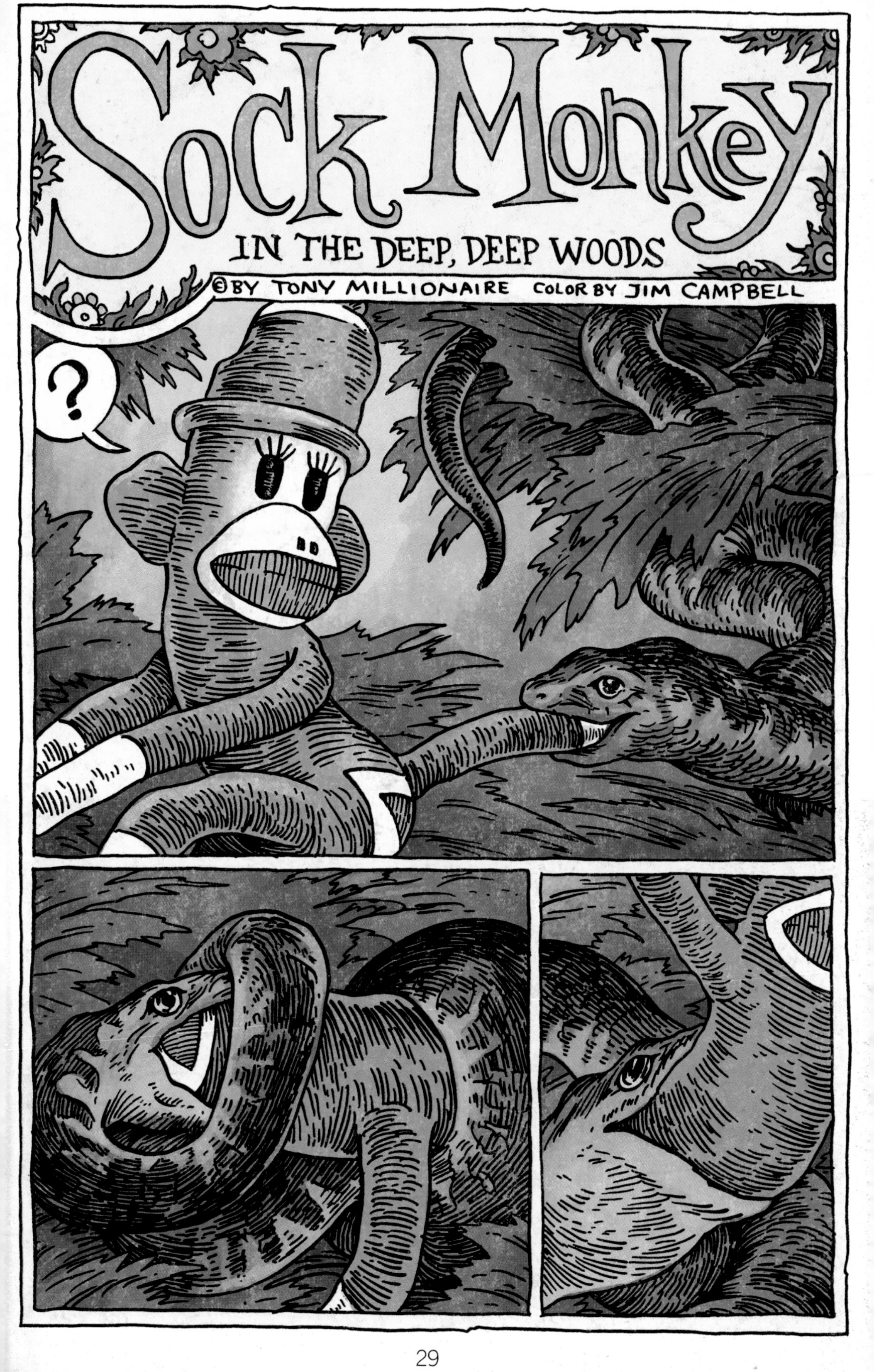
Sock Monkey
IN THE DEEP, DEEP WOODS
©BY TONY MILLIONAIRE COLOR BY JIM CAMPBELL
?

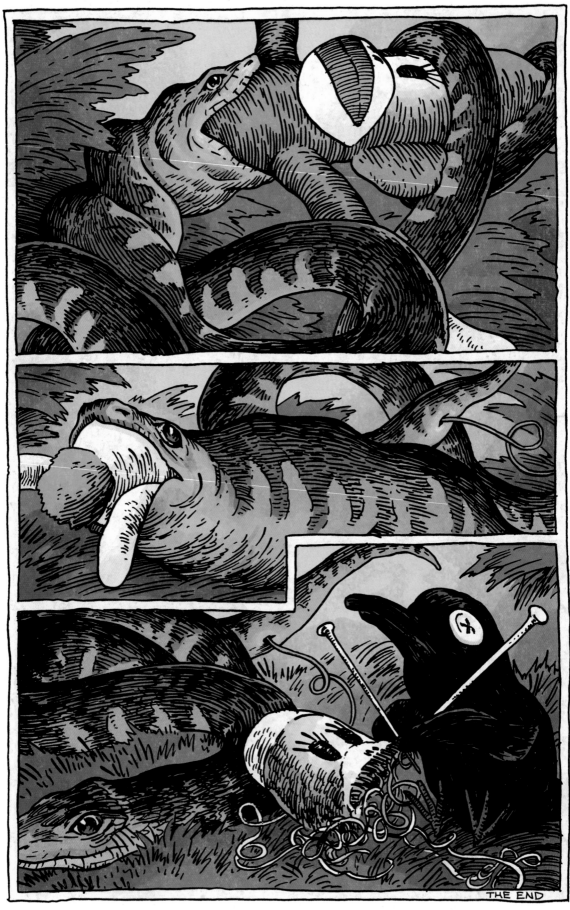

THE END

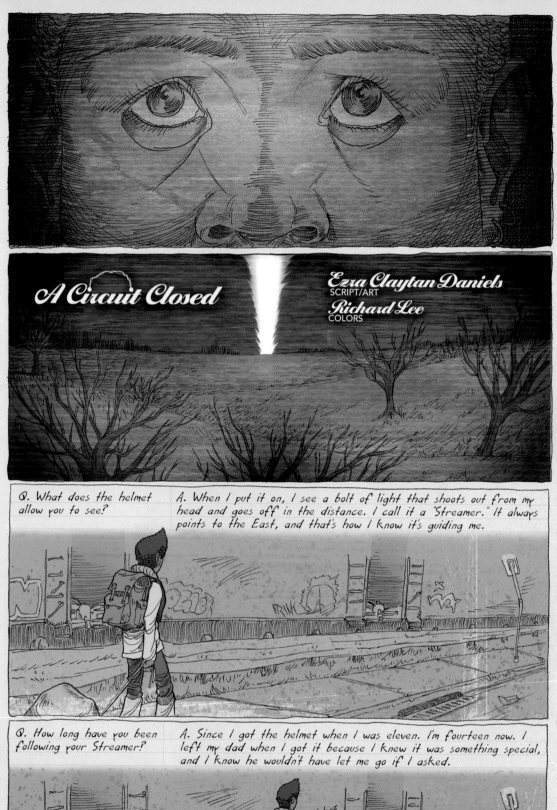

A Circuit Closed

Ezra Claytan Daniels
SCRIPT/ART

Richard Lee
COLORS

Q. What does the helmet allow you to see?

A. When I put it on, I see a bolt of light that shoots out from my head and goes off in the distance. I call it a "Streamer." It always points to the East, and that's how I know it's guiding me.

Q. How long have you been following your Streamer?

A. Since I got the helmet when I was eleven. I'm fourteen now. I left my dad when I got it because I knew it was something special, and I know he wouldn't have let me go if I asked.

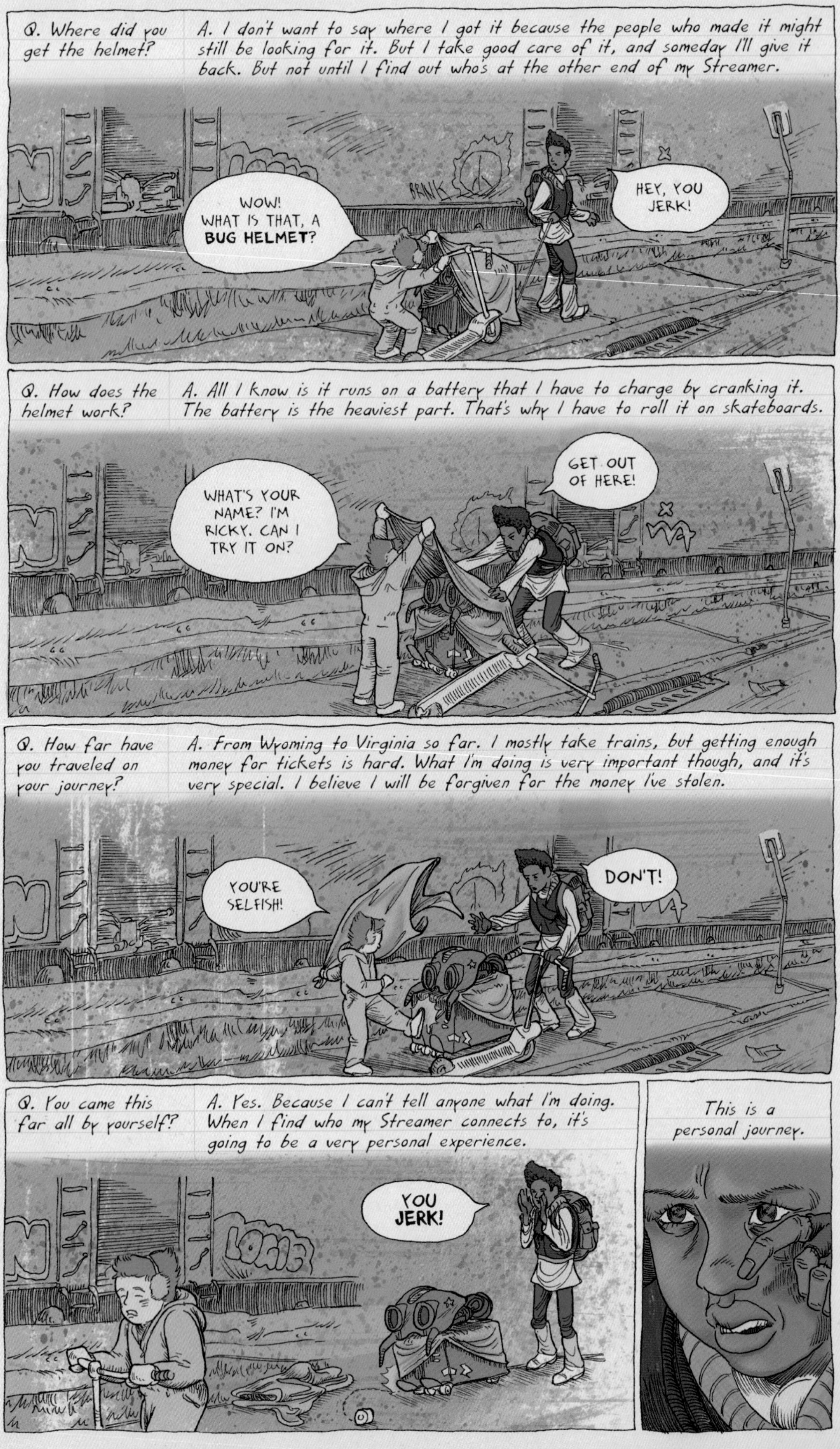

Q. Where did you get the helmet?
A. I don't want to say where I got it because the people who made it might still be looking for it. But I take good care of it, and someday I'll give it back. But not until I find out who's at the other end of my Streamer.
WOW! WHAT IS THAT, A BUG HELMET?
HEY, YOU JERK!
Q. How does the helmet work?
A. All I know is it runs on a battery that I have to charge by cranking it. The battery is the heaviest part. That's why I have to roll it on skateboards.
WHAT'S YOUR NAME? I'M RICKY. CAN I TRY IT ON?
GET OUT OF HERE!
Q. How far have you traveled on your journey?
A. From Wyoming to Virginia so far. I mostly take trains, but getting enough money for tickets is hard. What I'm doing is very important though, and it's very special. I believe I will be forgiven for the money I've stolen.
YOU'RE SELFISH!
DON'T!
Q. You came this far all by yourself?
A. Yes. Because I can't tell anyone what I'm doing. When I find who my Streamer connects to, it's going to be a very personal experience.
YOU JERK!
This is a personal journey.

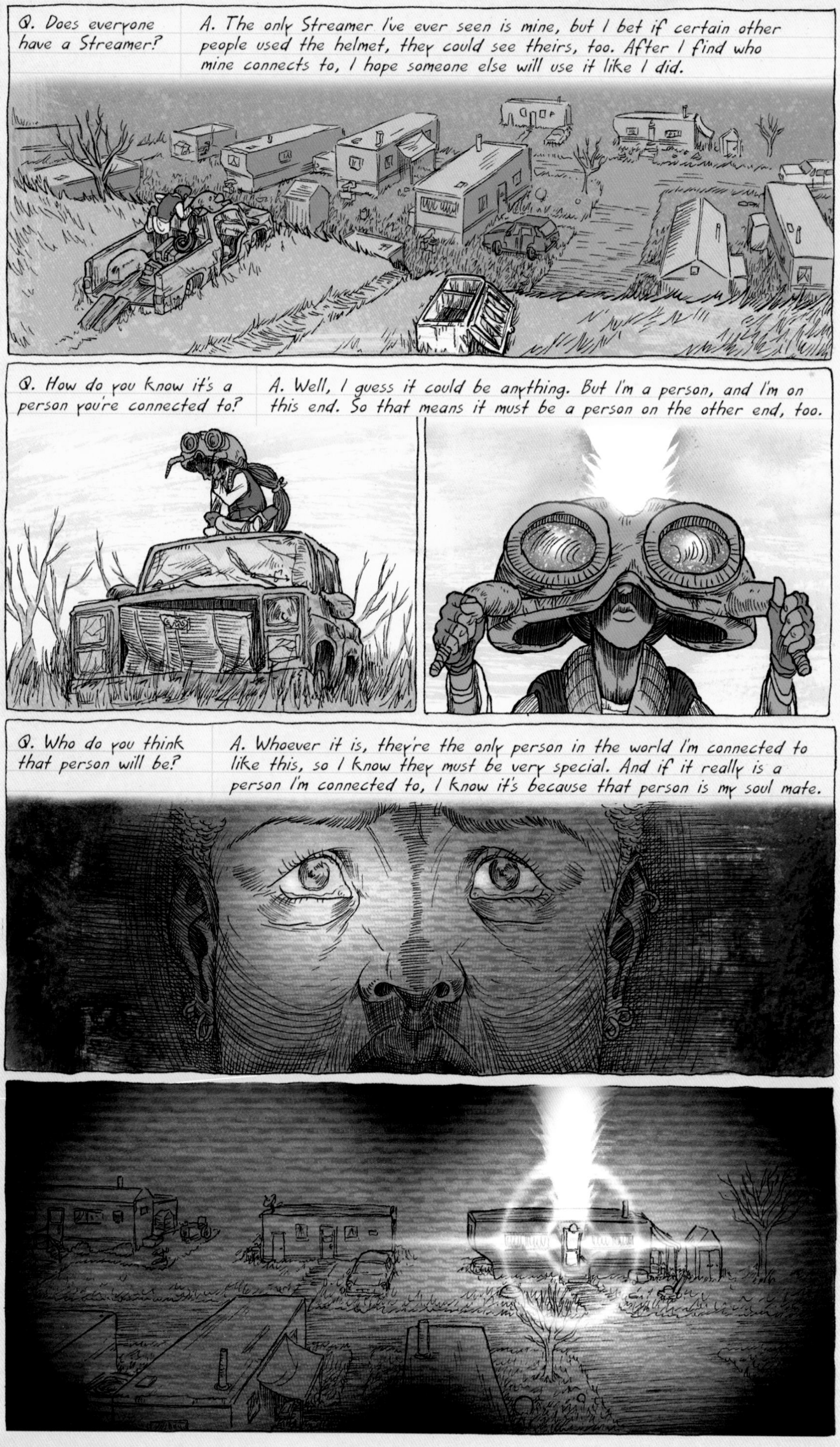
Q. Does everyone have a Streamer?
A. The only Streamer I've ever seen is mine, but I bet if certain other people used the helmet, they could see theirs, too. After I find who mine connects to, I hope someone else will use it like I did.
Q. How do you know it's a person you're connected to?
A. Well, I guess it could be anything. But I'm a person, and I'm on this end. So that means it must be a person on the other end, too.
Q. Who do you think that person will be?
A. Whoever it is, they're the only person in the world I'm connected to like this, so I know they must be very special. And if it really is a person I'm connected to, I know it's because that person is my soul mate.

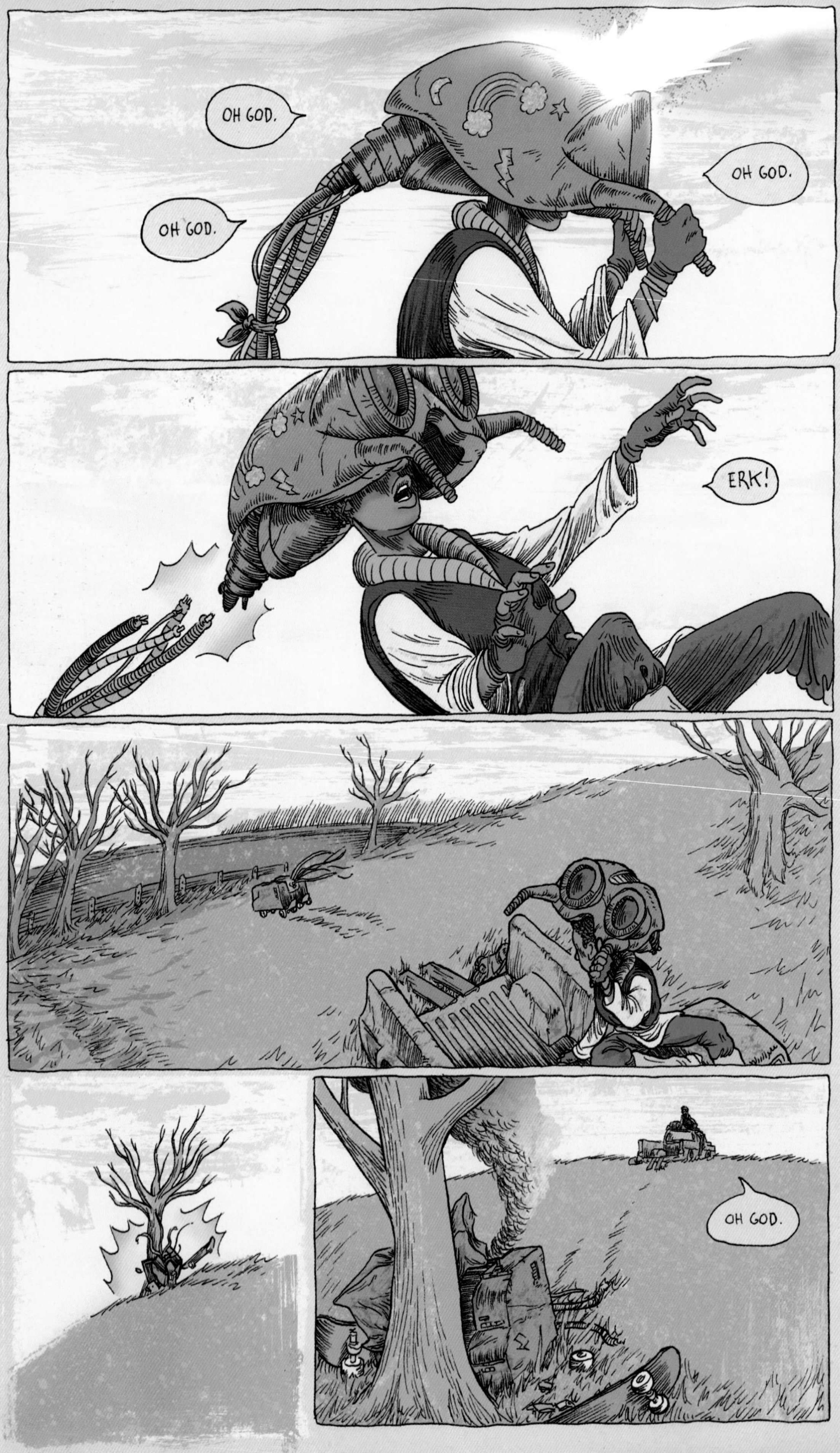
OH GOD.
OH GOD.
OH GOD.
ERK!
OH GOD.

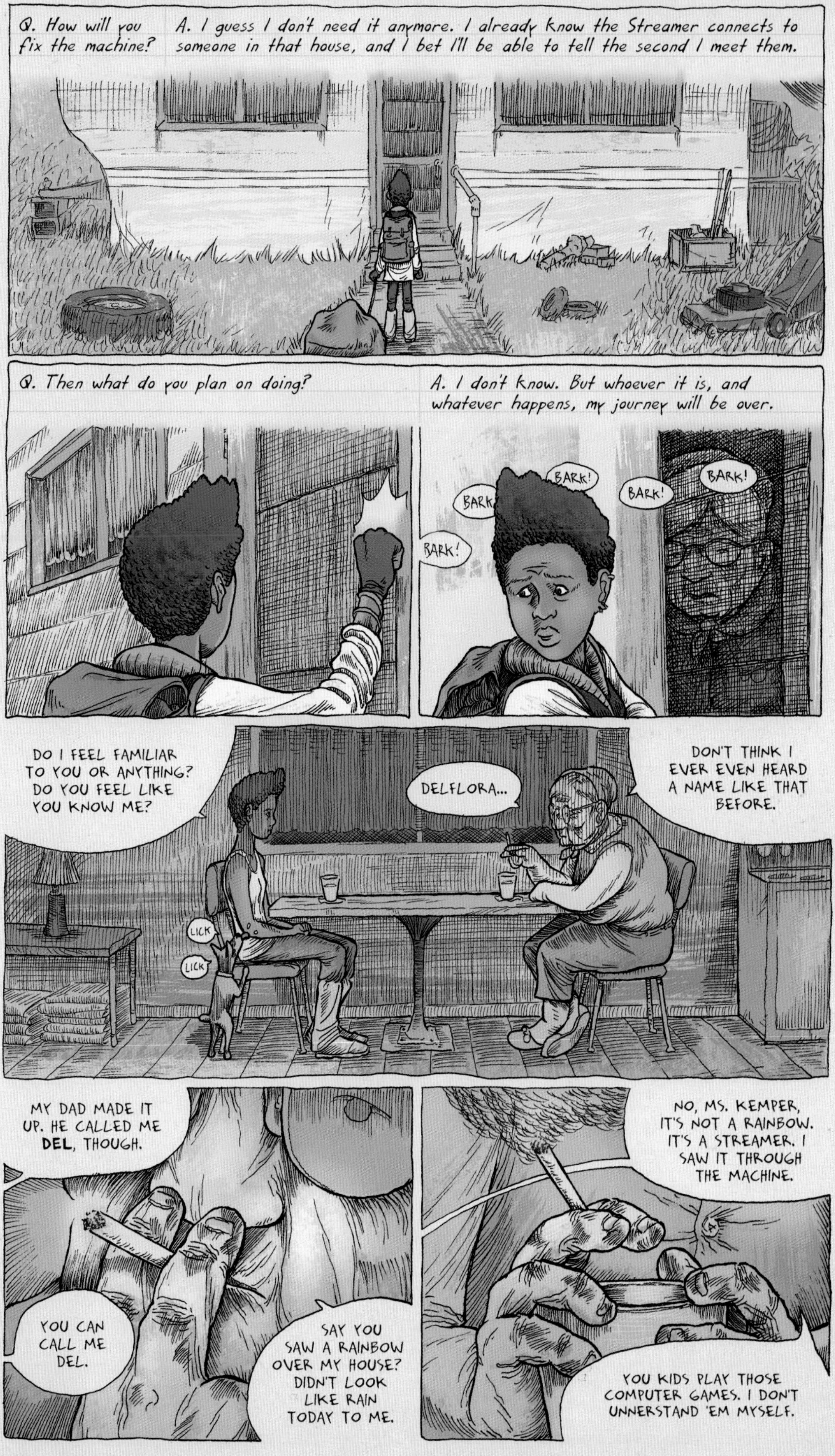
Q. How will you fix the machine?
A. I guess I don't need it anymore. I already know the Streamer connects to someone in that house, and I bet I'll be able to tell the second I meet them.
Q. Then what do you plan on doing?
A. I don't know. But whoever it is, and whatever happens, my journey will be over.
BARK!
BARK!
BARK!
BARK!
BARK!
DO I FEEL FAMILIAR TO YOU OR ANYTHING? DO YOU FEEL LIKE YOU KNOW ME?
DELFLORA...
DON'T THINK I EVER EVEN HEARD A NAME LIKE THAT BEFORE.
LICK
LICK
MY DAD MADE IT UP. HE CALLED ME DEL, THOUGH.
YOU CAN CALL ME DEL.
SAY YOU SAW A RAINBOW OVER MY HOUSE? DIDN'T LOOK LIKE RAIN TODAY TO ME.
NO, MS. KEMPER, IT'S NOT A RAINBOW. IT'S A STREAMER. I SAW IT THROUGH THE MACHINE.
YOU KIDS PLAY THOSE COMPUTER GAMES. I DON'T UNNERSTAND 'EM MYSELF.

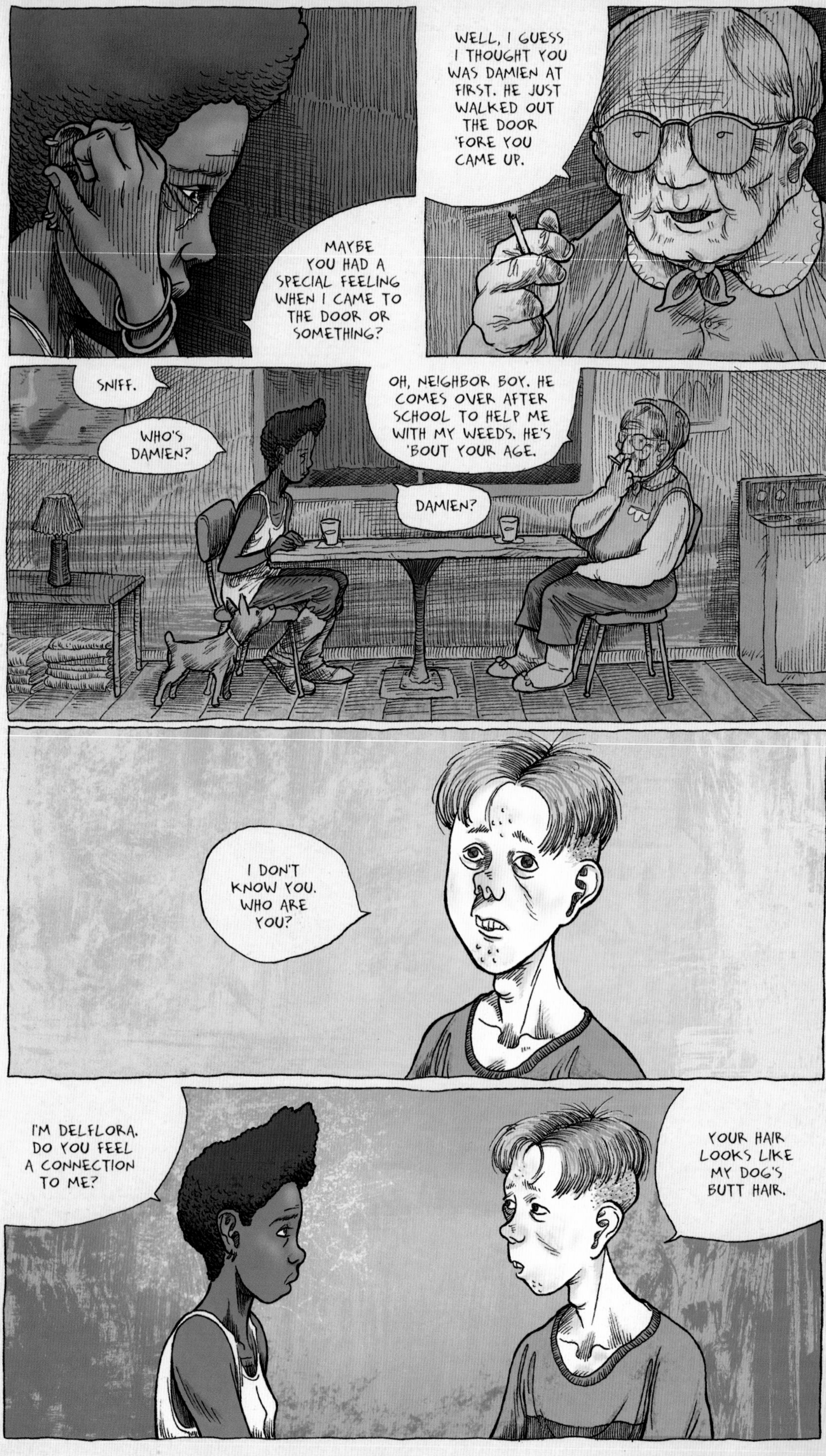

MAYBE YOU HAD A SPECIAL FEELING WHEN I CAME TO THE DOOR OR SOMETHING?
WELL, I GUESS I THOUGHT YOU WAS DAMIEN AT FIRST. HE JUST WALKED OUT THE DOOR 'FORE YOU CAME UP.
SNIFF.
WHO'S DAMIEN?
OH, NEIGHBOR BOY. HE COMES OVER AFTER SCHOOL TO HELP ME WITH MY WEEDS. HE'S 'BOUT YOUR AGE.
DAMIEN?
I DON'T KNOW YOU. WHO ARE YOU?
I'M DELFLORA. DO YOU FEEL A CONNECTION TO ME?
YOUR HAIR LOOKS LIKE MY DOG'S BUTT HAIR.

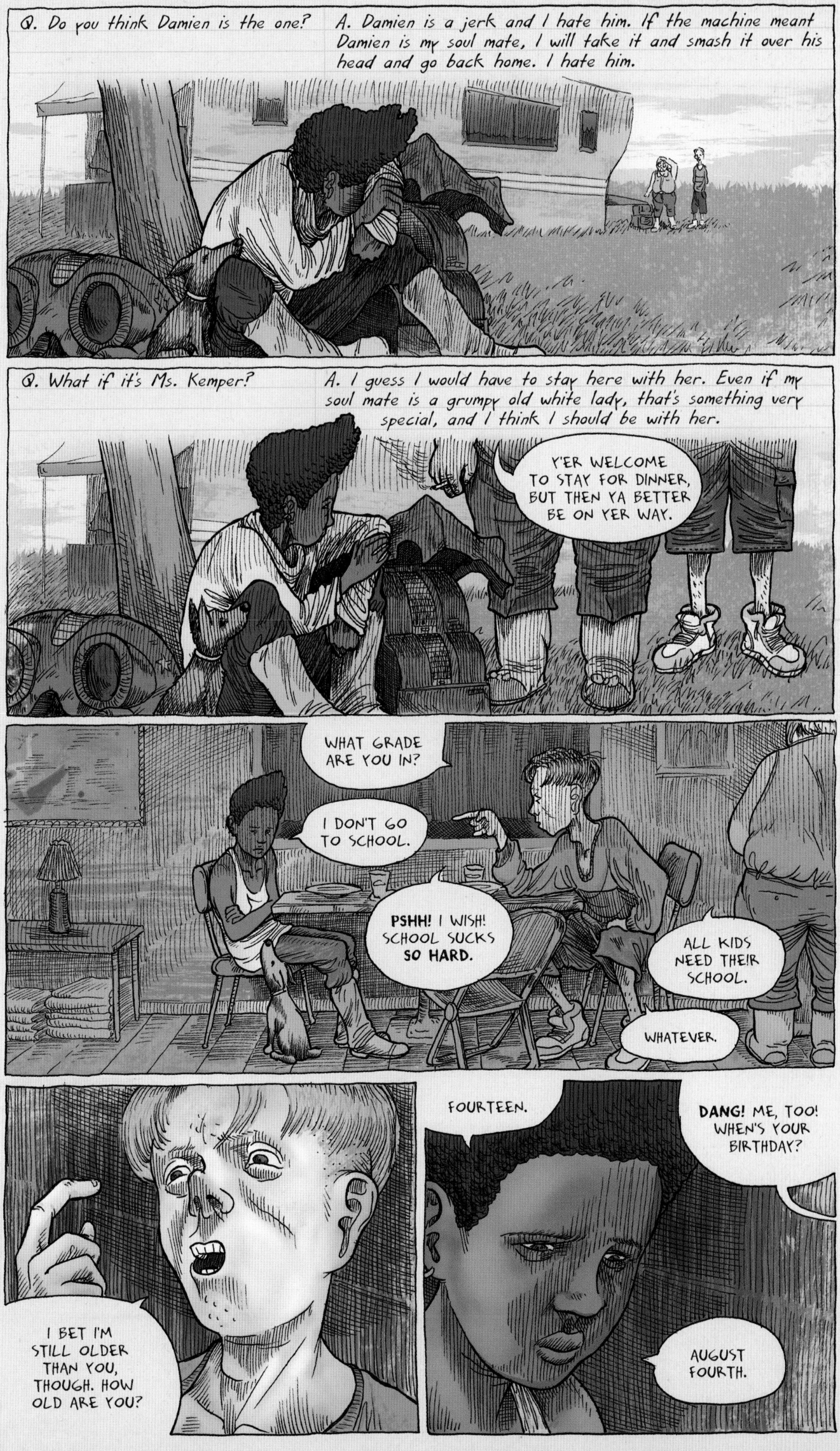
Q. Do you think Damien is the one?
A. Damien is a jerk and I hate him. If the machine meant Damien is my soul mate, I will take it and smash it over his head and go back home. I hate him.
Q. What if it's Ms. Kemper?
A. I guess I would have to stay here with her. Even if my soul mate is a grumpy old white lady, that's something very special, and I think I should be with her.
Y'ER WELCOME TO STAY FOR DINNER, BUT THEN YA BETTER BE ON YER WAY.
WHAT GRADE ARE YOU IN?
I DON'T GO TO SCHOOL.
PSHH! I WISH! SCHOOL SUCKS SO HARD.
ALL KIDS NEED THEIR SCHOOL.
WHATEVER.
I BET I'M STILL OLDER THAN YOU, THOUGH. HOW OLD ARE YOU?
FOURTEEN.
DANG! ME, TOO! WHEN'S YOUR BIRTHDAY?
AUGUST FOURTH.

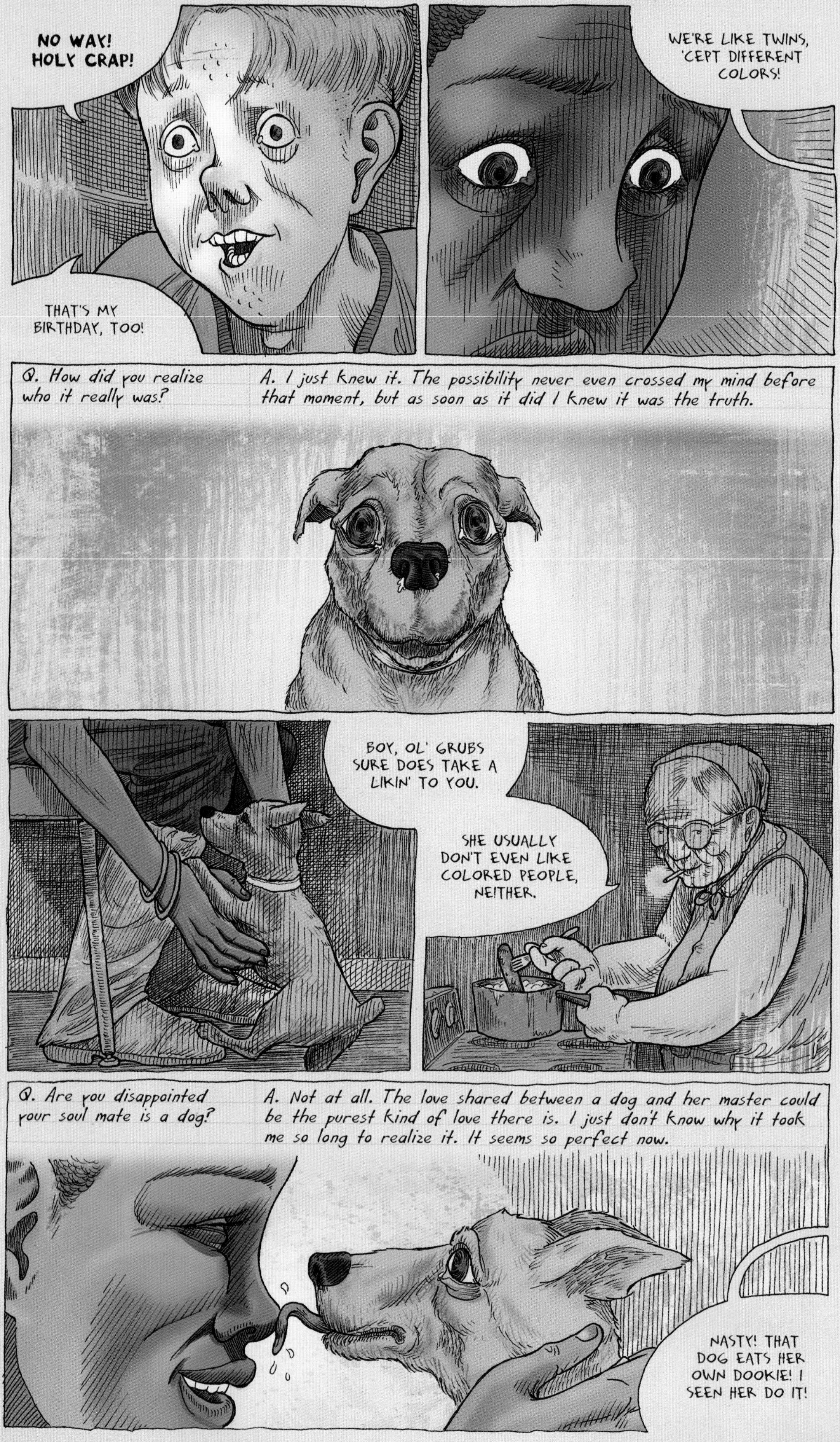
NO WAY! HOLY CRAP!
THAT'S MY BIRTHDAY, TOO!
WE'RE LIKE TWINS, 'CEPT DIFFERENT COLORS!
Q. How did you realize who it really was?
A. I just knew it. The possibility never even crossed my mind before that moment, but as soon as it did I knew it was the truth.
BOY, OL' GRUBS SURE DOES TAKE A LIKIN' TO YOU.
SHE USUALLY DON'T EVEN LIKE COLORED PEOPLE, NEITHER.
Q. Are you disappointed your soul mate is a dog?
A. Not at all. The love shared between a dog and her master could be the purest kind of love there is. I just don't know why it took me so long to realize it. It seems so perfect now.
NASTY! THAT DOG EATS HER OWN DOOKIE! I SEEN HER DO IT!

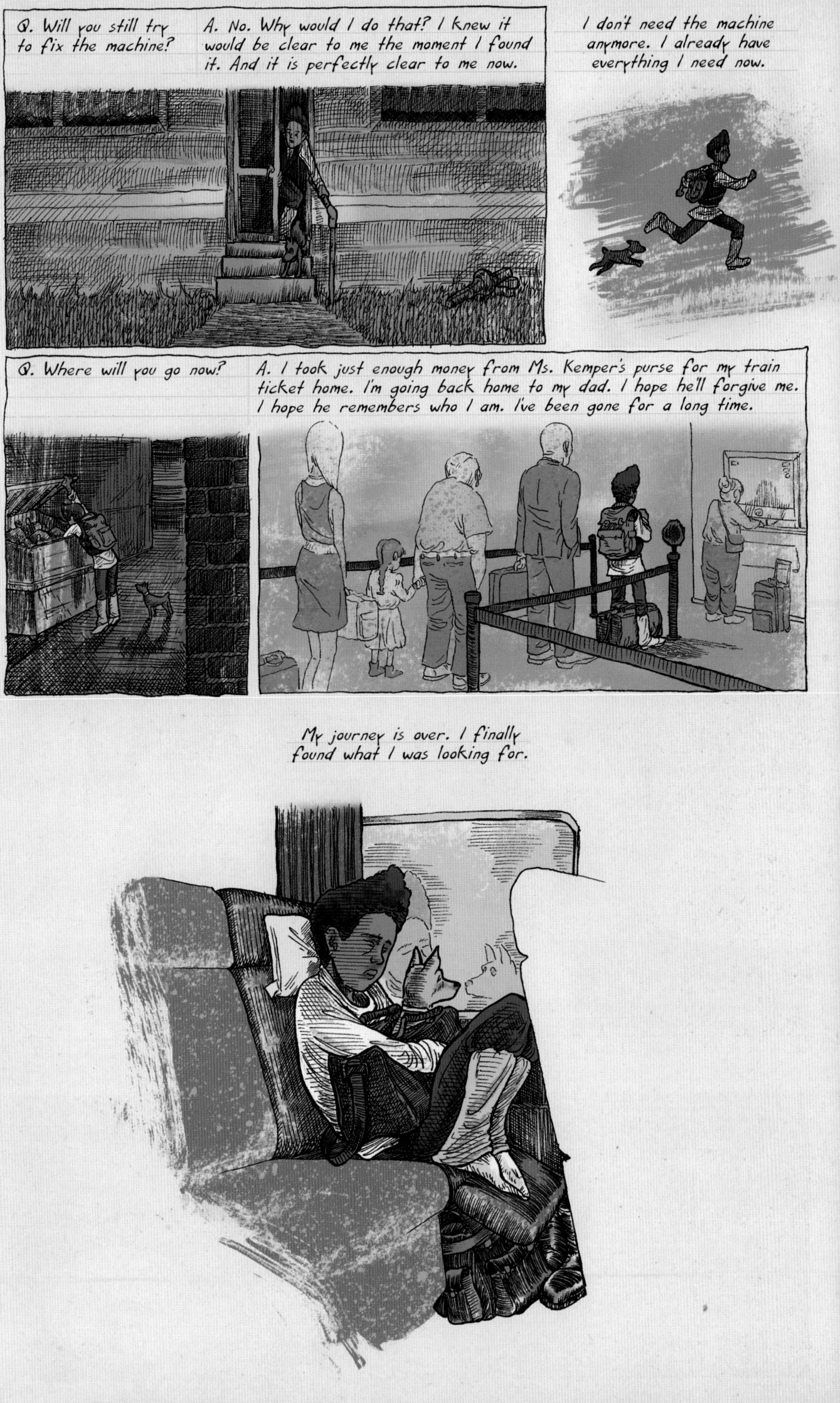
Q. Will you still try to fix the machine?
A. No. Why would I do that? I knew it would be clear to me the moment I found it. And it is perfectly clear to me now.
I don't need the machine anymore. I already have everything I need now.
Q. Where will you go now?
A. I took just enough money from Ms. Kemper's purse for my train ticket home. I'm going back home to my dad. I hope he'll forgive me. I hope he remembers who I am. I've been gone for a long time.
My journey is over. I finally found what I was looking for.

WELL, WHERE'D SHE GO?!

ALL'S I KNOW IS, I SAID SHE COULD STAY OVERNIGHT AND THE LITTLE WHORE TOOK OFF WITH FORTY DOLLARS AND STOLE MY DOG!

AND TO TOP IT OFF, SHE JUST LEFT HER BUSTED COMPUTER GAME SITTIN' ON MY LAWN!

OH.

...WHAT THE CRAP?

WELL, GO PLAY WITH IT IN YOUR OWN YARD!

DAMIEN, YOU BEEN MESSIN' OUT THERE ALL DAY! GO HOME!

BUT I'M ALMOST DONE! ALL'S WAS BUSTED WAS SOME WIRES!

WAIT, I THINK I'MA GET IT TO WORK!

Q. Where do you think it leads? A. I bet I already know where it leads. It's what led her to me. It's how we're connected. I just know it.

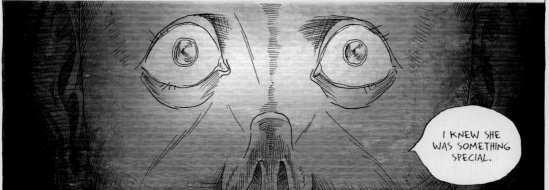

I KNEW SHE WAS SOMETHING SPECIAL.

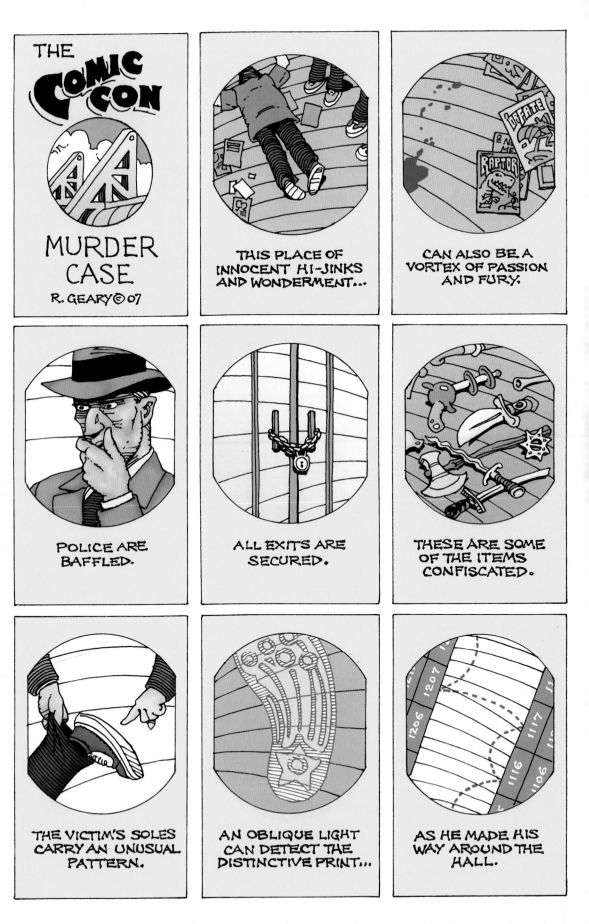

THE COMIC CON

MURDER CASE

R. GEARY © 07

THIS PLACE OF INNOCENT HI-JINKS AND WONDERMENT...

CAN ALSO BE A VORTEX OF PASSION AND FURY.

POLICE ARE BAFFLED.

ALL EXITS ARE SECURED.

THESE ARE SOME OF THE ITEMS CONFISCATED.

THE VICTIM'S SOLES CARRY AN UNUSUAL PATTERN.

AN OBLIQUE LIGHT CAN DETECT THE DISTINCTIVE PRINT...

AS HE MADE HIS WAY AROUND THE HALL.

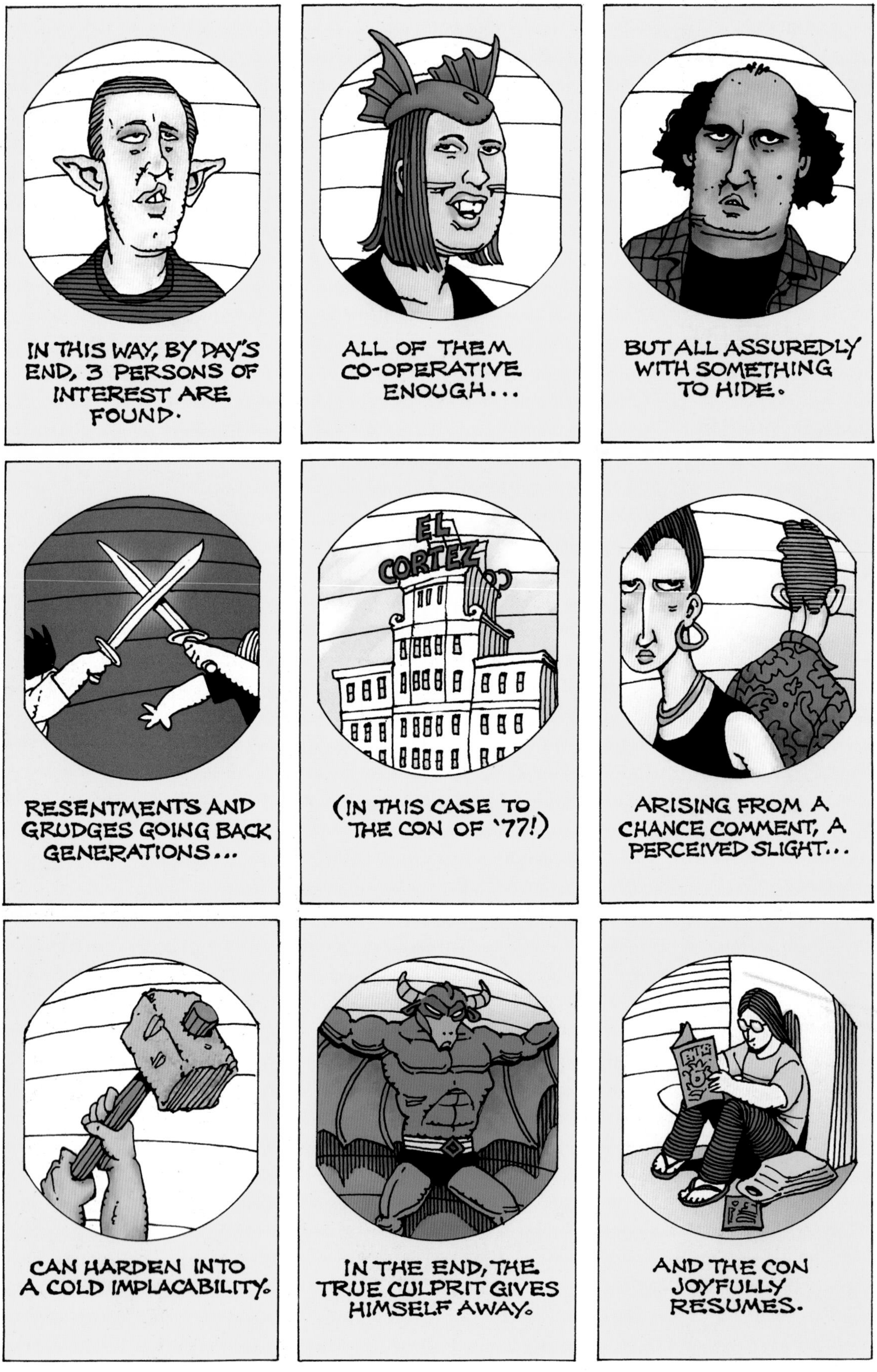
IN THIS WAY, BY DAY'S END, 3 PERSONS OF INTEREST ARE FOUND.
ALL OF THEM CO-OPERATIVE ENOUGH...
BUT ALL ASSUREDLY WITH SOMETHING TO HIDE.
RESENTMENTS AND GRUDGES GOING BACK GENERATIONS...
EL CORTEZ
(IN THIS CASE TO THE CON OF '77!)
ARISING FROM A CHANCE COMMENT, A PERCEIVED SLIGHT...
CAN HARDEN INTO A COLD IMPLACABILITY.
IN THE END, THE TRUE CULPRIT GIVES HIMSELF AWAY.
AND THE CON JOYFULLY RESUMES.

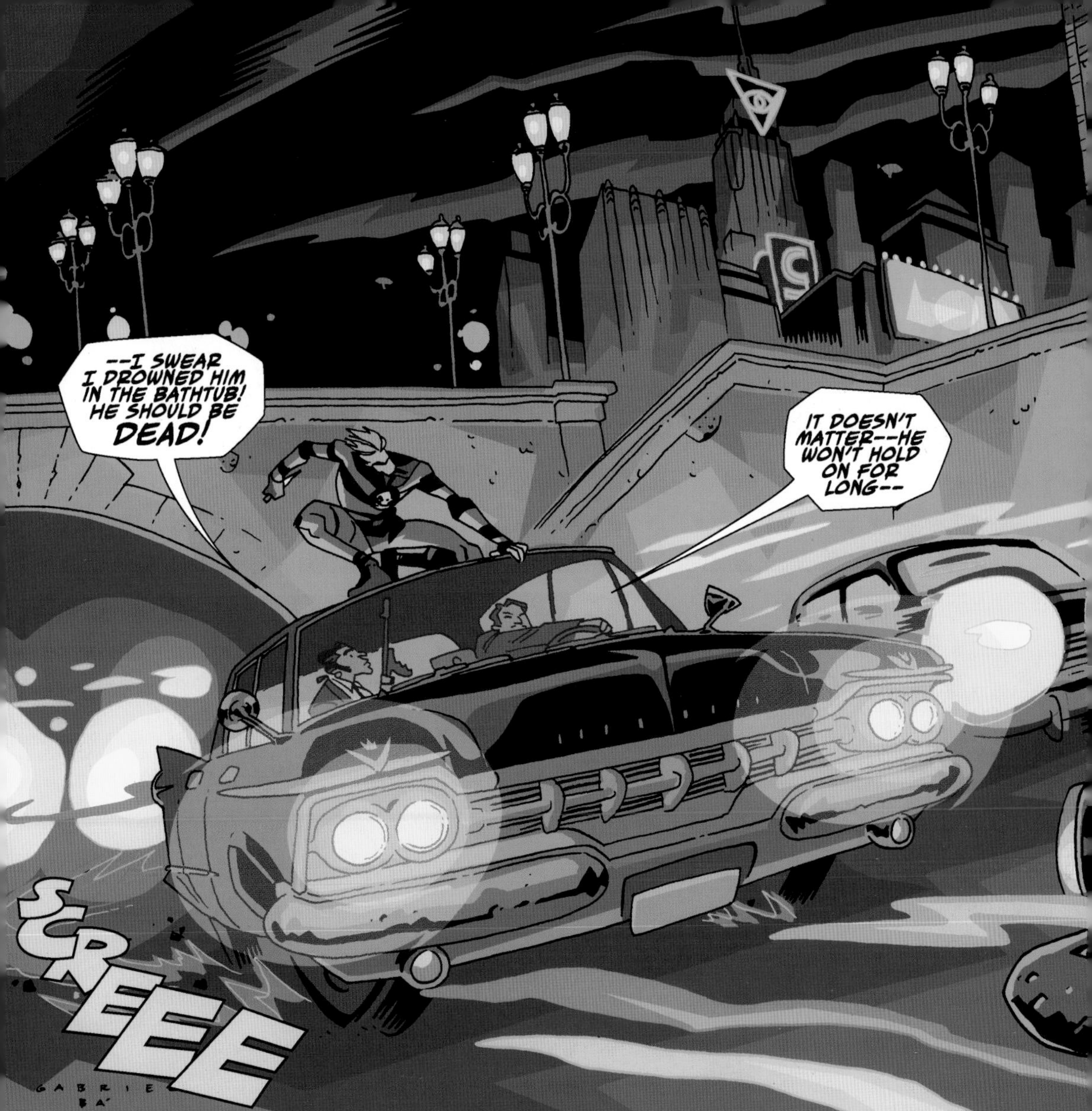
--I SWEAR I DROWNED HIM IN THE BATHTUB! HE SHOULD BE DEAD!
IT DOESN'T MATTER--HE WON'T HOLD ON FOR LONG--
SCREEE
GABRIEL BÁ

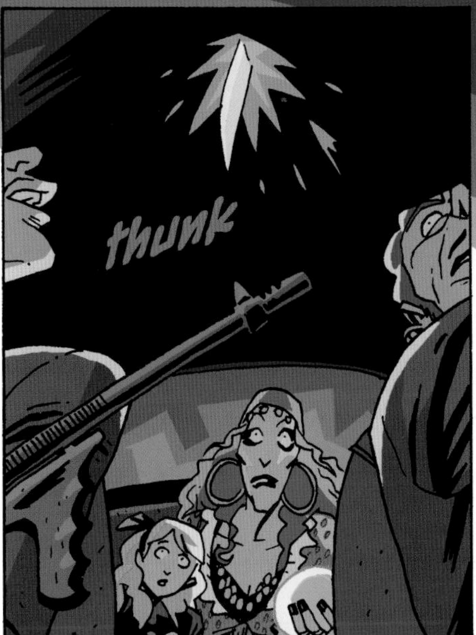
thunk

SAFE & SOUND

FEATURING
THE KRAKEN
FORMERLY OF
THE UMBRELLA ACADEMY

By Gerard Way
and Gabriel Bá
With Dave Stewart
and Nate Piekos

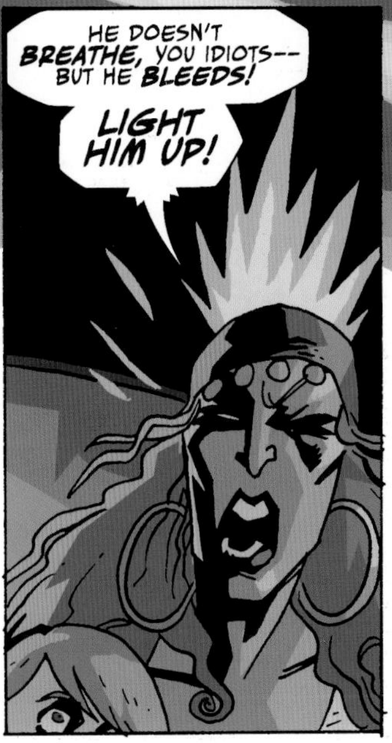
HE DOESN'T BREATHE, YOU IDIOTS--BUT HE BLEEDS!
LIGHT HIM UP!

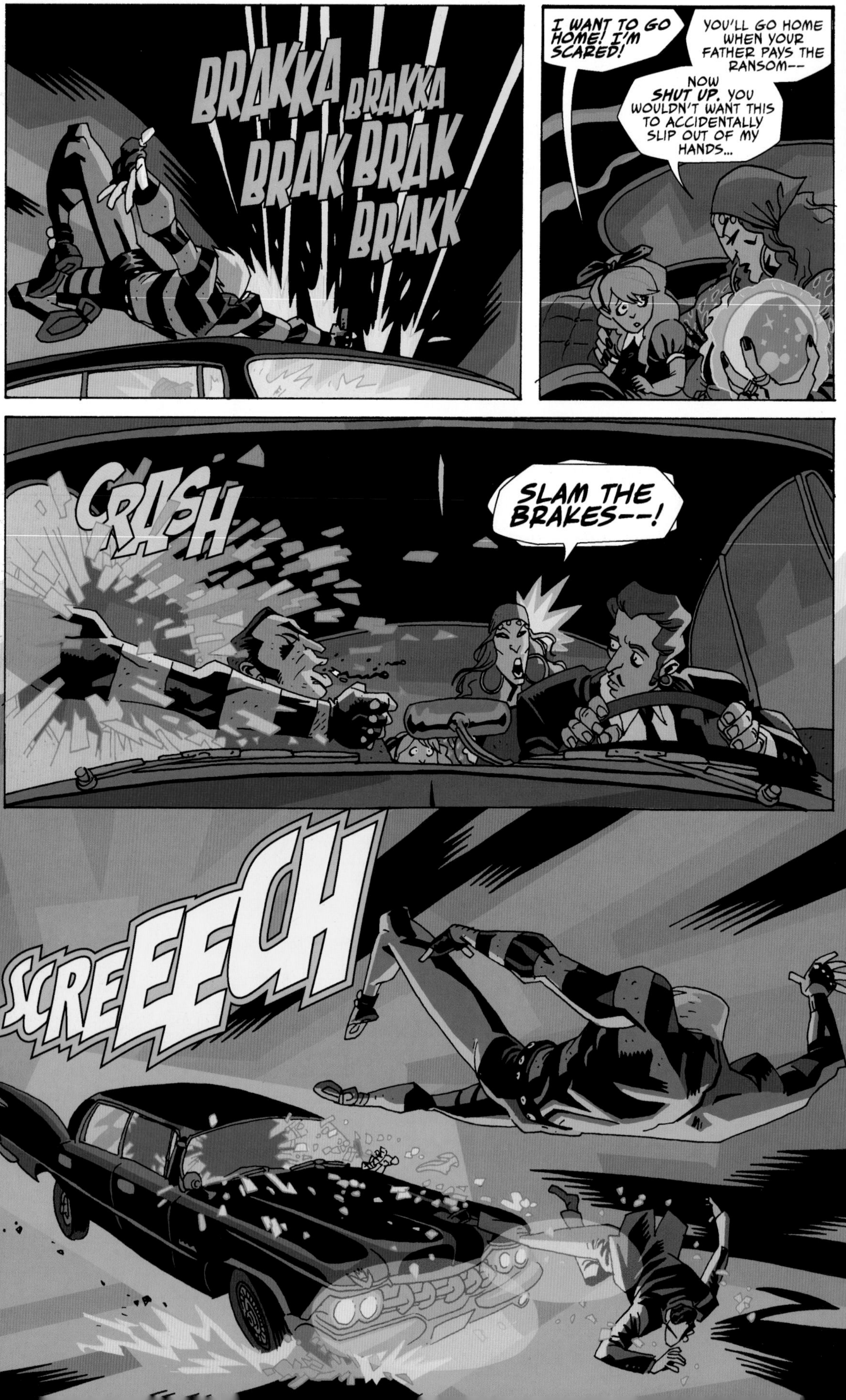
BRAKKA BRAKKA
BRAK BRAK
BRAKK
I WANT TO GO HOME! I'M SCARED!
YOU'LL GO HOME WHEN YOUR FATHER PAYS THE RANSOM--
NOW SHUT UP. YOU WOULDN'T WANT THIS TO ACCIDENTALLY SLIP OUT OF MY HANDS...
CRASH
SLAM THE BRAKES--!
SCREEECH

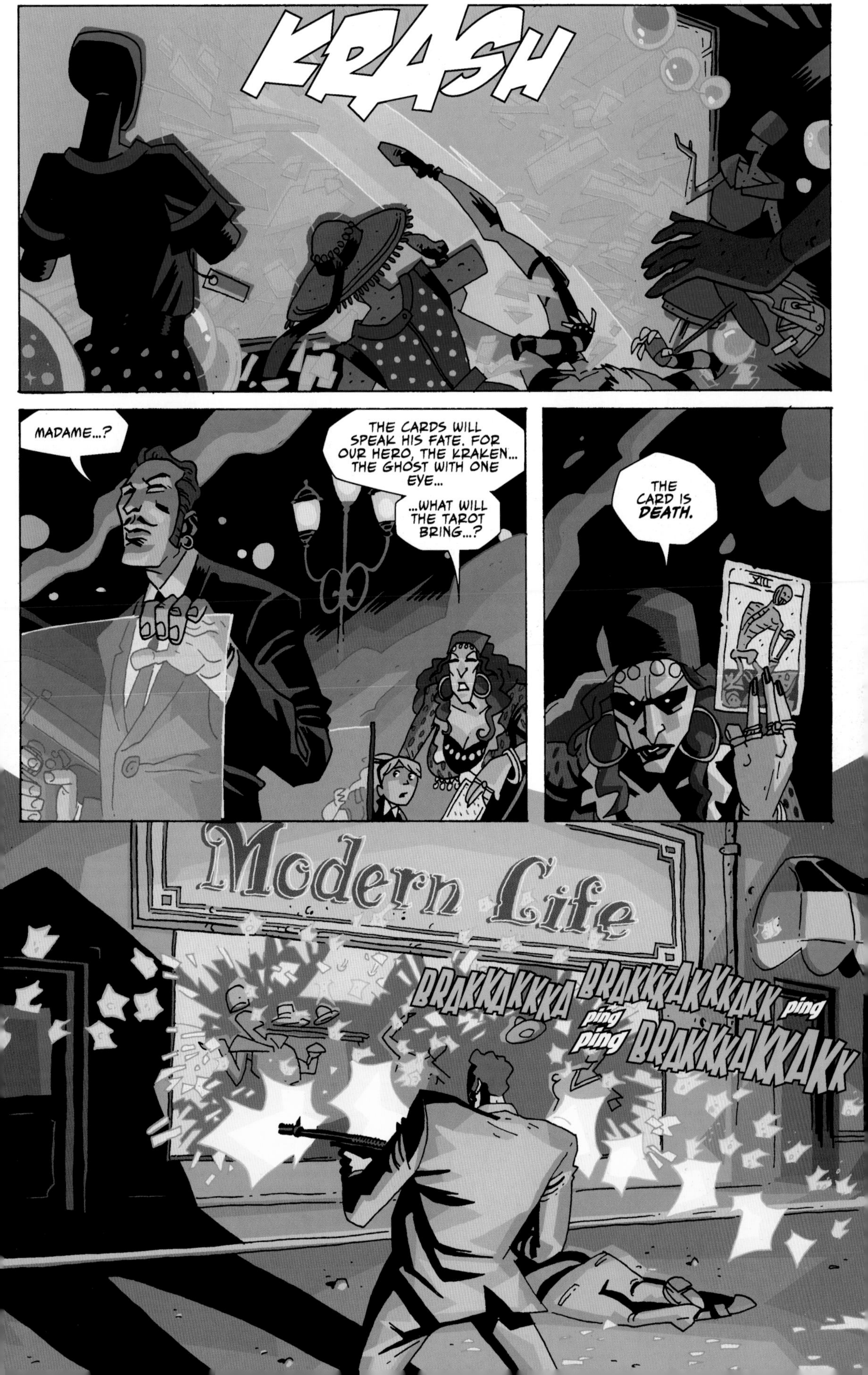
KRASH
MADAME...?
THE CARDS WILL SPEAK HIS FATE. FOR OUR HERO, THE KRAKEN... THE GHOST WITH ONE EYE...
...WHAT WILL THE TAROT BRING...?
THE CARD IS *DEATH.*
Modern Life
BRAKKAKKKA BRAKKKAKKKAKK ping
ping
ping BRAKKKAKKAKK

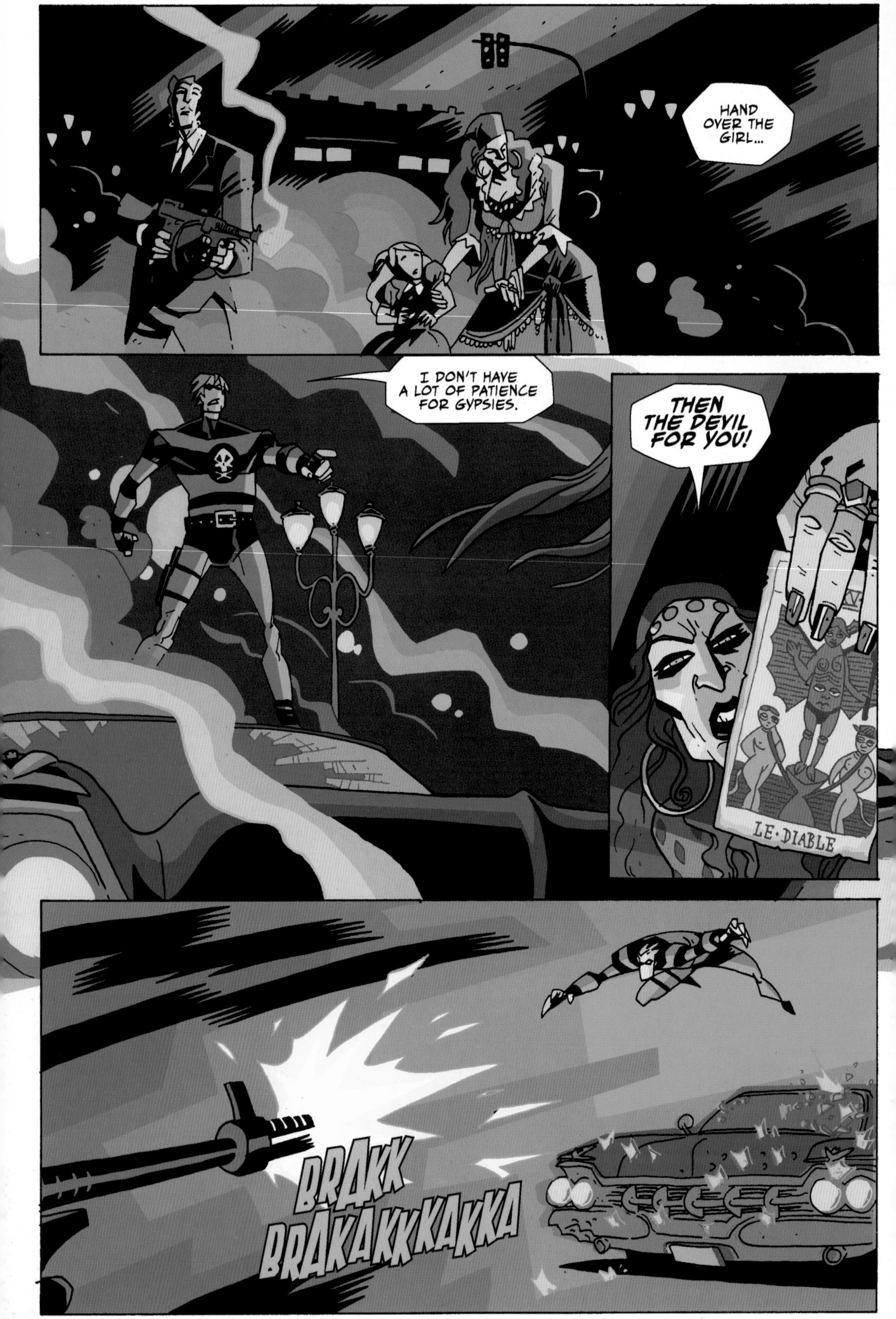
HAND OVER THE GIRL...
I DON'T HAVE A LOT OF PATIENCE FOR GYPSIES.
THEN THE DEVIL FOR YOU!
LE·DIABLE
BRAKK BRAKAKKKAKKA

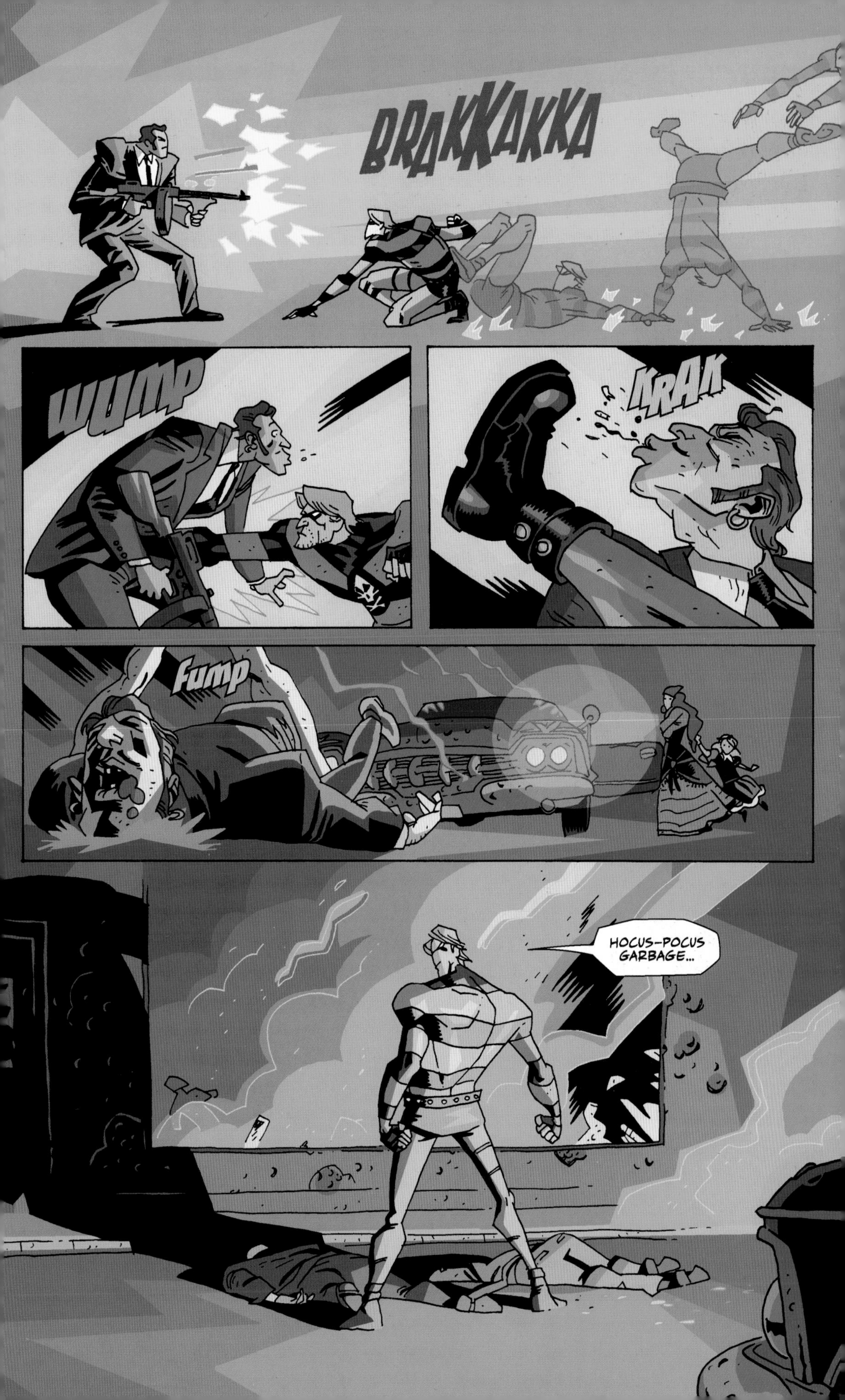
BRAKKAKKA
WUMP
KRAK
FUMP
HOCUS-POCUS GARBAGE...

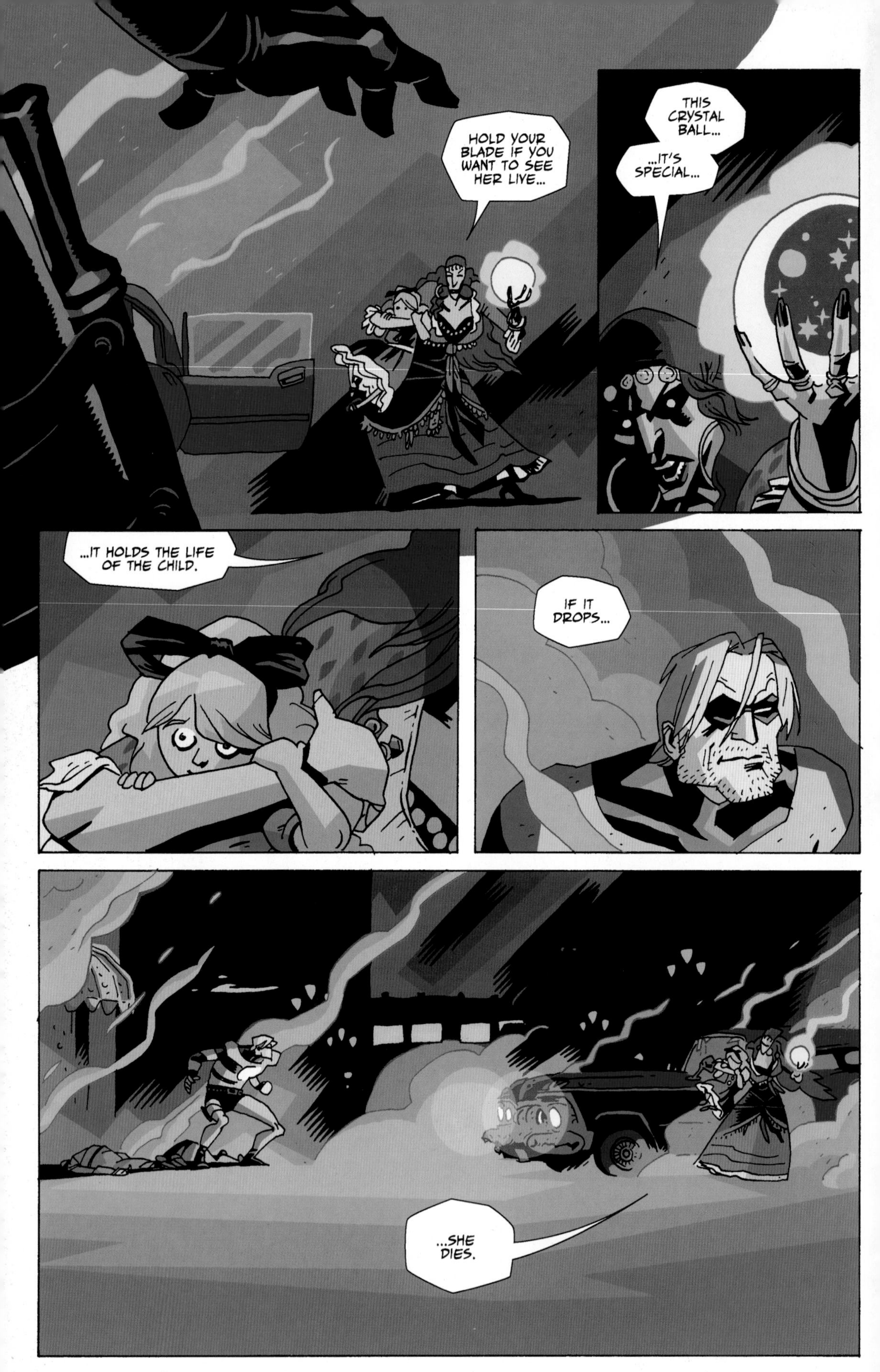
HOLD YOUR BLADE IF YOU WANT TO SEE HER LIVE...
THIS CRYSTAL BALL...
...IT'S SPECIAL...
...IT HOLDS THE LIFE OF THE CHILD.
IF IT DROPS...
...SHE DIES.

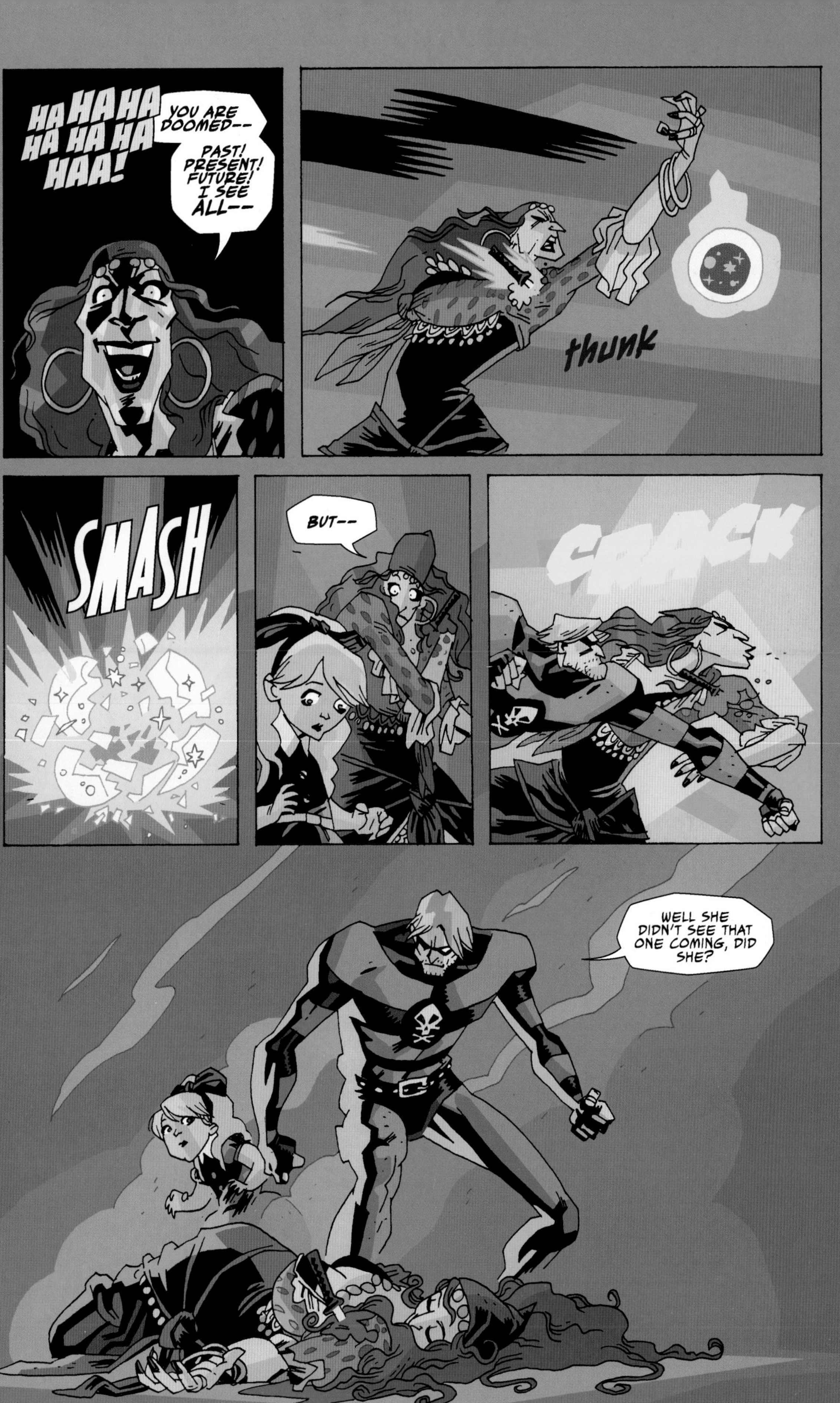
HA HA HA
HA HA HA
HAA!
YOU ARE DOOMED--
PAST! PRESENT! FUTURE! I SEE ALL--
thunk
SMASH
BUT--
CRACK
WELL SHE DIDN'T SEE THAT ONE COMING, DID SHE?

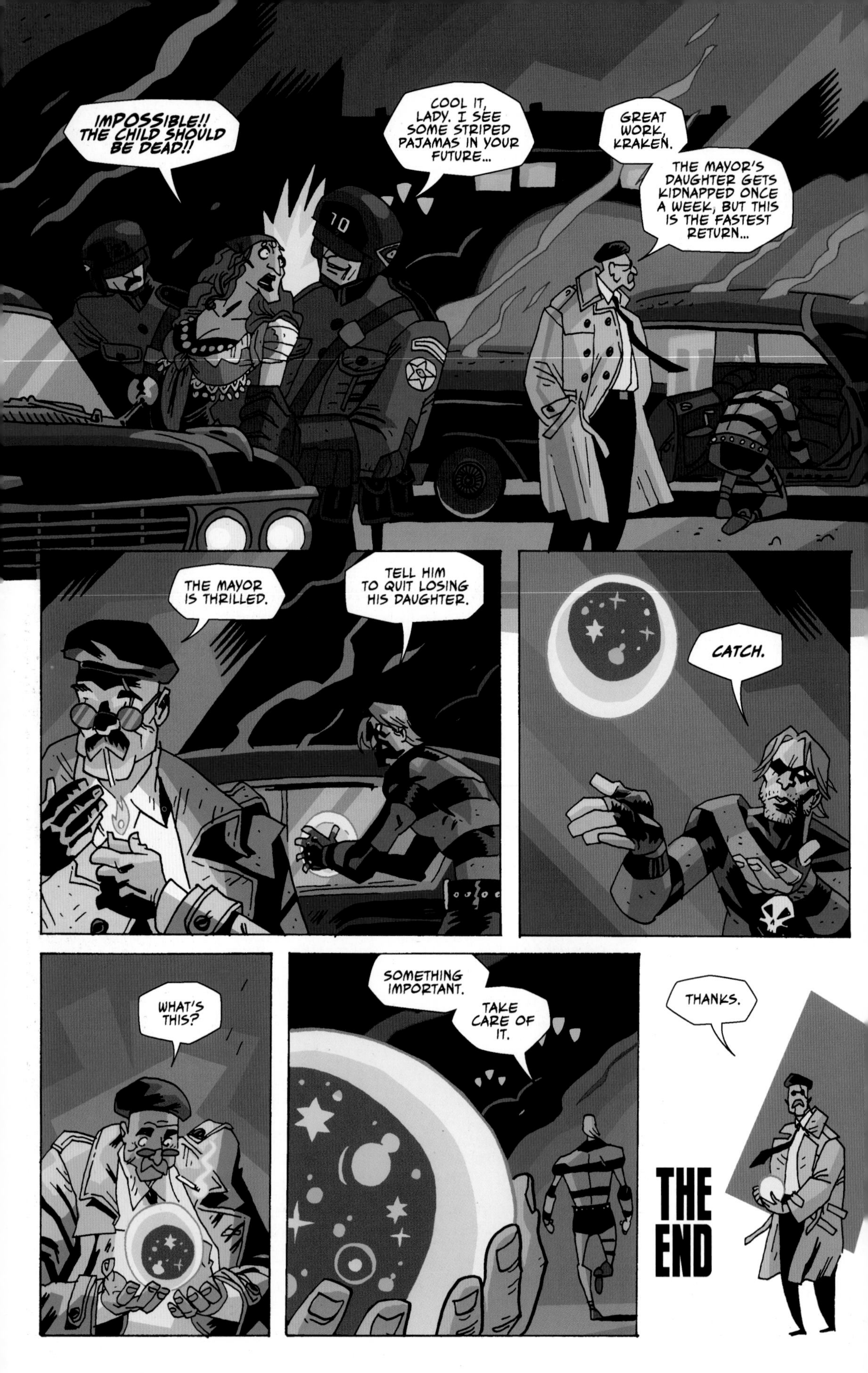
IMPOSSIBLE!! THE CHILD SHOULD BE DEAD!!
COOL IT, LADY. I SEE SOME STRIPED PAJAMAS IN YOUR FUTURE...
GREAT WORK, KRAKEN.
THE MAYOR'S DAUGHTER GETS KIDNAPPED ONCE A WEEK, BUT THIS IS THE FASTEST RETURN...
THE MAYOR IS THRILLED.
TELL HIM TO QUIT LOSING HIS DAUGHTER.
CATCH.
WHAT'S THIS?
SOMETHING IMPORTANT.
TAKE CARE OF IT.
THANKS.
THE END

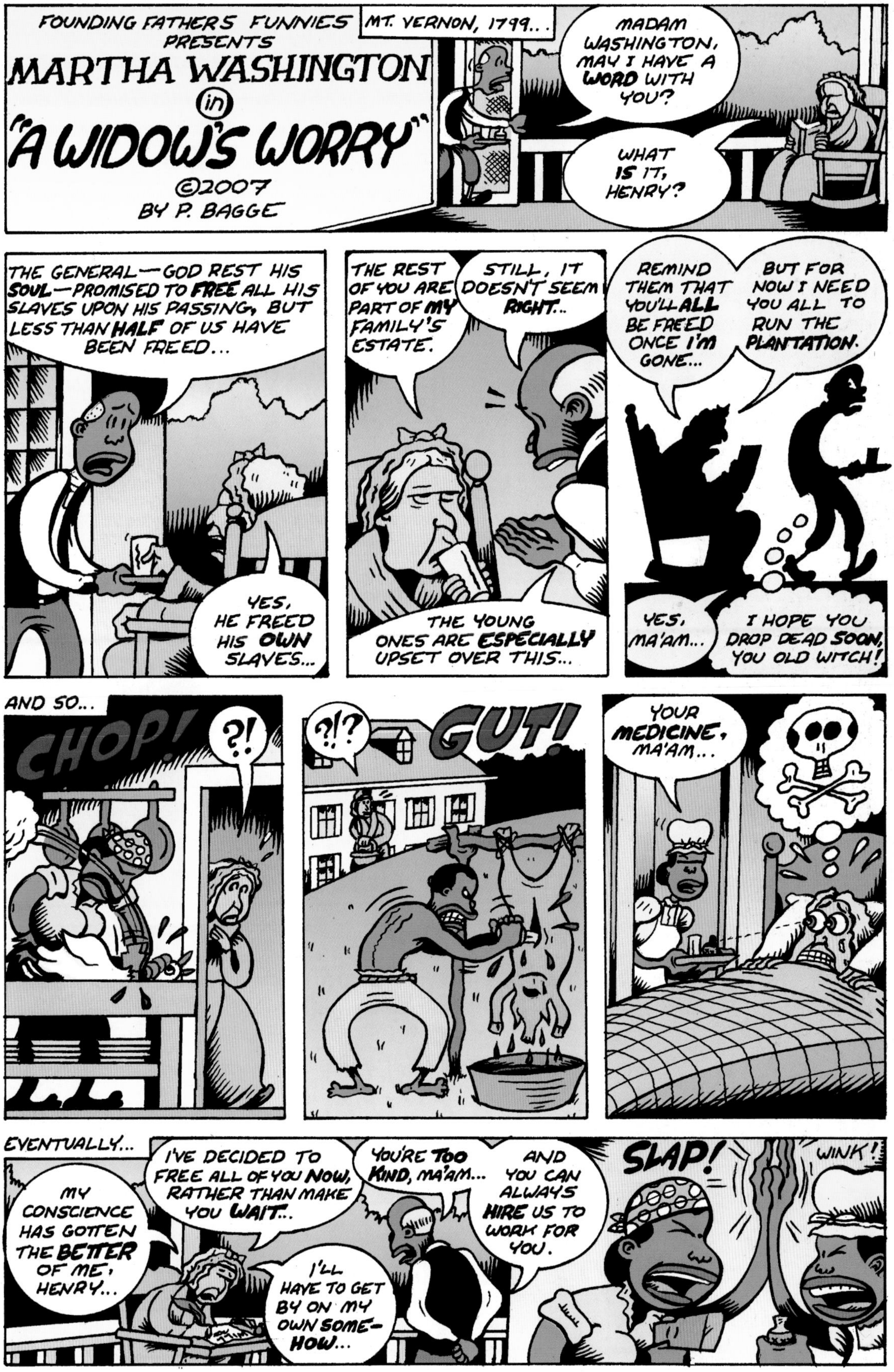

FOUNDING FATHERS FUNNIES PRESENTS
MARTHA WASHINGTON
in
"A WIDOW'S WORRY"
©2007
BY P. BAGGE
MT. VERNON, 1799...
MADAM WASHINGTON, MAY I HAVE A WORD WITH YOU?
WHAT IS IT, HENRY?
THE GENERAL—GOD REST HIS SOUL—PROMISED TO FREE ALL HIS SLAVES UPON HIS PASSING, BUT LESS THAN HALF OF US HAVE BEEN FREED...
YES, HE FREED HIS OWN SLAVES...
THE REST OF YOU ARE PART OF MY FAMILY'S ESTATE.
STILL, IT DOESN'T SEEM RIGHT...
THE YOUNG ONES ARE ESPECIALLY UPSET OVER THIS...
REMIND THEM THAT YOU'LL ALL BE FREED ONCE I'M GONE...
BUT FOR NOW I NEED YOU ALL TO RUN THE PLANTATION.
YES, MA'AM...
I HOPE YOU DROP DEAD SOON, YOU OLD WITCH!
AND SO...
CHOP!
?!
?!?
GUT!
YOUR MEDICINE, MA'AM...
EVENTUALLY...
MY CONSCIENCE HAS GOTTEN THE BETTER OF ME, HENRY...
I'VE DECIDED TO FREE ALL OF YOU NOW, RATHER THAN MAKE YOU WAIT...
I'LL HAVE TO GET BY ON MY OWN SOMEHOW...
YOU'RE TOO KIND, MA'AM...
AND YOU CAN ALWAYS HIRE US TO WORK FOR YOU.
SLAP!
WINK!

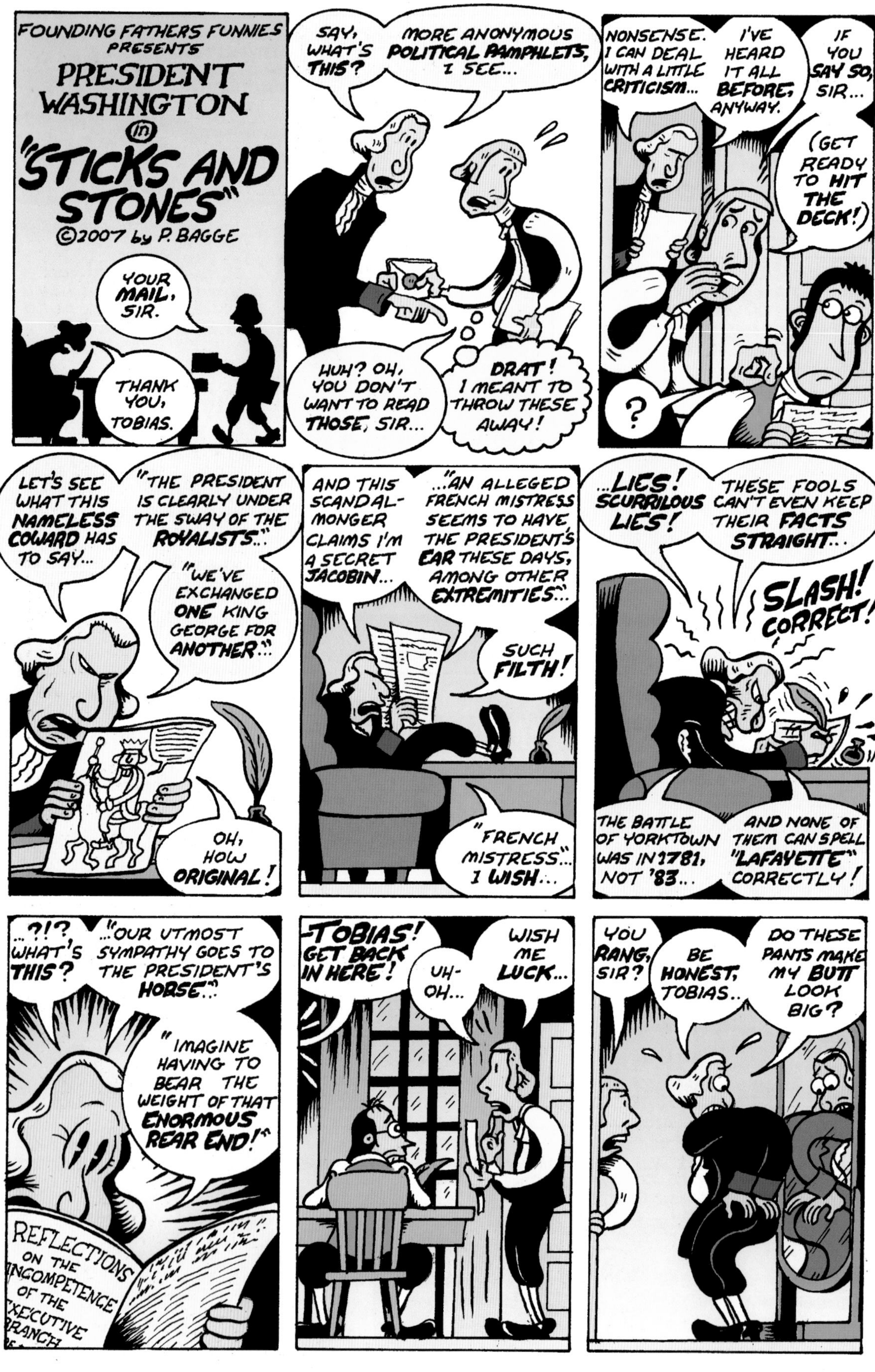
FOUNDING FATHERS FUNNIES PRESENTS
PRESIDENT WASHINGTON in "STICKS AND STONES"
©2007 by P. BAGGE
YOUR MAIL, SIR.
THANK YOU, TOBIAS.
SAY, WHAT'S THIS?
MORE ANONYMOUS POLITICAL PAMPHLETS, I SEE...
HUH? OH, YOU DON'T WANT TO READ THOSE, SIR...
DRAT! I MEANT TO THROW THESE AWAY!
NONSENSE. I CAN DEAL WITH A LITTLE CRITICISM...
I'VE HEARD IT ALL BEFORE, ANYWAY.
IF YOU SAY SO, SIR...
(GET READY TO HIT THE DECK!)
?
LET'S SEE WHAT THIS NAMELESS COWARD HAS TO SAY...
"THE PRESIDENT IS CLEARLY UNDER THE SWAY OF THE ROYALISTS..."
"WE'VE EXCHANGED ONE KING GEORGE FOR ANOTHER..."
OH, HOW ORIGINAL!
AND THIS SCANDAL-MONGER CLAIMS I'M A SECRET JACOBIN...
..."AN ALLEGED FRENCH MISTRESS SEEMS TO HAVE THE PRESIDENT'S EAR THESE DAYS, AMONG OTHER EXTREMITIES..."
SUCH FILTH!
"FRENCH MISTRESS"... I WISH...
...LIES! SCURRILOUS LIES!
THESE FOOLS CAN'T EVEN KEEP THEIR FACTS STRAIGHT...
SLASH! CORRECT!
THE BATTLE OF YORKTOWN WAS IN 1781, NOT '83...
AND NONE OF THEM CAN SPELL "LAFAYETTE" CORRECTLY!
...?!? WHAT'S THIS?
..."OUR UTMOST SYMPATHY GOES TO THE PRESIDENT'S HORSE..."
"IMAGINE HAVING TO BEAR THE WEIGHT OF THAT ENORMOUS REAR END!"
REFLECTIONS ON THE INCOMPETENCE OF THE EXECUTIVE BRANCH
TOBIAS! GET BACK IN HERE!
UH-OH...
WISH ME LUCK...
YOU RANG, SIR?
BE HONEST, TOBIAS...
DO THESE PANTS MAKE MY BUTT LOOK BIG?

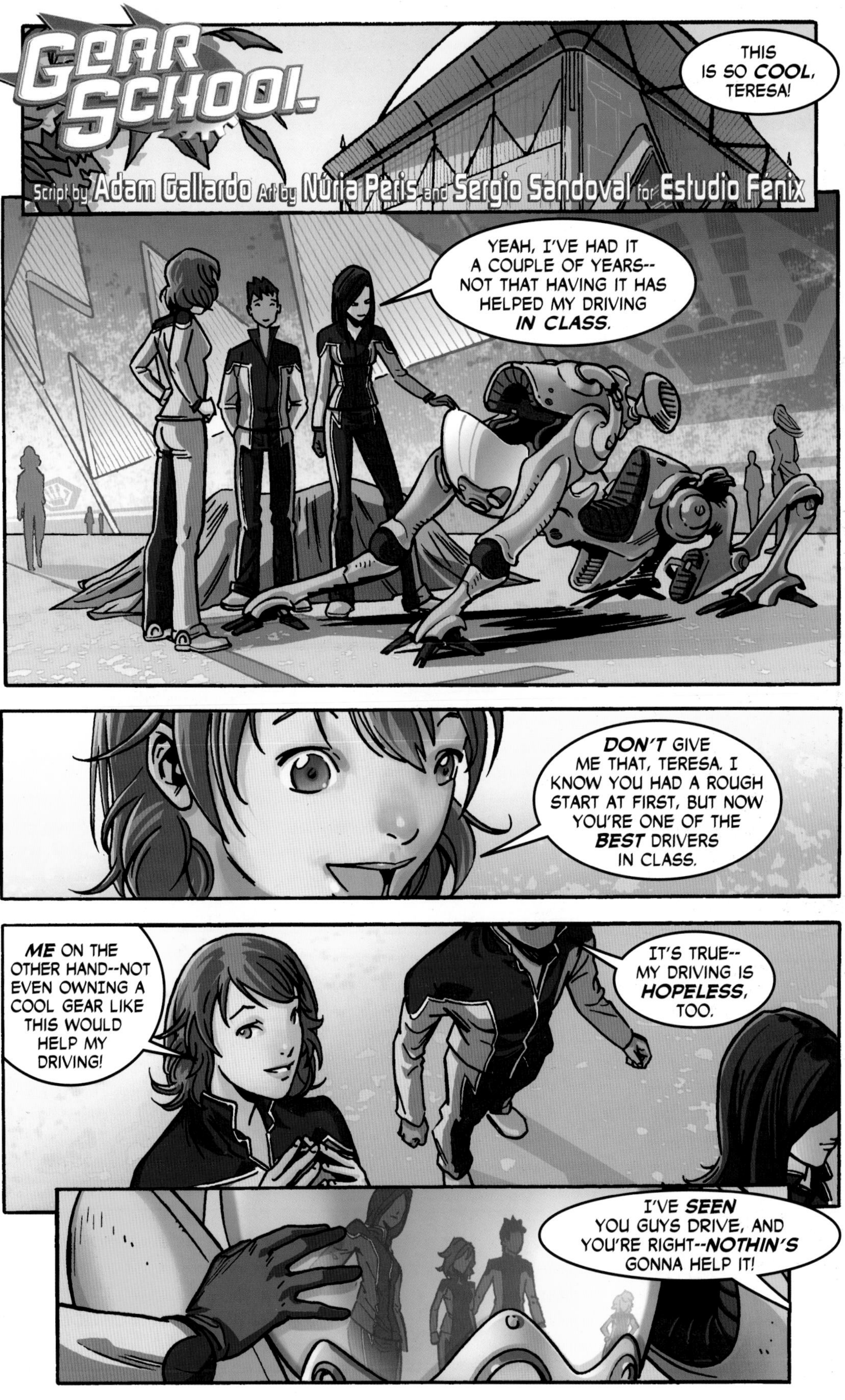
GEAR SCHOOL
Script by Adam Gallardo Art by Núria Peris and Sergio Sandoval for Estudio Fénix
THIS IS SO COOL, TERESA!
YEAH, I'VE HAD IT A COUPLE OF YEARS--NOT THAT HAVING IT HAS HELPED MY DRIVING IN CLASS.
DON'T GIVE ME THAT, TERESA. I KNOW YOU HAD A ROUGH START AT FIRST, BUT NOW YOU'RE ONE OF THE BEST DRIVERS IN CLASS.
ME ON THE OTHER HAND--NOT EVEN OWNING A COOL GEAR LIKE THIS WOULD HELP MY DRIVING!
IT'S TRUE--MY DRIVING IS HOPELESS, TOO.
I'VE SEEN YOU GUYS DRIVE, AND YOU'RE RIGHT--NOTHIN'S GONNA HELP IT!

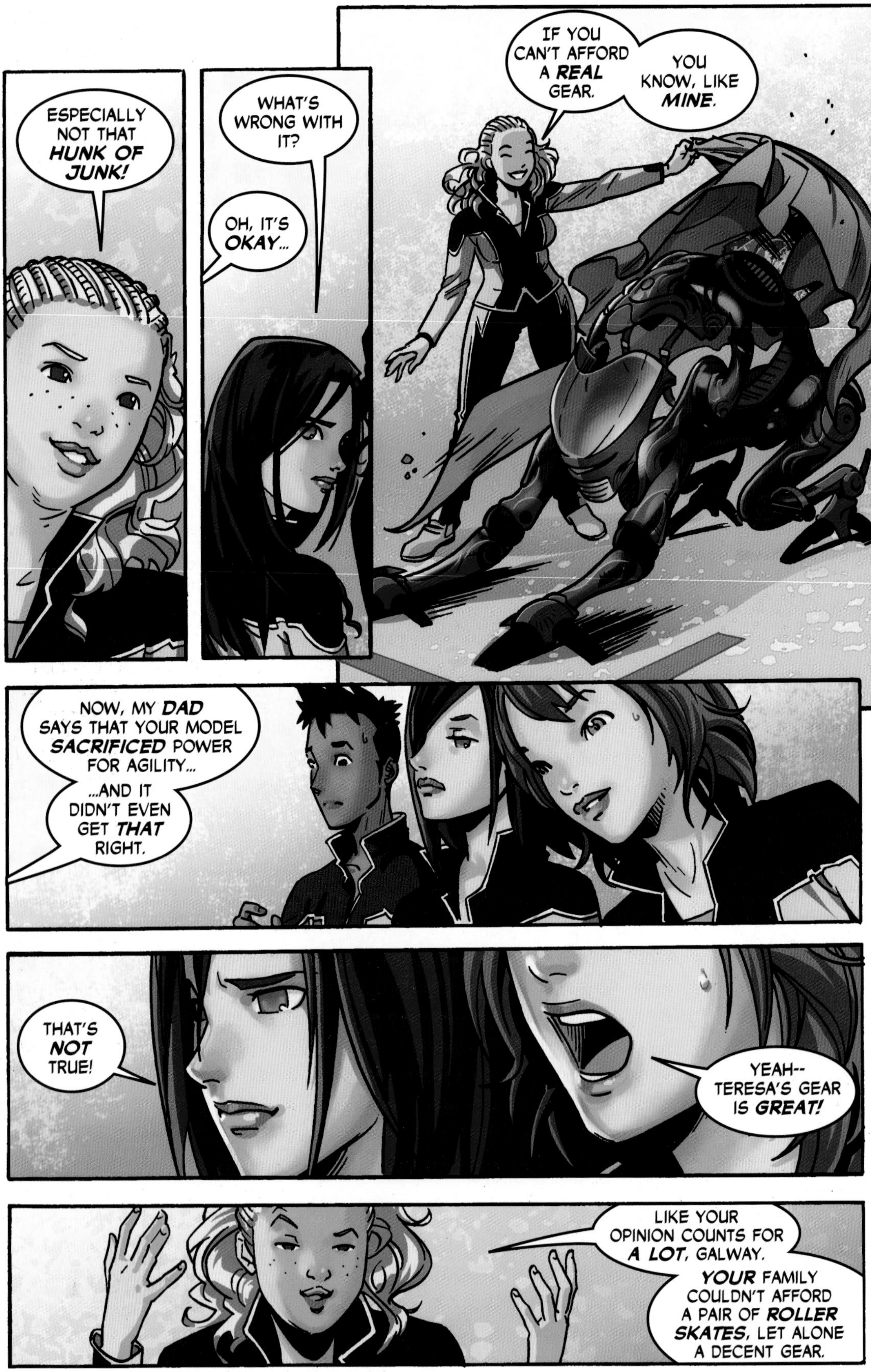
ESPECIALLY NOT THAT HUNK OF JUNK!
WHAT'S WRONG WITH IT?
OH, IT'S OKAY...
IF YOU CAN'T AFFORD A REAL GEAR.
YOU KNOW, LIKE MINE.
NOW, MY DAD SAYS THAT YOUR MODEL SACRIFICED POWER FOR AGILITY...
...AND IT DIDN'T EVEN GET THAT RIGHT.
THAT'S NOT TRUE!
YEAH-- TERESA'S GEAR IS GREAT!
LIKE YOUR OPINION COUNTS FOR A LOT, GALWAY.
YOUR FAMILY COULDN'T AFFORD A PAIR OF ROLLER SKATES, LET ALONE A DECENT GEAR.

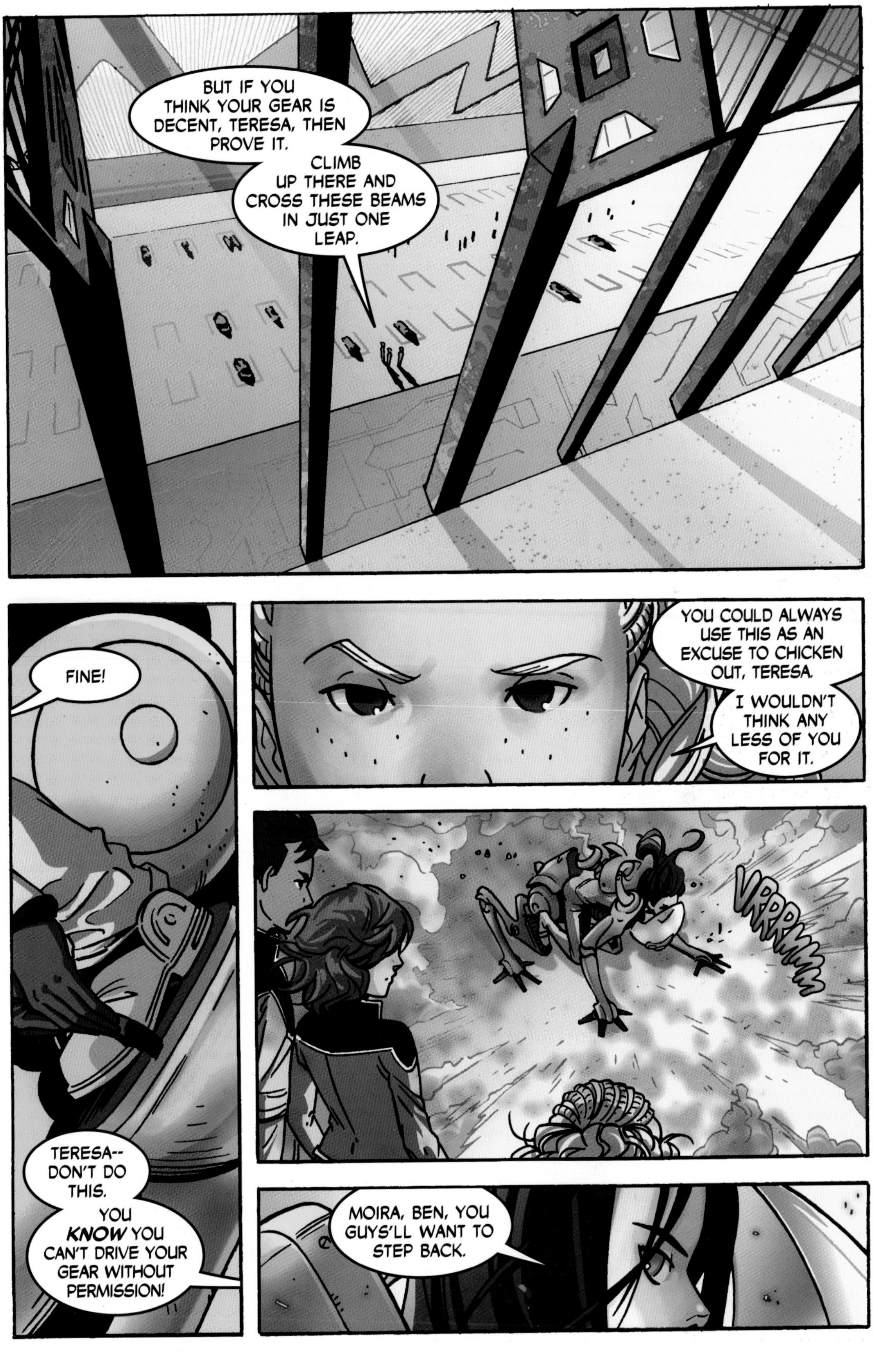
BUT IF YOU THINK YOUR GEAR IS DECENT, TERESA, THEN PROVE IT.
CLIMB UP THERE AND CROSS THESE BEAMS IN JUST ONE LEAP.
FINE!
YOU COULD ALWAYS USE THIS AS AN EXCUSE TO CHICKEN OUT, TERESA.
I WOULDN'T THINK ANY LESS OF YOU FOR IT.
VRRRMMM
TERESA-- DON'T DO THIS.
YOU **KNOW** YOU CAN'T DRIVE YOUR GEAR WITHOUT PERMISSION!
MOIRA, BEN, YOU GUYS'LL WANT TO STEP BACK.

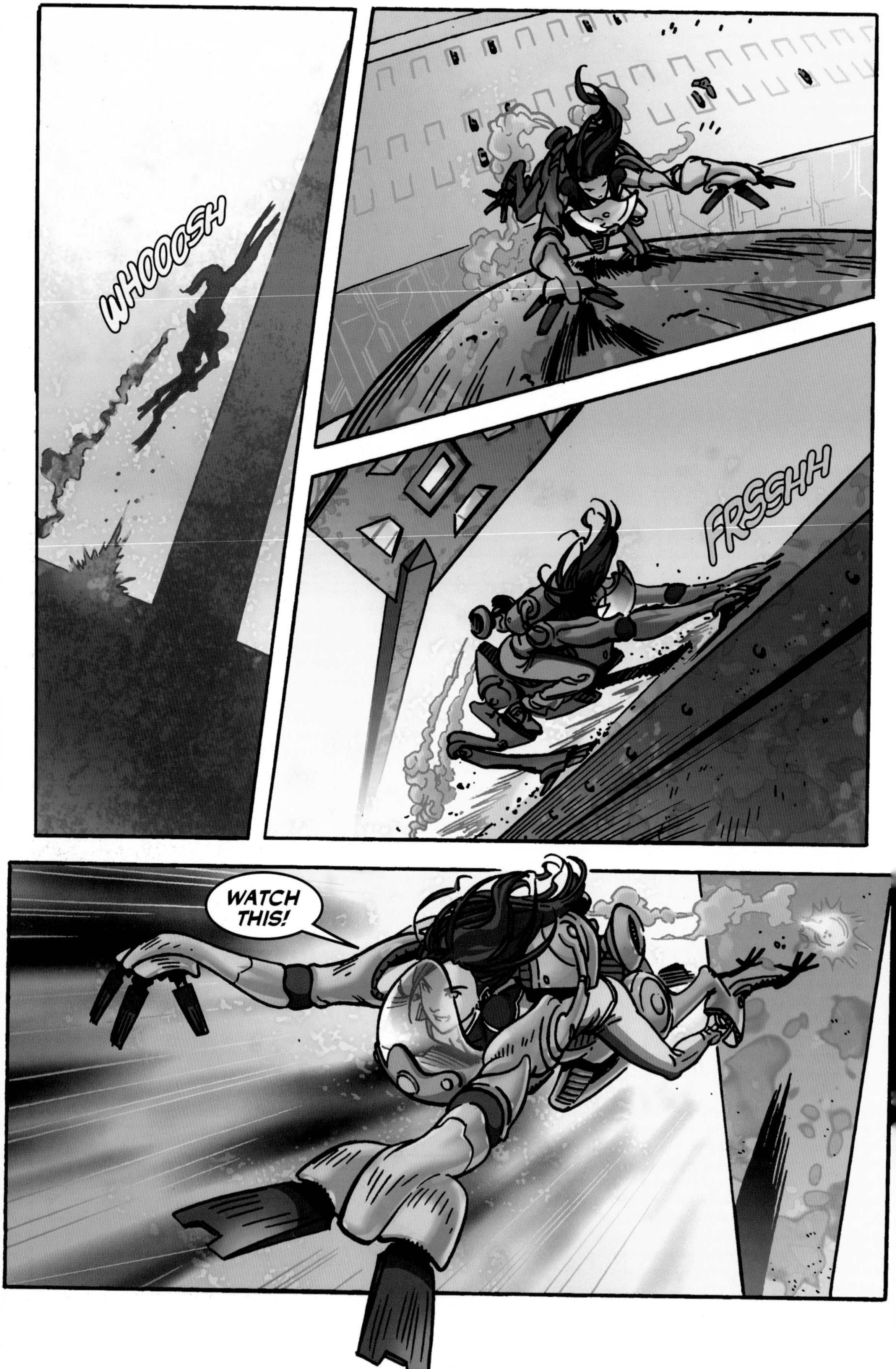
WHOOOOSH
FRSSHH
WATCH THIS!

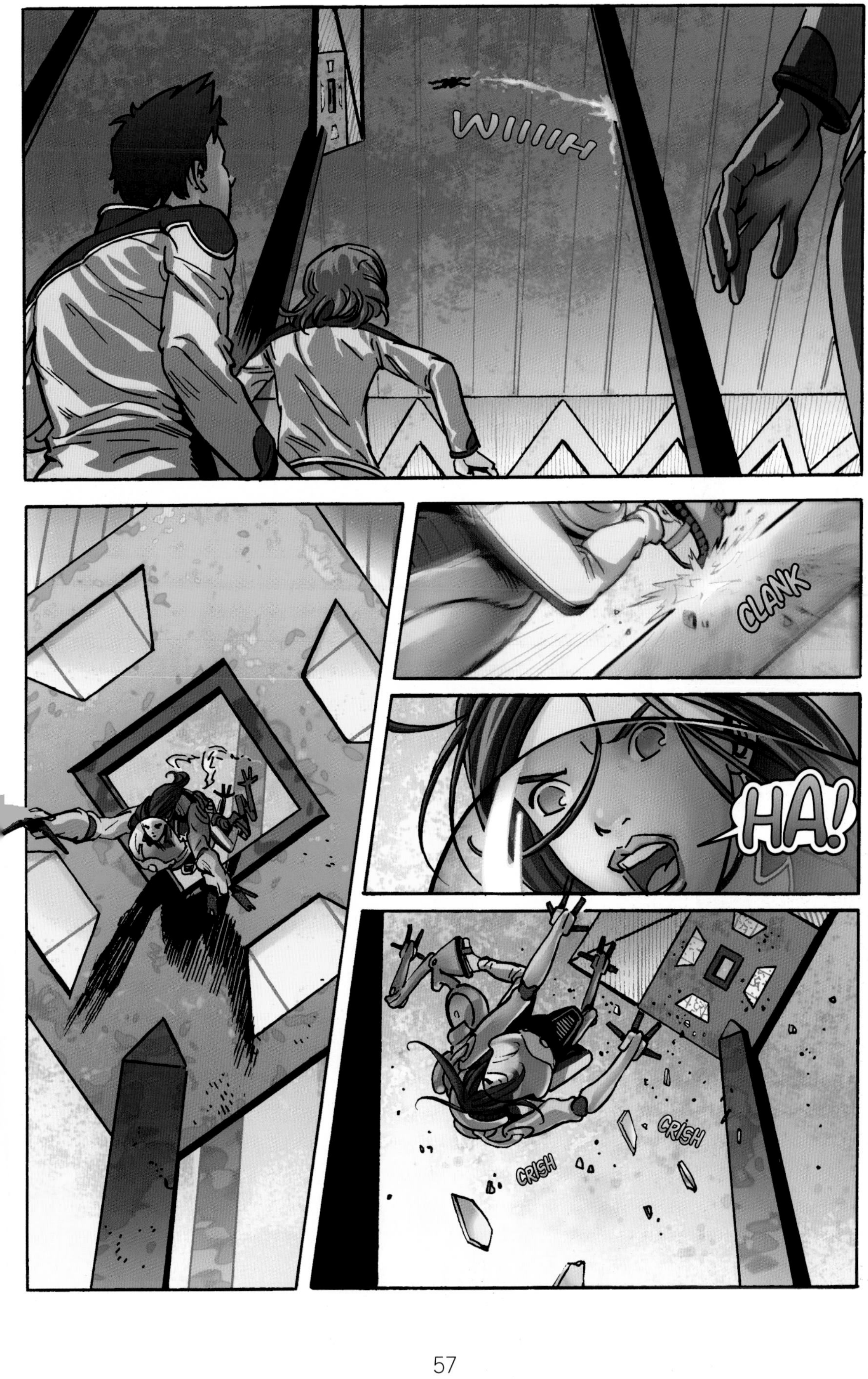
WIIIIH
CLANK
HA!
CRISH
CRISH

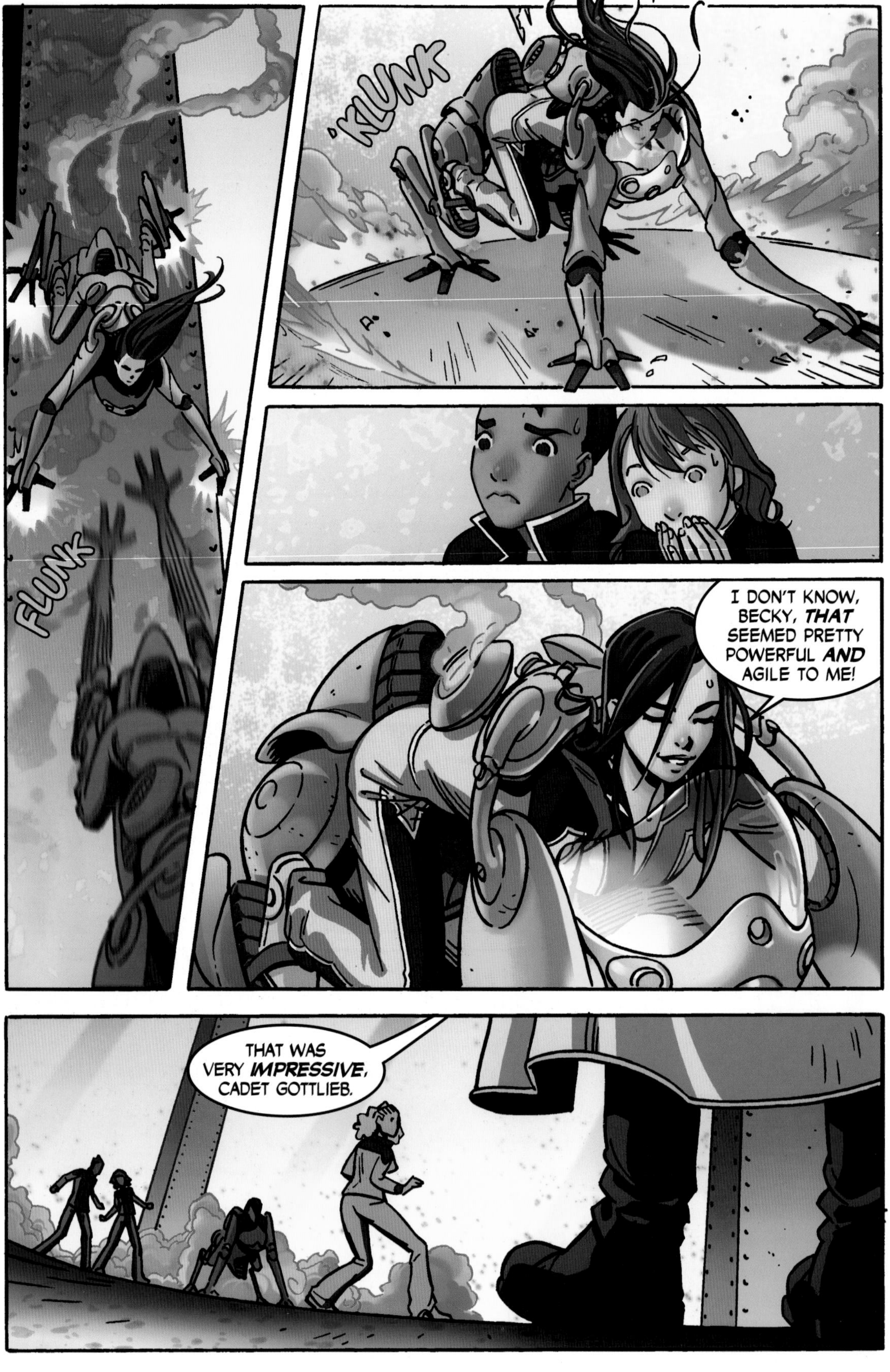
KLUNK
FLUNK
I DON'T KNOW, BECKY, THAT SEEMED PRETTY POWERFUL AND AGILE TO ME!
THAT WAS VERY IMPRESSIVE, CADET GOTTLIEB.

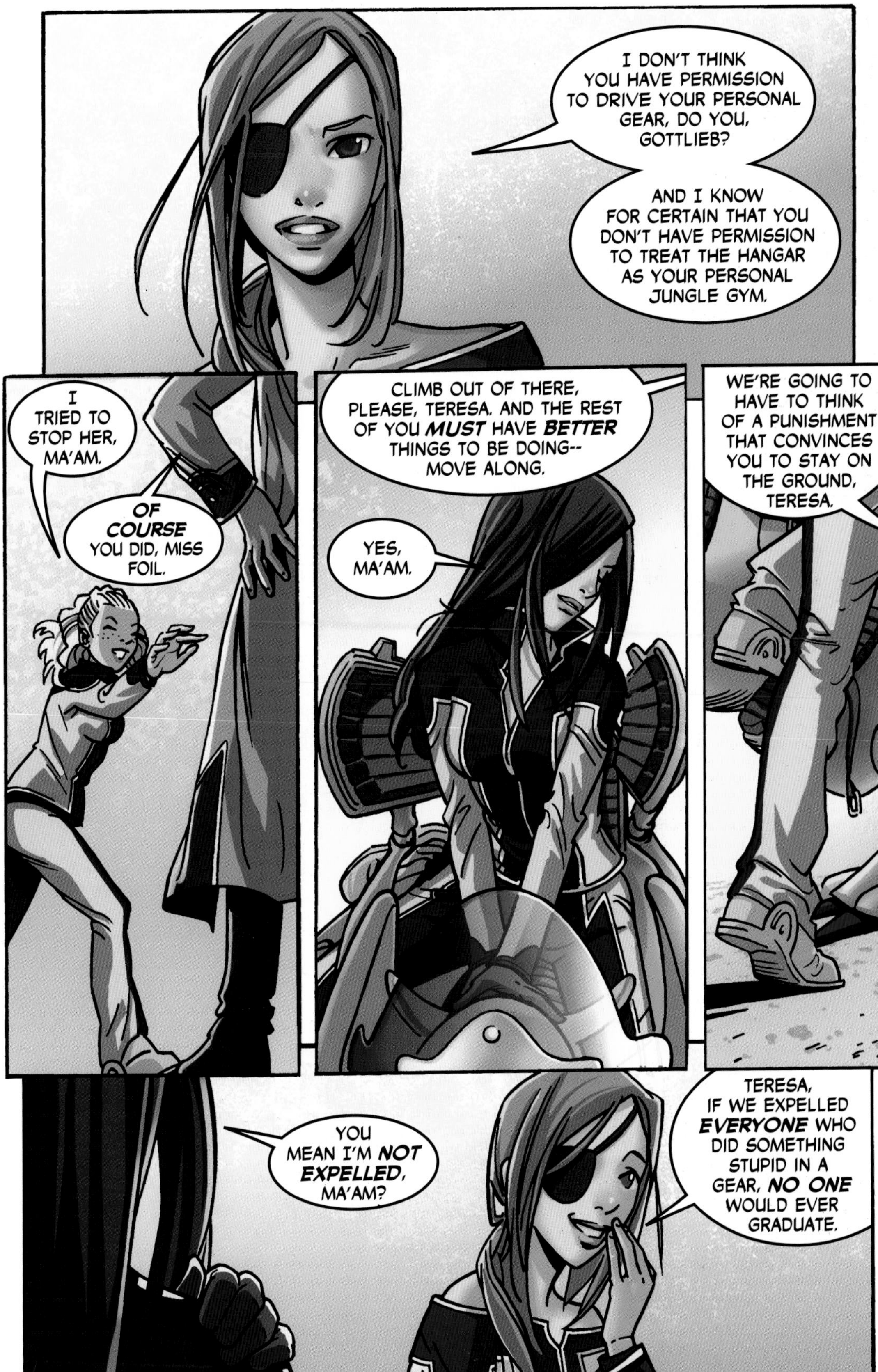
I DON'T THINK YOU HAVE PERMISSION TO DRIVE YOUR PERSONAL GEAR, DO YOU, GOTTLIEB?
AND I KNOW FOR CERTAIN THAT YOU DON'T HAVE PERMISSION TO TREAT THE HANGAR AS YOUR PERSONAL JUNGLE GYM.
I TRIED TO STOP HER, MA'AM.
OF COURSE YOU DID, MISS FOIL.
CLIMB OUT OF THERE, PLEASE, TERESA. AND THE REST OF YOU MUST HAVE BETTER THINGS TO BE DOING-- MOVE ALONG.
YES, MA'AM.
WE'RE GOING TO HAVE TO THINK OF A PUNISHMENT THAT CONVINCES YOU TO STAY ON THE GROUND, TERESA.
YOU MEAN I'M NOT EXPELLED, MA'AM?
TERESA, IF WE EXPELLED EVERYONE WHO DID SOMETHING STUPID IN A GEAR, NO ONE WOULD EVER GRADUATE.

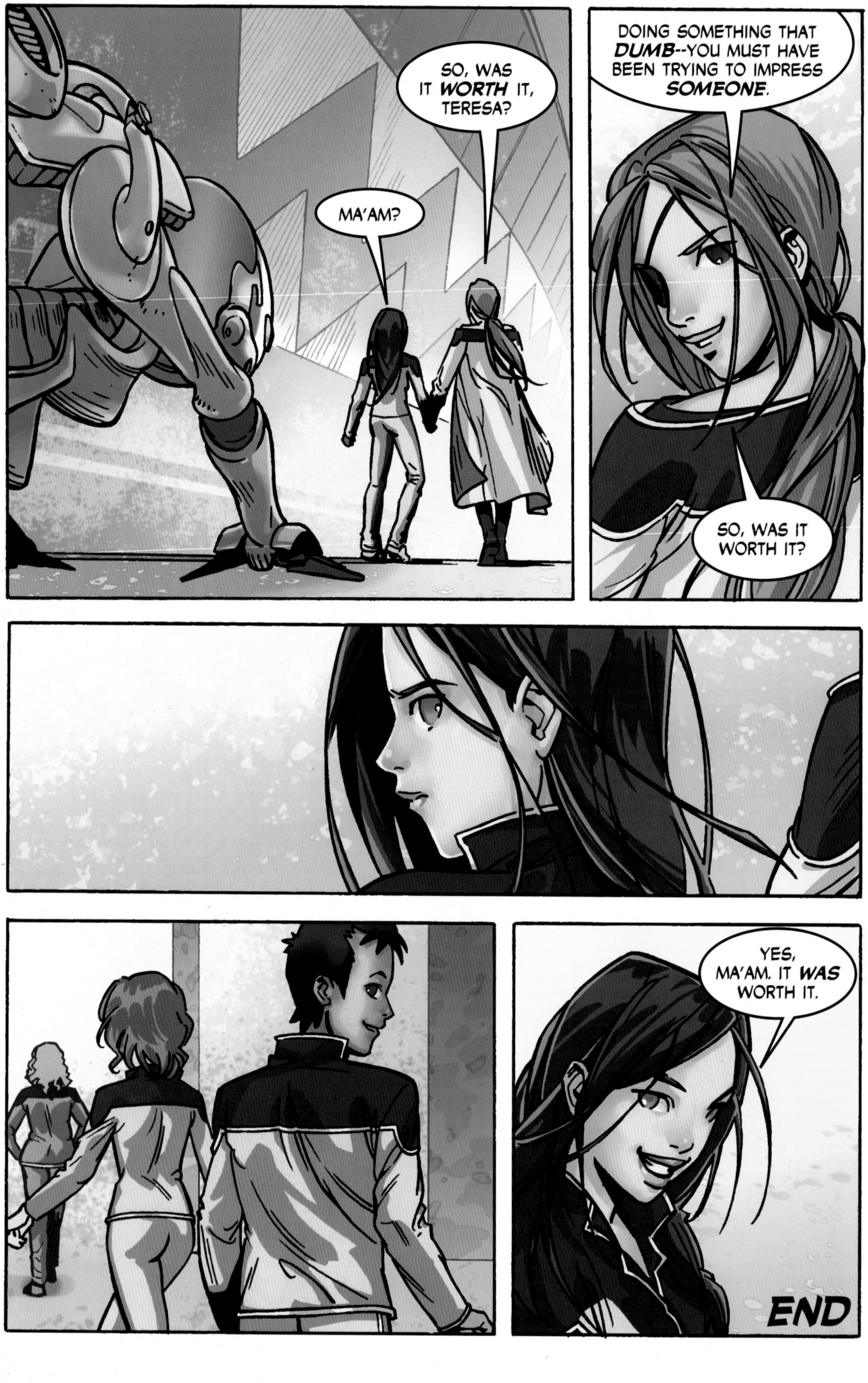
MA'AM?
SO, WAS IT WORTH IT, TERESA?
DOING SOMETHING THAT DUMB--YOU MUST HAVE BEEN TRYING TO IMPRESS SOMEONE.
SO, WAS IT WORTH IT?
YES, MA'AM. IT WAS WORTH IT.
END

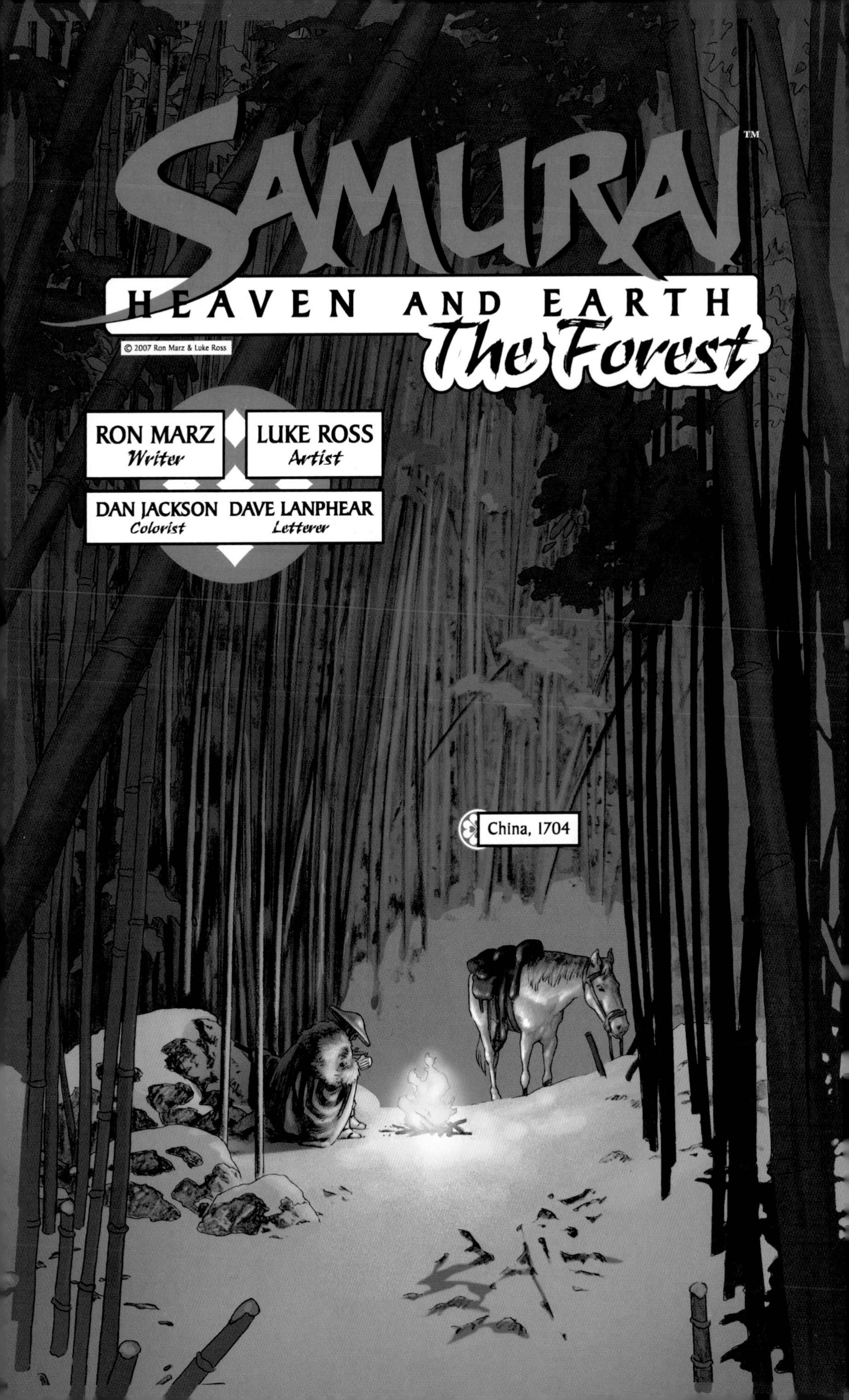
SAMURAI™
HEAVEN AND EARTH
The Forest
© 2007 Ron Marz & Luke Ross
RON MARZ Writer
LUKE ROSS Artist
DAN JACKSON Colorist
DAVE LANPHEAR Letterer
China, 1704

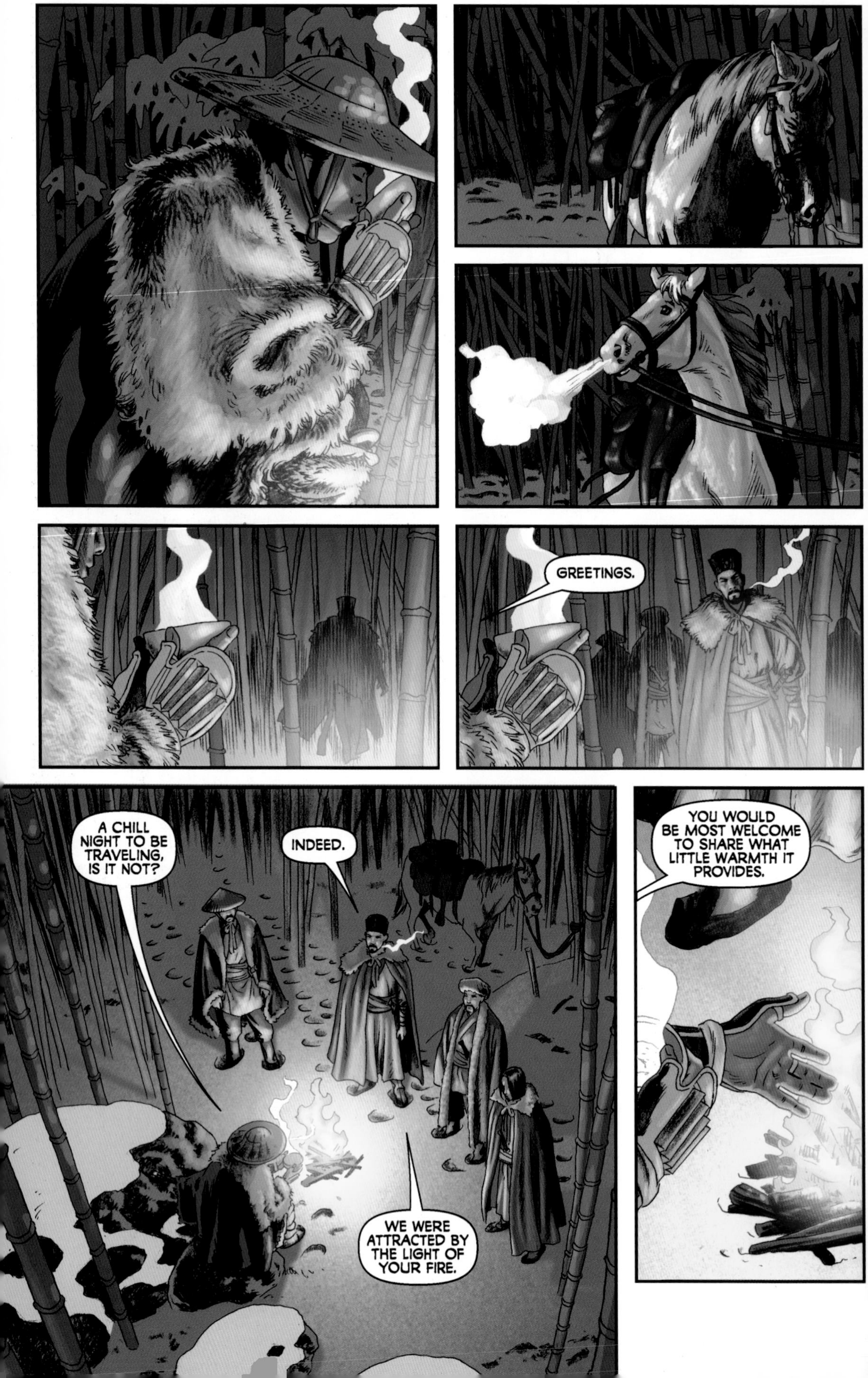
GREETINGS.
A CHILL NIGHT TO BE TRAVELING, IS IT NOT?
INDEED.
WE WERE ATTRACTED BY THE LIGHT OF YOUR FIRE.
YOU WOULD BE MOST WELCOME TO SHARE WHAT LITTLE WARMTH IT PROVIDES.

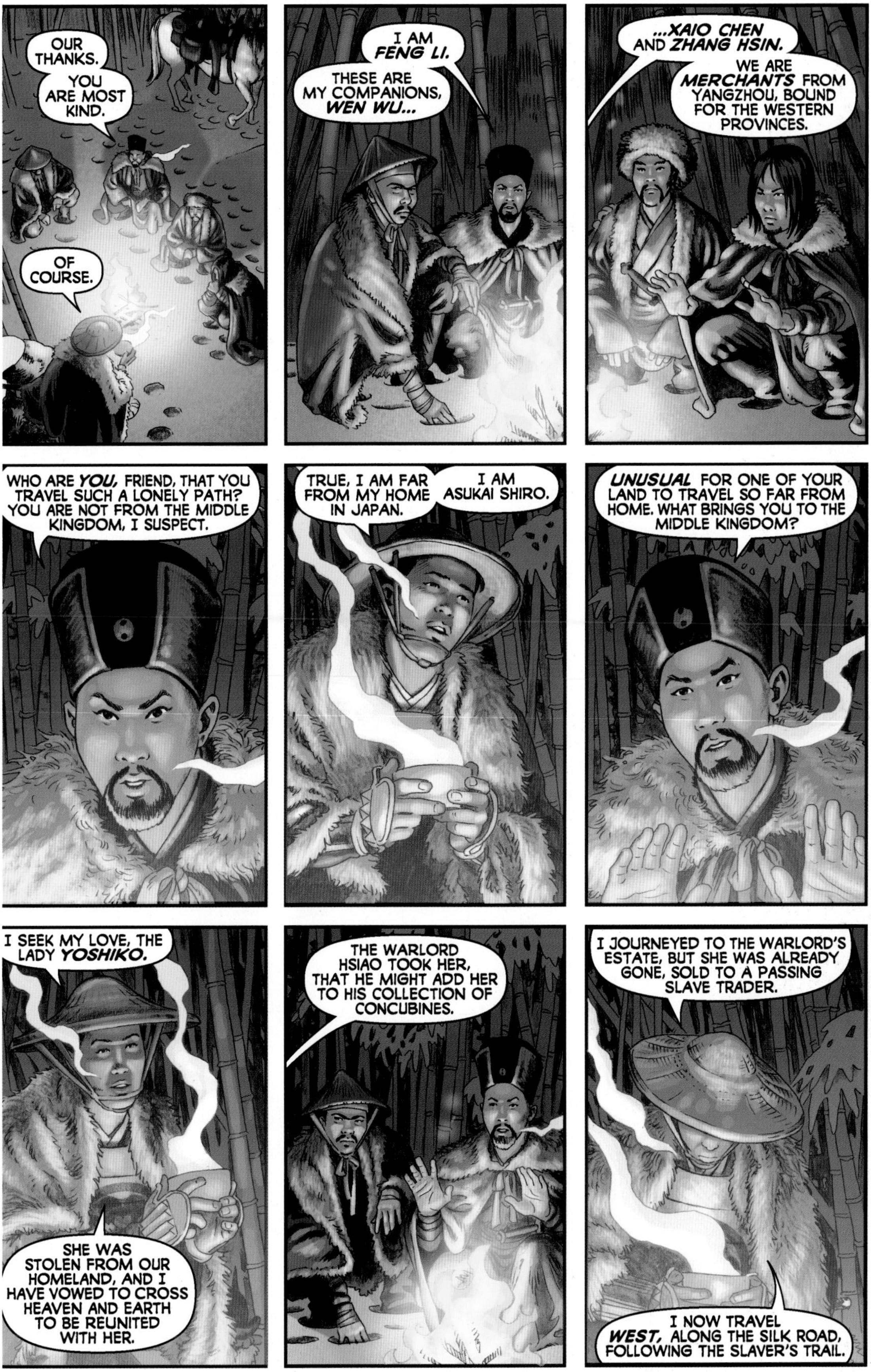
OUR THANKS.
YOU ARE MOST KIND.
OF COURSE.
I AM FENG LI.
THESE ARE MY COMPANIONS, WEN WU...
...XAIO CHEN AND ZHANG HSIN.
WE ARE MERCHANTS FROM YANGZHOU, BOUND FOR THE WESTERN PROVINCES.
WHO ARE YOU, FRIEND, THAT YOU TRAVEL SUCH A LONELY PATH? YOU ARE NOT FROM THE MIDDLE KINGDOM, I SUSPECT.
TRUE, I AM FAR FROM MY HOME IN JAPAN.
I AM ASUKAI SHIRO.
UNUSUAL FOR ONE OF YOUR LAND TO TRAVEL SO FAR FROM HOME. WHAT BRINGS YOU TO THE MIDDLE KINGDOM?
I SEEK MY LOVE, THE LADY YOSHIKO.
SHE WAS STOLEN FROM OUR HOMELAND, AND I HAVE VOWED TO CROSS HEAVEN AND EARTH TO BE REUNITED WITH HER.
THE WARLORD HSIAO TOOK HER, THAT HE MIGHT ADD HER TO HIS COLLECTION OF CONCUBINES.
I JOURNEYED TO THE WARLORD'S ESTATE, BUT SHE WAS ALREADY GONE, SOLD TO A PASSING SLAVE TRADER.
I NOW TRAVEL WEST, ALONG THE SILK ROAD, FOLLOWING THE SLAVER'S TRAIL.

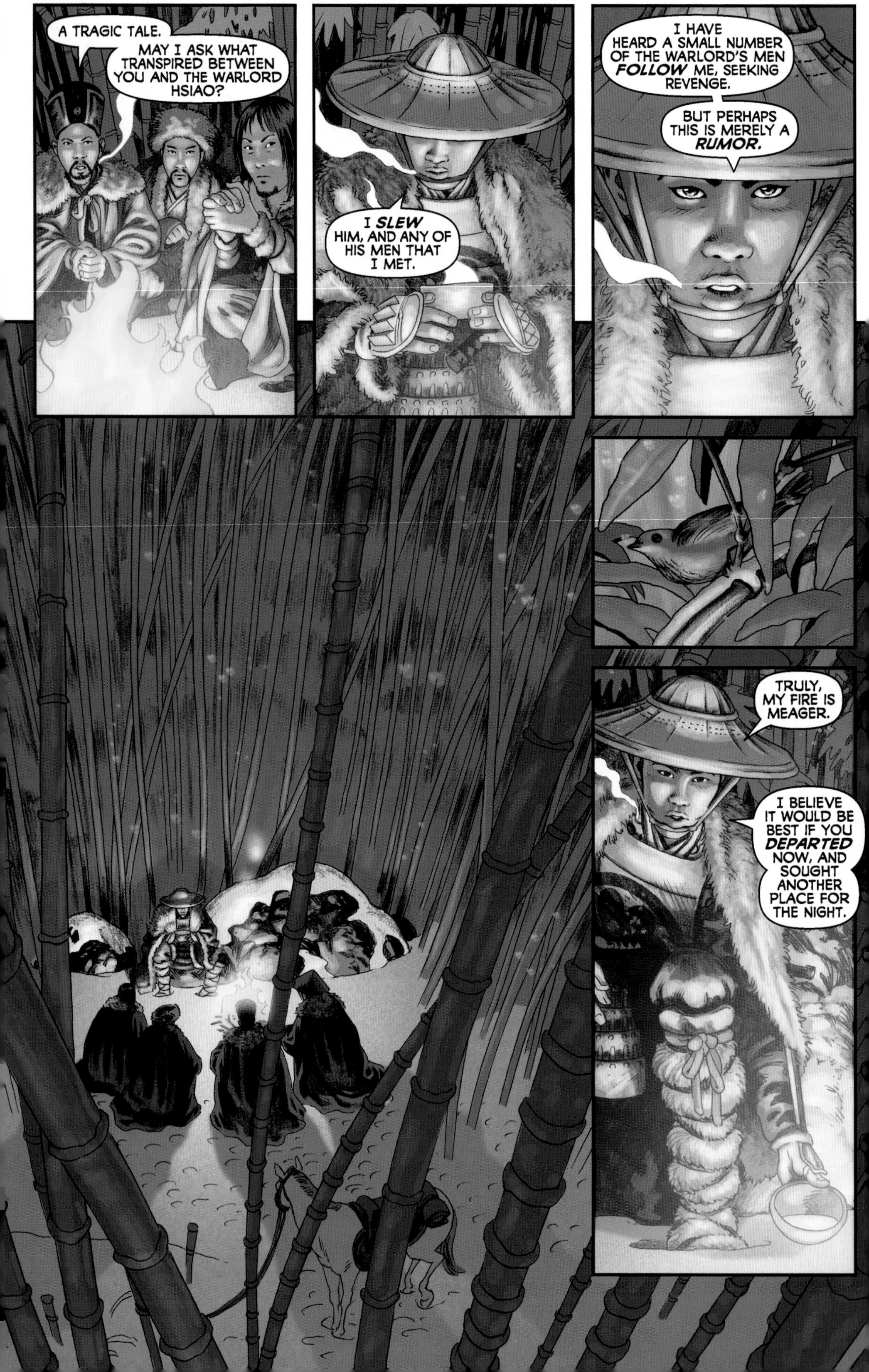
A TRAGIC TALE.
MAY I ASK WHAT TRANSPIRED BETWEEN YOU AND THE WARLORD HSIAO?
I SLEW HIM, AND ANY OF HIS MEN THAT I MET.
I HAVE HEARD A SMALL NUMBER OF THE WARLORD'S MEN FOLLOW ME, SEEKING REVENGE.
BUT PERHAPS THIS IS MERELY A RUMOR.
TRULY, MY FIRE IS MEAGER.
I BELIEVE IT WOULD BE BEST IF YOU DEPARTED NOW, AND SOUGHT ANOTHER PLACE FOR THE NIGHT.

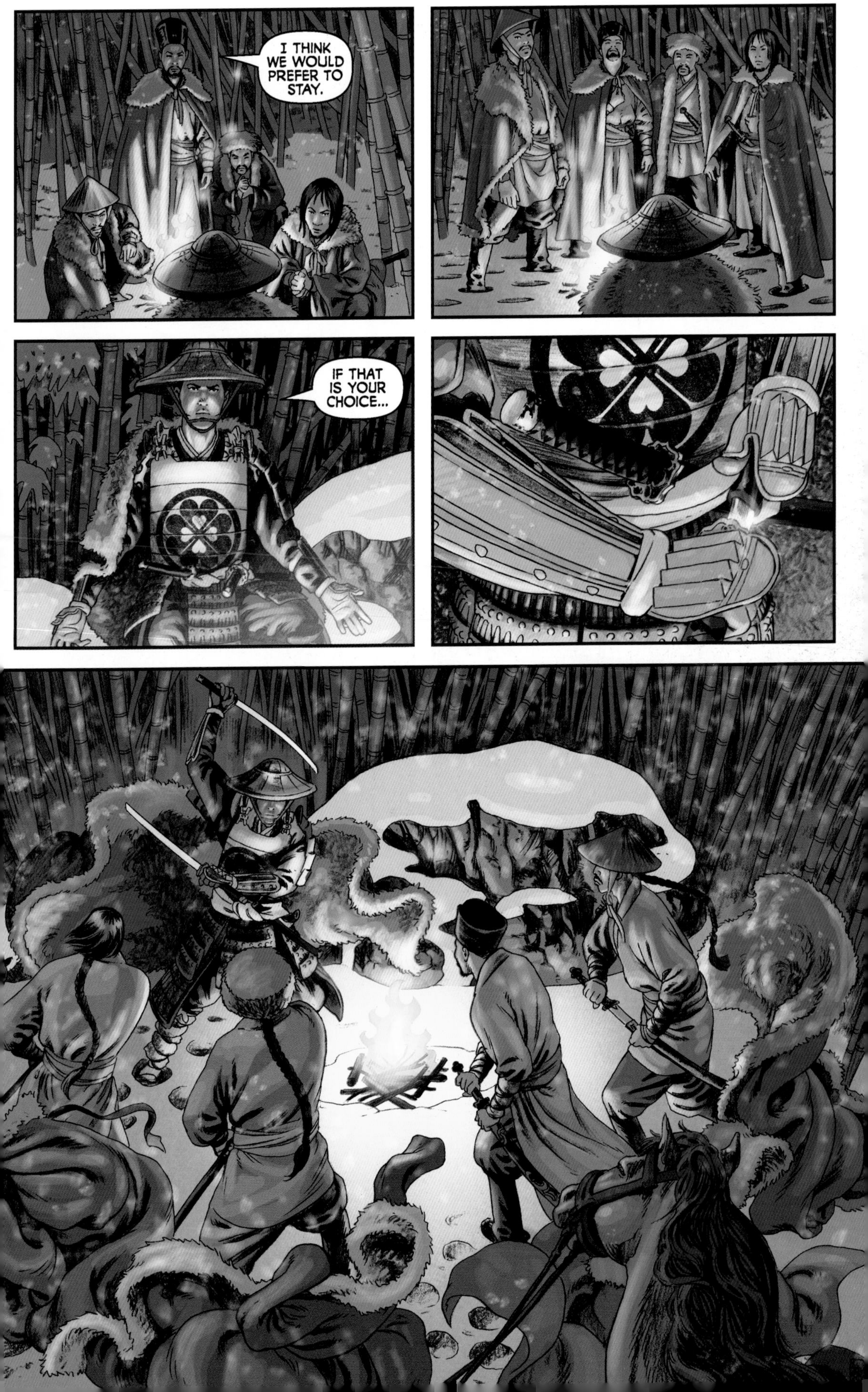
I THINK WE WOULD PREFER TO STAY.
IF THAT IS YOUR CHOICE...

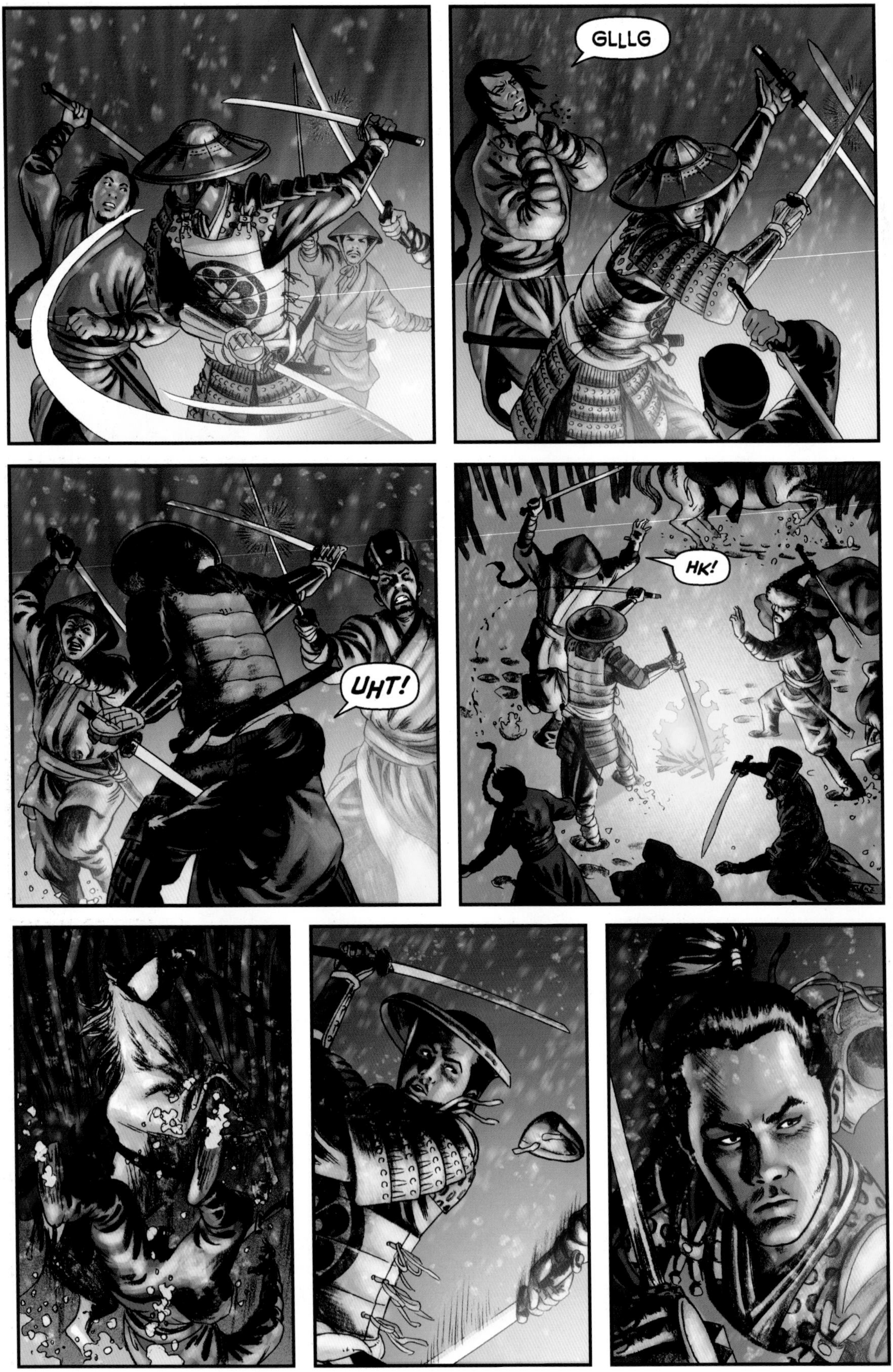
GLLLG
UHT!
HK!

WHH?

COWARD OF A BARBARIAN!

HRRK

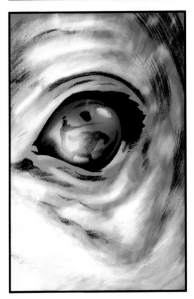

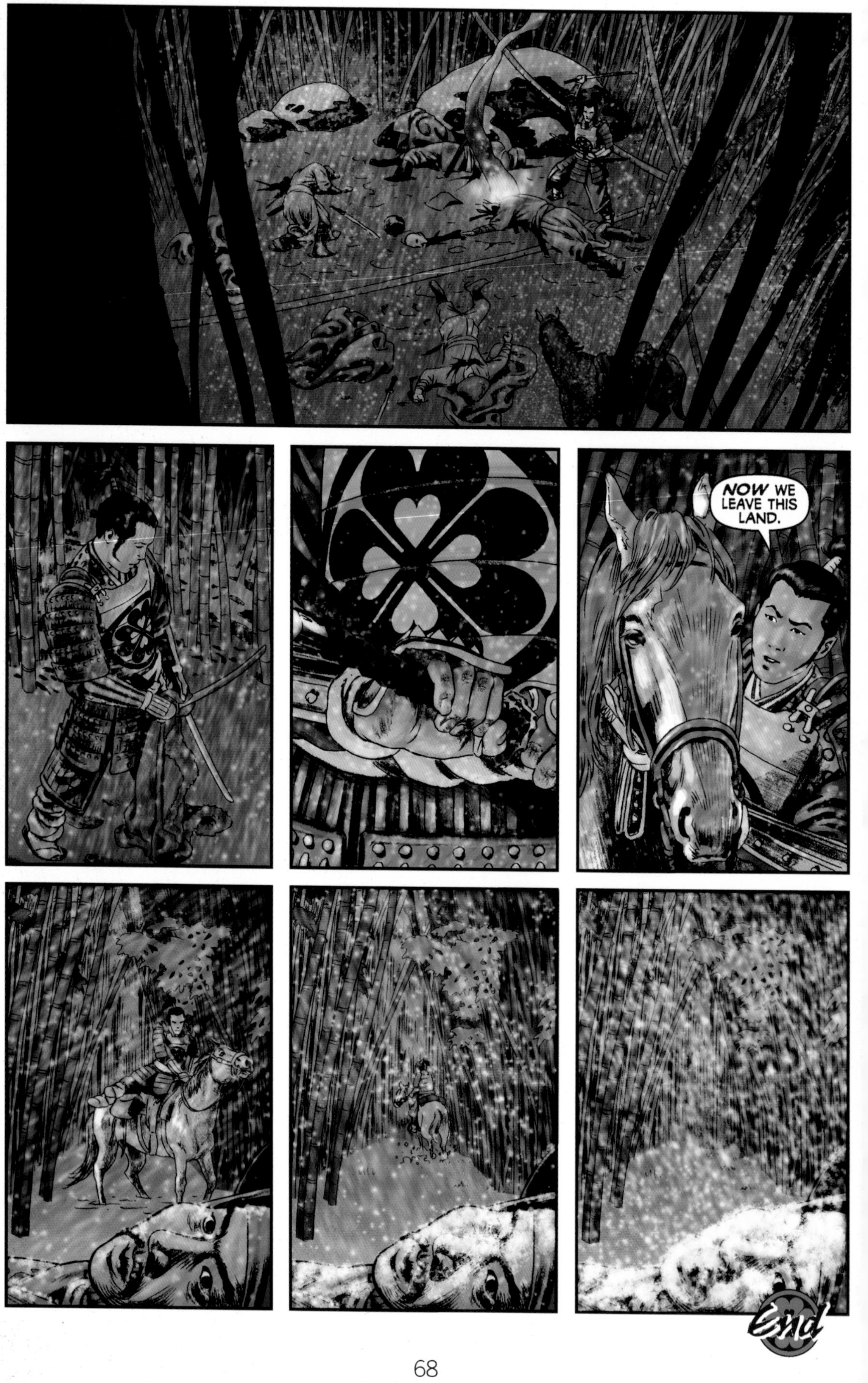
NOW WE LEAVE THIS LAND.
End

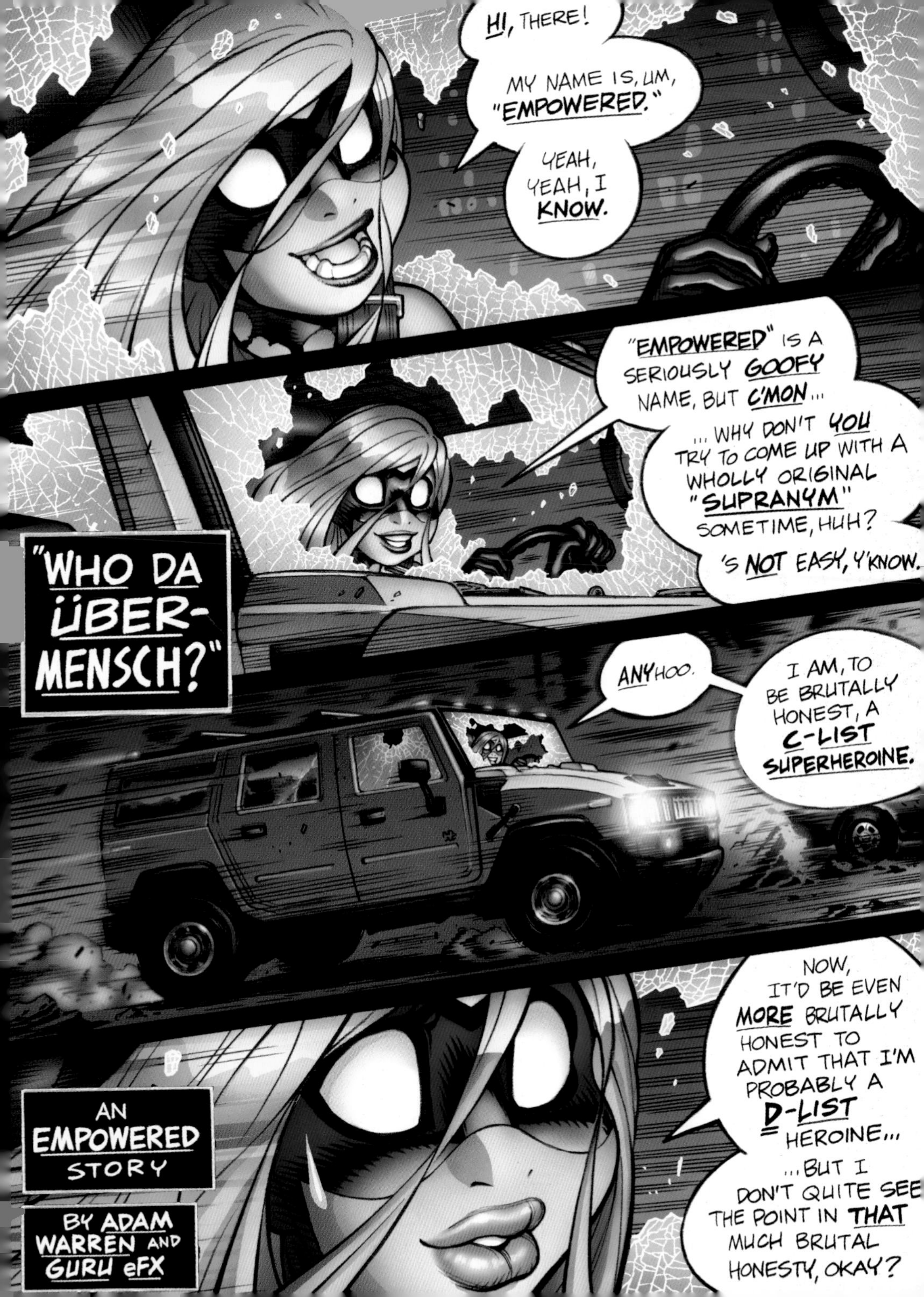
HI, THERE!
MY NAME IS, UM, "EMPOWERED."
YEAH, YEAH, I KNOW.
"EMPOWERED" IS A SERIOUSLY GOOFY NAME, BUT C'MON...
...WHY DON'T YOU TRY TO COME UP WITH A WHOLLY ORIGINAL "SUPRANYM" SOMETIME, HUH?
'S NOT EASY, Y'KNOW.
"WHO DA ÜBER-MENSCH?"
ANYHOO.
I AM, TO BE BRUTALLY HONEST, A C-LIST SUPERHEROINE.
NOW, IT'D BE EVEN MORE BRUTALLY HONEST TO ADMIT THAT I'M PROBABLY A D-LIST HEROINE...
...BUT I DON'T QUITE SEE THE POINT IN THAT MUCH BRUTAL HONESTY, OKAY?
AN EMPOWERED STORY
BY ADAM WARREN AND GURU eFX

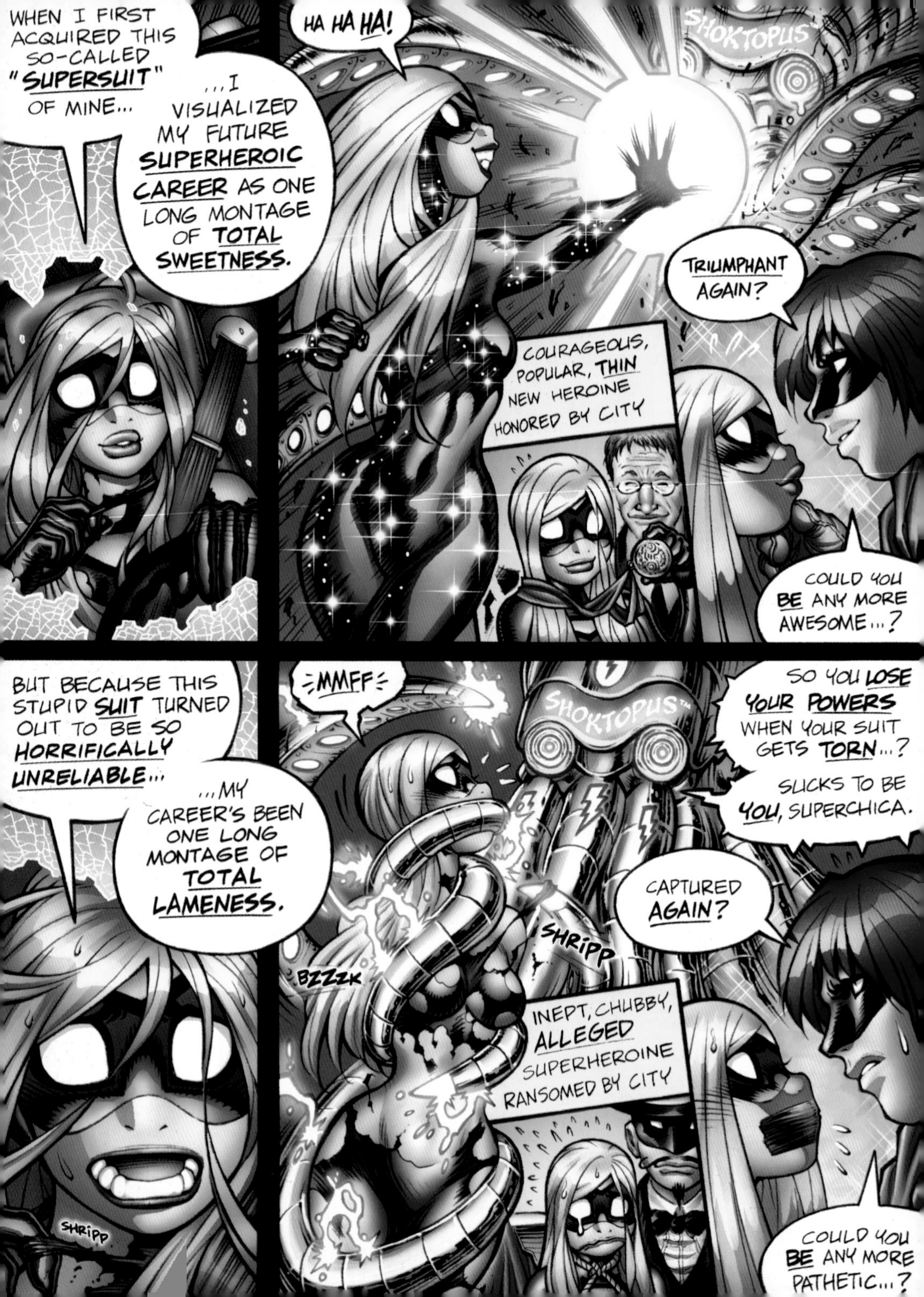
WHEN I FIRST ACQUIRED THIS SO-CALLED "SUPERSUIT" OF MINE...
...I VISUALIZED MY FUTURE SUPERHEROIC CAREER AS ONE LONG MONTAGE OF TOTAL SWEETNESS.
HA HA HA!
SHOKTOPUS™
TRIUMPHANT AGAIN?
COURAGEOUS, POPULAR, THIN NEW HEROINE HONORED BY CITY
COULD YOU BE ANY MORE AWESOME...?
BUT BECAUSE THIS STUPID SUIT TURNED OUT TO BE SO HORRIFICALLY UNRELIABLE...
...MY CAREER'S BEEN ONE LONG MONTAGE OF TOTAL LAMENESS.
SHRIPP
MMFF
SHOKTOPUS™
SO YOU LOSE YOUR POWERS WHEN YOUR SUIT GETS TORN...?
SUCKS TO BE YOU, SUPERCHICA.
CAPTURED AGAIN?
SHRIPP
BZZZK
INEPT, CHUBBY, ALLEGED SUPERHEROINE RANSOMED BY CITY
COULD YOU BE ANY MORE PATHETIC...?

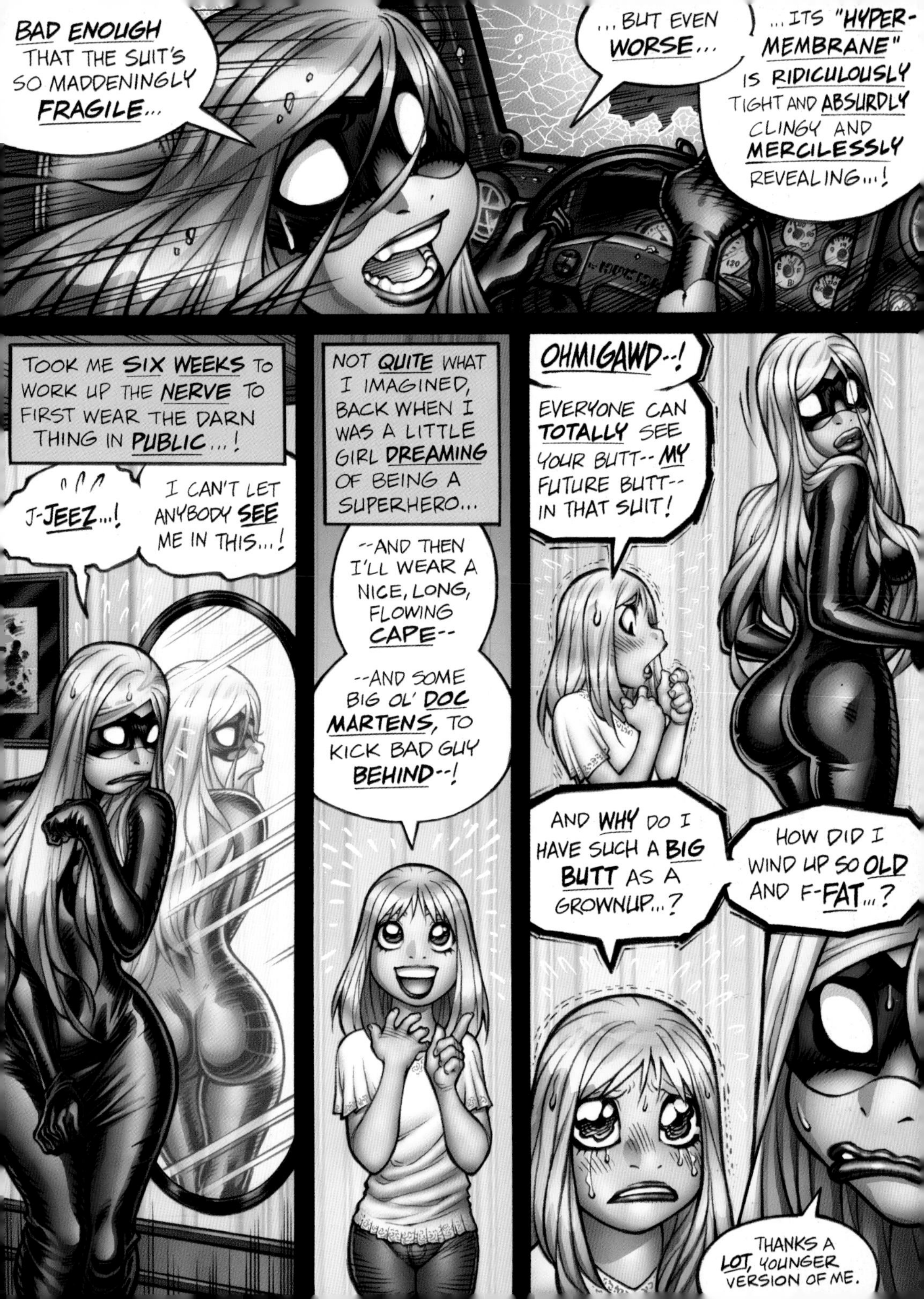

BAD ENOUGH THAT THE SUIT'S SO MADDENINGLY FRAGILE...
...BUT EVEN WORSE...
...ITS "HYPER-MEMBRANE" IS RIDICULOUSLY TIGHT AND ABSURDLY CLINGY AND MERCILESSLY REVEALING...!
TOOK ME SIX WEEKS TO WORK UP THE NERVE TO FIRST WEAR THE DARN THING IN PUBLIC...!
J-JEEZ...!
I CAN'T LET ANYBODY SEE ME IN THIS...!
NOT QUITE WHAT I IMAGINED, BACK WHEN I WAS A LITTLE GIRL DREAMING OF BEING A SUPERHERO...
--AND THEN I'LL WEAR A NICE, LONG, FLOWING CAPE--
--AND SOME BIG OL' DOC MARTENS, TO KICK BAD GUY BEHIND--!
OHMIGAWD--!
EVERYONE CAN TOTALLY SEE YOUR BUTT--MY FUTURE BUTT--IN THAT SUIT!
AND WHY DO I HAVE SUCH A BIG BUTT AS A GROWNUP...?
HOW DID I WIND UP SO OLD AND F-FAT...?
THANKS A LOT, YOUNGER VERSION OF ME.

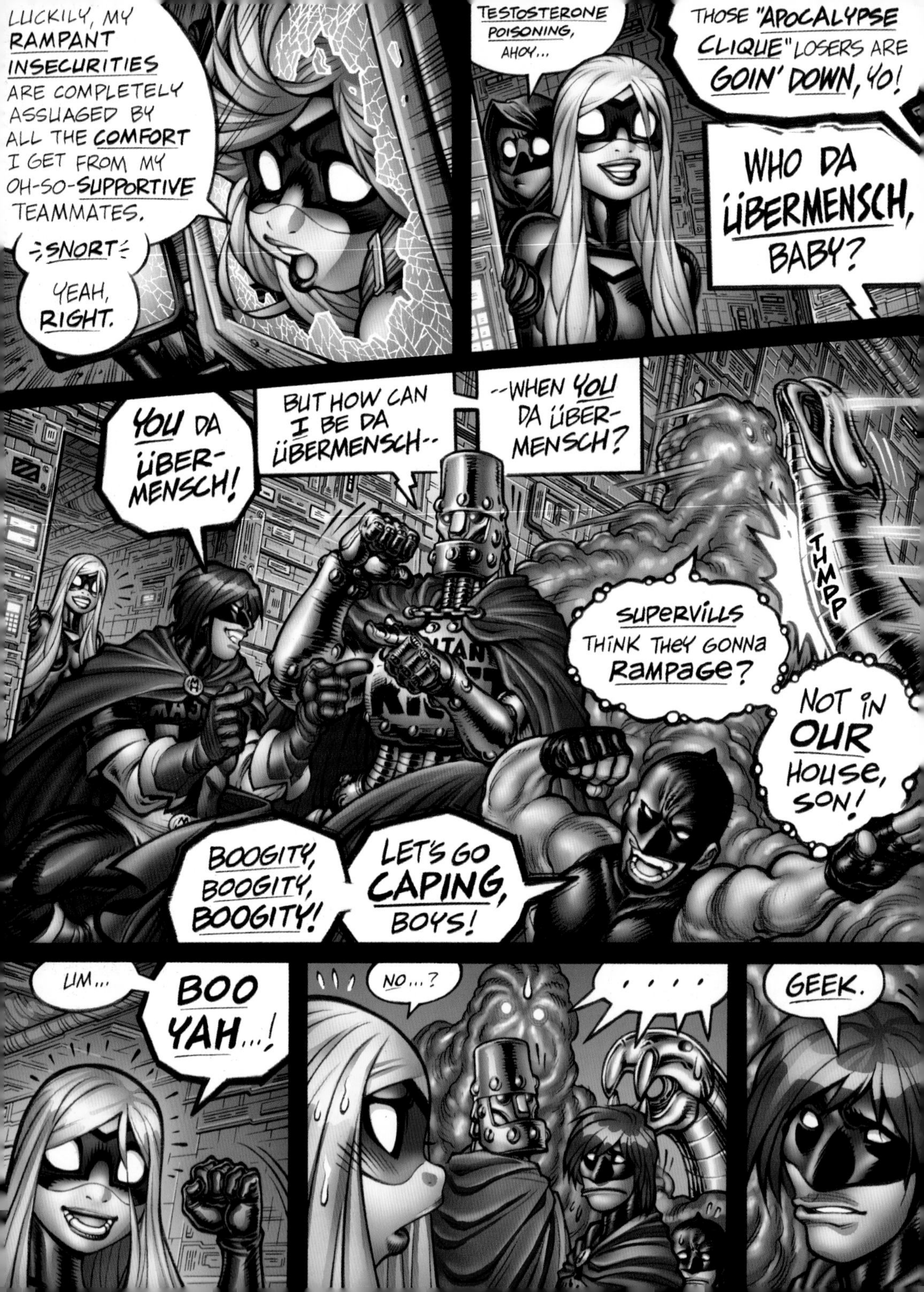
LUCKILY, MY RAMPANT INSECURITIES ARE COMPLETELY ASSUAGED BY ALL THE COMFORT I GET FROM MY OH-SO-SUPPORTIVE TEAMMATES.
SNORT
YEAH, RIGHT.
TESTOSTERONE POISONING, AHOY...
THOSE "APOCALYPSE CLIQUE" LOSERS ARE GOIN' DOWN, YO!
WHO DA ÜBERMENSCH, BABY?
YOU DA ÜBER-MENSCH!
BUT HOW CAN I BE DA ÜBERMENSCH--
--WHEN YOU DA ÜBER-MENSCH?
THMPP
SUPERVILLS THINK THEY GONNA RAMPAGE?
NOT IN OUR HOUSE, SON!
BOOGITY, BOOGITY, BOOGITY!
LET'S GO CAPING, BOYS!
UM...
BOO YAH...!
NO...?
. . . .
GEEK.

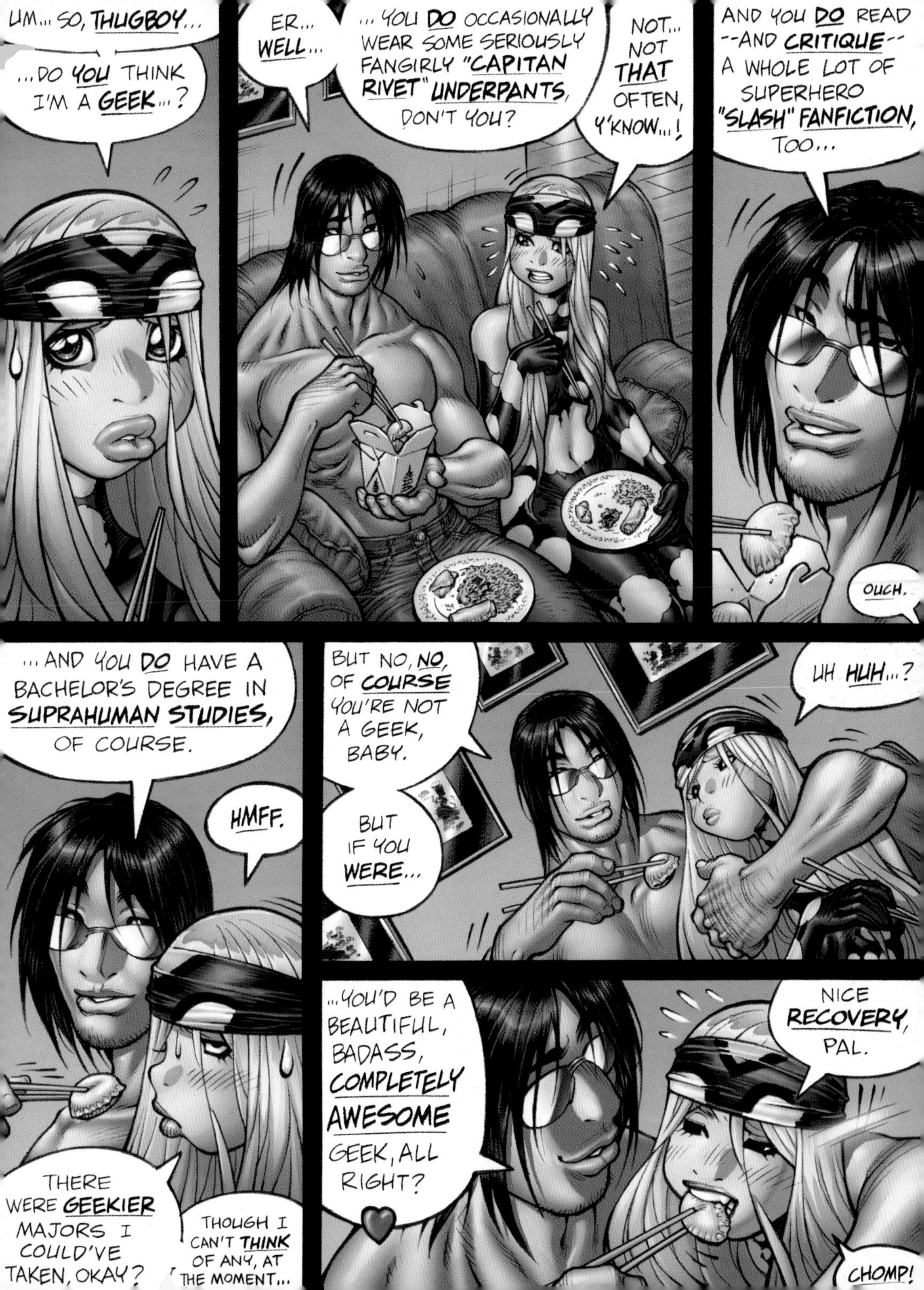
UM... SO, THUGBOY...
...DO YOU THINK I'M A GEEK...?
ER... WELL...
...YOU DO OCCASIONALLY WEAR SOME SERIOUSLY FANGIRLY "CAPITAN RIVET" UNDERPANTS, DON'T YOU?
NOT... NOT THAT OFTEN, Y'KNOW...!
AND YOU DO READ --AND CRITIQUE-- A WHOLE LOT OF SUPERHERO "SLASH" FANFICTION, TOO...
OUCH.
...AND YOU DO HAVE A BACHELOR'S DEGREE IN SUPRAHUMAN STUDIES, OF COURSE.
HMFF.
THERE WERE GEEKIER MAJORS I COULD'VE TAKEN, OKAY?
THOUGH I CAN'T THINK OF ANY, AT THE MOMENT...
BUT NO, NO, OF COURSE YOU'RE NOT A GEEK, BABY.
UH HUH...?
BUT IF YOU WERE...
...YOU'D BE A BEAUTIFUL, BADASS, COMPLETELY AWESOME GEEK, ALL RIGHT?
NICE RECOVERY, PAL.
CHOMP!

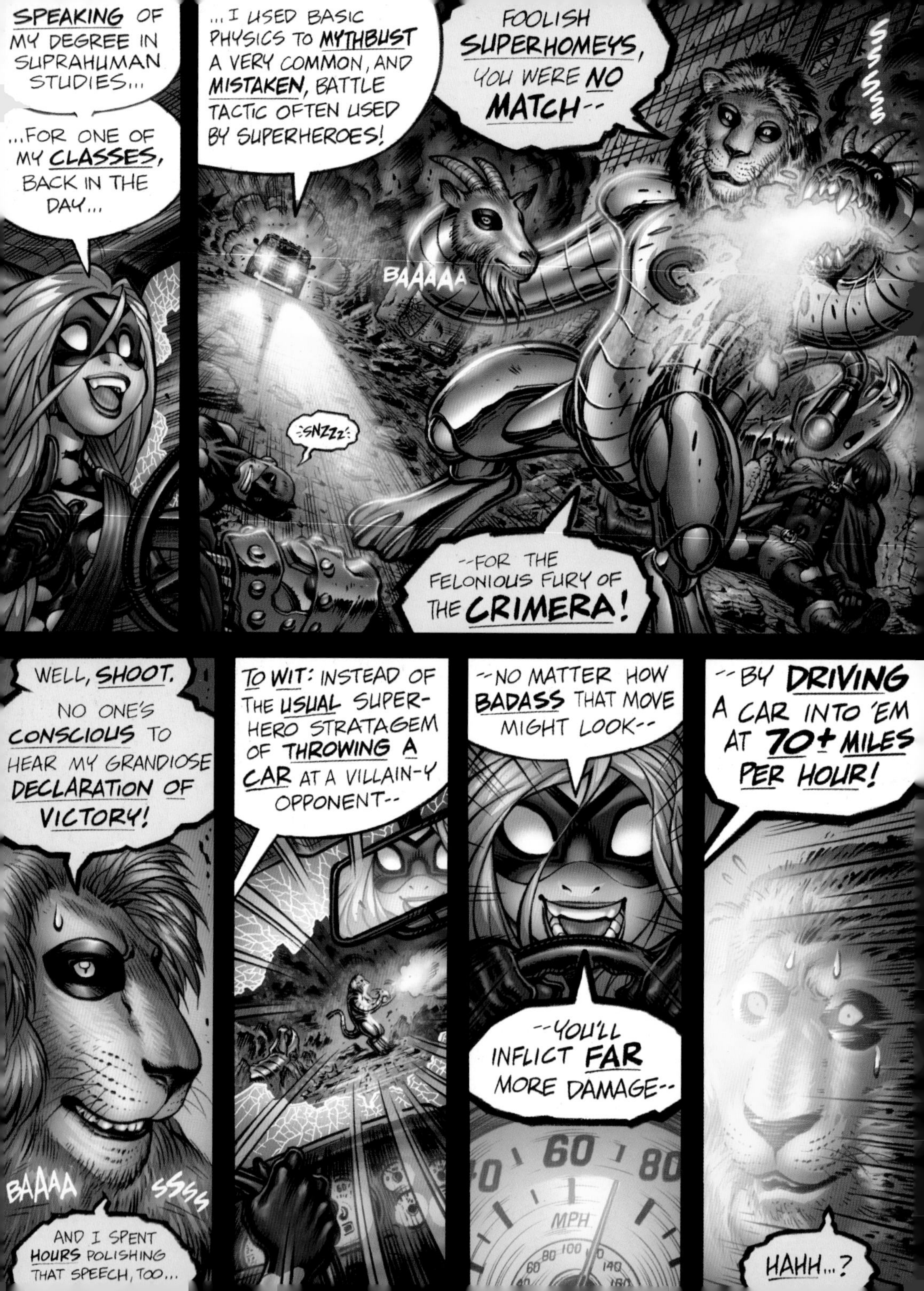
SPEAKING OF MY DEGREE IN SUPRAHUMAN STUDIES...
...FOR ONE OF MY CLASSES, BACK IN THE DAY...
...I USED BASIC PHYSICS TO MYTHBUST A VERY COMMON, AND MISTAKEN, BATTLE TACTIC OFTEN USED BY SUPERHEROES!
FOOLISH SUPERHOMEYS, YOU WERE NO MATCH--
BAAAAA
SNZZZ
--FOR THE FELONIOUS FURY OF THE CRIMERA!
WELL, SHOOT. NO ONE'S CONSCIOUS TO HEAR MY GRANDIOSE DECLARATION OF VICTORY!
BAAAA
SSSS
AND I SPENT HOURS POLISHING THAT SPEECH, TOO...
TO WIT: INSTEAD OF THE USUAL SUPER-HERO STRATAGEM OF THROWING A CAR AT A VILLAIN-Y OPPONENT--
--NO MATTER HOW BADASS THAT MOVE MIGHT LOOK--
--YOU'LL INFLICT FAR MORE DAMAGE--
MPH
--BY DRIVING A CAR INTO 'EM AT 70+ MILES PER HOUR!
HAHH...?

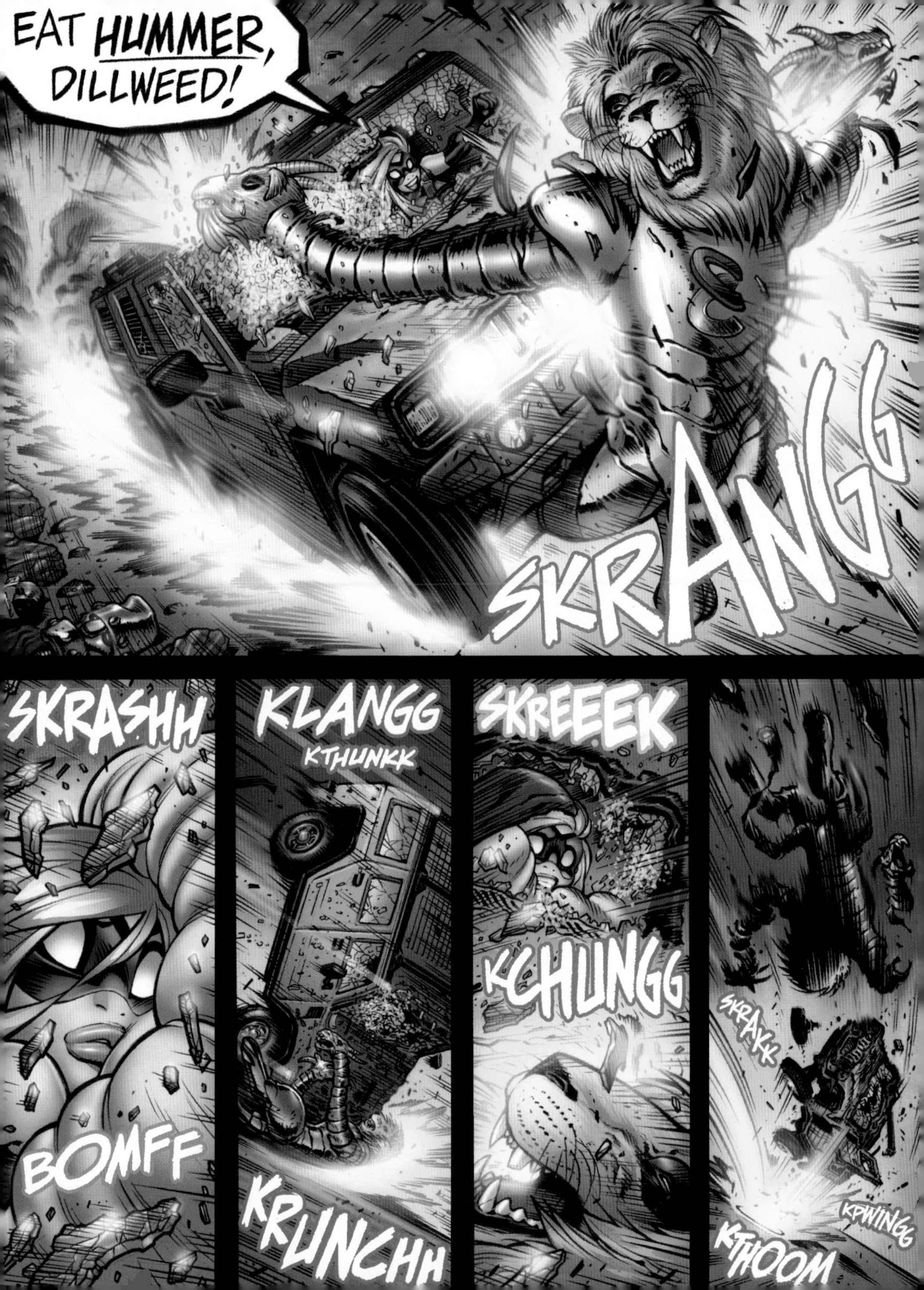
EAT HUMMER, DILLWEED!
SKRANGG
SKRASHH
BOMFF
KLANGG
KTHUNKK
KRUNCHH
SKREEEK
KCHUNGG
SKRAKK
KPWINGG
KTHOOM

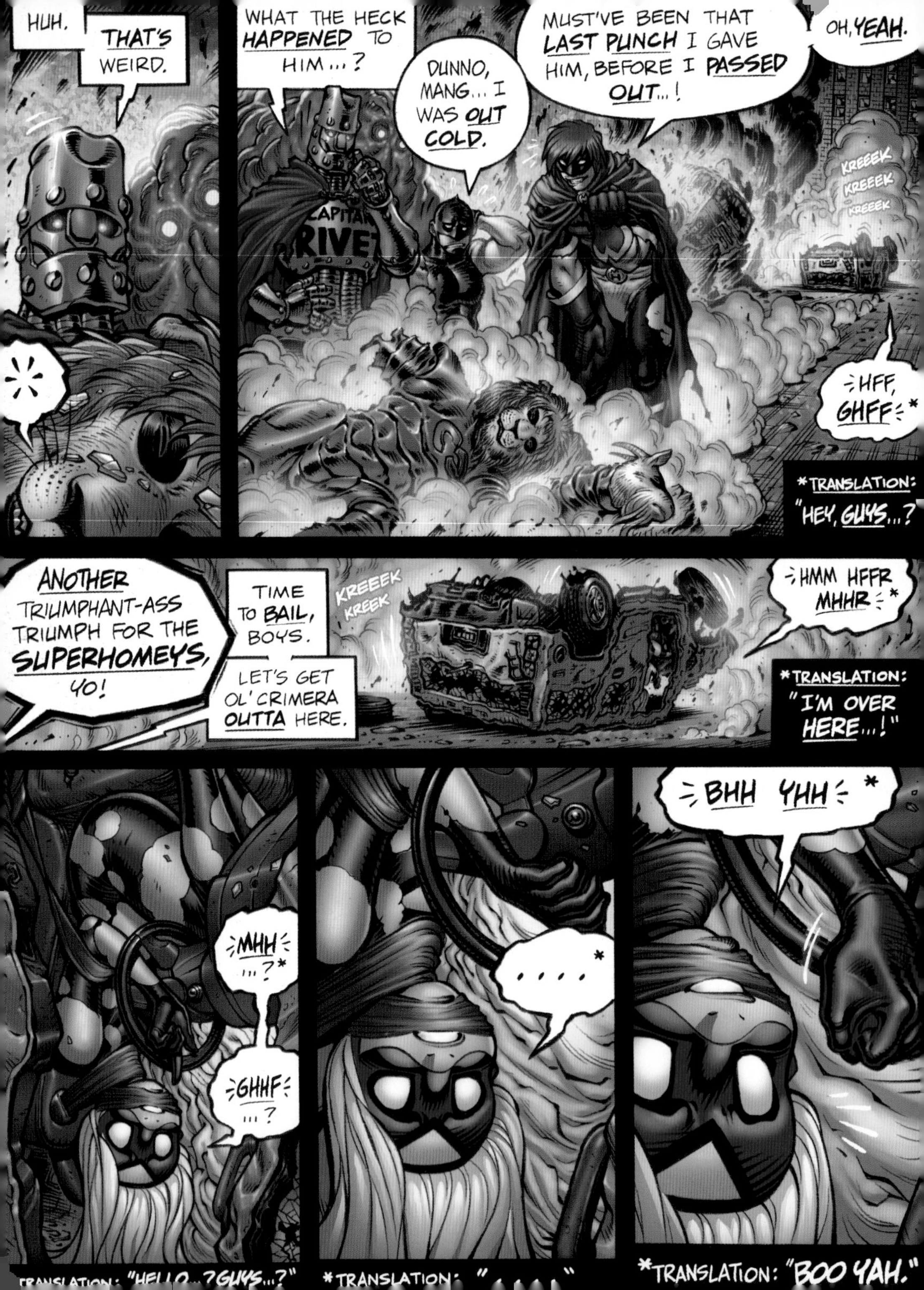
HUH.
THAT'S WEIRD.
WHAT THE HECK HAPPENED TO HIM...?
DUNNO, MANG... I WAS OUT COLD.
MUST'VE BEEN THAT LAST PUNCH I GAVE HIM, BEFORE I PASSED OUT...!
OH, YEAH.
CAPITAN RIVET
KREEEK KREEEK KREEEK
!
HFF, GHFF *
*TRANSLATION: "HEY, GUYS...?"
ANOTHER TRIUMPHANT-ASS TRIUMPH FOR THE SUPERHOMEYS, YO!
TIME TO BAIL, BOYS.
LET'S GET OL' CRIMERA OUTTA HERE.
KREEEK KREEK
HMM HFFR MHHR *
*TRANSLATION: "I'M OVER HERE...!"
MHH ...?*
GHHF ...?
. . . . *
BHH YHH *
TRANSLATION: "HELLO...?GUYS...?"
*TRANSLATION: " . . . . "
*TRANSLATION: "BOO YAH."

CHICKENHARE
RANDOM BONES BY CHRIS GRINE

IT'S JUST UP AHEAD.

I HOPE YOU TWO AREN'T DRAGGING ME OUT HERE JUST TO TRY TO SCARE ME, BECAUSE IT **WON'T** WORK.

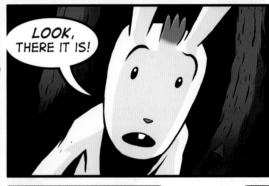

LOOK, THERE IT IS!

A MYSTERIOUS PILE OF SEEMINGLY RANDOM BONES.

I'M **SO** FRIGHTENED.

WHO DO YOU THINK MIGHT HAVE DONE **THIS**?

I HAVEN'T SEEN **ANYONE** BUT **US** ON THIS ISLAND.

NICE TRY, BUT IT'S OBVIOUS YOU TWO STACKED THESE UP TO TRY TO SCARE ME.

PATHETIC.

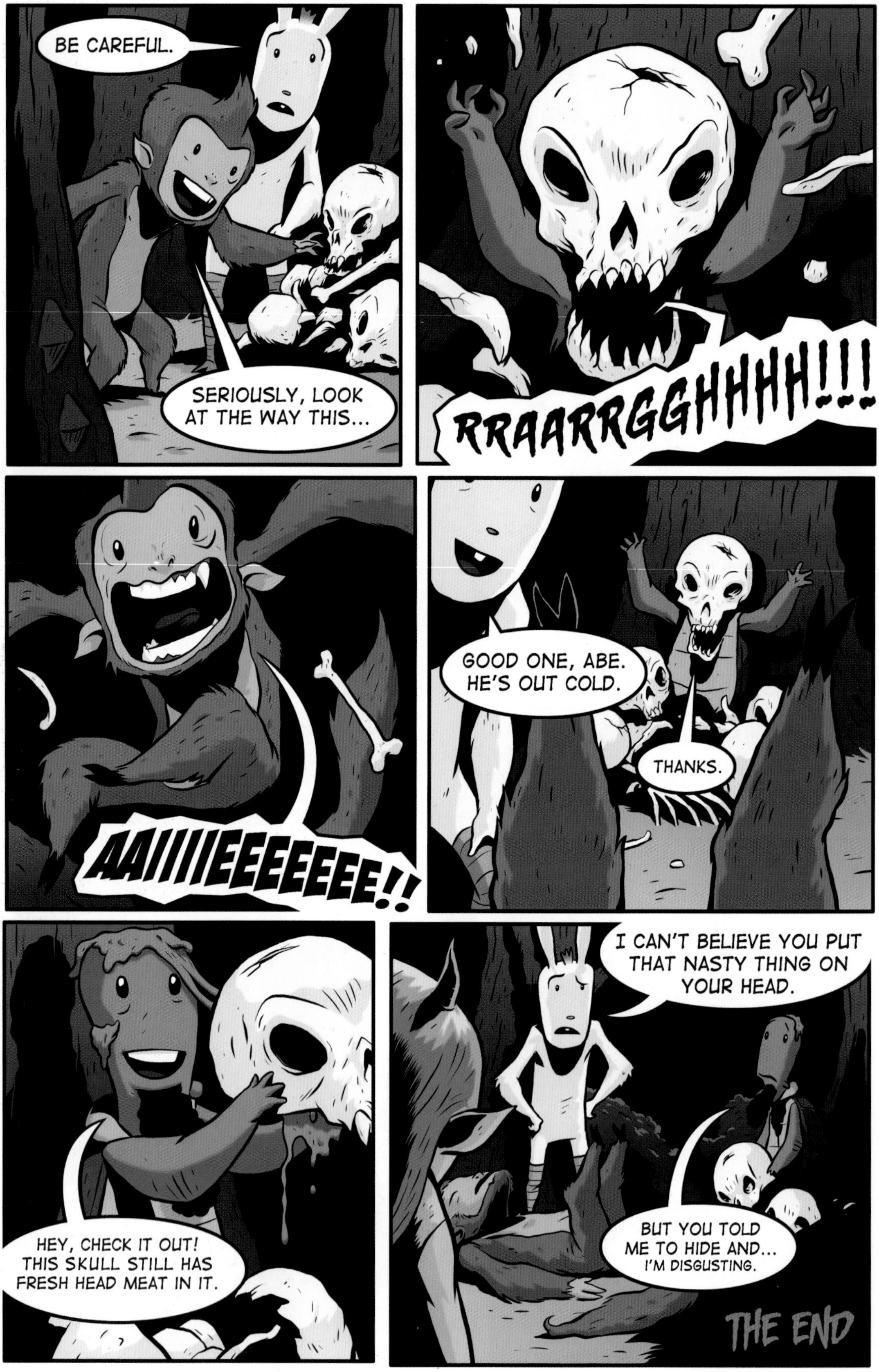
BE CAREFUL.
SERIOUSLY, LOOK AT THE WAY THIS...
RRAARRGGHHHH!!!
AAIIIIEEEEEEE!!
GOOD ONE, ABE. HE'S OUT COLD.
THANKS.
HEY, CHECK IT OUT! THIS SKULL STILL HAS FRESH HEAD MEAT IN IT.
I CAN'T BELIEVE YOU PUT THAT NASTY THING ON YOUR HEAD.
BUT YOU TOLD ME TO HIDE AND... I'M DISGUSTING.
THE END

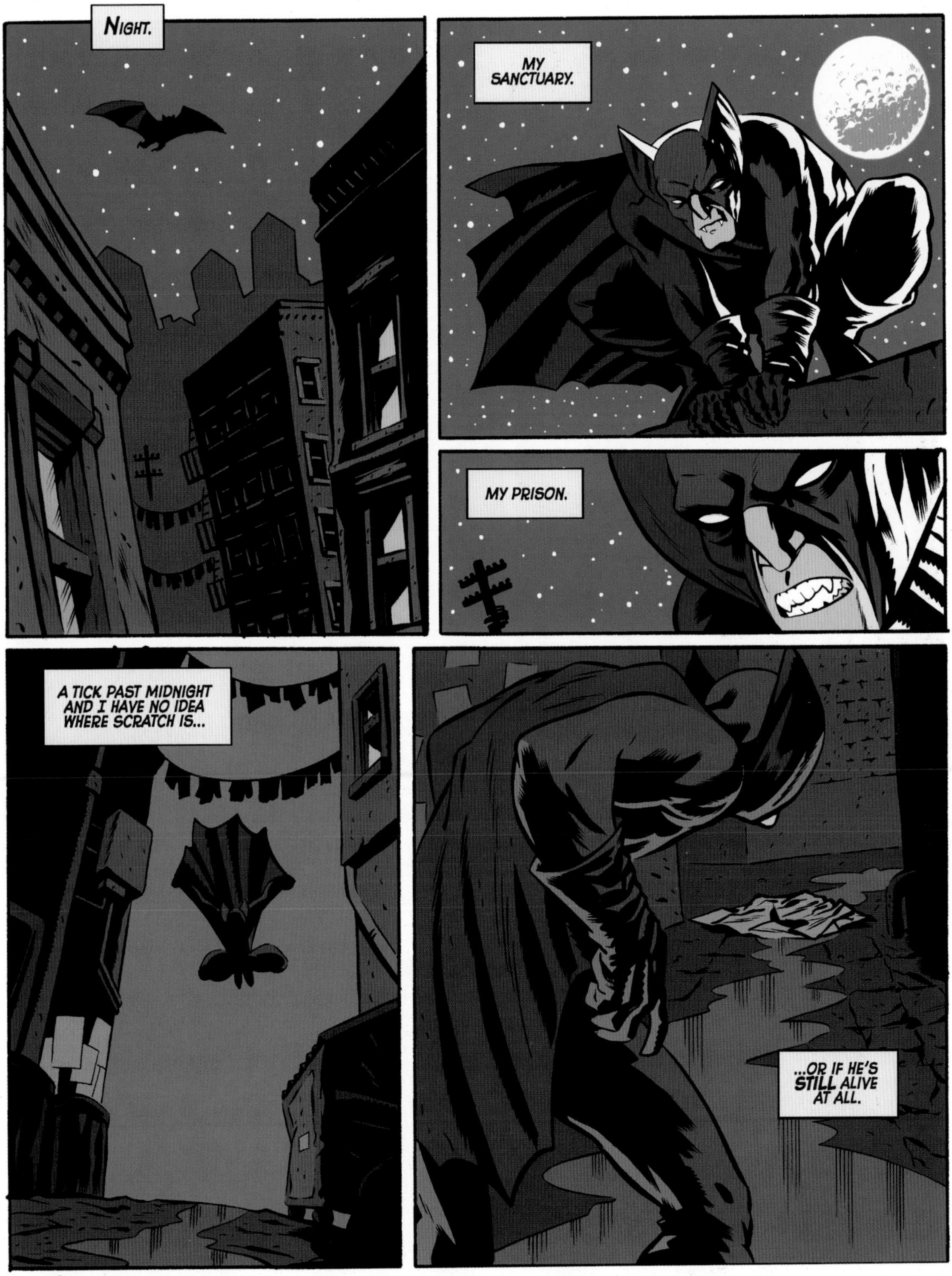
NIGHT.
MY SANCTUARY.
MY PRISON.
A TICK PAST MIDNIGHT AND I HAVE NO IDEA WHERE SCRATCH IS...
...OR IF HE'S STILL ALIVE AT ALL.

THE NOCTURNAL ADVENTURES OF SCRATCH AND SUCK

BY STEVE NILES & BRIAN CHURILLA

COLORS: JEREMY SHEPHERD

LETTERS: NATE PIEKOS

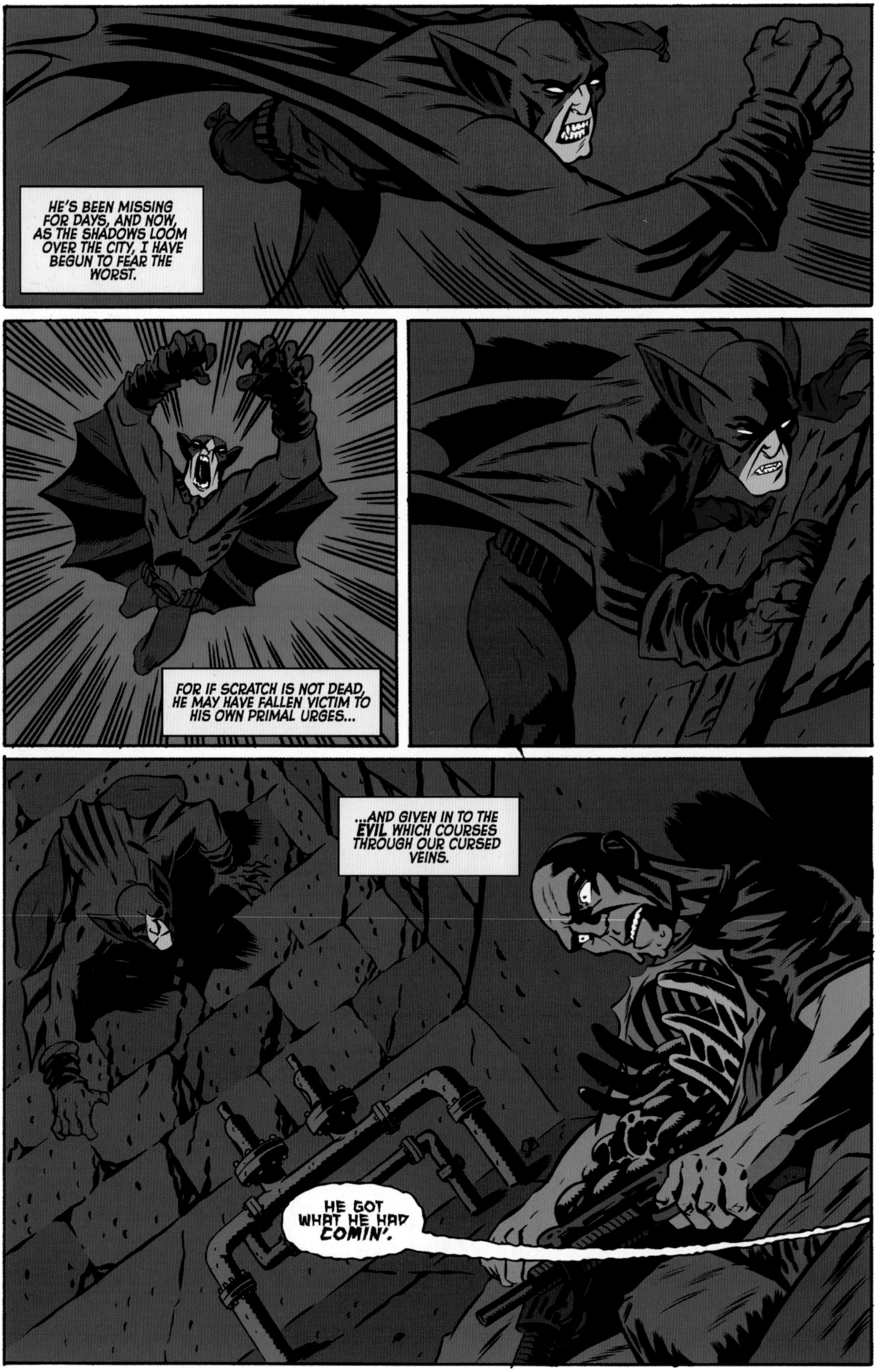
HE'S BEEN MISSING FOR DAYS, AND NOW, AS THE SHADOWS LOOM OVER THE CITY, I HAVE BEGUN TO FEAR THE WORST.
FOR IF SCRATCH IS NOT DEAD, HE MAY HAVE FALLEN VICTIM TO HIS OWN PRIMAL URGES...
...AND GIVEN IN TO THE EVIL WHICH COURSES THROUGH OUR CURSED VEINS.
HE GOT WHAT HE HAD COMIN'.

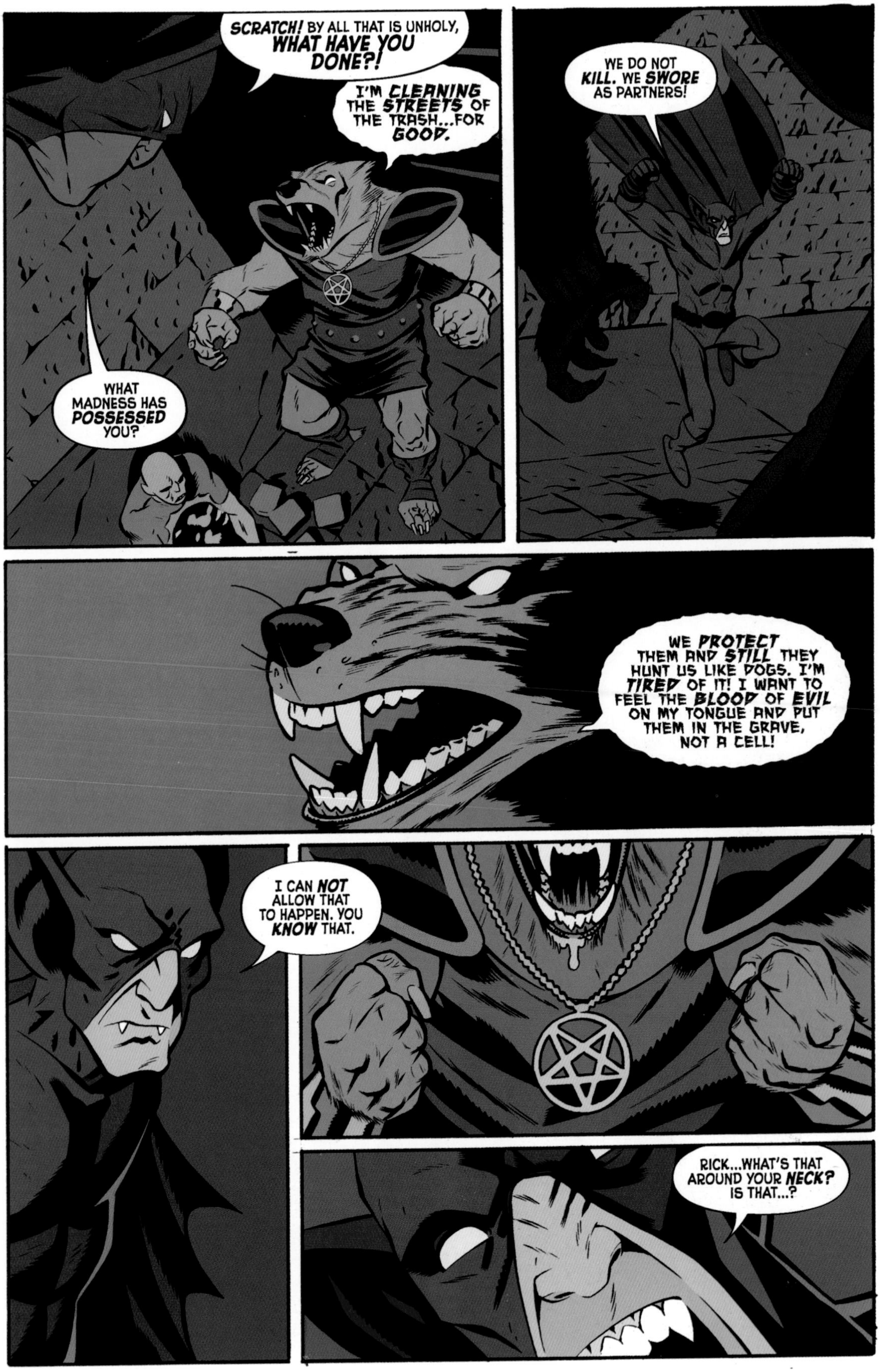
SCRATCH! BY ALL THAT IS UNHOLY, WHAT HAVE YOU DONE?!
I'M CLEANING THE STREETS OF THE TRASH...FOR GOOD.
WHAT MADNESS HAS POSSESSED YOU?
WE DO NOT KILL. WE SWORE AS PARTNERS!
WE PROTECT THEM AND STILL THEY HUNT US LIKE DOGS. I'M TIRED OF IT! I WANT TO FEEL THE BLOOD OF EVIL ON MY TONGUE AND PUT THEM IN THE GRAVE, NOT A CELL!
I CAN NOT ALLOW THAT TO HAPPEN. YOU KNOW THAT.
RICK...WHAT'S THAT AROUND YOUR NECK? IS THAT...?

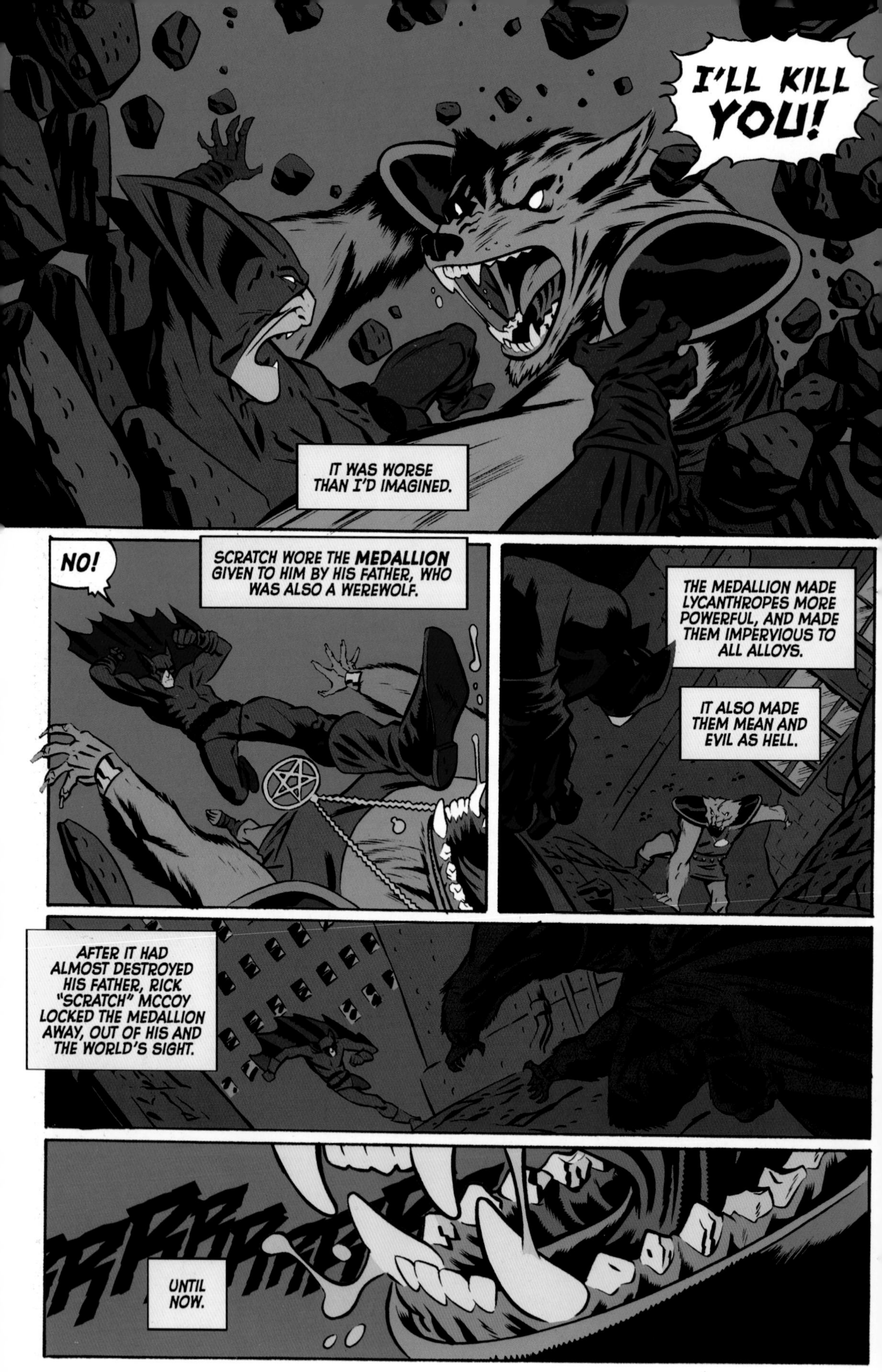
I'LL KILL YOU!
IT WAS WORSE THAN I'D IMAGINED.
NO!
SCRATCH WORE THE MEDALLION GIVEN TO HIM BY HIS FATHER, WHO WAS ALSO A WEREWOLF.
THE MEDALLION MADE LYCANTHROPES MORE POWERFUL, AND MADE THEM IMPERVIOUS TO ALL ALLOYS.
IT ALSO MADE THEM MEAN AND EVIL AS HELL.
AFTER IT HAD ALMOST DESTROYED HIS FATHER, RICK "SCRATCH" MCCOY LOCKED THE MEDALLION AWAY, OUT OF HIS AND THE WORLD'S SIGHT.
UNTIL NOW.

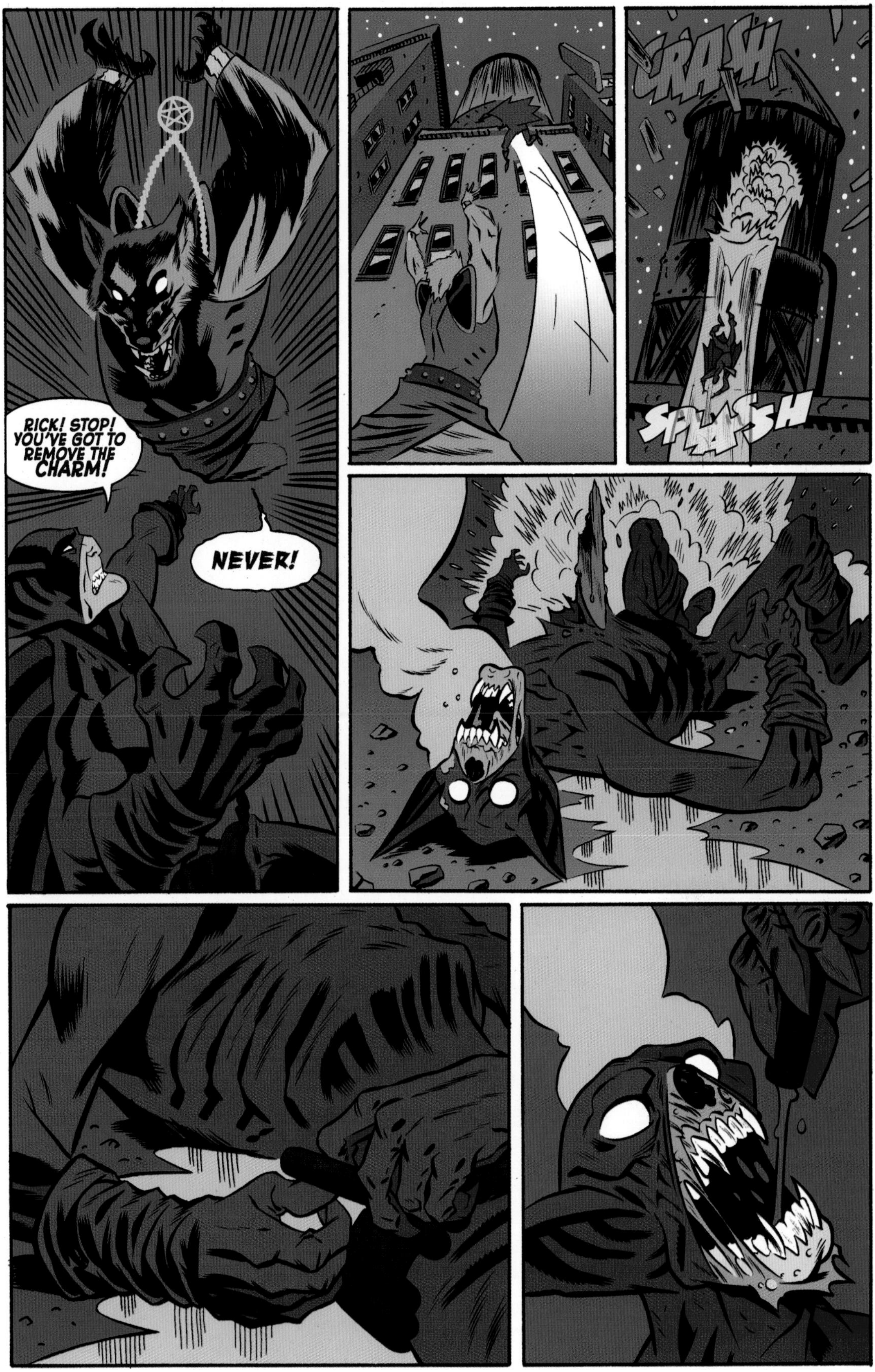
RICK! STOP! YOU'VE GOT TO REMOVE THE CHARM!
NEVER!
CRASH
SPLASH

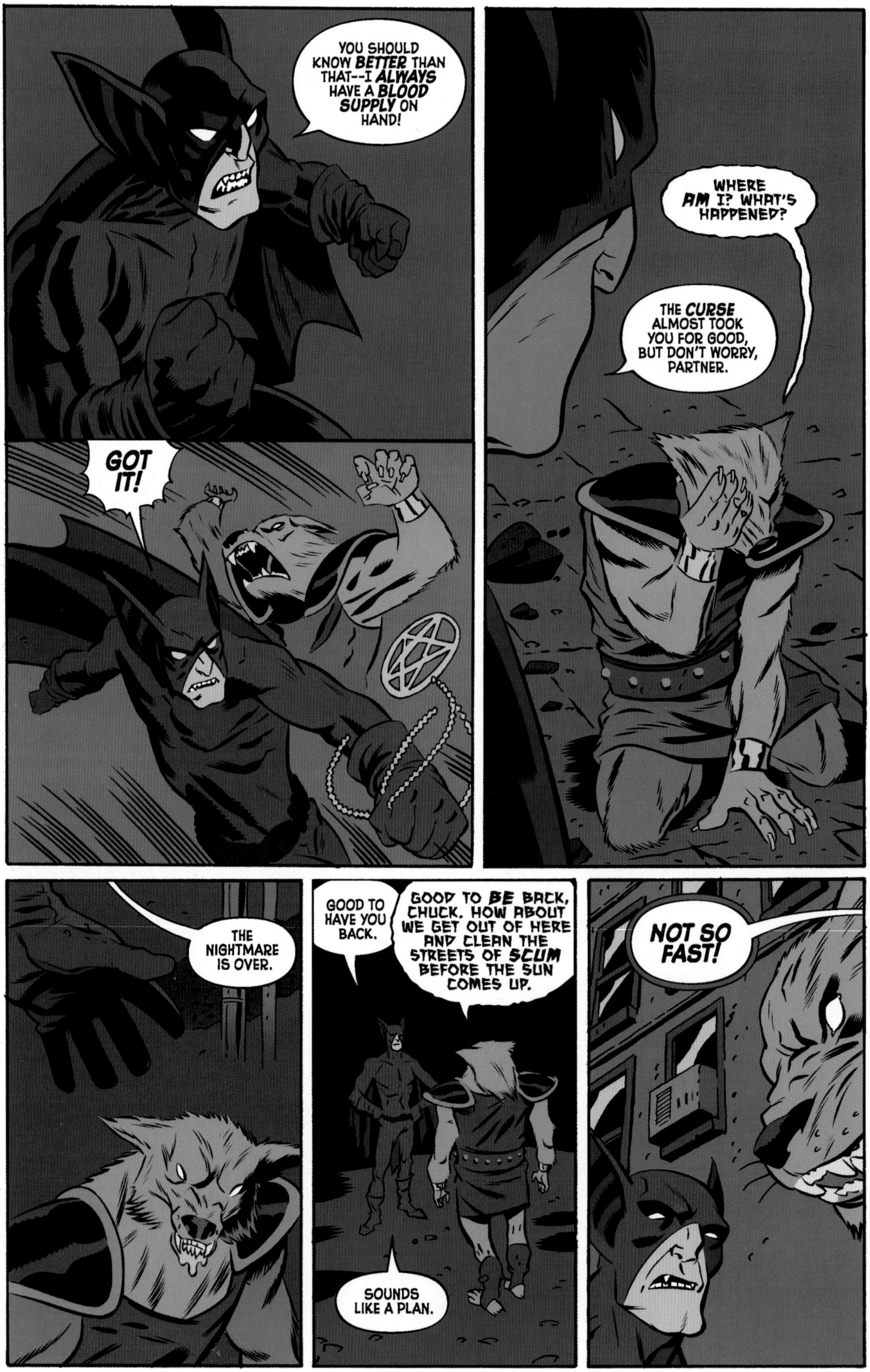
YOU SHOULD KNOW BETTER THAN THAT--I ALWAYS HAVE A BLOOD SUPPLY ON HAND!
GOT IT!
WHERE AM I? WHAT'S HAPPENED?
THE CURSE ALMOST TOOK YOU FOR GOOD, BUT DON'T WORRY, PARTNER.
THE NIGHTMARE IS OVER.
GOOD TO HAVE YOU BACK.
GOOD TO BE BACK, CHUCK. HOW ABOUT WE GET OUT OF HERE AND CLEAN THE STREETS OF SCUM BEFORE THE SUN COMES UP.
SOUNDS LIKE A PLAN.
NOT SO FAST!

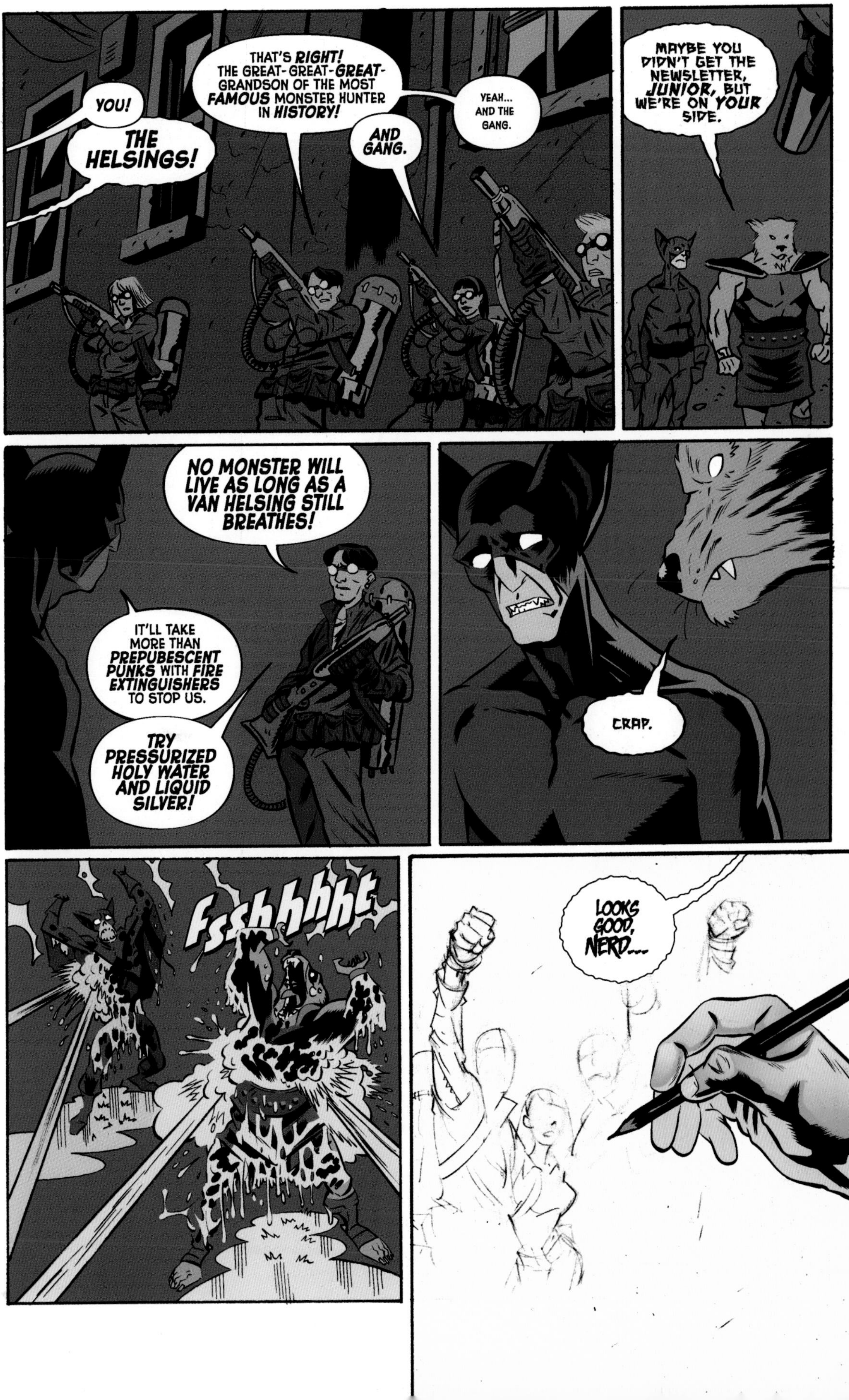
YOU!
THE HELSINGS!
THAT'S RIGHT! THE GREAT-GREAT-GREAT-GRANDSON OF THE MOST FAMOUS MONSTER HUNTER IN HISTORY!
AND GANG.
YEAH... AND THE GANG.
MAYBE YOU DIDN'T GET THE NEWSLETTER, JUNIOR, BUT WE'RE ON YOUR SIDE.
NO MONSTER WILL LIVE AS LONG AS A VAN HELSING STILL BREATHES!
IT'LL TAKE MORE THAN PREPUBESCENT PUNKS WITH FIRE EXTINGUISHERS TO STOP US.
TRY PRESSURIZED HOLY WATER AND LIQUID SILVER!
CRAP.
Fsshhhht
LOOKS GOOD, NERD...

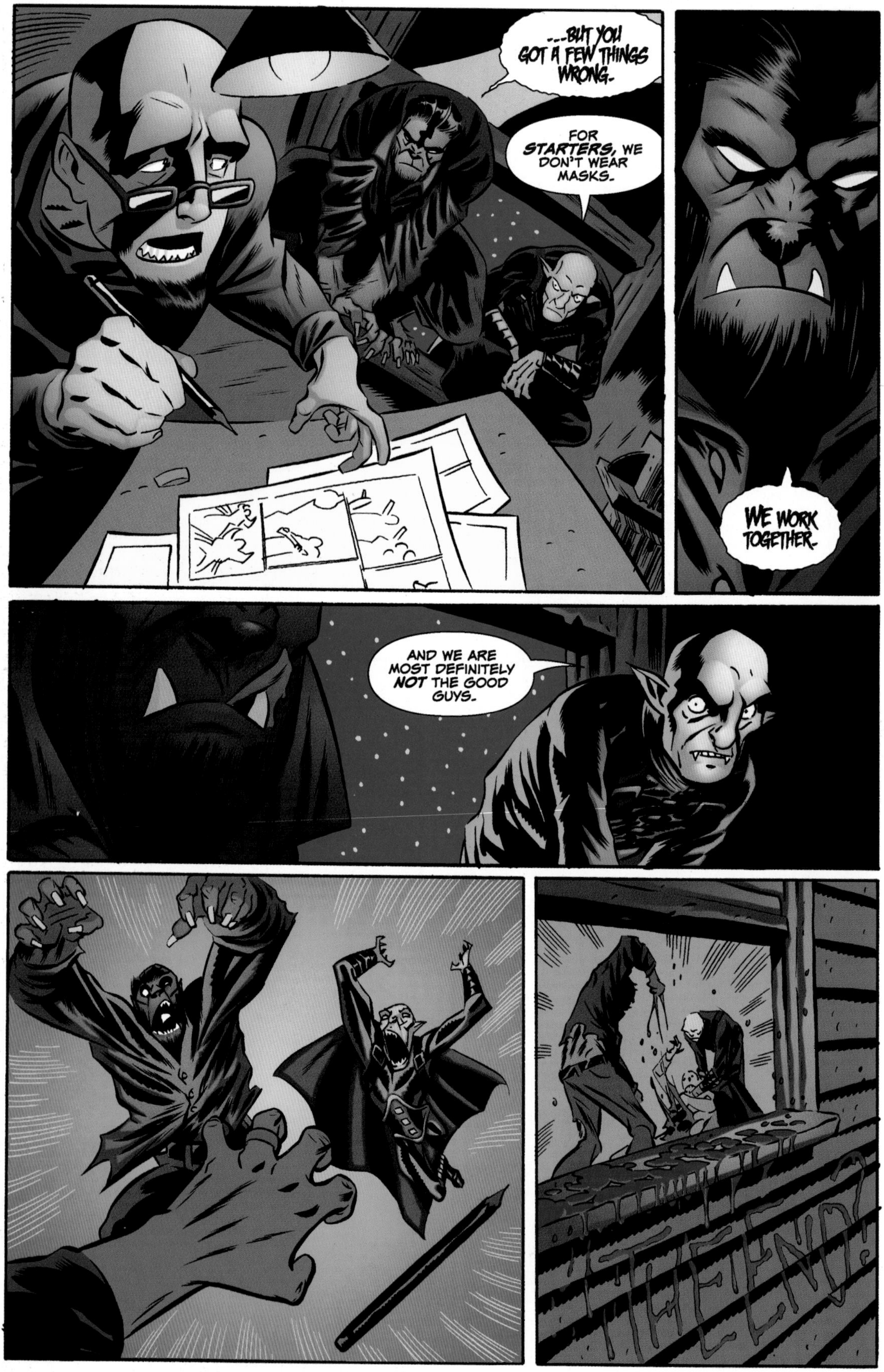
...BUT YOU GOT A FEW THINGS WRONG.
FOR STARTERS, WE DON'T WEAR MASKS.
WE WORK TOGETHER.
AND WE ARE MOST DEFINITELY NOT THE GOOD GUYS.
THE END?

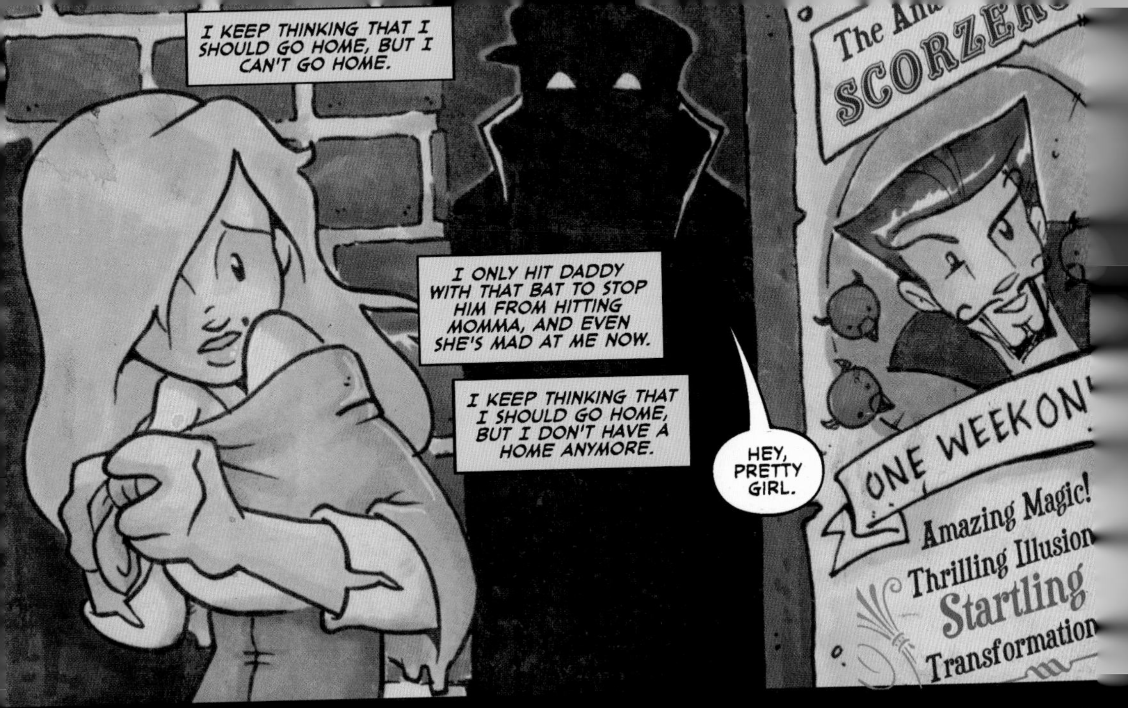

I KEEP THINKING THAT I SHOULD GO HOME, BUT I CAN'T GO HOME.
I ONLY HIT DADDY WITH THAT BAT TO STOP HIM FROM HITTING MOMMA, AND EVEN SHE'S MAD AT ME NOW.
I KEEP THINKING THAT I SHOULD GO HOME, BUT I DON'T HAVE A HOME ANYMORE.
HEY, PRETTY GIRL.
Amazing Magic!
Thrilling Illusion
Startling
Transformation

TRICKS OF THE TRADE

ART BY KATIE COOK WRITTEN BY BRODIE H. BROCKIE

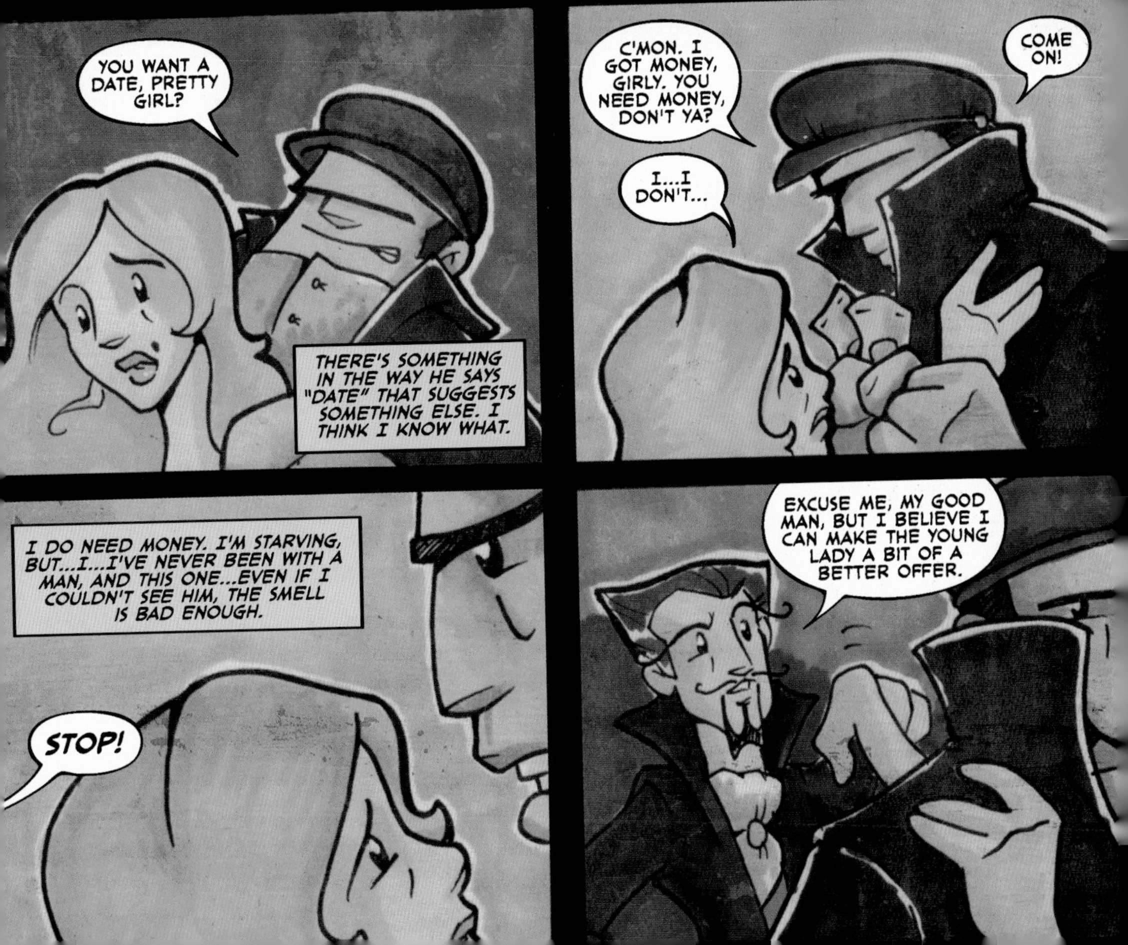

YOU WANT A DATE, PRETTY GIRL?
THERE'S SOMETHING IN THE WAY HE SAYS "DATE" THAT SUGGESTS SOMETHING ELSE. I THINK I KNOW WHAT.
C'MON. I GOT MONEY, GIRLY. YOU NEED MONEY, DON'T YA?
COME ON!
I...I DON'T...
I DO NEED MONEY. I'M STARVING, BUT...I...I'VE NEVER BEEN WITH A MAN, AND THIS ONE...EVEN IF I COULDN'T SEE HIM, THE SMELL IS BAD ENOUGH.
STOP!
EXCUSE ME, MY GOOD MAN, BUT I BELIEVE I CAN MAKE THE YOUNG LADY A BIT OF A BETTER OFFER.

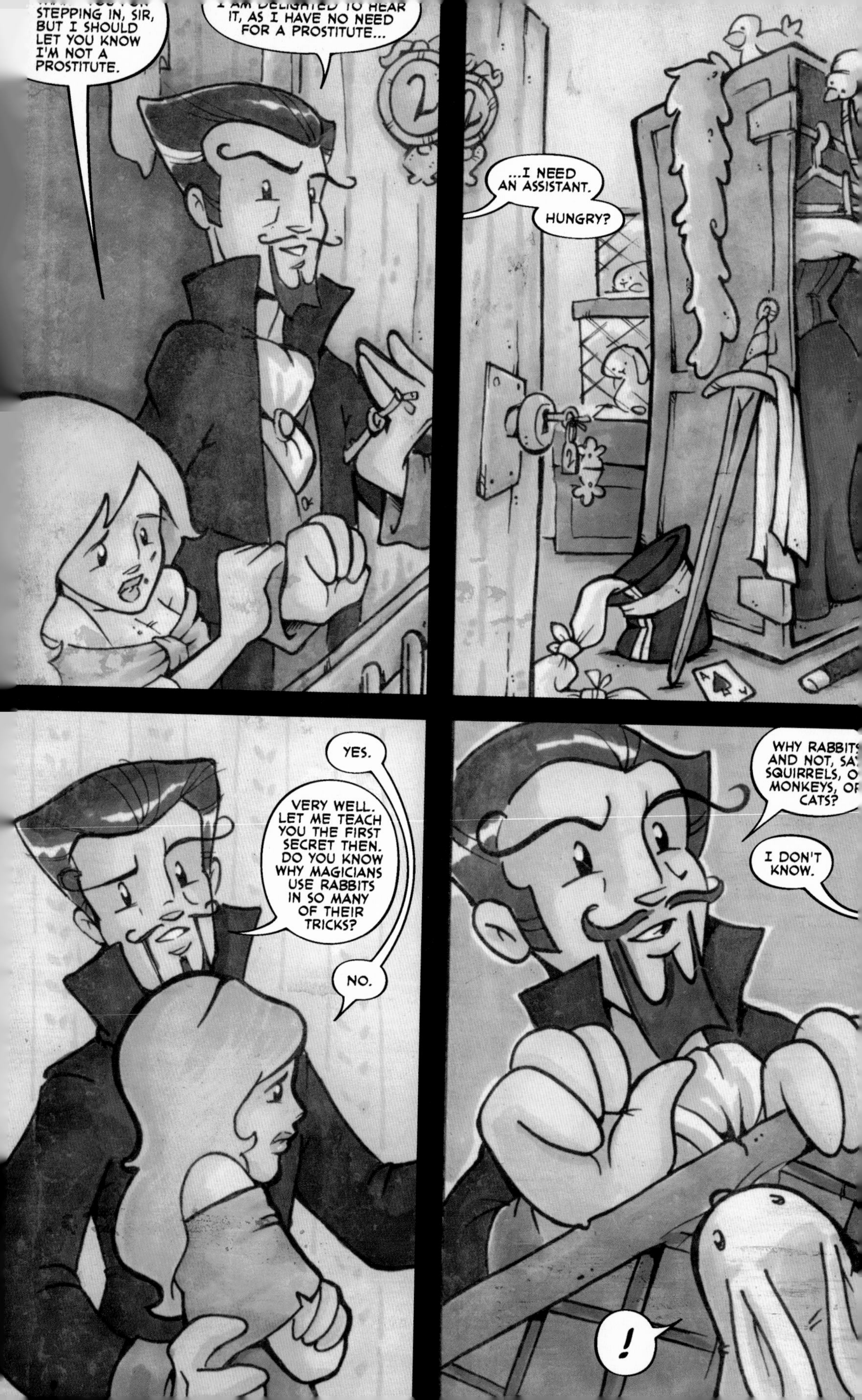
STEPPING IN, SIR, BUT I SHOULD LET YOU KNOW I'M NOT A PROSTITUTE.
I AM DELIGHTED TO HEAR IT, AS I HAVE NO NEED FOR A PROSTITUTE...
...I NEED AN ASSISTANT.
HUNGRY?
YES.
VERY WELL. LET ME TEACH YOU THE FIRST SECRET THEN. DO YOU KNOW WHY MAGICIANS USE RABBITS IN SO MANY OF THEIR TRICKS?
NO.
WHY RABBITS AND NOT, SA SQUIRRELS, O MONKEYS, OF CATS?
I DON'T KNOW.
!

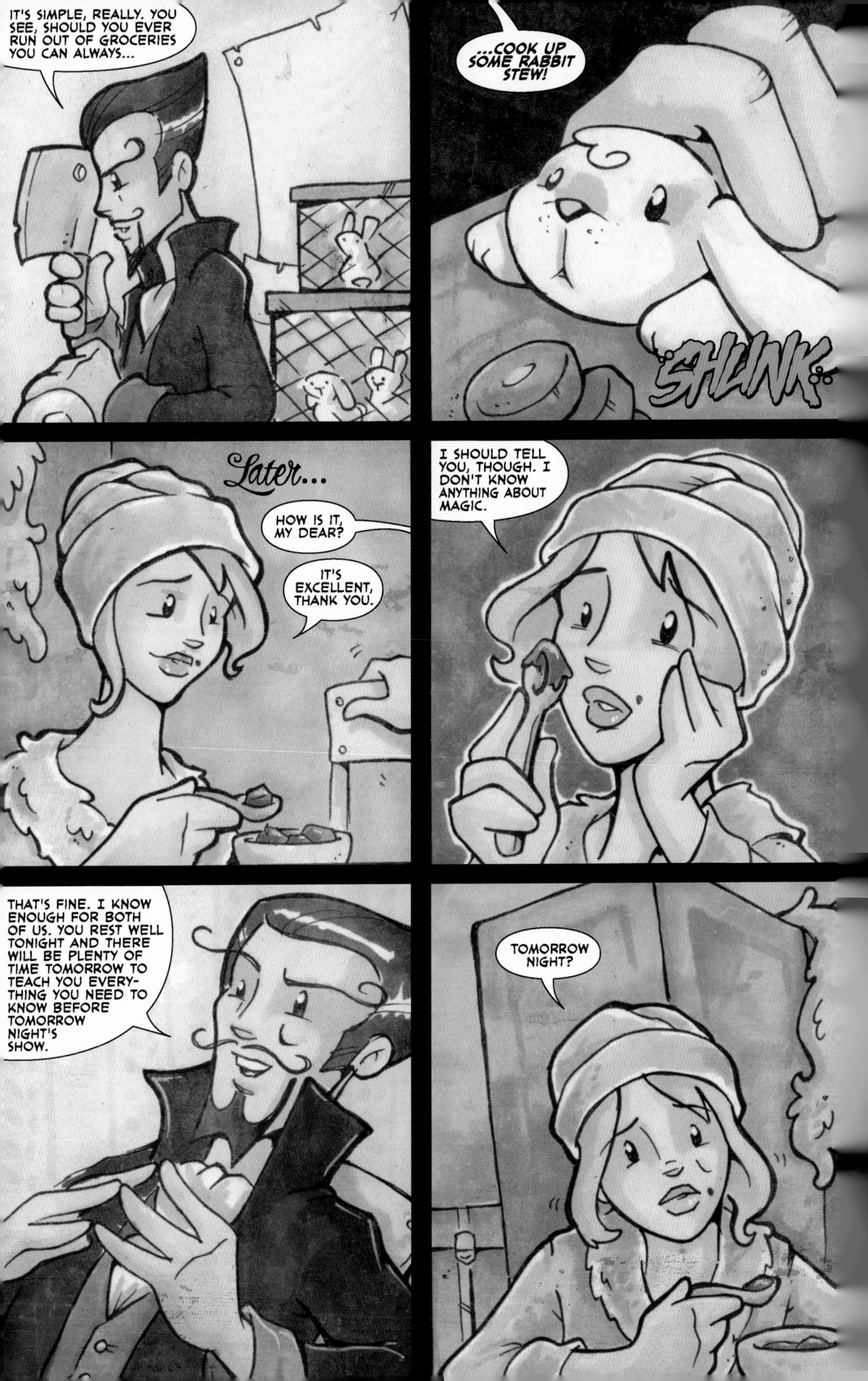
IT'S SIMPLE, REALLY. YOU SEE, SHOULD YOU EVER RUN OUT OF GROCERIES YOU CAN ALWAYS...
...COOK UP SOME RABBIT STEW!
SHLINK
Later...
HOW IS IT, MY DEAR?
IT'S EXCELLENT, THANK YOU.
I SHOULD TELL YOU, THOUGH. I DON'T KNOW ANYTHING ABOUT MAGIC.
THAT'S FINE. I KNOW ENOUGH FOR BOTH OF US. YOU REST WELL TONIGHT AND THERE WILL BE PLENTY OF TIME TOMORROW TO TEACH YOU EVERYTHING YOU NEED TO KNOW BEFORE TOMORROW NIGHT'S SHOW.
TOMORROW NIGHT?

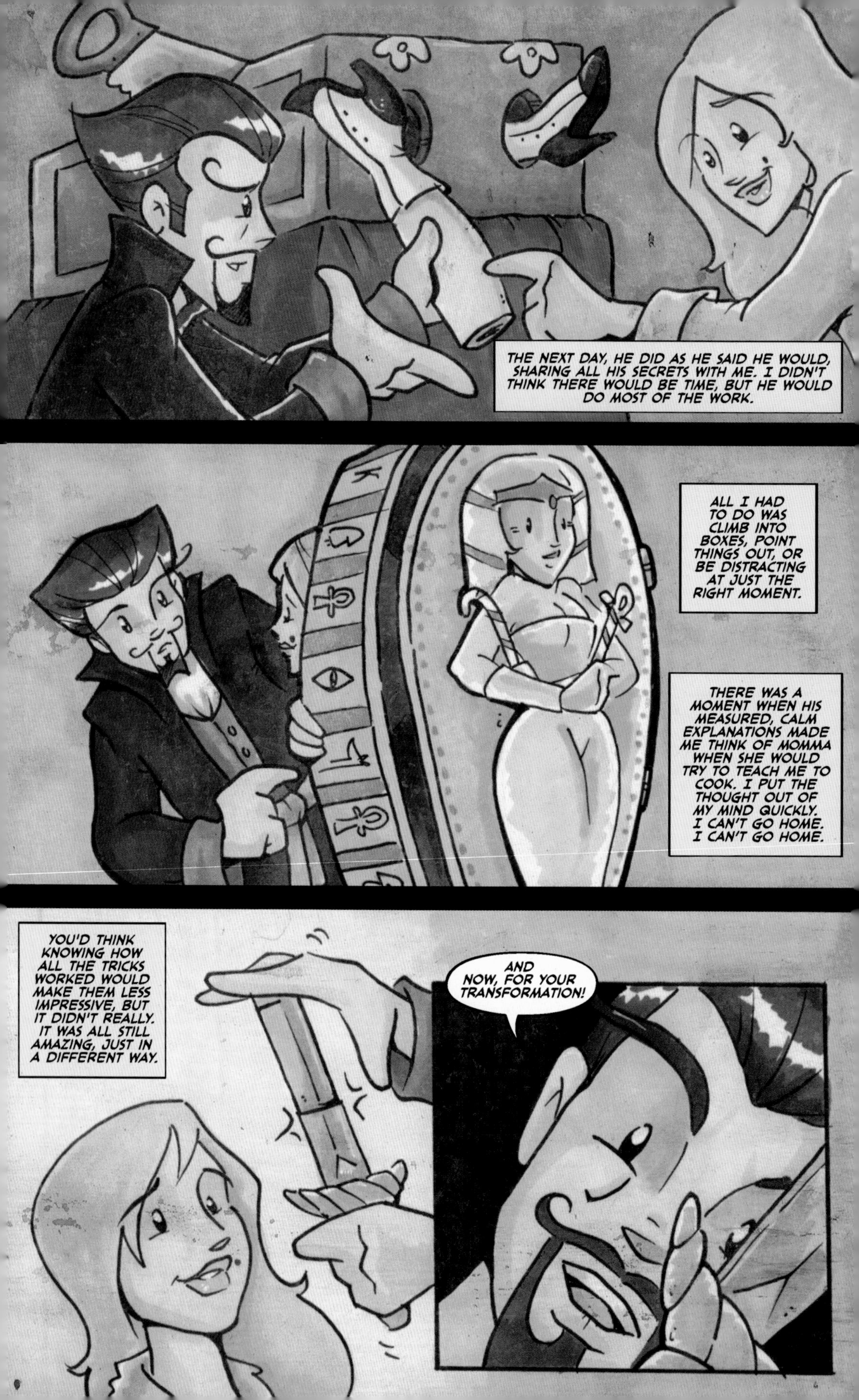
THE NEXT DAY, HE DID AS HE SAID HE WOULD, SHARING ALL HIS SECRETS WITH ME. I DIDN'T THINK THERE WOULD BE TIME, BUT HE WOULD DO MOST OF THE WORK.
ALL I HAD TO DO WAS CLIMB INTO BOXES, POINT THINGS OUT, OR BE DISTRACTING AT JUST THE RIGHT MOMENT.
THERE WAS A MOMENT WHEN HIS MEASURED, CALM EXPLANATIONS MADE ME THINK OF MOMMA WHEN SHE WOULD TRY TO TEACH ME TO COOK. I PUT THE THOUGHT OUT OF MY MIND QUICKLY. I CAN'T GO HOME. I CAN'T GO HOME.
YOU'D THINK KNOWING HOW ALL THE TRICKS WORKED WOULD MAKE THEM LESS IMPRESSIVE, BUT IT DIDN'T REALLY. IT WAS ALL STILL AMAZING, JUST IN A DIFFERENT WAY.
AND NOW, FOR YOUR TRANSFORMATION!

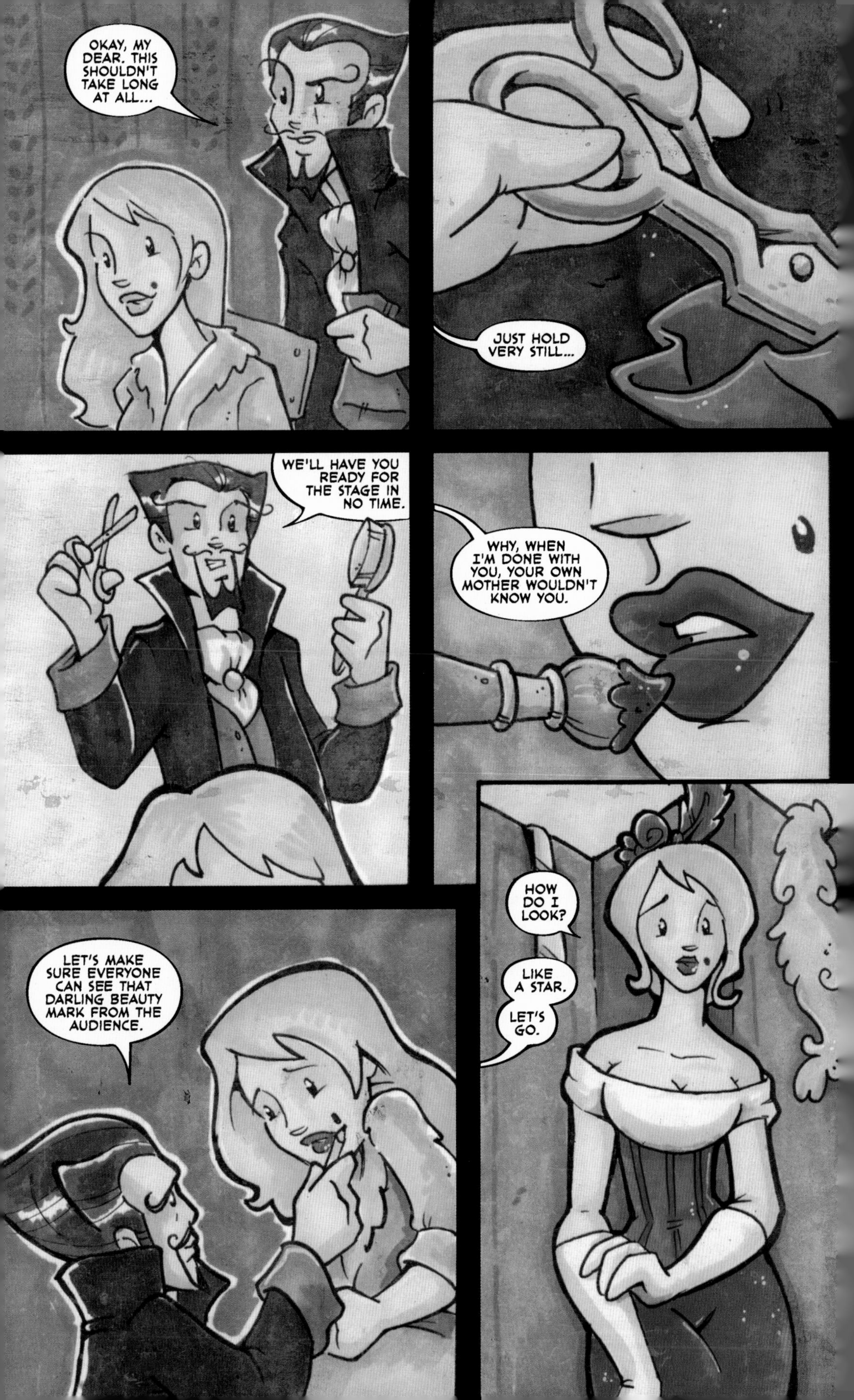
OKAY, MY DEAR. THIS SHOULDN'T TAKE LONG AT ALL...
JUST HOLD VERY STILL...
WE'LL HAVE YOU READY FOR THE STAGE IN NO TIME.
WHY, WHEN I'M DONE WITH YOU, YOUR OWN MOTHER WOULDN'T KNOW YOU.
LET'S MAKE SURE EVERYONE CAN SEE THAT DARLING BEAUTY MARK FROM THE AUDIENCE.
HOW DO I LOOK?
LIKE A STAR.
LET'S GO.

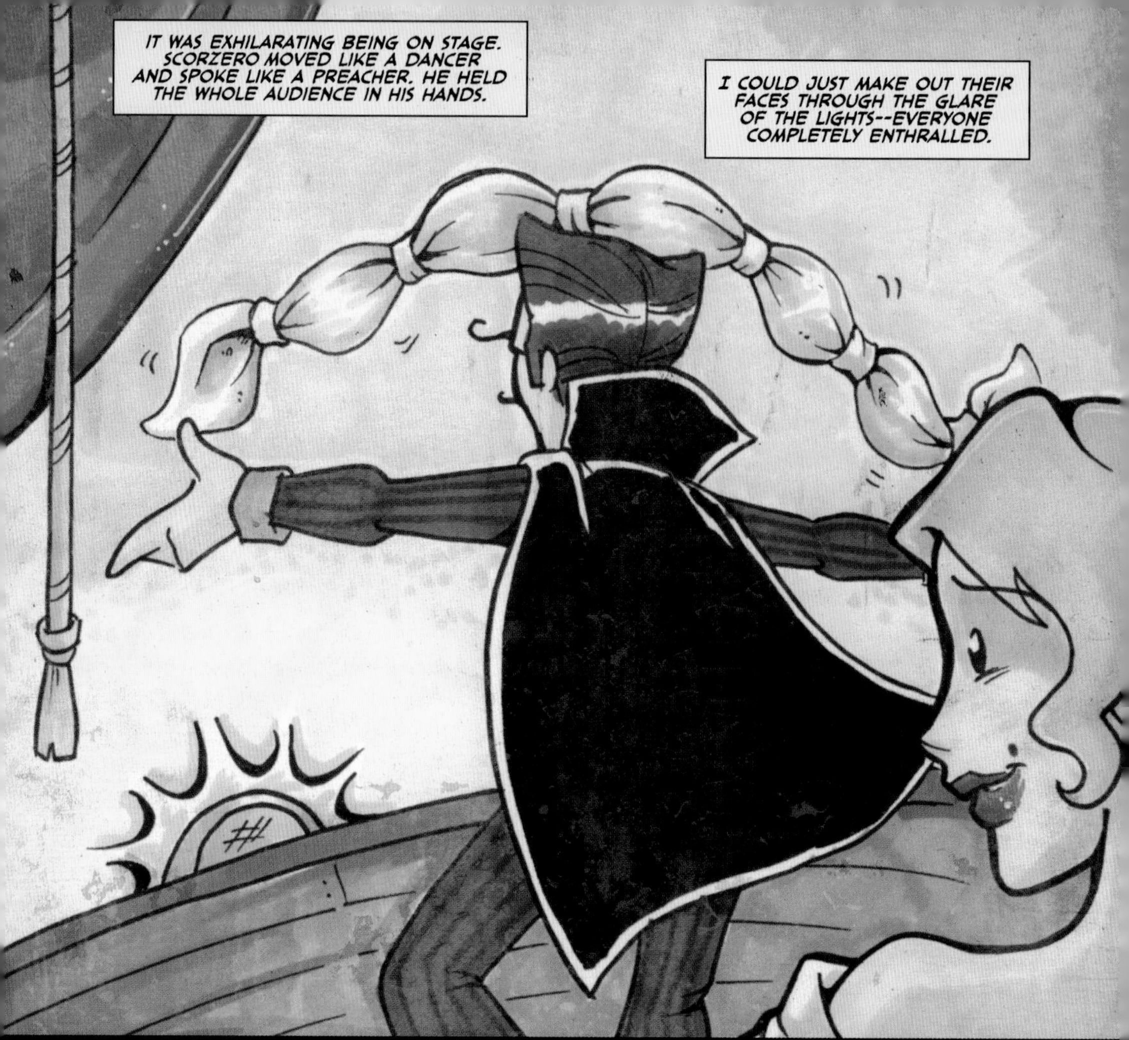
IT WAS EXHILARATING BEING ON STAGE. SCORZERO MOVED LIKE A DANCER AND SPOKE LIKE A PREACHER. HE HELD THE WHOLE AUDIENCE IN HIS HANDS.
I COULD JUST MAKE OUT THEIR FACES THROUGH THE GLARE OF THE LIGHTS--EVERYONE COMPLETELY ENTHRALLED.

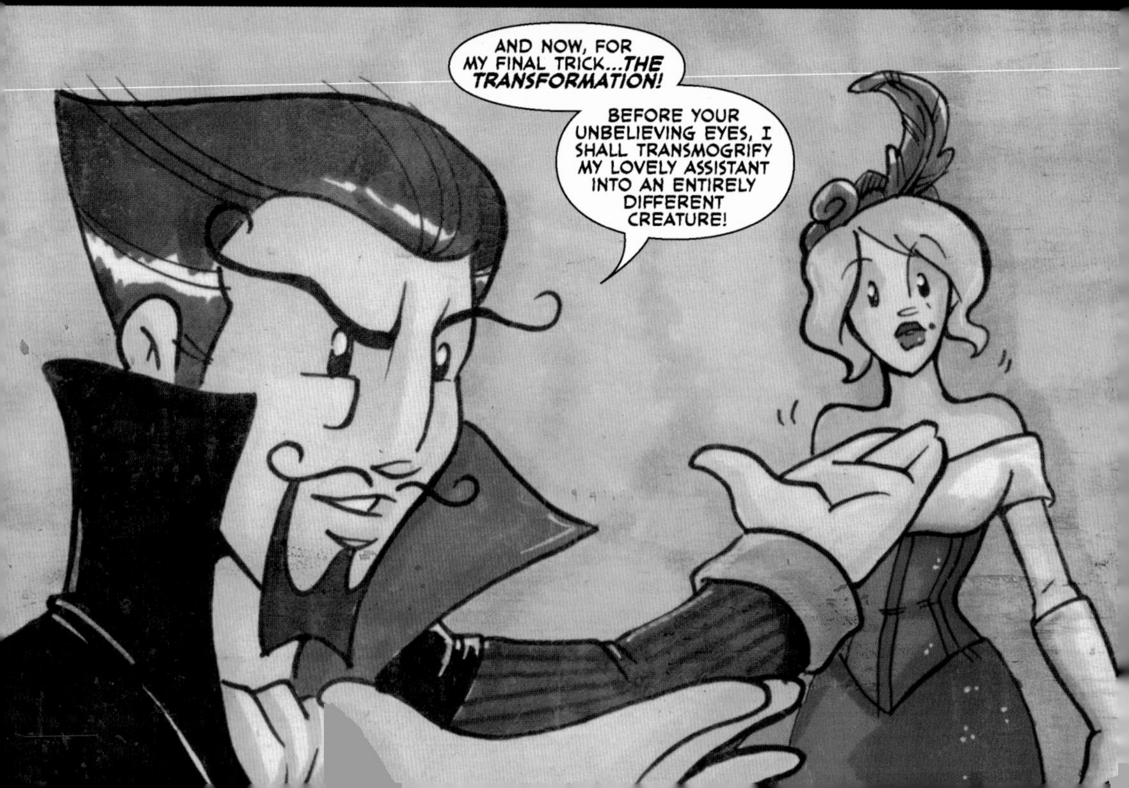
AND NOW, FOR MY FINAL TRICK...*THE TRANSFORMATION!*
BEFORE YOUR UNBELIEVING EYES, I SHALL TRANSMOGRIFY MY LOVELY ASSISTANT INTO AN ENTIRELY DIFFERENT CREATURE!

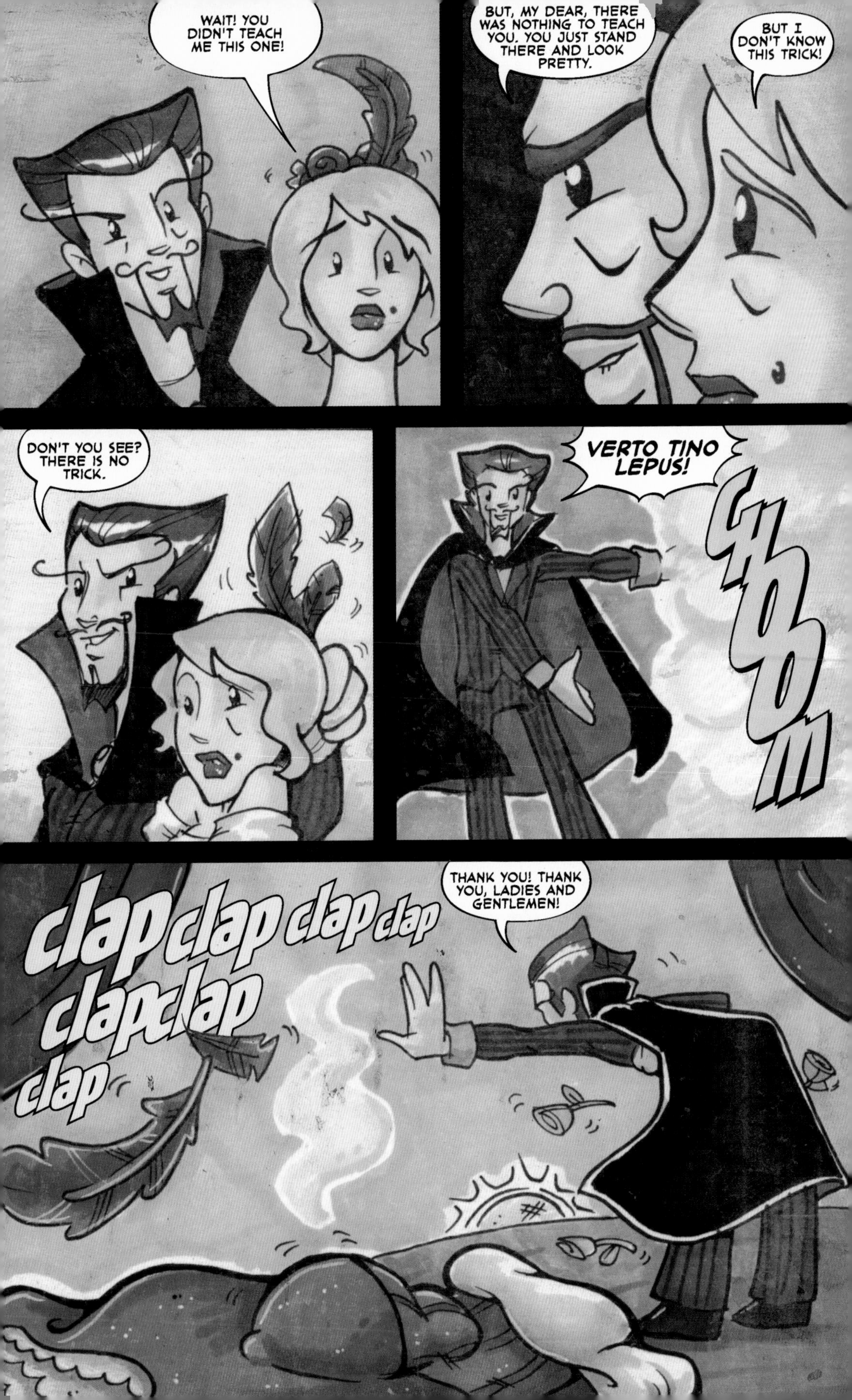
WAIT! YOU DIDN'T TEACH ME THIS ONE!
BUT, MY DEAR, THERE WAS NOTHING TO TEACH YOU. YOU JUST STAND THERE AND LOOK PRETTY.
BUT I DON'T KNOW THIS TRICK!
DON'T YOU SEE? THERE IS NO TRICK.
VERTO TINO LEPUS!
CHOOOM
clap clap clap clap
clapclap
clap
THANK YOU! THANK YOU, LADIES AND GENTLEMEN!

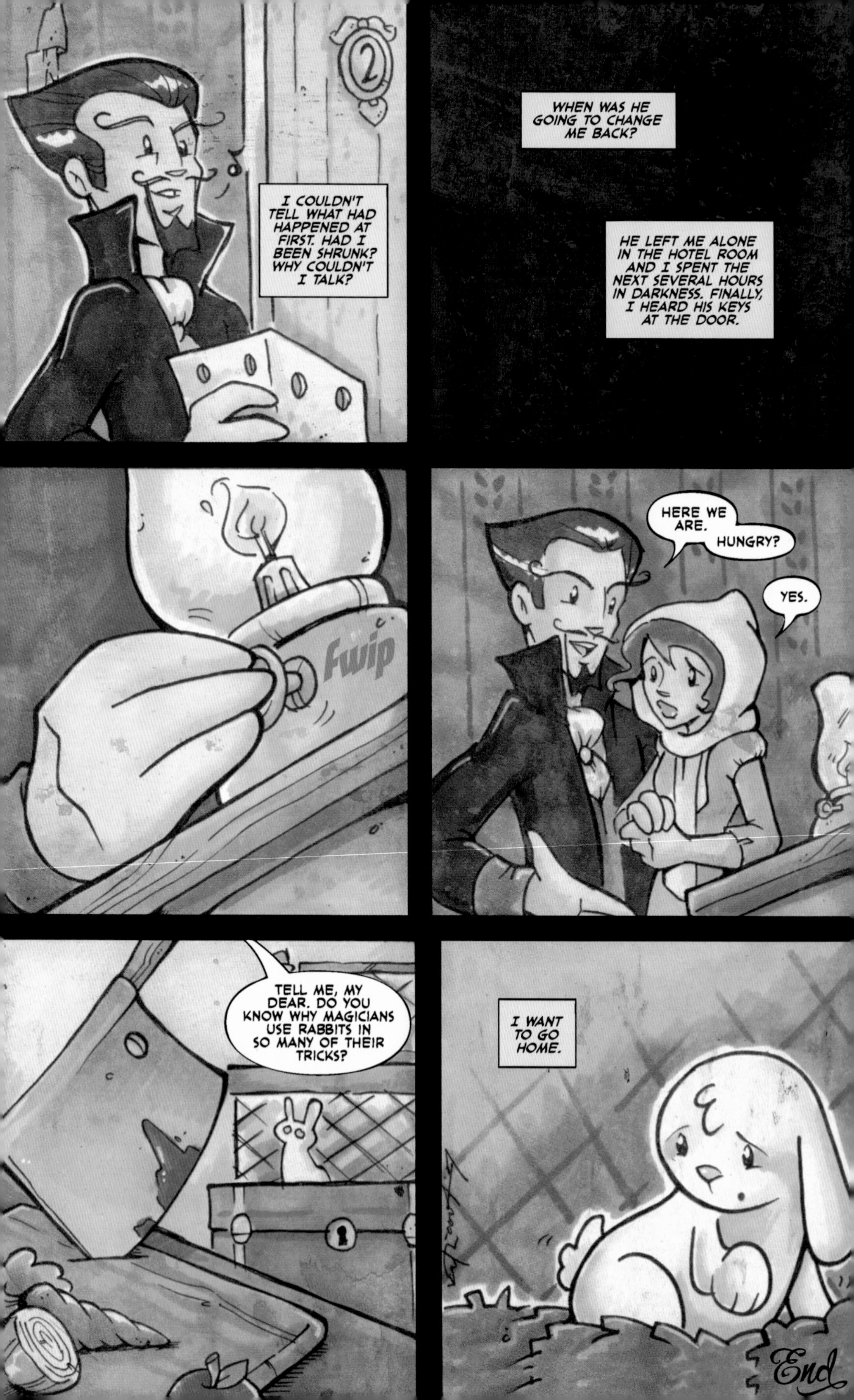
I COULDN'T TELL WHAT HAD HAPPENED AT FIRST. HAD I BEEN SHRUNK? WHY COULDN'T I TALK?
WHEN WAS HE GOING TO CHANGE ME BACK?
HE LEFT ME ALONE IN THE HOTEL ROOM AND I SPENT THE NEXT SEVERAL HOURS IN DARKNESS. FINALLY, I HEARD HIS KEYS AT THE DOOR.
Fwip
HERE WE ARE.
HUNGRY?
YES.
TELL ME, MY DEAR. DO YOU KNOW WHY MAGICIANS USE RABBITS IN SO MANY OF THEIR TRICKS?
I WANT TO GO HOME.
End

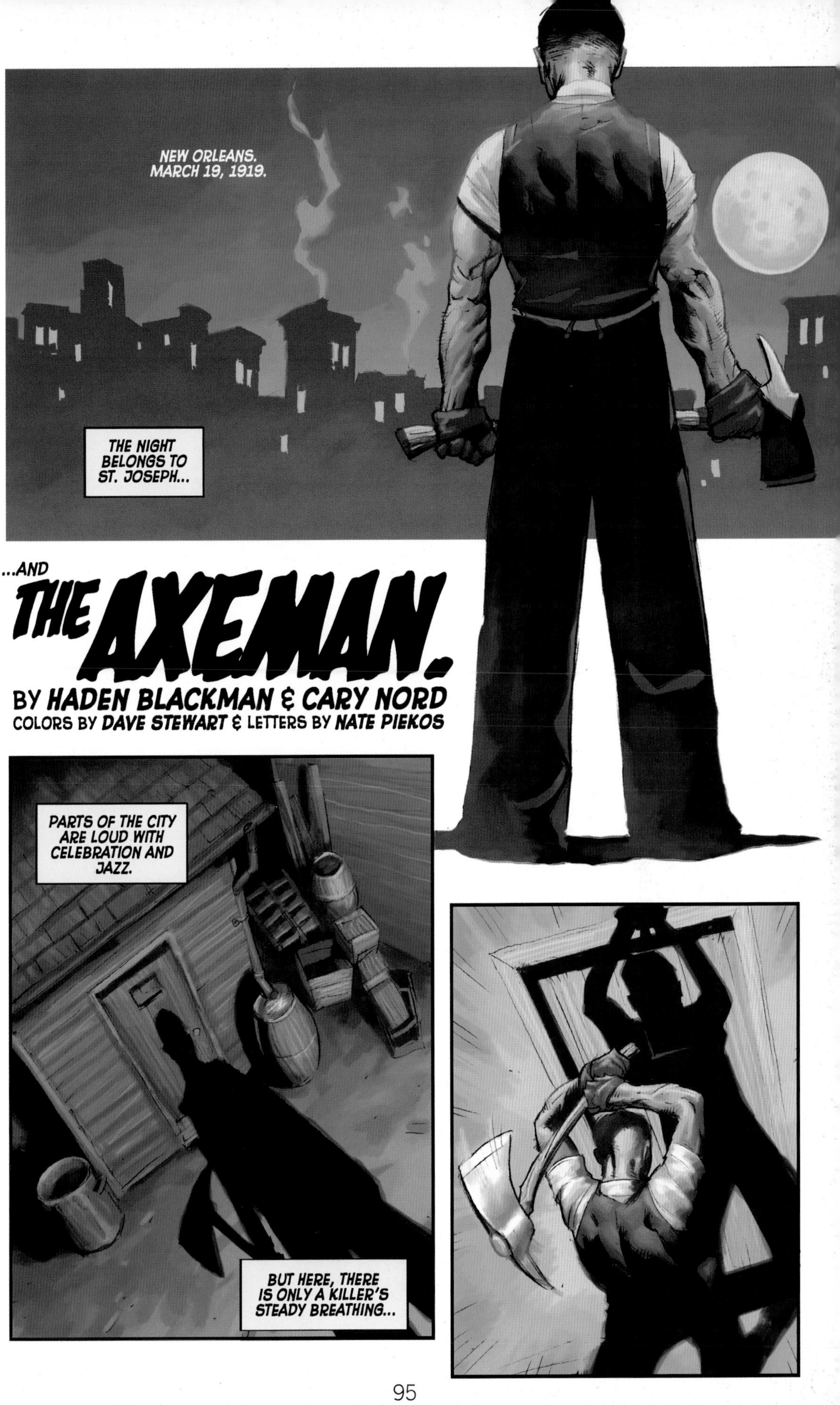
NEW ORLEANS. MARCH 19, 1919.
THE NIGHT BELONGS TO ST. JOSEPH...
...AND THE AXEMAN.
BY HADEN BLACKMAN & CARY NORD
COLORS BY DAVE STEWART & LETTERS BY NATE PIEKOS
PARTS OF THE CITY ARE LOUD WITH CELEBRATION AND JAZZ.
BUT HERE, THERE IS ONLY A KILLER'S STEADY BREATHING...

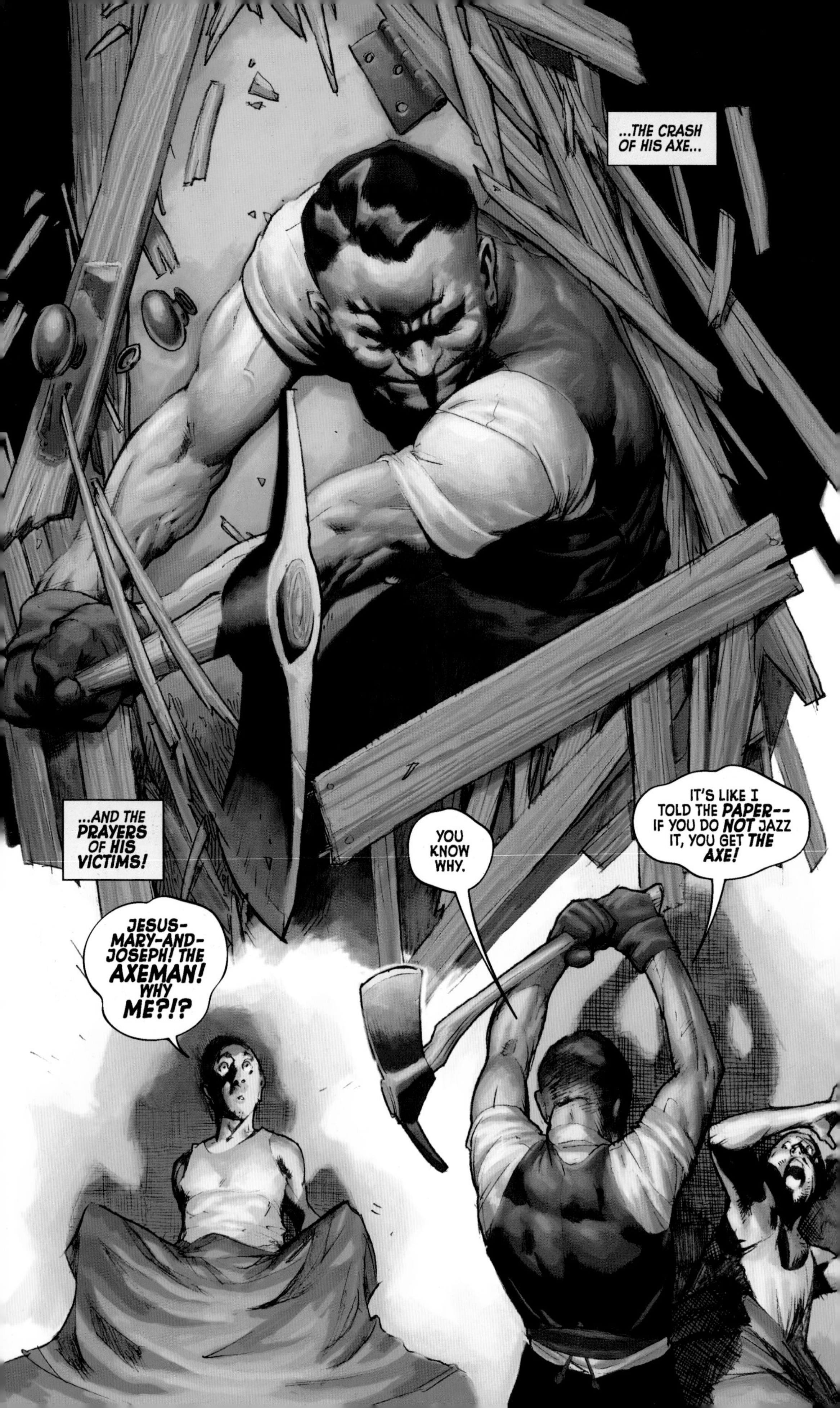
...THE CRASH OF HIS AXE...
...AND THE PRAYERS OF HIS VICTIMS!
JESUS-MARY-AND-JOSEPH! THE AXEMAN! WHY ME?!?
YOU KNOW WHY.
IT'S LIKE I TOLD THE PAPER-- IF YOU DO NOT JAZZ IT, YOU GET THE AXE!

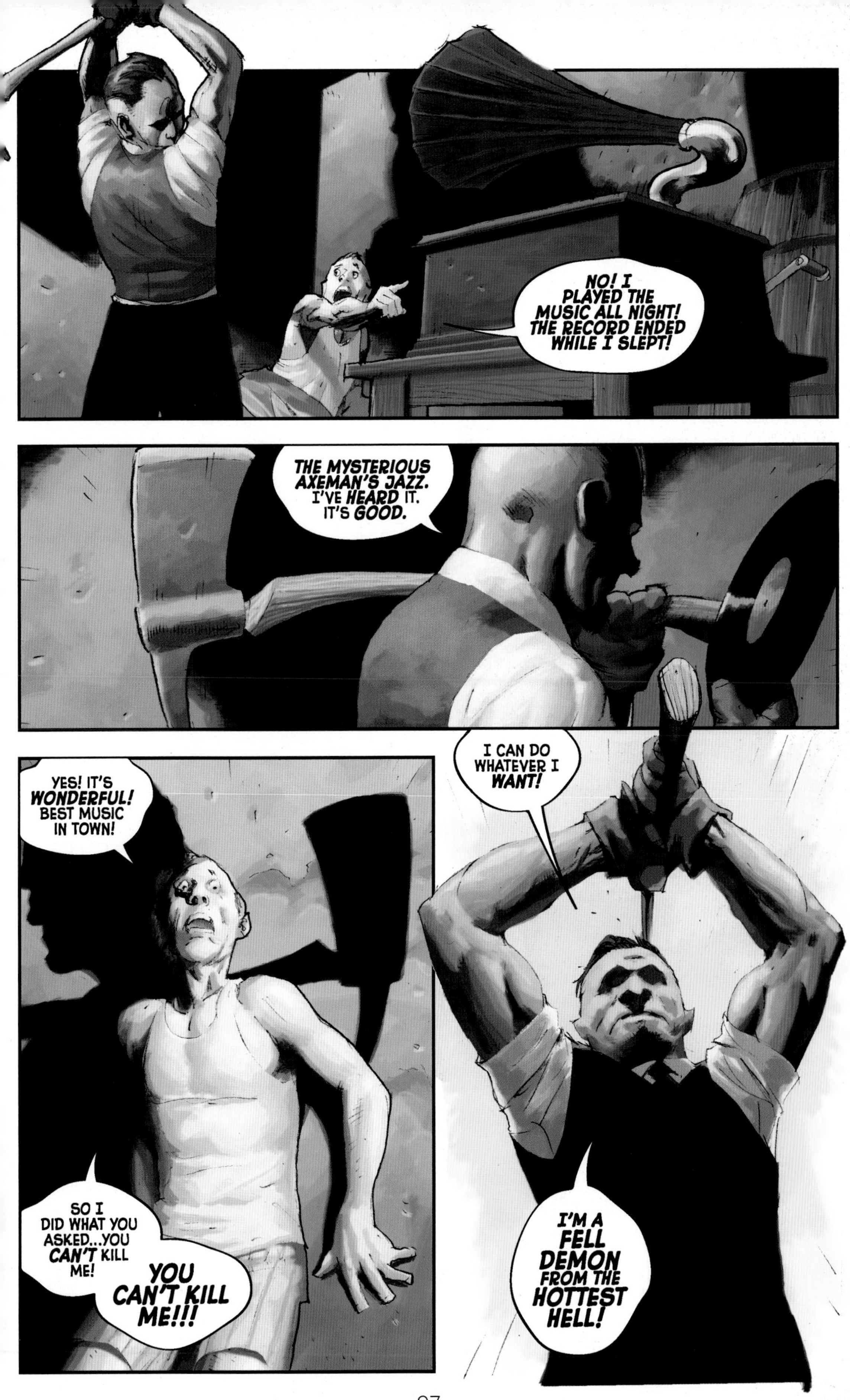
NO! I PLAYED THE MUSIC ALL NIGHT! THE RECORD ENDED WHILE I SLEPT!
THE MYSTERIOUS AXEMAN'S JAZZ. I'VE HEARD IT. IT'S GOOD.
YES! IT'S WONDERFUL! BEST MUSIC IN TOWN!
I CAN DO WHATEVER I WANT!
SO I DID WHAT YOU ASKED...YOU CAN'T KILL ME!
YOU CAN'T KILL ME!!!
I'M A FELL DEMON FROM THE HOTTEST HELL!

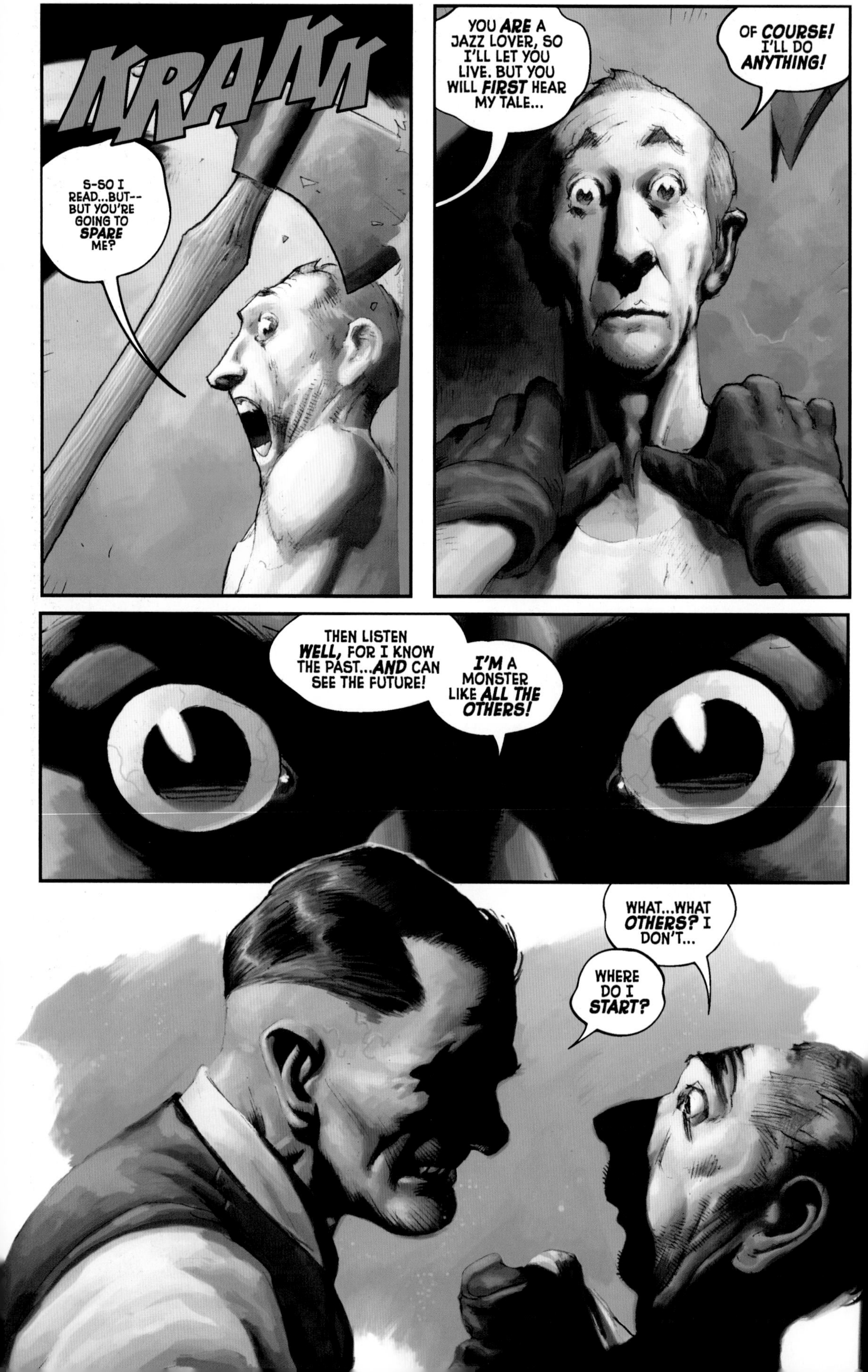
KRANK
S-SO I READ...BUT--BUT YOU'RE GOING TO SPARE ME?
YOU ARE A JAZZ LOVER, SO I'LL LET YOU LIVE. BUT YOU WILL FIRST HEAR MY TALE...
OF COURSE! I'LL DO ANYTHING!
THEN LISTEN WELL, FOR I KNOW THE PAST...AND CAN SEE THE FUTURE!
I'M A MONSTER LIKE ALL THE OTHERS!
WHAT...WHAT OTHERS? I DON'T...
WHERE DO I START?

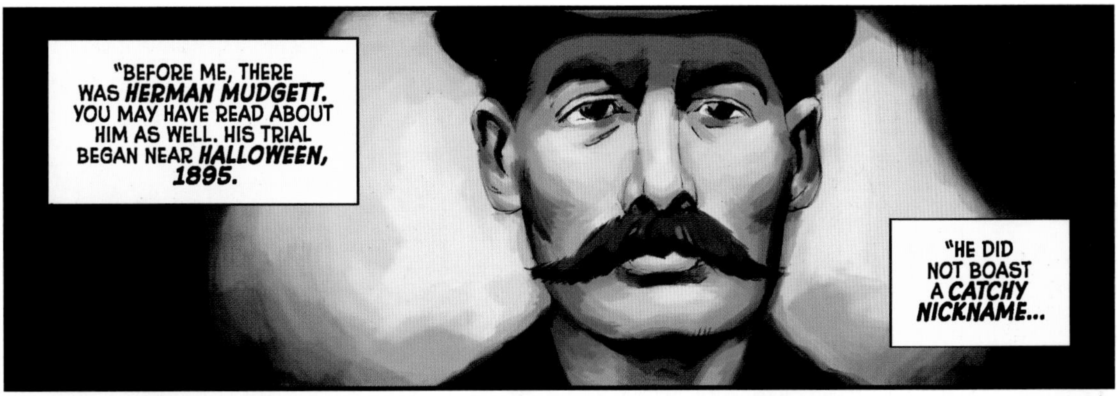
"BEFORE ME, THERE WAS HERMAN MUDGETT. YOU MAY HAVE READ ABOUT HIM AS WELL. HIS TRIAL BEGAN NEAR HALLOWEEN, 1895.
"HE DID NOT BOAST A CATCHY NICKNAME...

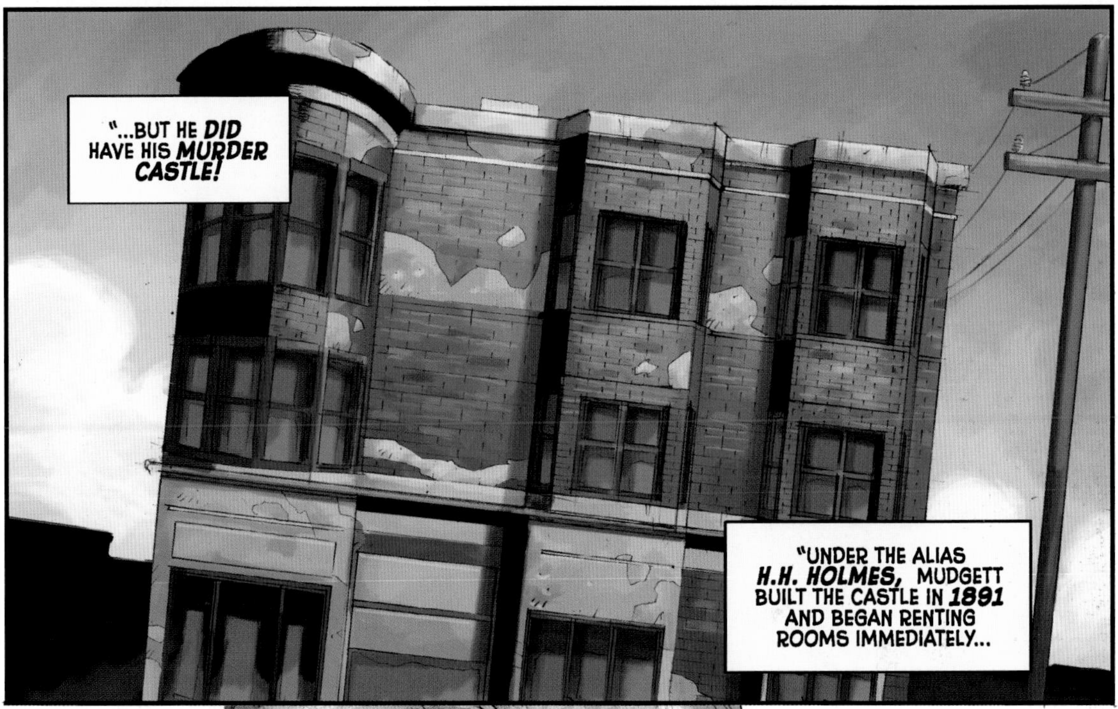
"...BUT HE DID HAVE HIS MURDER CASTLE!
"UNDER THE ALIAS H.H. HOLMES, MUDGETT BUILT THE CASTLE IN 1891 AND BEGAN RENTING ROOMS IMMEDIATELY...

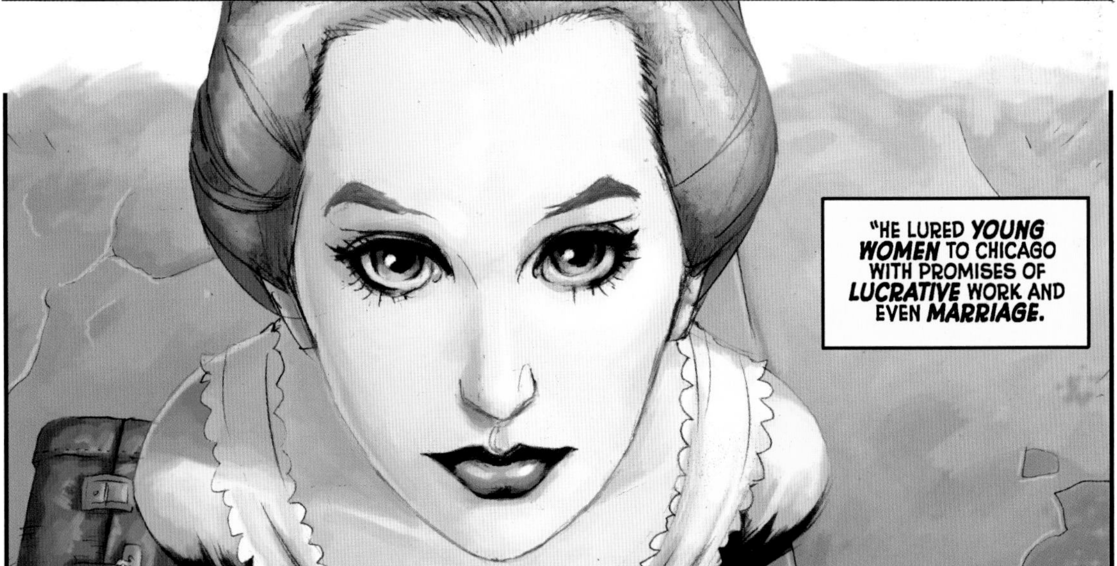
"HE LURED YOUNG WOMEN TO CHICAGO WITH PROMISES OF LUCRATIVE WORK AND EVEN MARRIAGE.

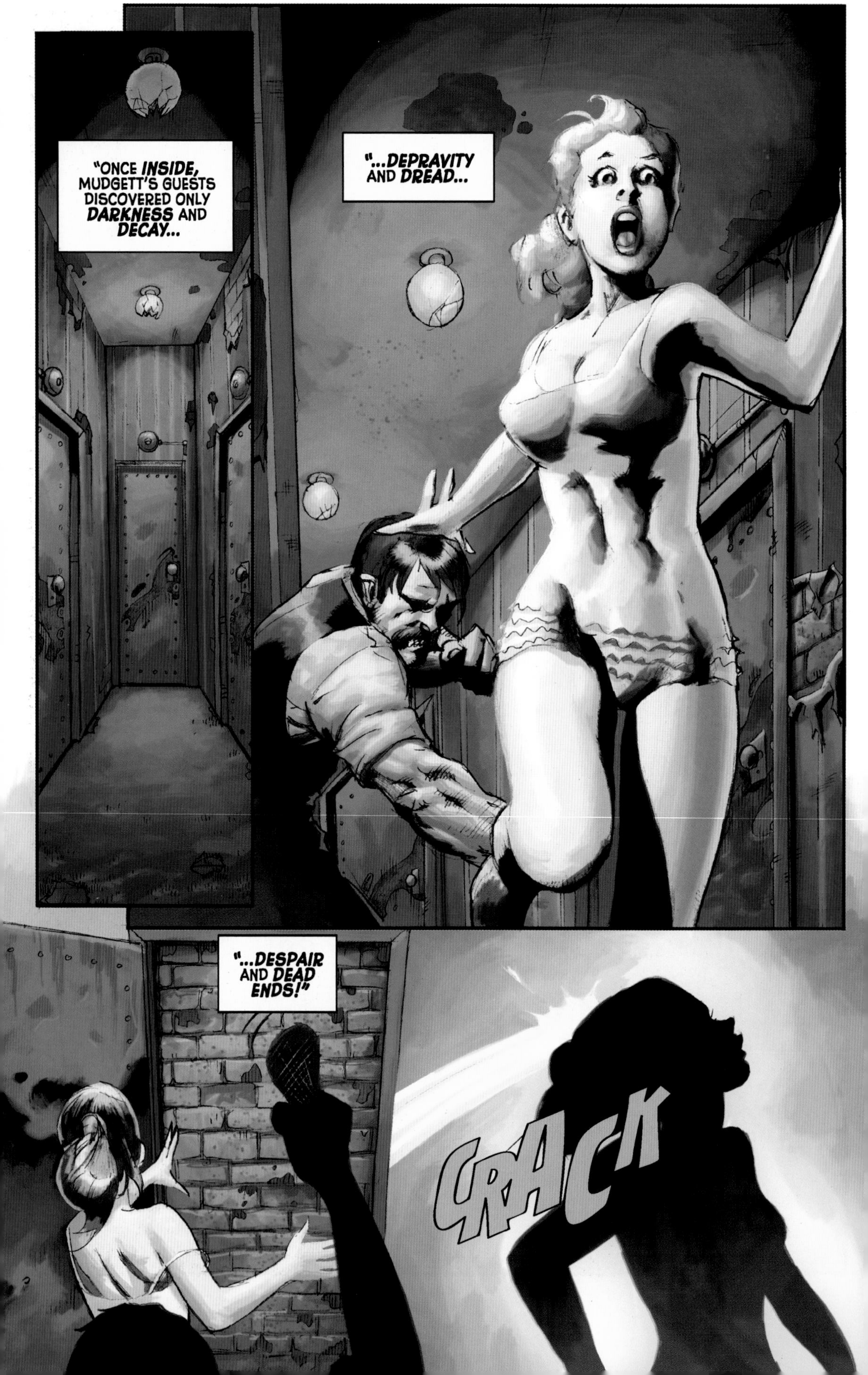
"ONCE INSIDE, MUDGETT'S GUESTS DISCOVERED ONLY DARKNESS AND DECAY...
"...DEPRAVITY AND DREAD...
"...DESPAIR AND DEAD ENDS!"
CRACK

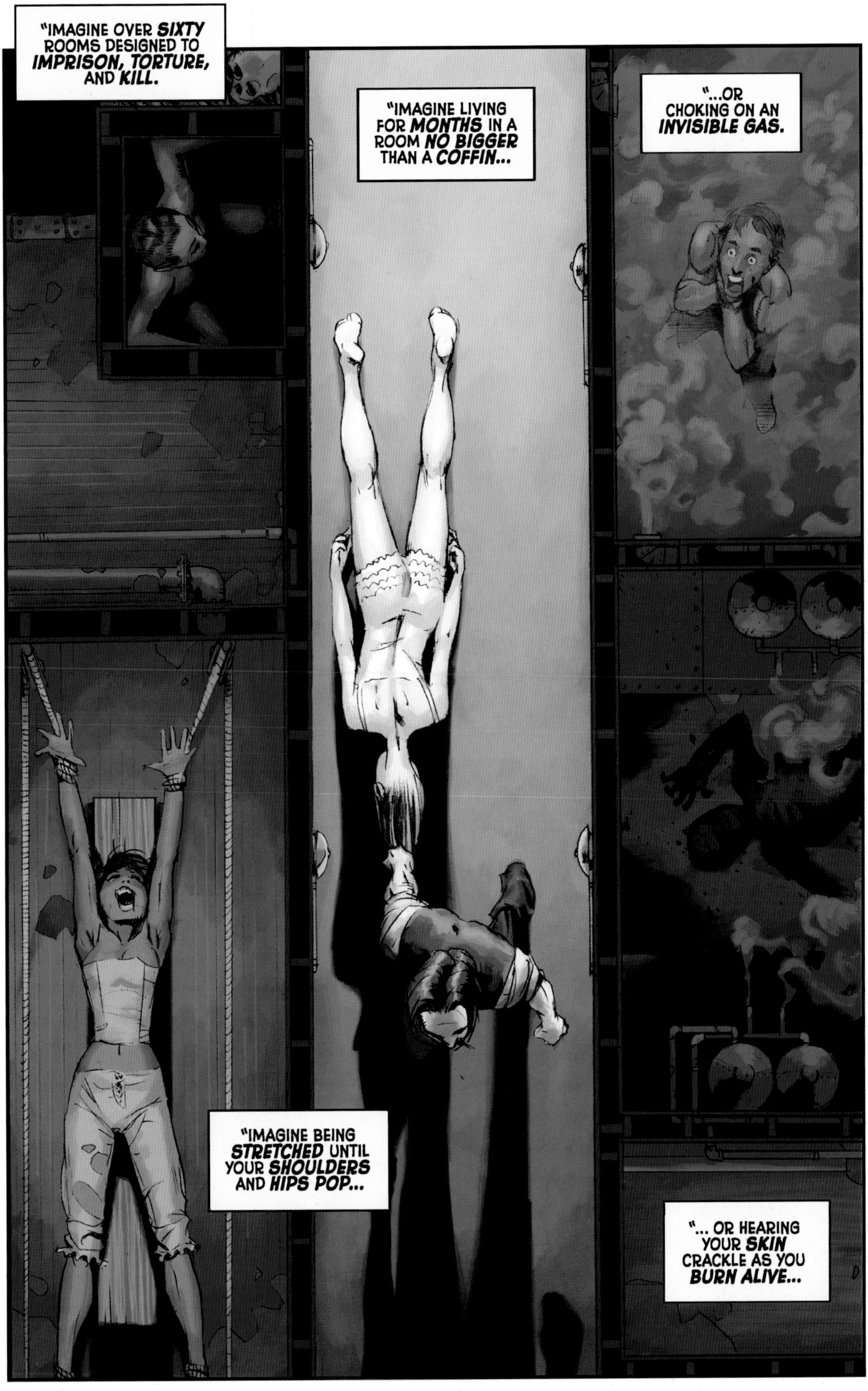
"IMAGINE OVER SIXTY ROOMS DESIGNED TO IMPRISON, TORTURE, AND KILL.
"IMAGINE LIVING FOR MONTHS IN A ROOM NO BIGGER THAN A COFFIN...
"...OR CHOKING ON AN INVISIBLE GAS.
"IMAGINE BEING STRETCHED UNTIL YOUR SHOULDERS AND HIPS POP...
"... OR HEARING YOUR SKIN CRACKLE AS YOU BURN ALIVE...

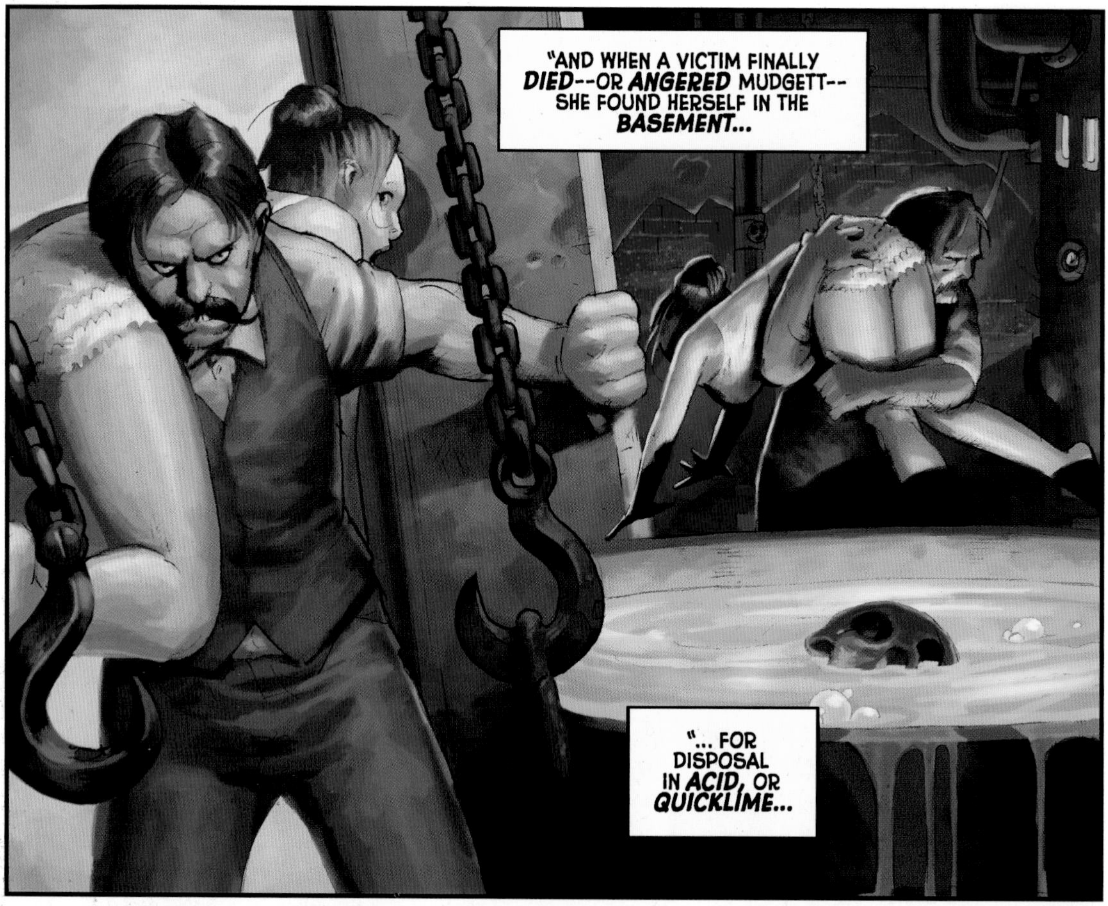
"AND WHEN A VICTIM FINALLY DIED--OR ANGERED MUDGETT--SHE FOUND HERSELF IN THE BASEMENT...
"... FOR DISPOSAL IN ACID, OR QUICKLIME...

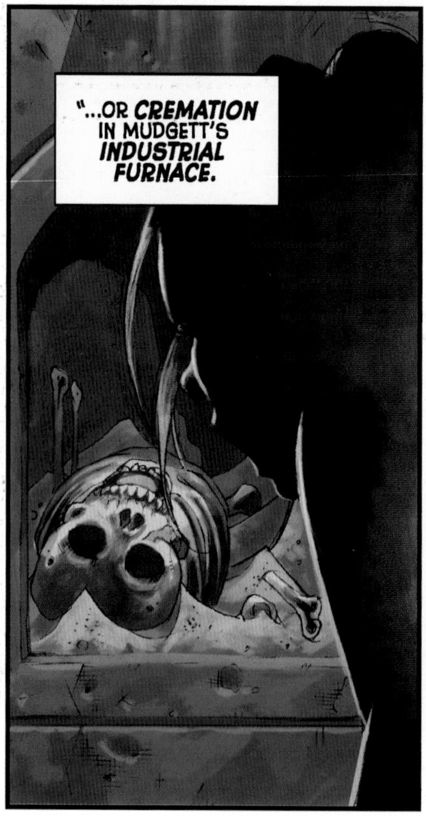
"...OR CREMATION IN MUDGETT'S INDUSTRIAL FURNACE.

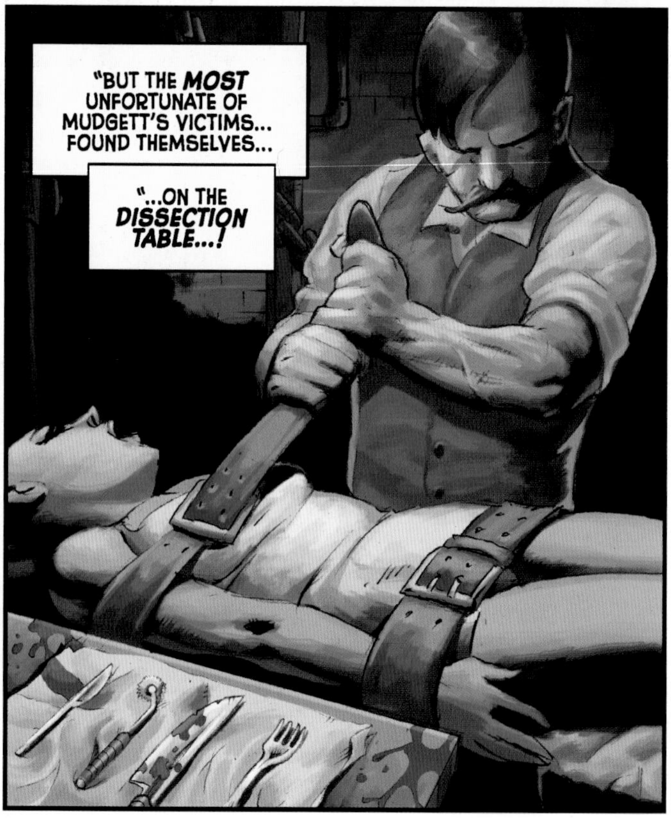
"BUT THE MOST UNFORTUNATE OF MUDGETT'S VICTIMS... FOUND THEMSELVES...
"...ON THE DISSECTION TABLE...!

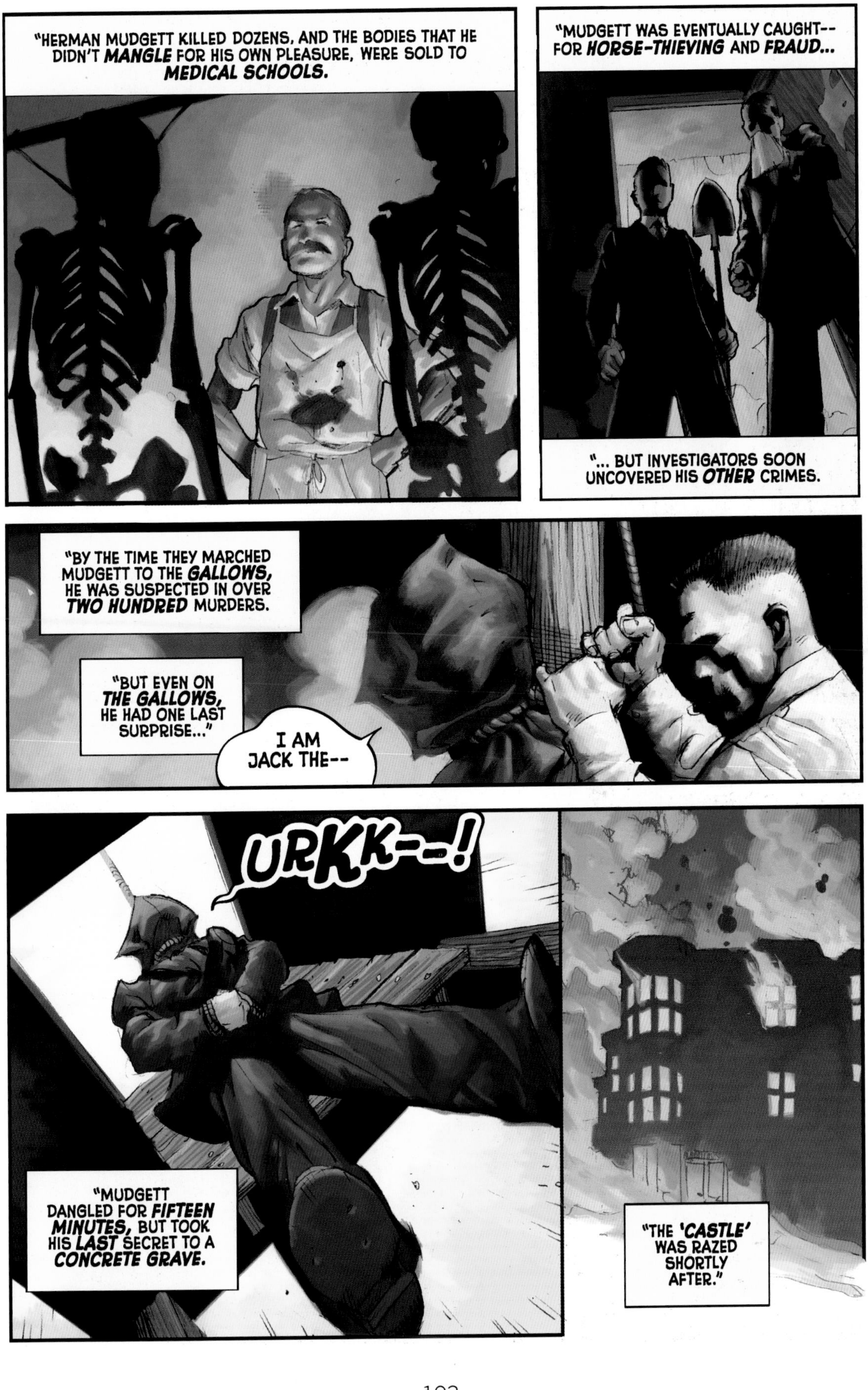
"HERMAN MUDGETT KILLED DOZENS, AND THE BODIES THAT HE DIDN'T MANGLE FOR HIS OWN PLEASURE, WERE SOLD TO MEDICAL SCHOOLS.
"MUDGETT WAS EVENTUALLY CAUGHT-- FOR HORSE-THIEVING AND FRAUD...
"... BUT INVESTIGATORS SOON UNCOVERED HIS OTHER CRIMES.
"BY THE TIME THEY MARCHED MUDGETT TO THE GALLOWS, HE WAS SUSPECTED IN OVER TWO HUNDRED MURDERS.
"BUT EVEN ON THE GALLOWS, HE HAD ONE LAST SURPRISE..."
I AM JACK THE--
URKK--!
"MUDGETT DANGLED FOR FIFTEEN MINUTES, BUT TOOK HIS LAST SECRET TO A CONCRETE GRAVE.
"THE 'CASTLE' WAS RAZED SHORTLY AFTER."

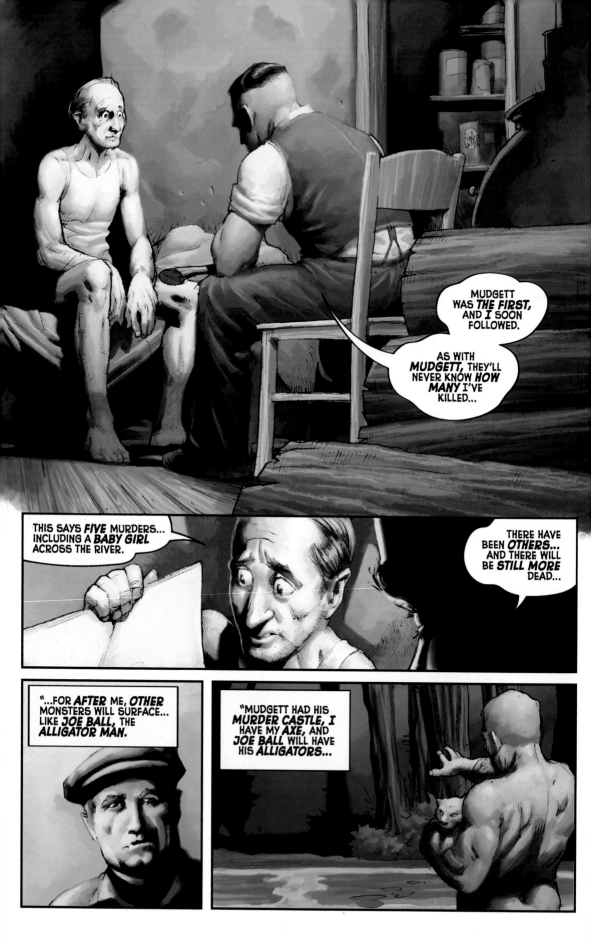

MUDGETT WAS *THE FIRST*, AND *I* SOON FOLLOWED.

AS WITH *MUDGETT*, THEY'LL NEVER KNOW *HOW MANY* I'VE KILLED...

THIS SAYS *FIVE* MURDERS... INCLUDING A *BABY GIRL* ACROSS THE RIVER.

THERE HAVE BEEN *OTHERS*... AND THERE WILL BE *STILL MORE* DEAD...

"...FOR *AFTER* ME, *OTHER* MONSTERS WILL SURFACE... LIKE *JOE BALL*, THE *ALLIGATOR MAN*.

"MUDGETT HAD HIS *MURDER CASTLE*, I HAVE MY *AXE*, AND *JOE BALL* WILL HAVE HIS *ALLIGATORS*...

"*FEEDING TIME* WILL BE ENTERTAINMENT AT JOE BALL'S *BAR...*

"...THE *SOCIABLE INN.*

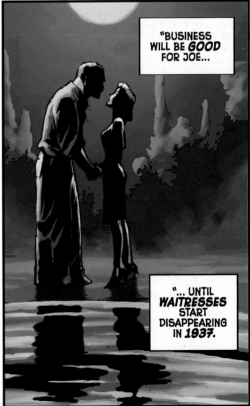

"BUSINESS WILL BE *GOOD* FOR JOE...

"... UNTIL *WAITRESSES* START DISAPPEARING IN *1937.*

"BY *LATE 1938,* THE AUTHORITIES WILL SUSPECT BALL OF *MURDER...*"

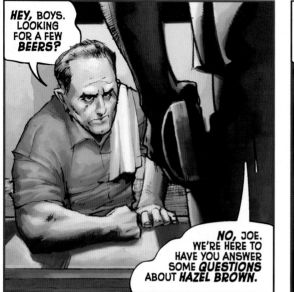

HEY, BOYS. LOOKING FOR A FEW *BEERS?*

NO, JOE. WE'RE HERE TO HAVE YOU ANSWER SOME *QUESTIONS* ABOUT *HAZEL BROWN.*

THEN I'LL POUR ONE FOR *MYSELF.*

JOE, PUT DOWN THE GUN!

BLAMMM

106

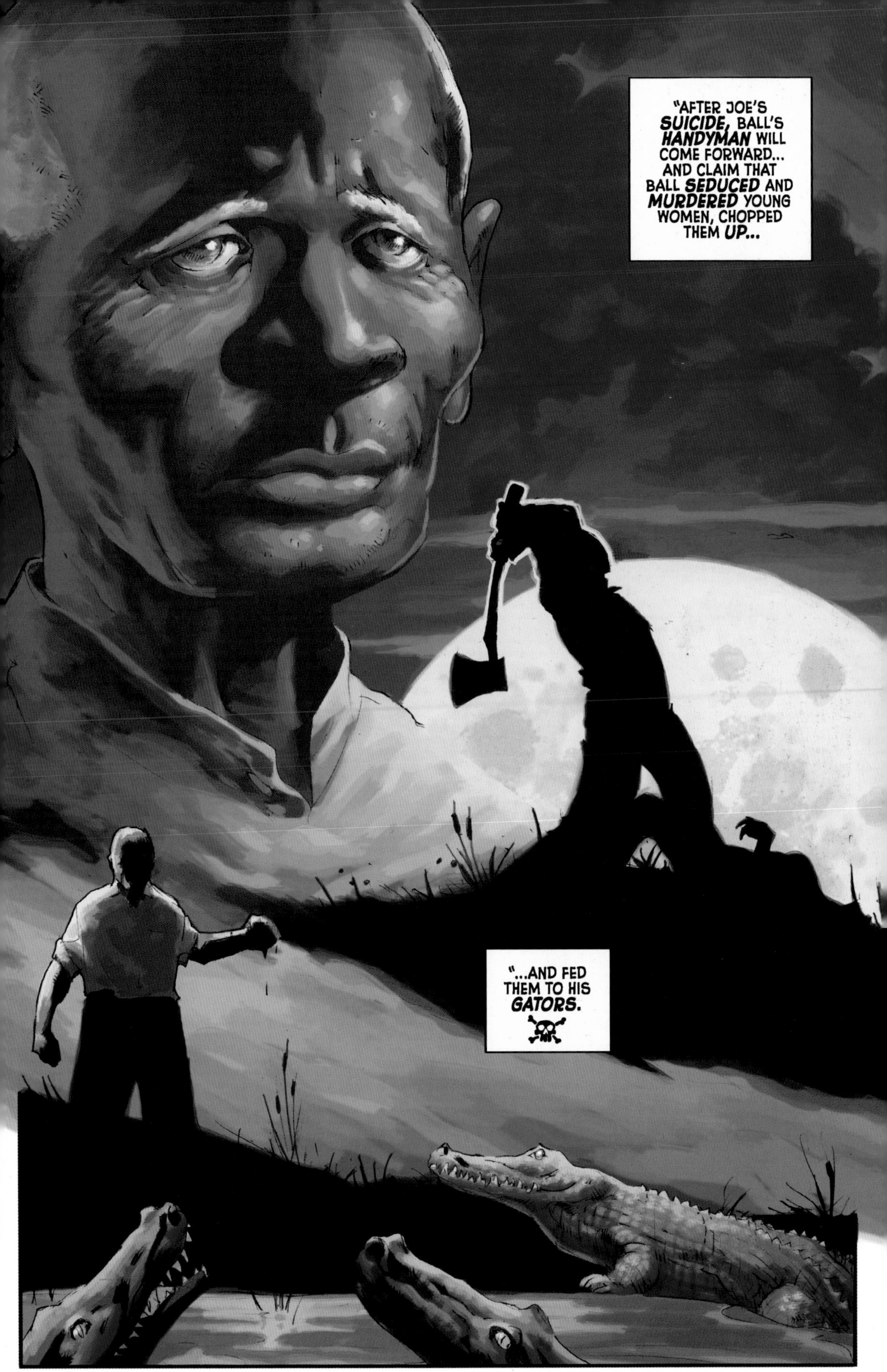
"AFTER JOE'S SUICIDE, BALL'S HANDYMAN WILL COME FORWARD... AND CLAIM THAT BALL SEDUCED AND MURDERED YOUNG WOMEN, CHOPPED THEM UP...
"...AND FED THEM TO HIS GATORS.

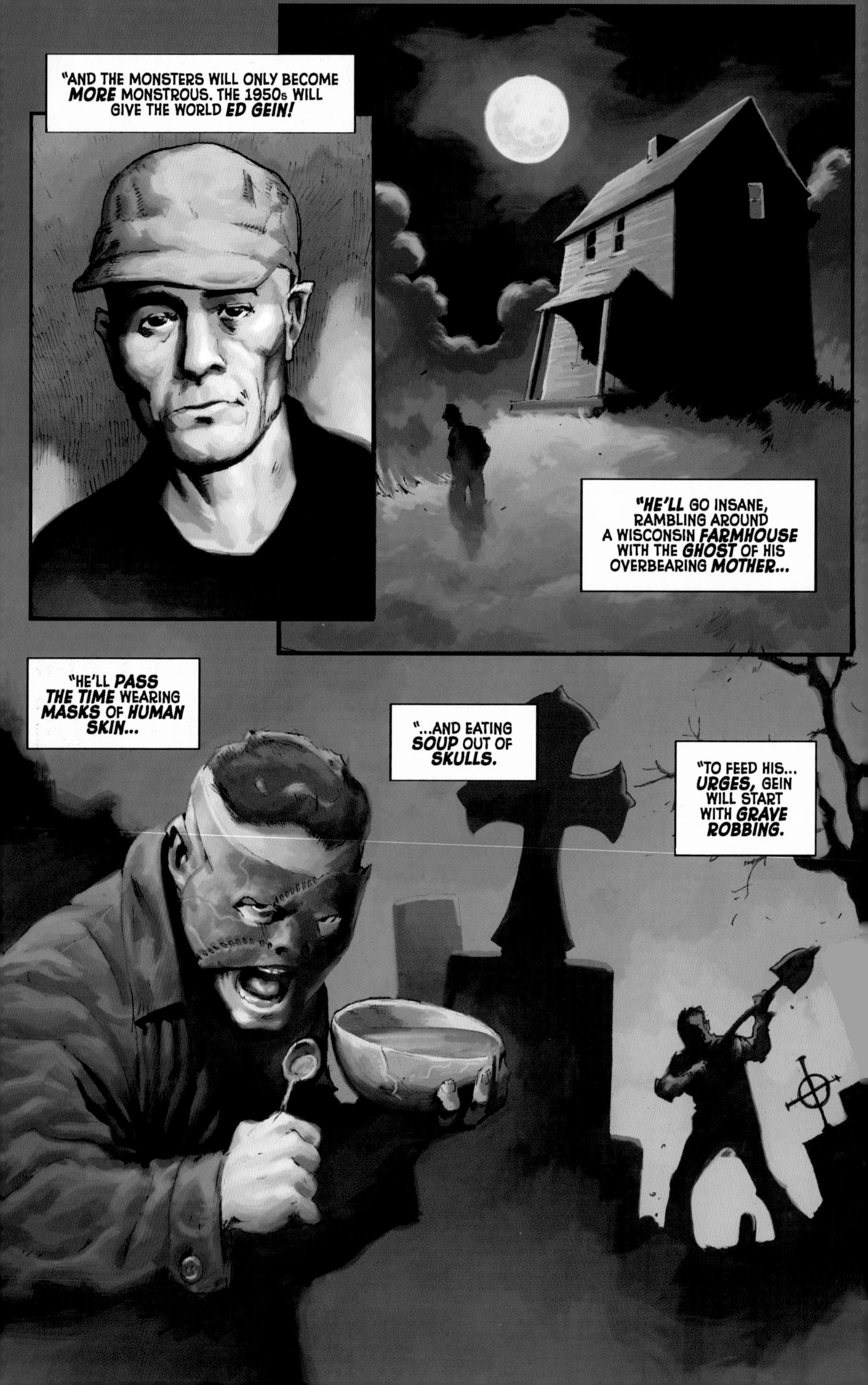
"AND THE MONSTERS WILL ONLY BECOME MORE MONSTROUS. THE 1950s WILL GIVE THE WORLD ED GEIN!
"HE'LL GO INSANE, RAMBLING AROUND A WISCONSIN FARMHOUSE WITH THE GHOST OF HIS OVERBEARING MOTHER...
"HE'LL PASS THE TIME WEARING MASKS OF HUMAN SKIN...
"...AND EATING SOUP OUT OF SKULLS.
"TO FEED HIS... URGES, GEIN WILL START WITH GRAVE ROBBING.

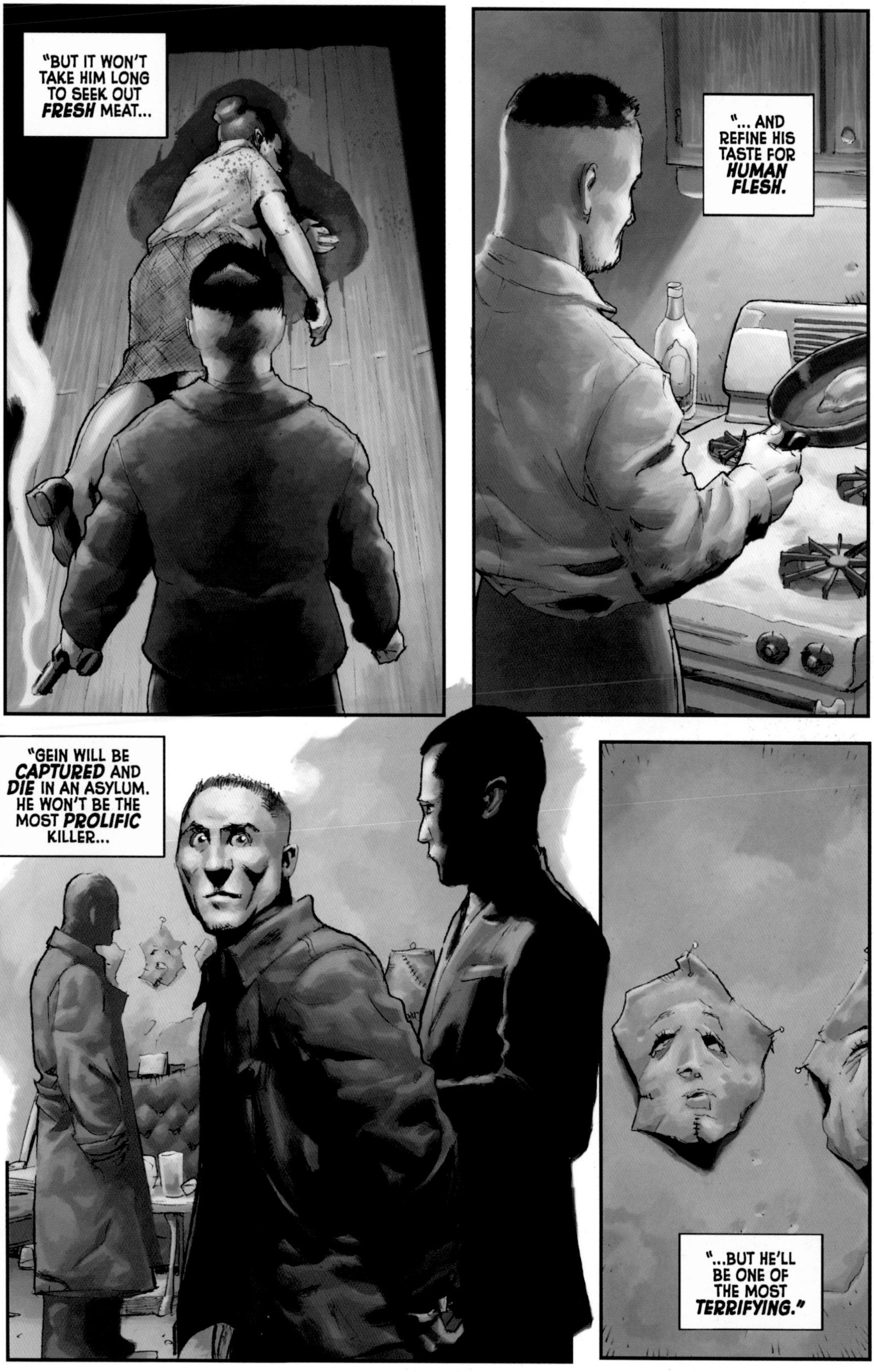
"BUT IT WON'T TAKE HIM LONG TO SEEK OUT FRESH MEAT...
"... AND REFINE HIS TASTE FOR HUMAN FLESH.
"GEIN WILL BE CAPTURED AND DIE IN AN ASYLUM. HE WON'T BE THE MOST PROLIFIC KILLER...
"...BUT HE'LL BE ONE OF THE MOST TERRIFYING."

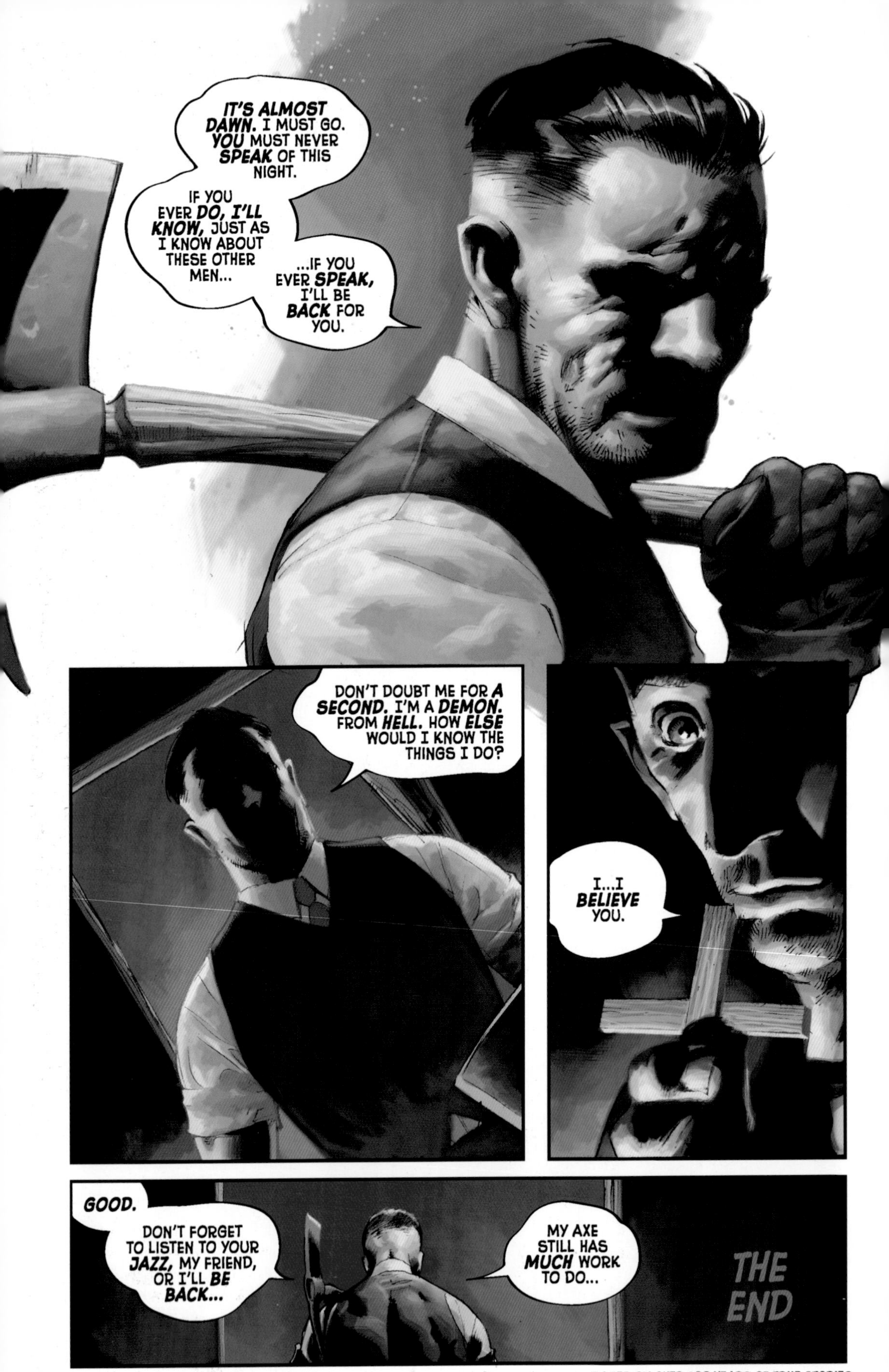
IT'S ALMOST DAWN. I MUST GO. YOU MUST NEVER SPEAK OF THIS NIGHT.
IF YOU EVER DO, I'LL KNOW, JUST AS I KNOW ABOUT THESE OTHER MEN...
...IF YOU EVER SPEAK, I'LL BE BACK FOR YOU.
DON'T DOUBT ME FOR A SECOND. I'M A DEMON. FROM HELL. HOW ELSE WOULD I KNOW THE THINGS I DO?
I...I BELIEVE YOU.
GOOD.
DON'T FORGET TO LISTEN TO YOUR JAZZ, MY FRIEND, OR I'LL BE BACK...
MY AXE STILL HAS MUCH WORK TO DO...
THE END
BASED ON OVER 100 YEARS OF TRUE STORIES.

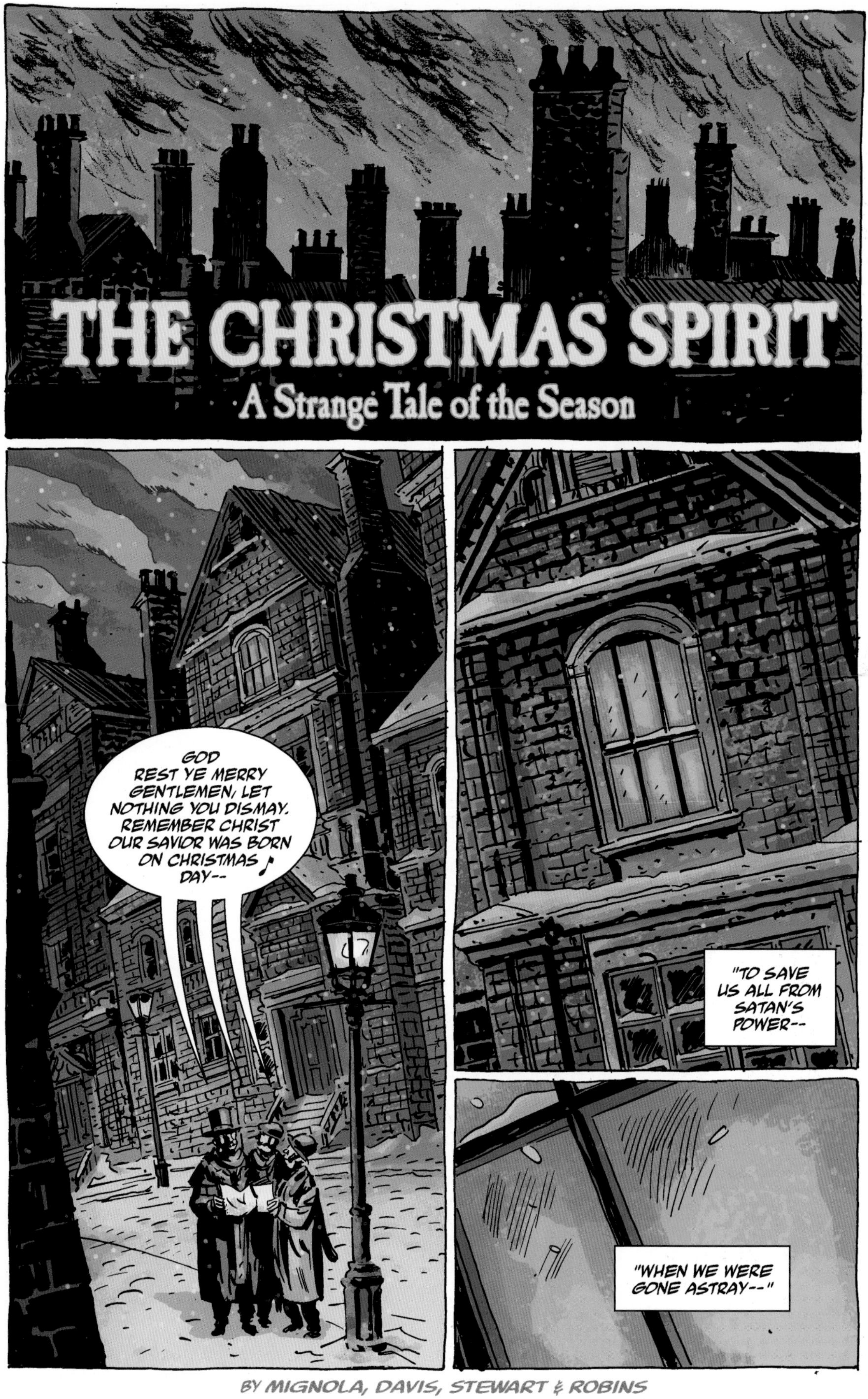
THE CHRISTMAS SPIRIT
A Strange Tale of the Season
GOD REST YE MERRY GENTLEMEN, LET NOTHING YOU DISMAY. REMEMBER CHRIST OUR SAVIOR WAS BORN ON CHRISTMAS DAY--
"TO SAVE US ALL FROM SATAN'S POWER--
"WHEN WE WERE GONE ASTRAY--"

BY MIGNOLA, DAVIS, STEWART & ROBINS

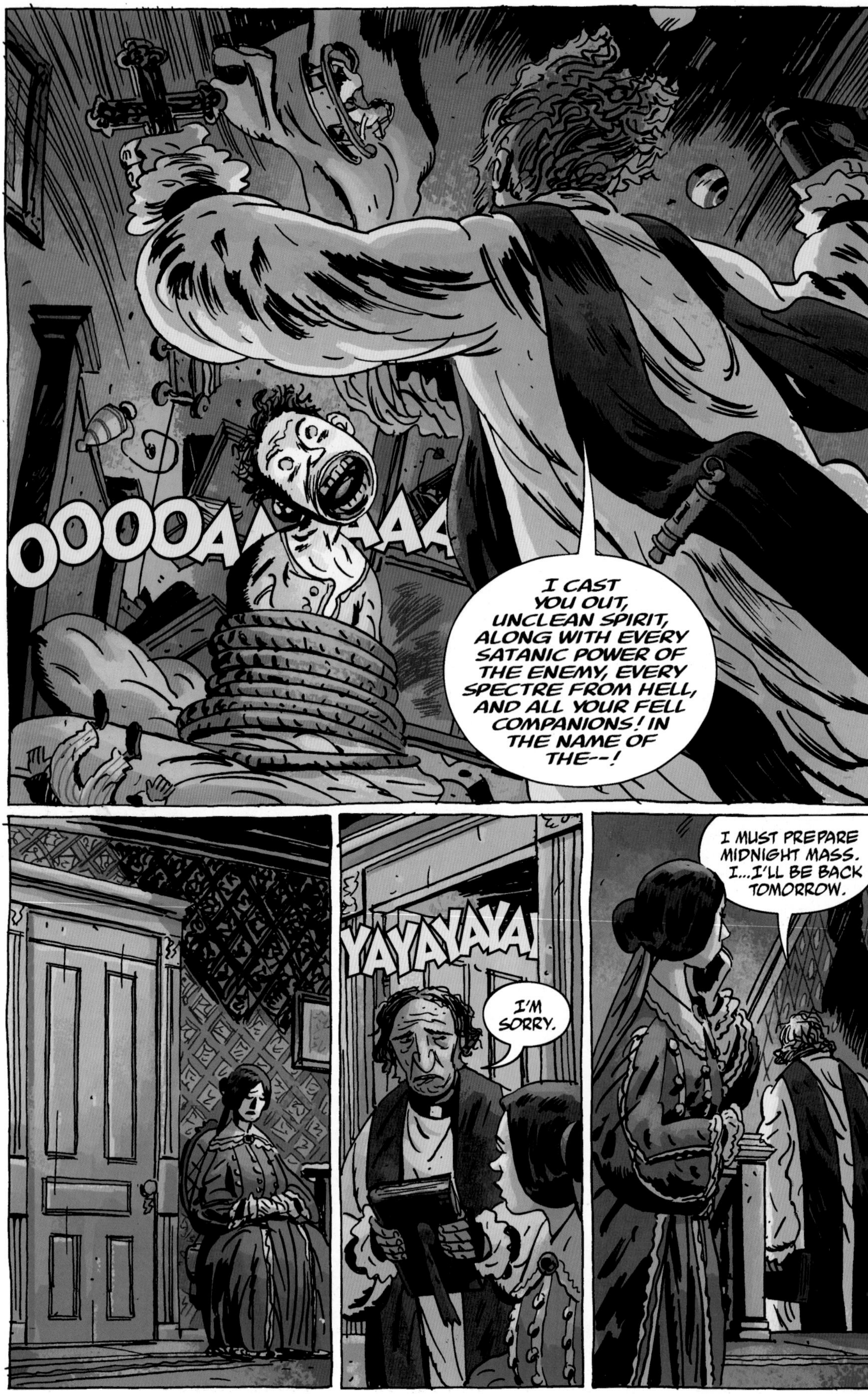

OOOOAAAAAA
I CAST YOU OUT, UNCLEAN SPIRIT, ALONG WITH EVERY SATANIC POWER OF THE ENEMY, EVERY SPECTRE FROM HELL, AND ALL YOUR FELL COMPANIONS! IN THE NAME OF THE--!
YAYAYAYA!
I'M SORRY.
I MUST PREPARE MIDNIGHT MASS. I...I'LL BE BACK TOMORROW.

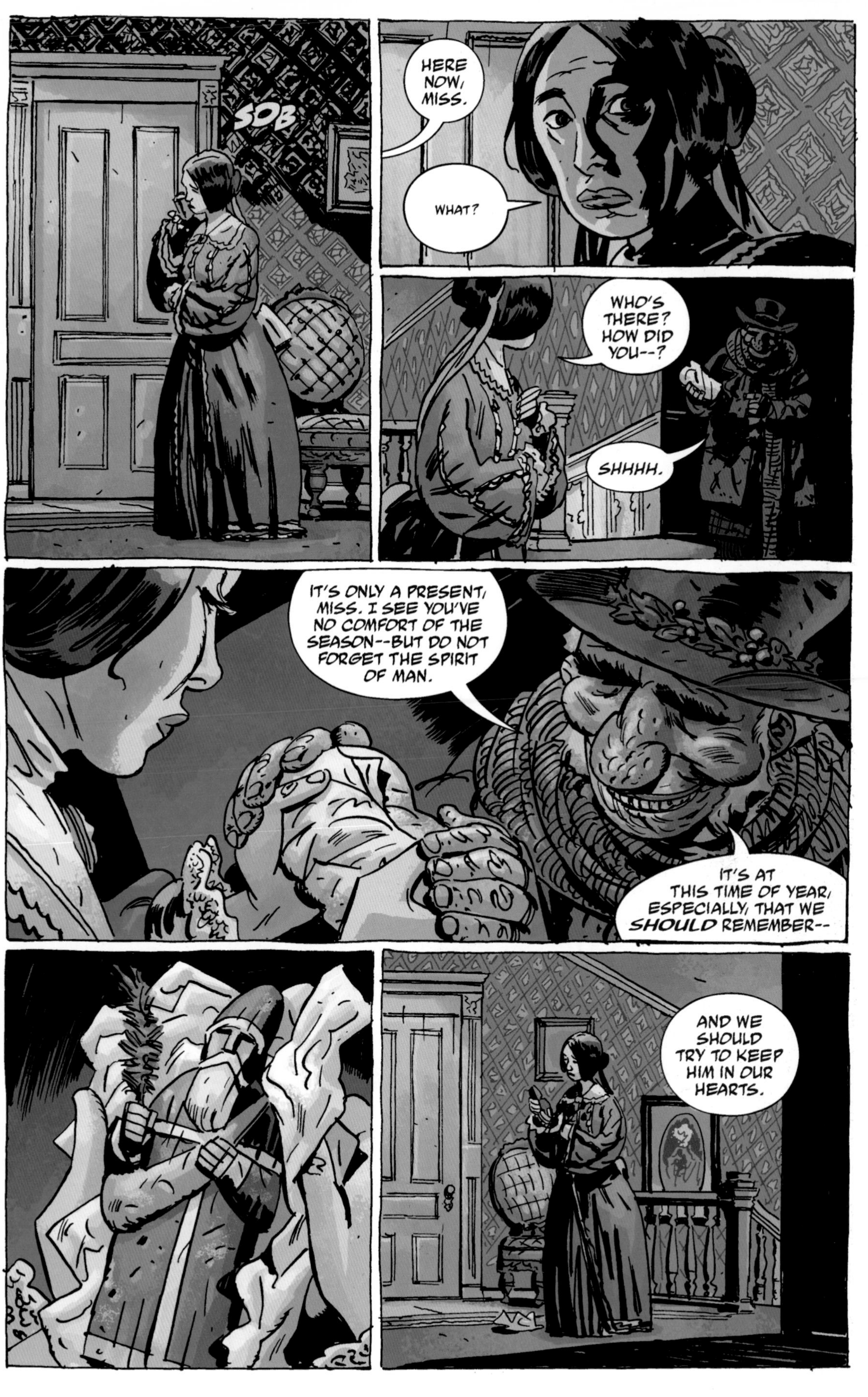
SOB
HERE NOW, MISS.
WHAT?
WHO'S THERE? HOW DID YOU--?
SHHHH.
IT'S ONLY A PRESENT, MISS. I SEE YOU'VE NO COMFORT OF THE SEASON--BUT DO NOT FORGET THE SPIRIT OF MAN.
IT'S AT THIS TIME OF YEAR, ESPECIALLY, THAT WE *SHOULD* REMEMBER--
AND WE SHOULD TRY TO KEEP HIM IN OUR HEARTS.

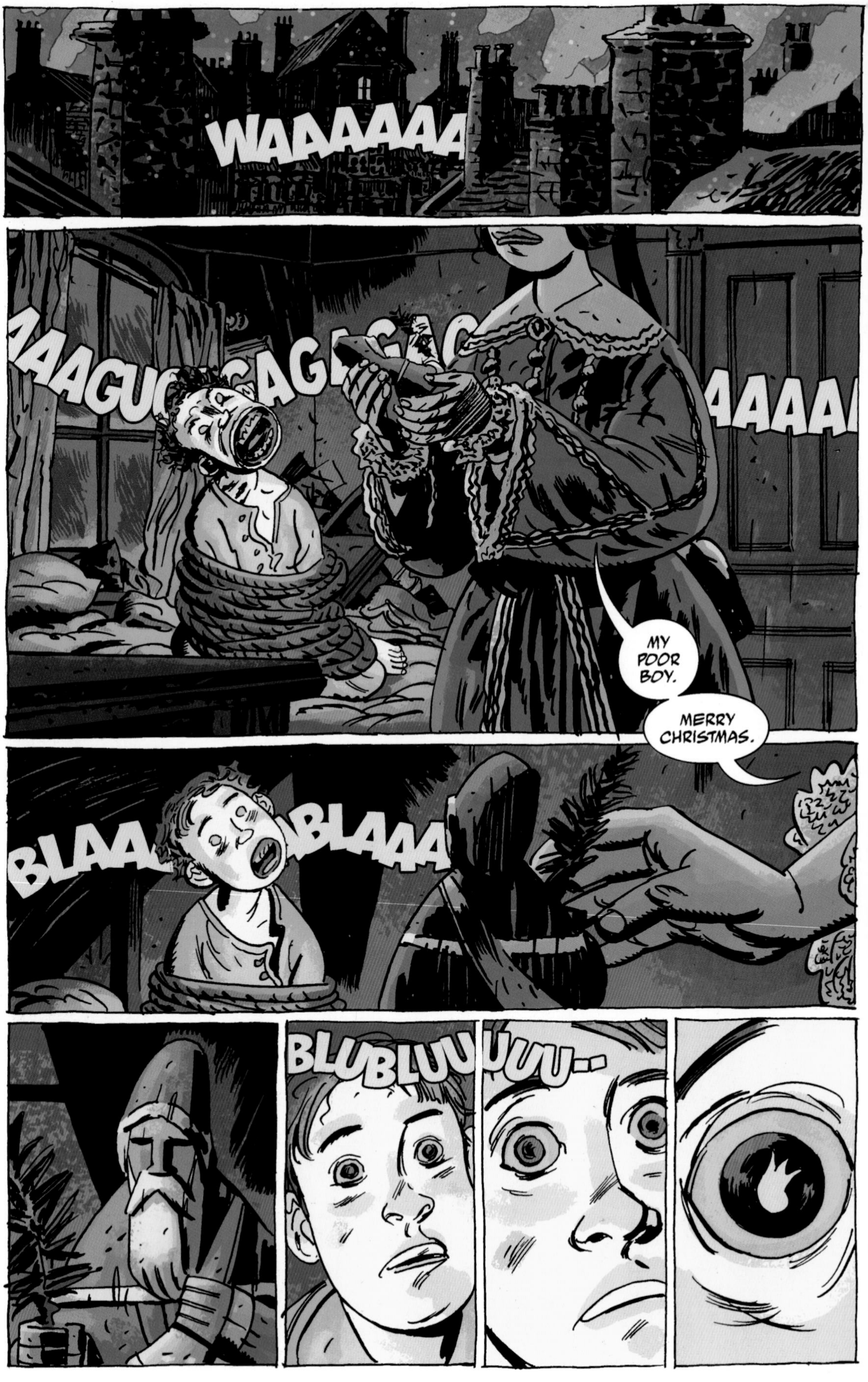

WAAAAAA
AAAGUGAGAGAGAG
AAAAA
MY POOR BOY.
MERRY CHRISTMAS.
BLAAABLAAA
BLUBLUUUUU--

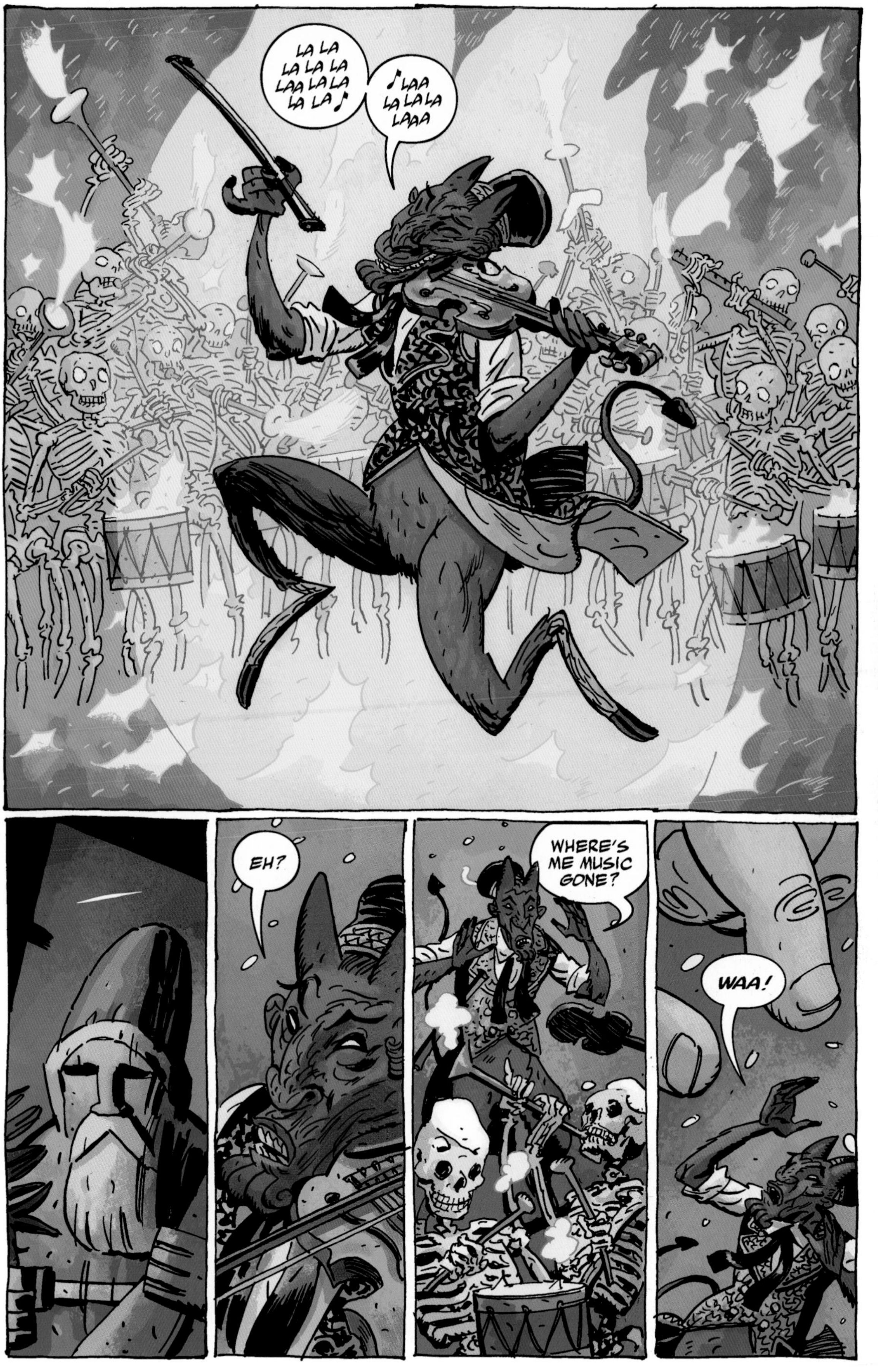
LA LA
LA LA LA
LAA LA LA
LA LA ♪
♪LAA
LA LA LA
LAAA
EH?
WHERE'S
ME MUSIC
GONE?
WAA!

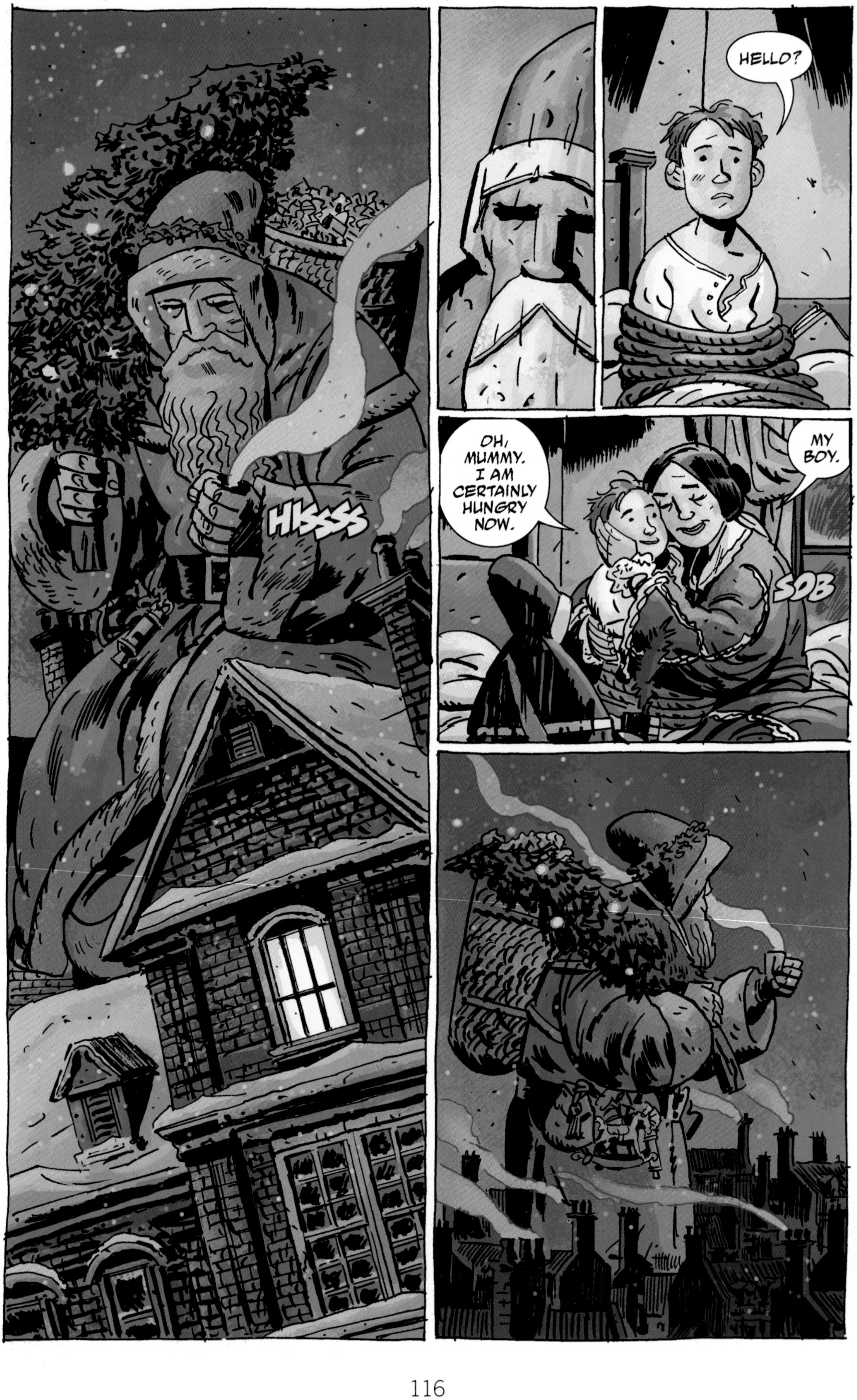
HISSSS
HELLO?
OH, MUMMY. I AM CERTAINLY HUNGRY NOW.
MY BOY.
SOB

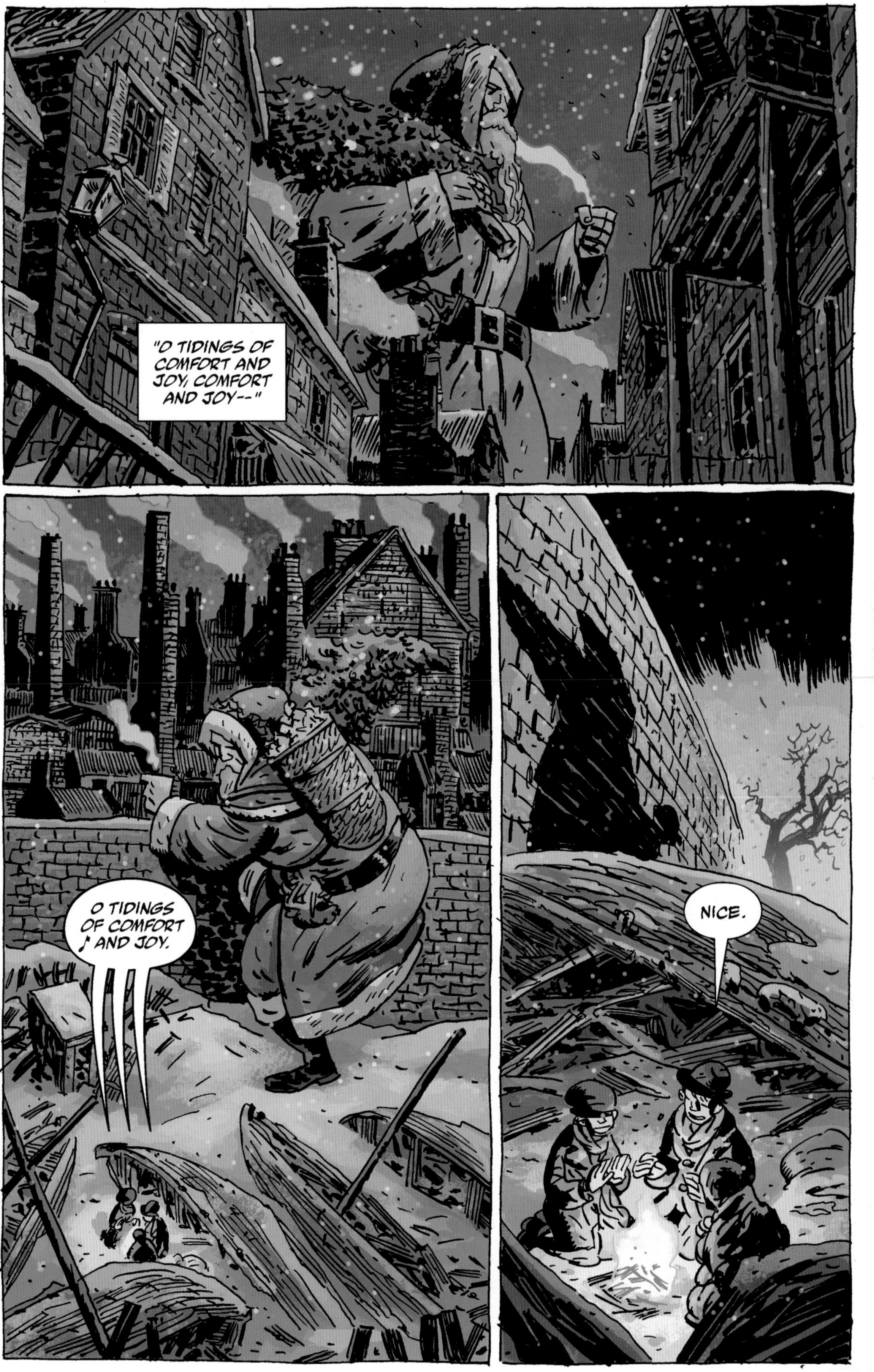
"O TIDINGS OF COMFORT AND JOY, COMFORT AND JOY--"
O TIDINGS OF COMFORT ♪ AND JOY.
NICE.

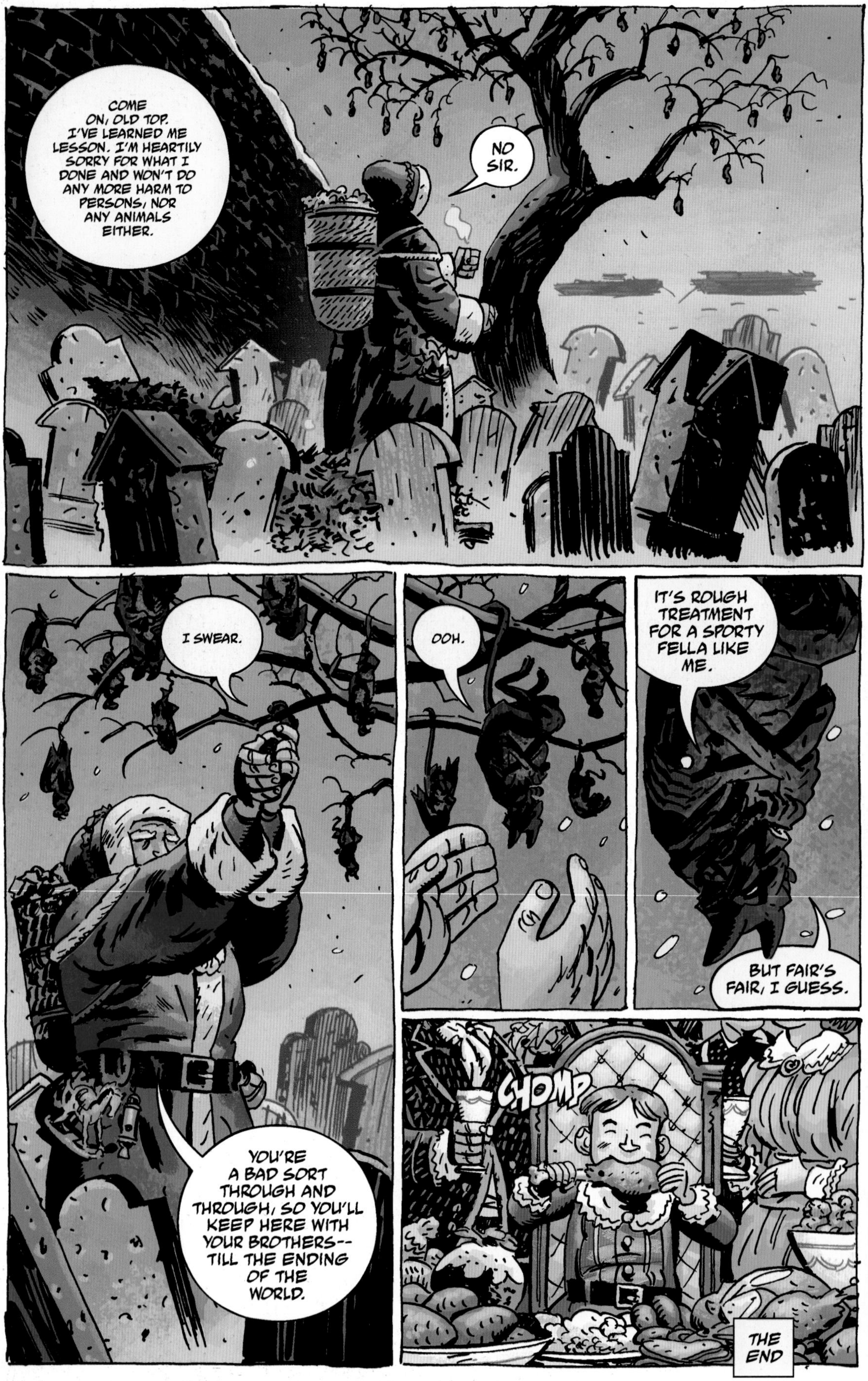
COME ON, OLD TOP. I'VE LEARNED ME LESSON. I'M HEARTILY SORRY FOR WHAT I DONE AND WON'T DO ANY MORE HARM TO PERSONS, NOR ANY ANIMALS EITHER.
NO SIR.
I SWEAR.
YOU'RE A BAD SORT THROUGH AND THROUGH, SO YOU'LL KEEP HERE WITH YOUR BROTHERS-- TILL THE ENDING OF THE WORLD.
OOH.
IT'S ROUGH TREATMENT FOR A SPORTY FELLA LIKE ME.
BUT FAIR'S FAIR, I GUESS.
CHOMP
THE END

MATTHEW BERNIER

EAT THE WALLS

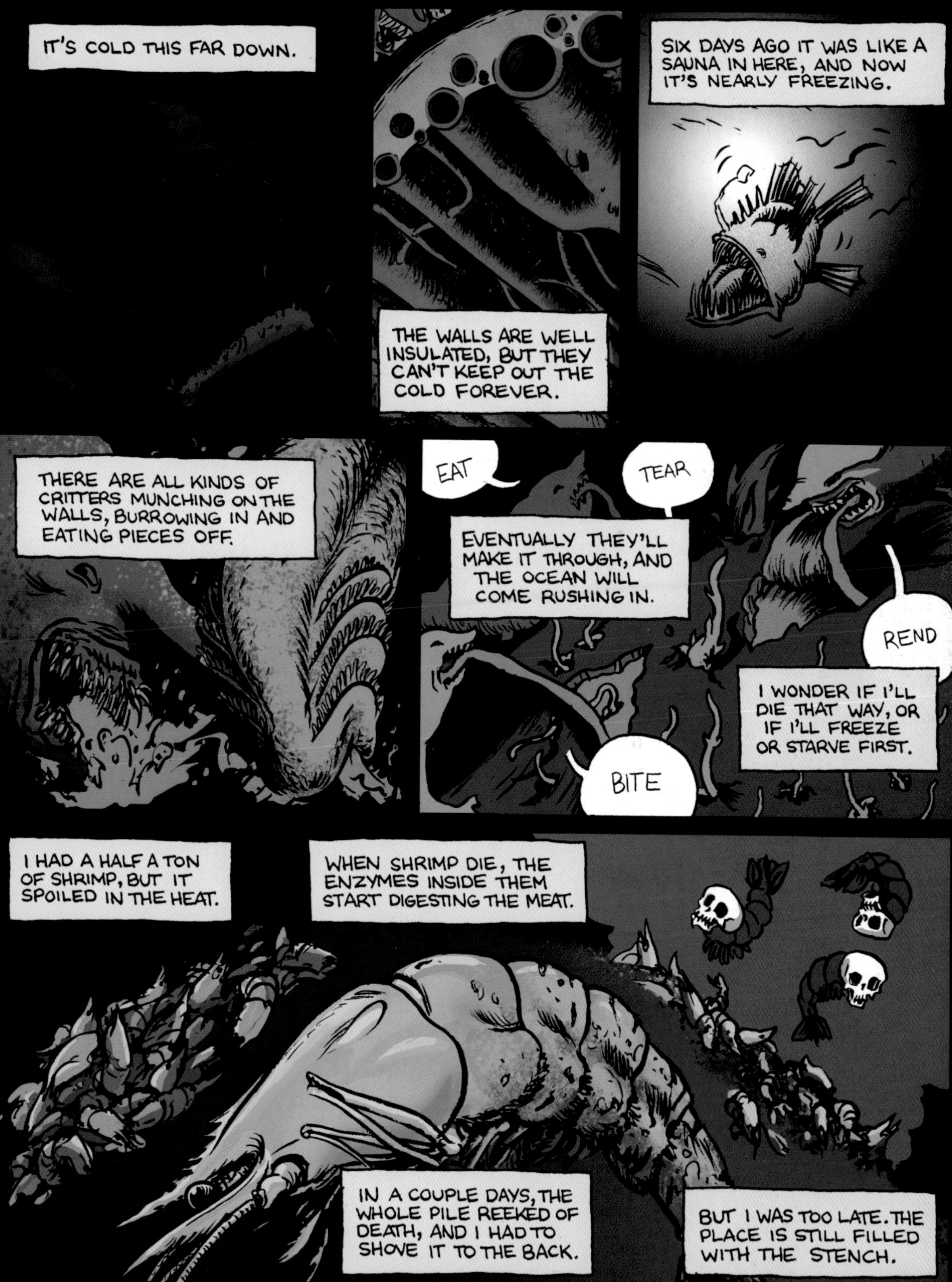

IT'S COLD THIS FAR DOWN.
THE WALLS ARE WELL INSULATED, BUT THEY CAN'T KEEP OUT THE COLD FOREVER.
SIX DAYS AGO IT WAS LIKE A SAUNA IN HERE, AND NOW IT'S NEARLY FREEZING.
THERE ARE ALL KINDS OF CRITTERS MUNCHING ON THE WALLS, BURROWING IN AND EATING PIECES OFF.
EAT
TEAR
EVENTUALLY THEY'LL MAKE IT THROUGH, AND THE OCEAN WILL COME RUSHING IN.
REND
I WONDER IF I'LL DIE THAT WAY, OR IF I'LL FREEZE OR STARVE FIRST.
BITE
I HAD A HALF A TON OF SHRIMP, BUT IT SPOILED IN THE HEAT.
WHEN SHRIMP DIE, THE ENZYMES INSIDE THEM START DIGESTING THE MEAT.
IN A COUPLE DAYS, THE WHOLE PILE REEKED OF DEATH, AND I HAD TO SHOVE IT TO THE BACK.
BUT I WAS TOO LATE. THE PLACE IS STILL FILLED WITH THE STENCH.

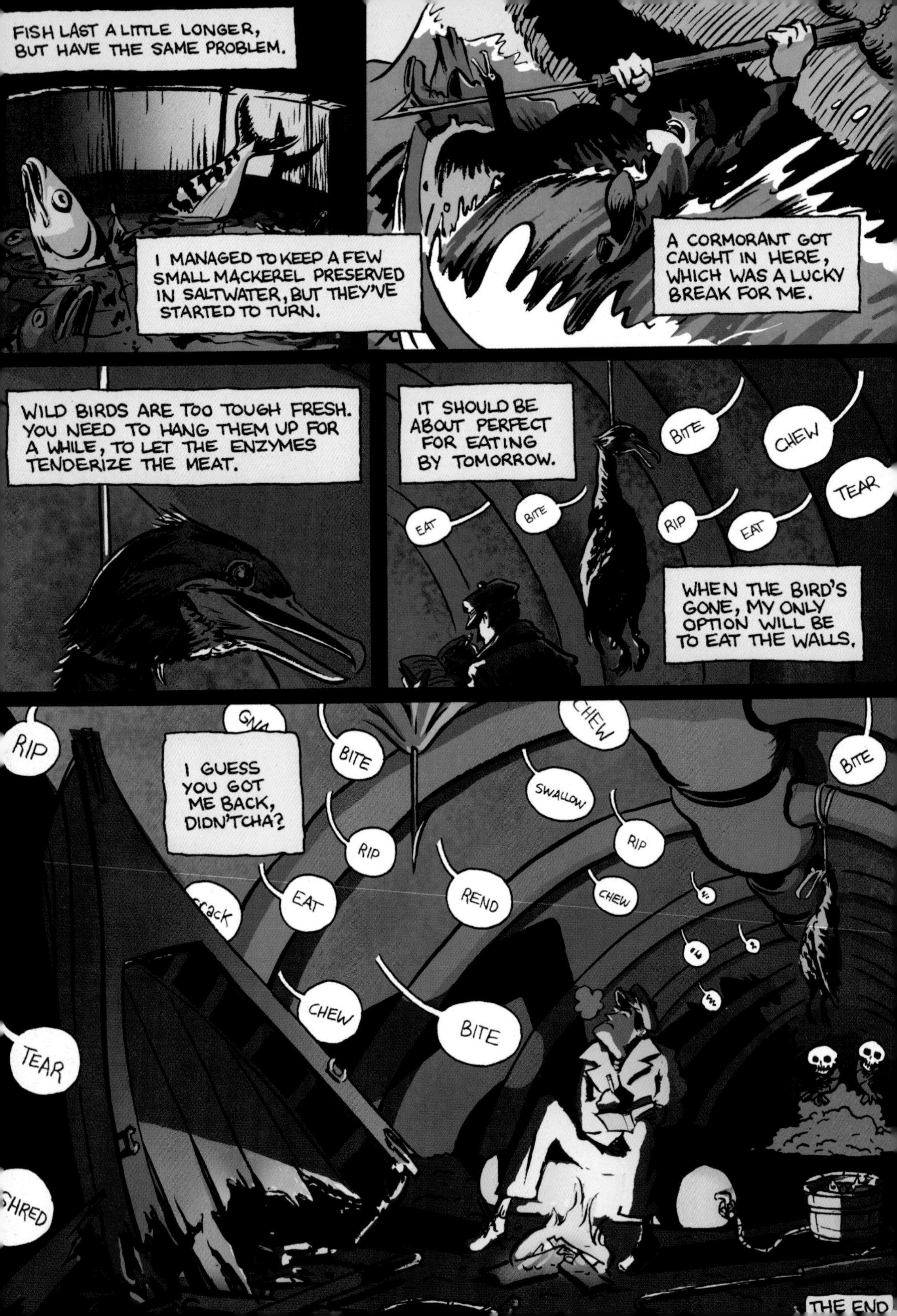

FISH LAST A LITTLE LONGER, BUT HAVE THE SAME PROBLEM.
I MANAGED TO KEEP A FEW SMALL MACKEREL PRESERVED IN SALTWATER, BUT THEY'VE STARTED TO TURN.
A CORMORANT GOT CAUGHT IN HERE, WHICH WAS A LUCKY BREAK FOR ME.
WILD BIRDS ARE TOO TOUGH FRESH. YOU NEED TO HANG THEM UP FOR A WHILE, TO LET THE ENZYMES TENDERIZE THE MEAT.
IT SHOULD BE ABOUT PERFECT FOR EATING BY TOMORROW.
BITE
CHEW
EAT
BITE
TEAR
RIP
EAT
WHEN THE BIRD'S GONE, MY ONLY OPTION WILL BE TO EAT THE WALLS.
RIP
I GUESS YOU GOT ME BACK, DIDN'TCHA?
BITE
CHEW
BITE
SWALLOW
RIP
RIP
EAT
REND
CHEW
CHEW
BITE
TEAR
THE END

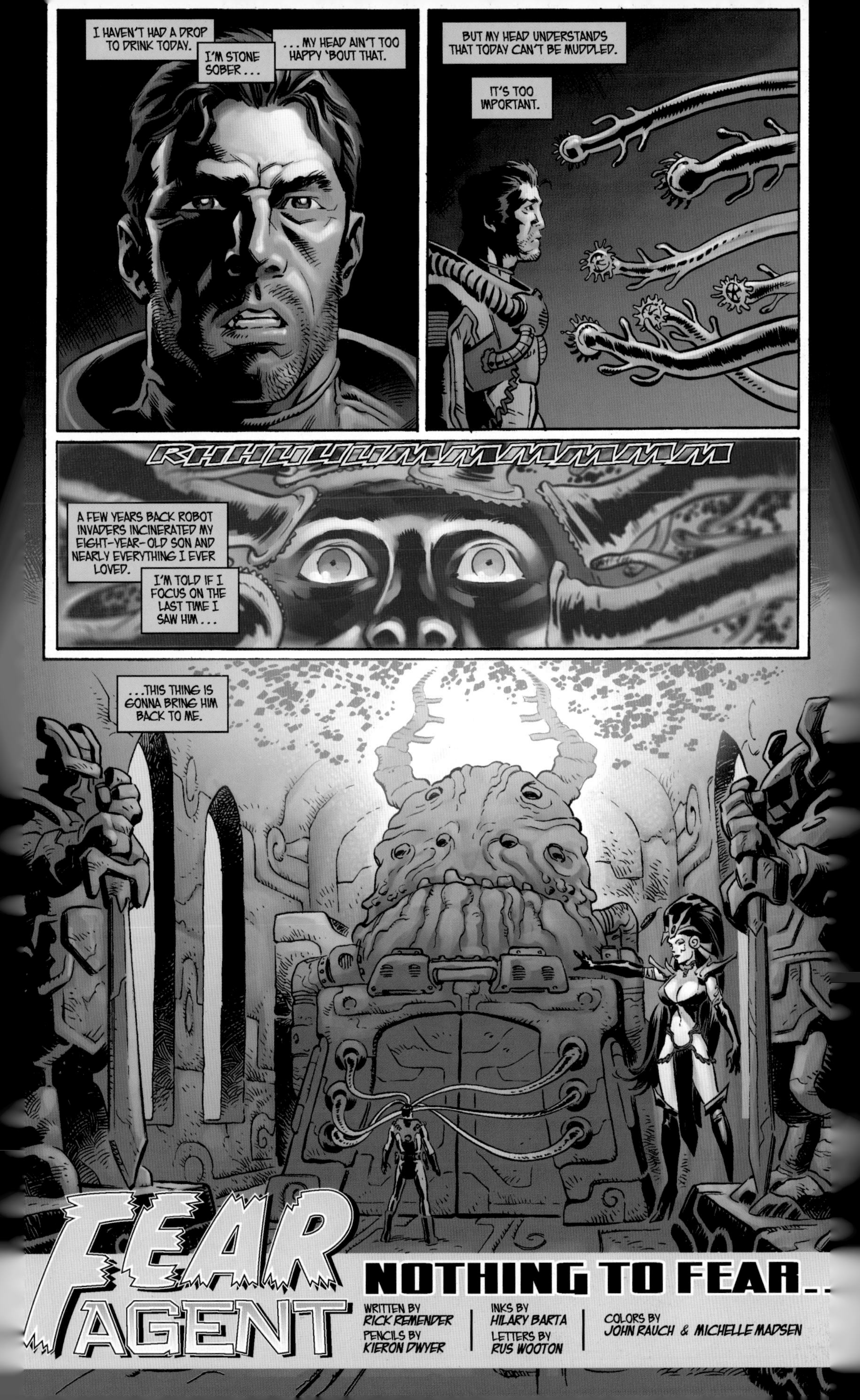
I HAVEN'T HAD A DROP TO DRINK TODAY.
I'M STONE SOBER . . .
. . . MY HEAD AIN'T TOO HAPPY 'BOUT THAT.
BUT MY HEAD UNDERSTANDS THAT TODAY CAN'T BE MUDDLED.
IT'S TOO IMPORTANT.
RHHUUUMMMMMMMMM
A FEW YEARS BACK ROBOT INVADERS INCINERATED MY EIGHT-YEAR-OLD SON AND NEARLY EVERYTHING I EVER LOVED.
I'M TOLD IF I FOCUS ON THE LAST TIME I SAW HIM . . .
. . . THIS THING IS GONNA BRING HIM BACK TO ME.
FEAR AGENT
NOTHING TO FEAR . . .
WRITTEN BY RICK REMENDER
PENCILS BY KIERON DWYER
INKS BY HILARY BARTA
LETTERS BY RUS WOOTON
COLORS BY JOHN RAUCH & MICHELLE MADSEN

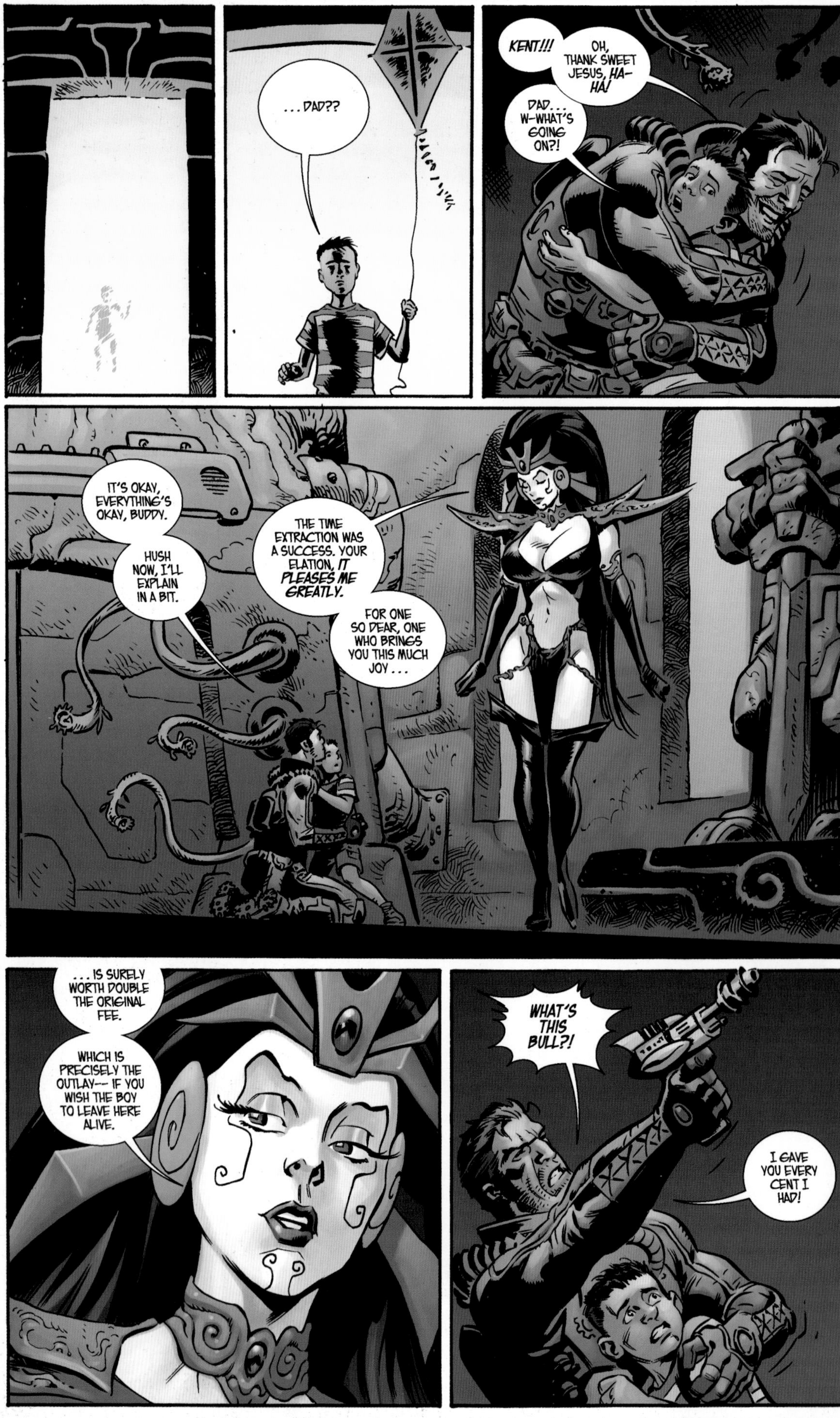
. . . DAD??
KENT!!!
OH, THANK SWEET JESUS, HA-HA!
DAD . . . W-WHAT'S GOING ON?!
IT'S OKAY, EVERYTHING'S OKAY, BUDDY.
HUSH NOW, I'LL EXPLAIN IN A BIT.
THE TIME EXTRACTION WAS A SUCCESS. YOUR ELATION, IT PLEASES ME GREATLY.
FOR ONE SO DEAR, ONE WHO BRINGS YOU THIS MUCH JOY . . .
. . . IS SURELY WORTH DOUBLE THE ORIGINAL FEE.
WHICH IS PRECISELY THE OUTLAY-- IF YOU WISH THE BOY TO LEAVE HERE ALIVE.
WHAT'S THIS BULL?!
I GAVE YOU EVERY CENT I HAD!

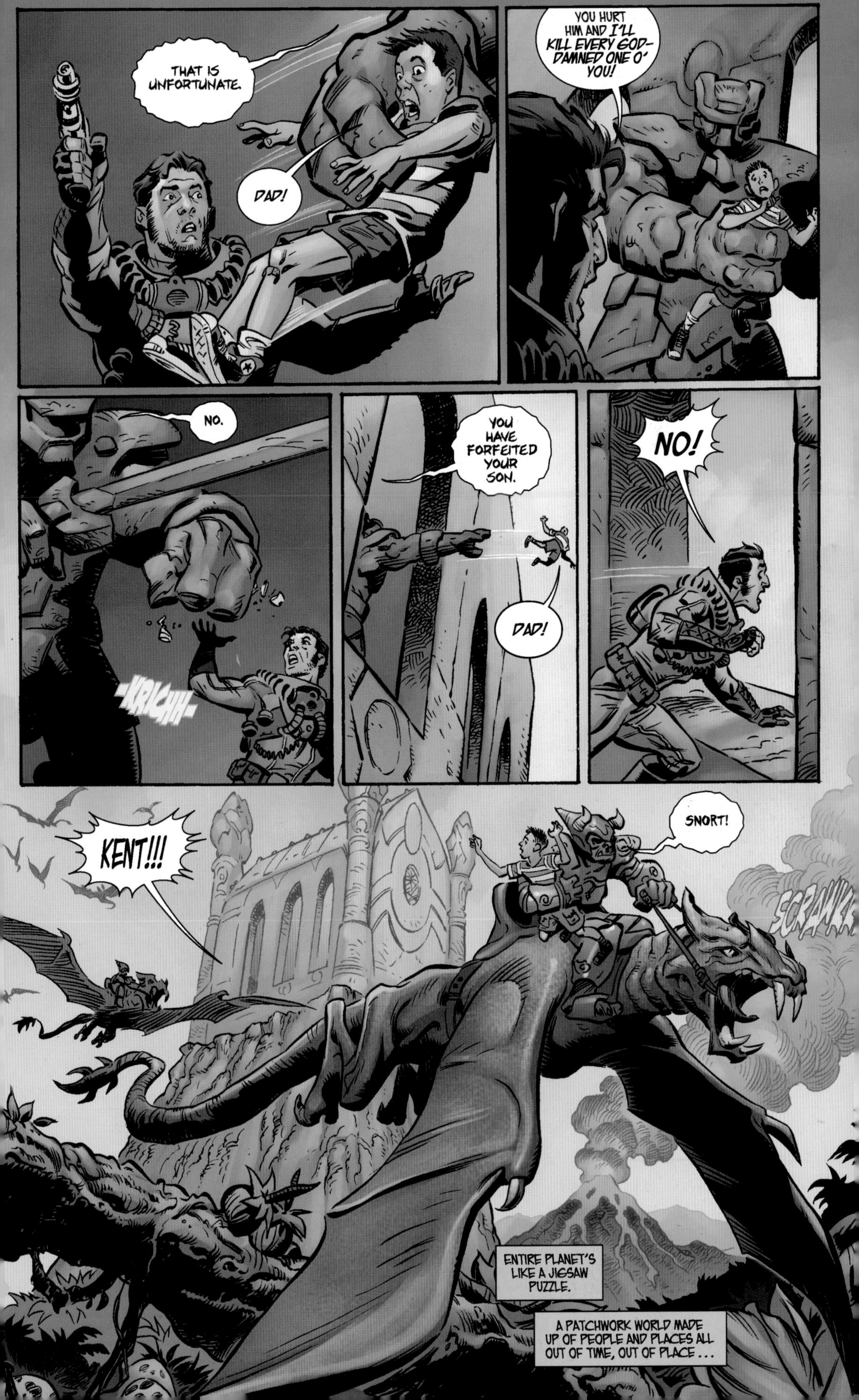
THAT IS UNFORTUNATE.
DAD!
YOU HURT HIM AND I'LL KILL EVERY GOD-DAMNED ONE O' YOU!
NO.
KRICHH
YOU HAVE FORFEITED YOUR SON.
DAD!
NO!
KENT!!!
SNORT!
ENTIRE PLANET'S LIKE A JIGSAW PUZZLE.
A PATCHWORK WORLD MADE UP OF PEOPLE AND PLACES ALL OUT OF TIME, OUT OF PLACE . . .

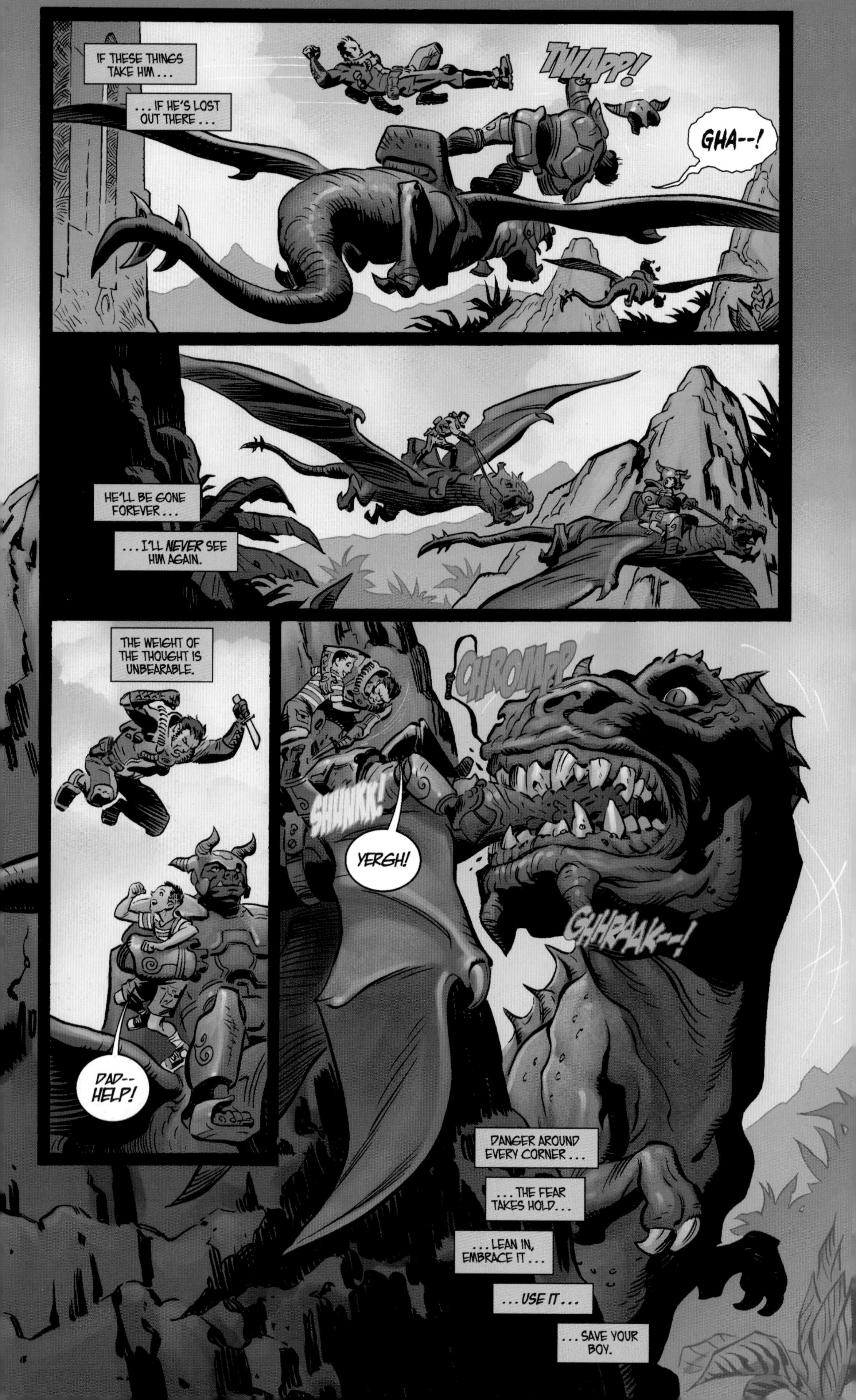
IF THESE THINGS TAKE HIM . . .
. . . IF HE'S LOST OUT THERE . . .
TWAPP!
GHA--!
HE'LL BE GONE FOREVER . . .
. . . I'LL NEVER SEE HIM AGAIN.
THE WEIGHT OF THE THOUGHT IS UNBEARABLE.
DAD-- HELP!
CHROMP!
SHUNKK!
YERGH!
GHHRAAK--!
DANGER AROUND EVERY CORNER . . .
. . . THE FEAR TAKES HOLD . . .
. . . LEAN IN, EMBRACE IT . . .
. . . USE IT . . .
. . . SAVE YOUR BOY.

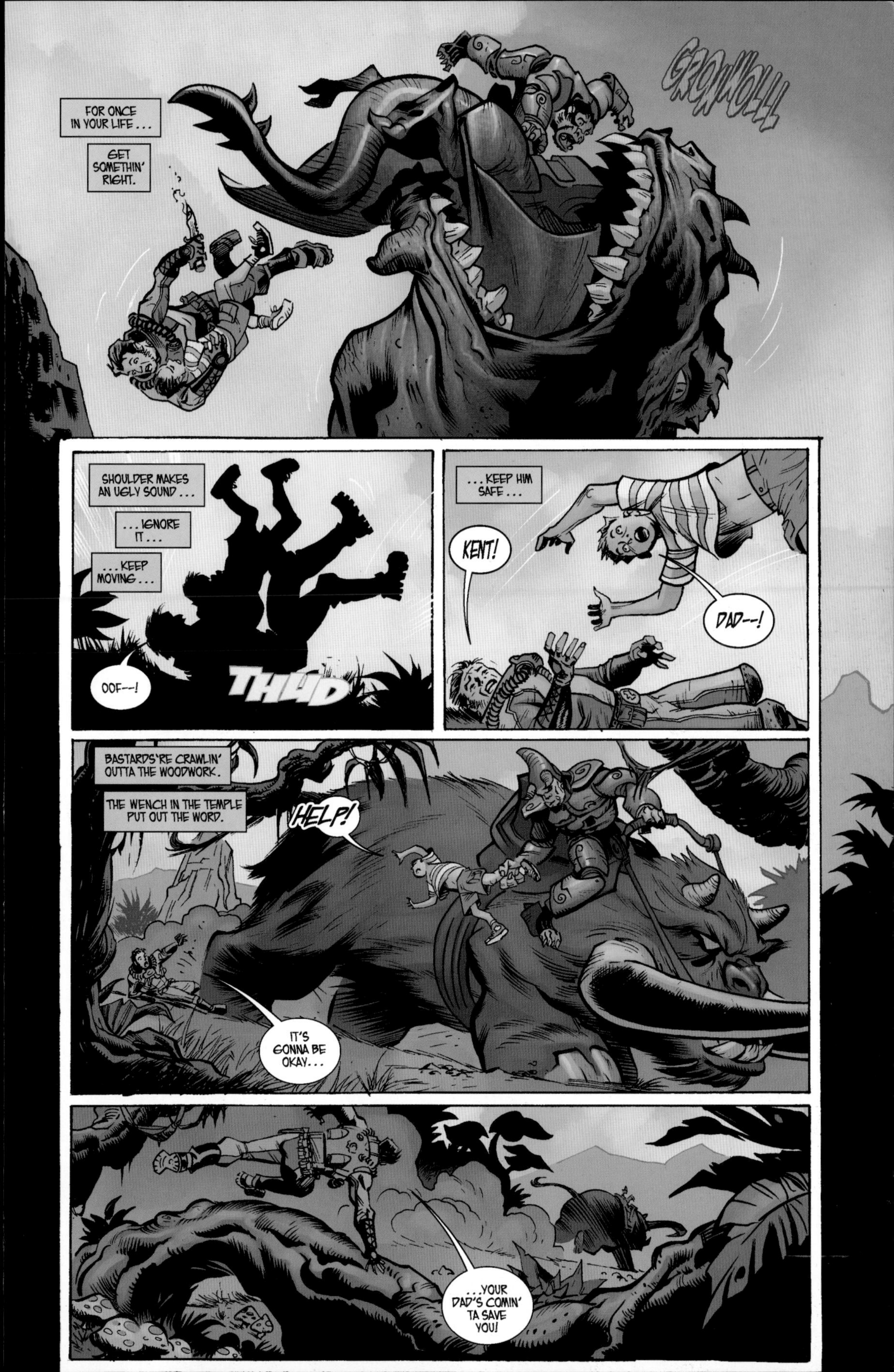
GROWOLL
FOR ONCE IN YOUR LIFE . . .
GET SOMETHIN' RIGHT.
SHOULDER MAKES AN UGLY SOUND . . .
. . . IGNORE IT . . .
. . . KEEP MOVING . . .
OOF--!
THUD
. . . KEEP HIM SAFE . . .
KENT!
DAD--!
BASTARDS'RE CRAWLIN' OUTTA THE WOODWORK.
THE WENCH IN THE TEMPLE PUT OUT THE WORD.
HELP!
IT'S GONNA BE OKAY . . .
. . . YOUR DAD'S COMIN' TA SAVE YOU!

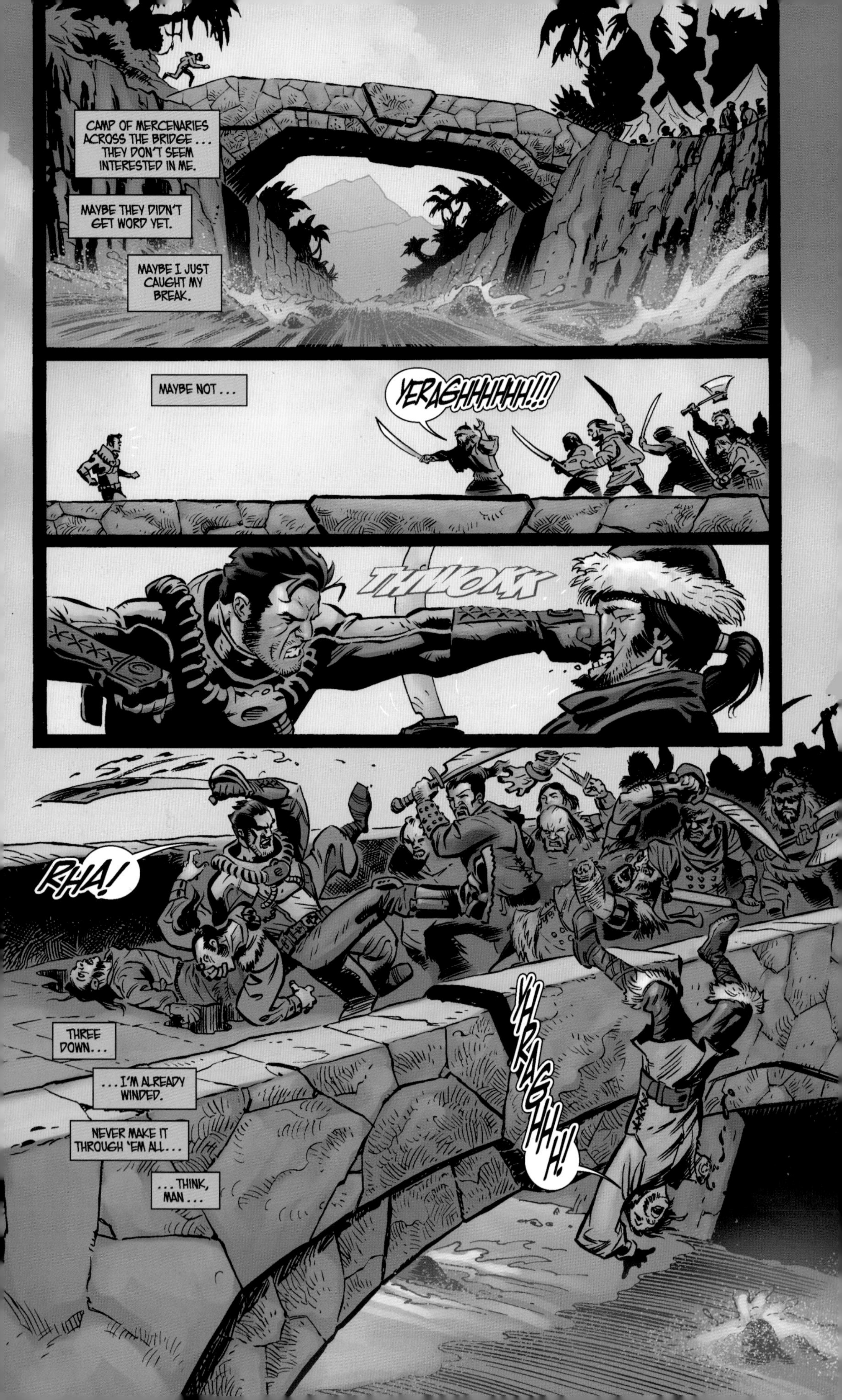
CAMP OF MERCENARIES ACROSS THE BRIDGE . . . THEY DON'T SEEM INTERESTED IN ME.
MAYBE THEY DIDN'T GET WORD YET.
MAYBE I JUST CAUGHT MY BREAK.
MAYBE NOT . . .
YERAGHHHHHH!!!
THWOKK
RHA!
THREE DOWN . . .
. . . I'M ALREADY WINDED.
NEVER MAKE IT THROUGH 'EM ALL . . .
. . . THINK, MAN . . .
YHRAGHHH!

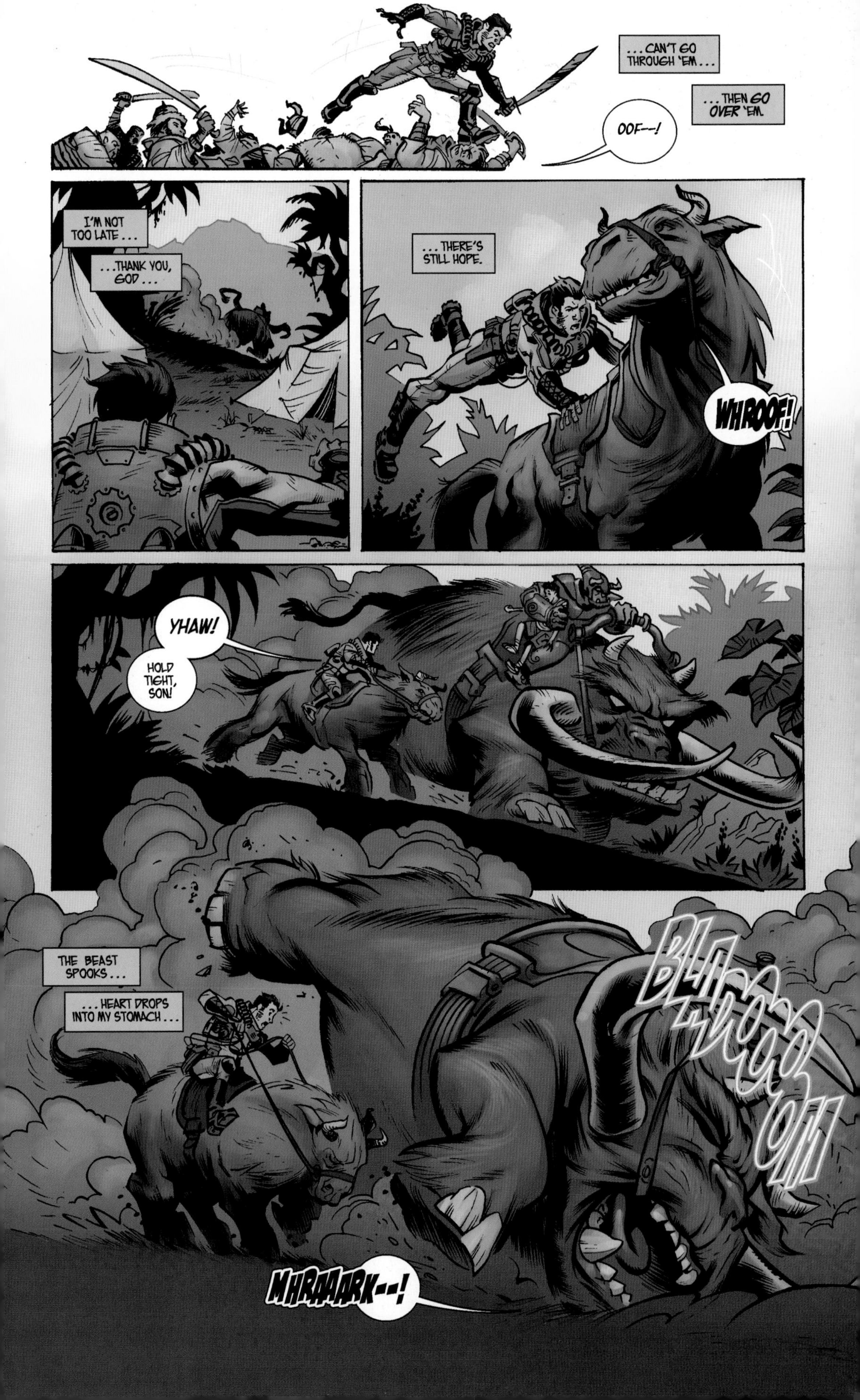
. . . CAN'T GO THROUGH 'EM . . .
. . . THEN GO OVER 'EM.
OOF--!
I'M NOT TOO LATE . . .
. . . THANK YOU, GOD . . .
. . . THERE'S STILL HOPE.
WHROOF!
YHAW!
HOLD TIGHT, SON!
THE BEAST SPOOKS . . .
. . . HEART DROPS INTO MY STOMACH . . .
MHRAAARK--!

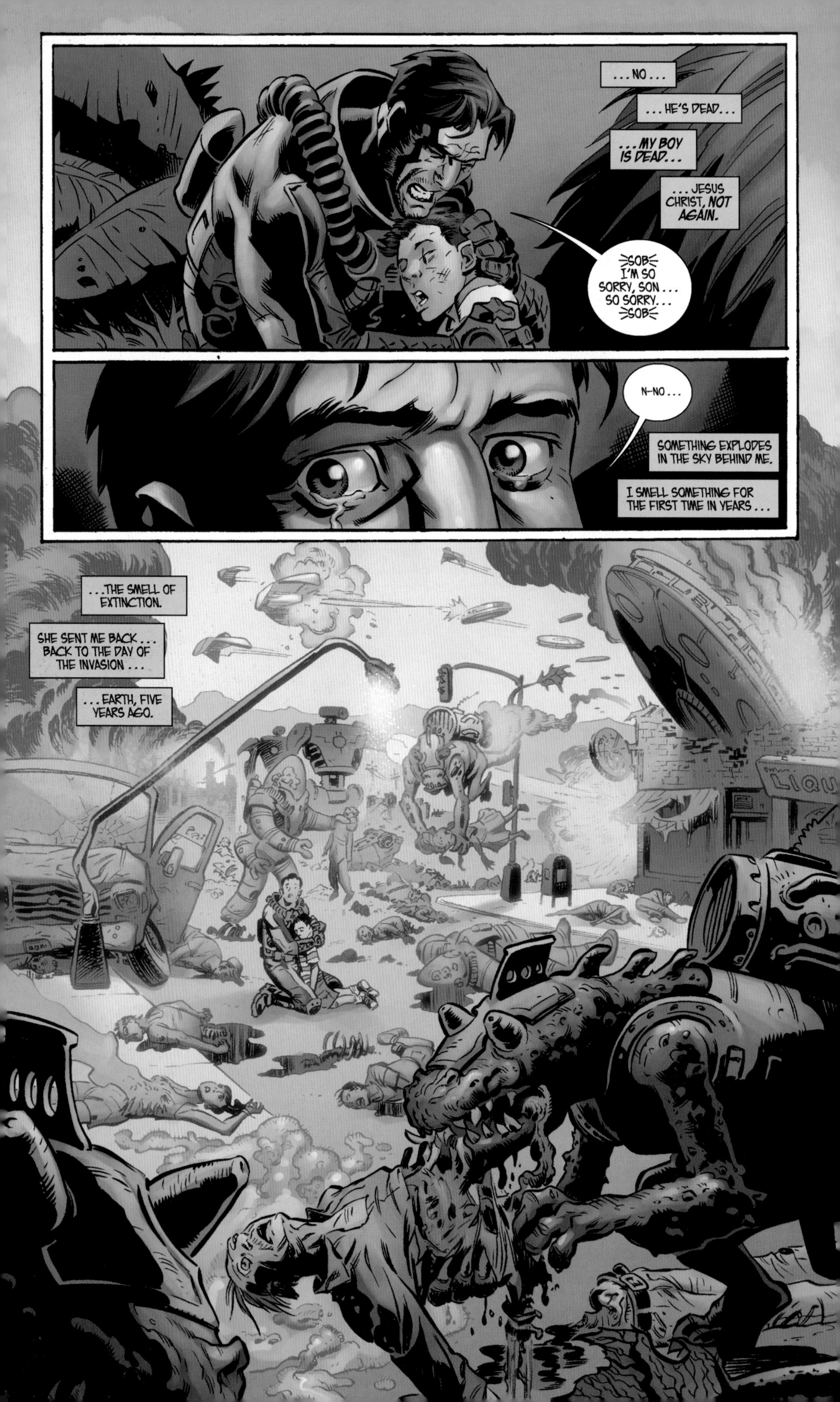

. . . NO . . .
. . . HE'S DEAD . . .
. . . MY BOY IS DEAD . . .
. . . JESUS CHRIST, NOT AGAIN.
SOB I'M SO SORRY, SON . . . SO SORRY . . . SOB
N-NO . . .
SOMETHING EXPLODES IN THE SKY BEHIND ME.
I SMELL SOMETHING FOR THE FIRST TIME IN YEARS . . .
. . . THE SMELL OF EXTINCTION.
SHE SENT ME BACK . . . BACK TO THE DAY OF THE INVASION . . .
. . . EARTH, FIVE YEARS AGO.

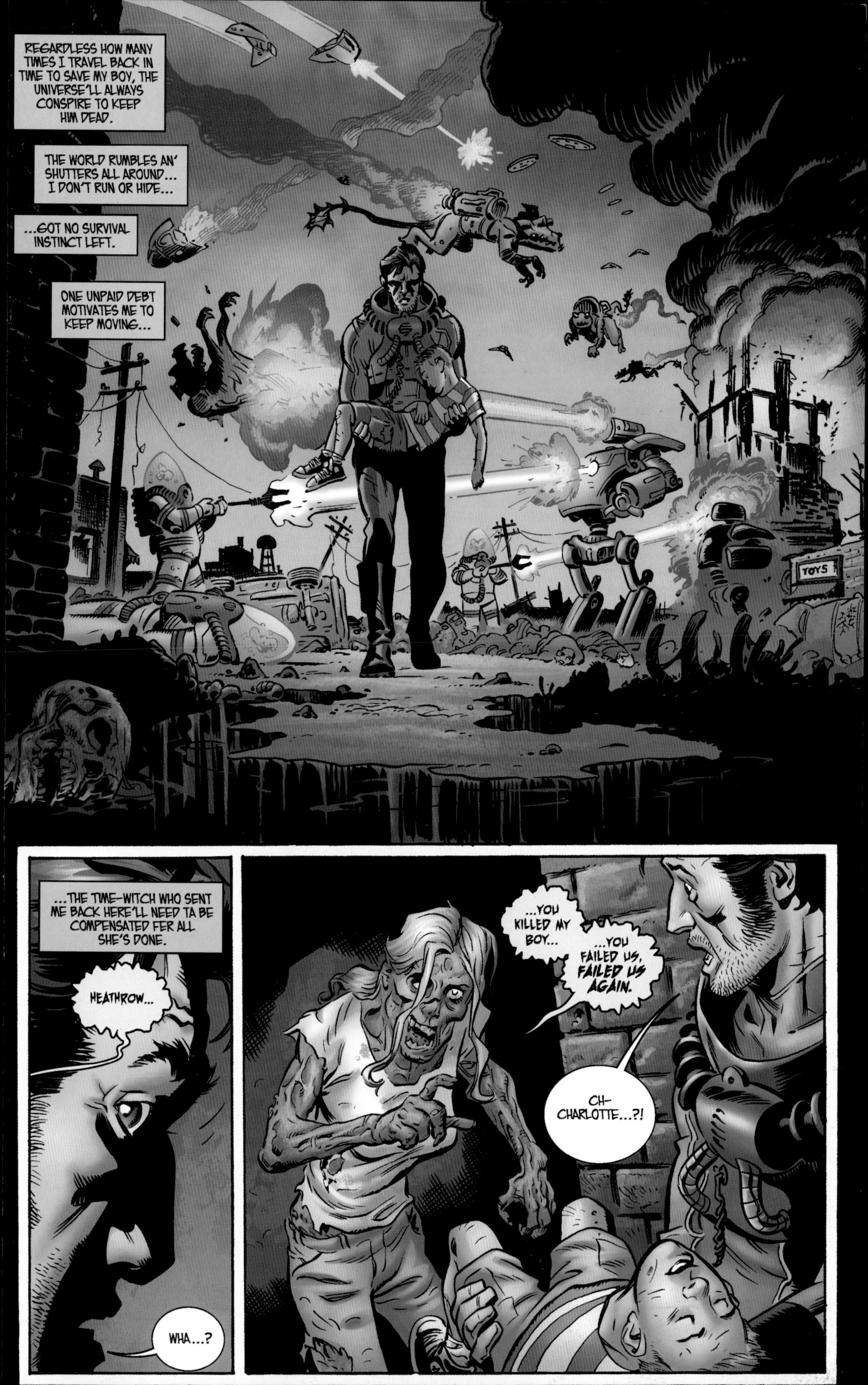
REGARDLESS HOW MANY TIMES I TRAVEL BACK IN TIME TO SAVE MY BOY, THE UNIVERSE'LL ALWAYS CONSPIRE TO KEEP HIM DEAD.
THE WORLD RUMBLES AN' SHUTTERS ALL AROUND... I DON'T RUN OR HIDE...
...GOT NO SURVIVAL INSTINCT LEFT.
ONE UNPAID DEBT MOTIVATES ME TO KEEP MOVING...
TOYS
...THE TIME-WITCH WHO SENT ME BACK HERE'LL NEED TA BE COMPENSATED FER ALL SHE'S DONE.
HEATHROW...
WHA...?
...YOU KILLED MY BOY...
...YOU FAILED US, FAILED US AGAIN.
CH-CHARLOTTE...?!

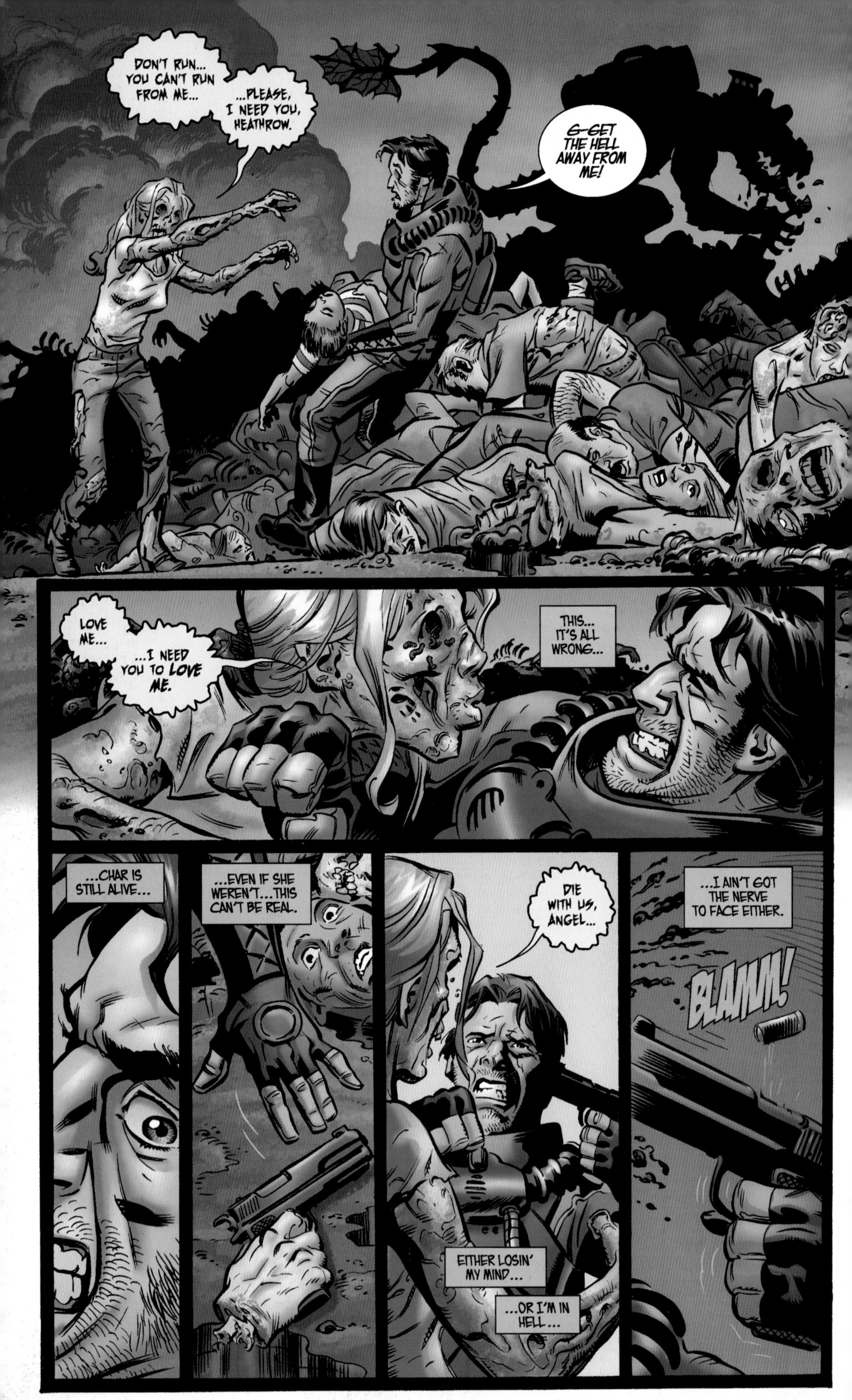
DON'T RUN... YOU CAN'T RUN FROM ME...
...PLEASE, I NEED YOU, HEATHROW.
G-GET THE HELL AWAY FROM ME!
LOVE ME...
...I NEED YOU TO LOVE ME.
THIS... IT'S ALL WRONG...
...CHAR IS STILL ALIVE...
...EVEN IF SHE WEREN'T...THIS CAN'T BE REAL.
DIE WITH US, ANGEL...
EITHER LOSIN' MY MIND...
...OR I'M IN HELL...
...I AIN'T GOT THE NERVE TO FACE EITHER.
BLAMM!

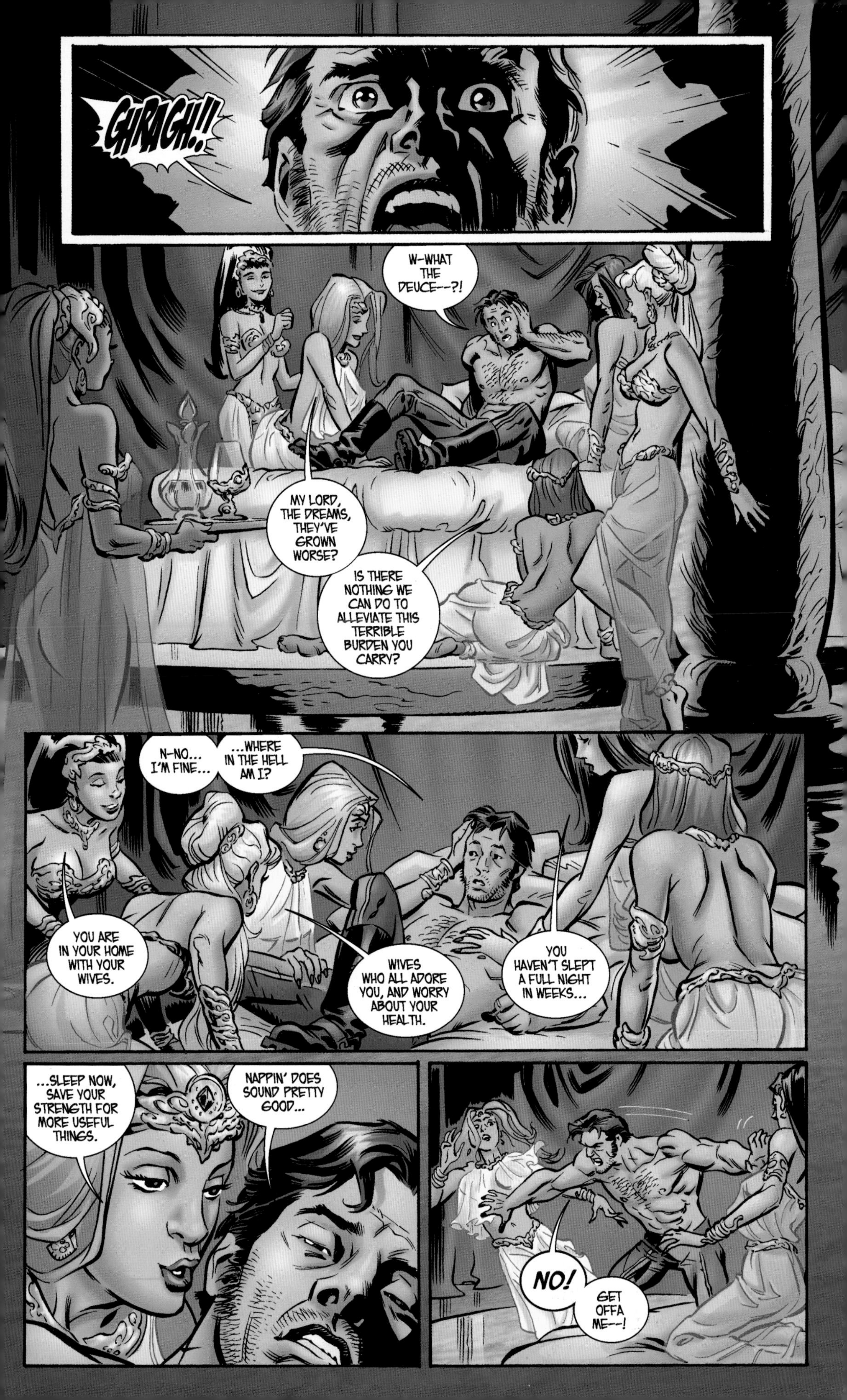
GHRAGH!!
W-WHAT THE DEUCE--?!
MY LORD, THE DREAMS, THEY'VE GROWN WORSE?
IS THERE NOTHING WE CAN DO TO ALLEVIATE THIS TERRIBLE BURDEN YOU CARRY?
N-NO... I'M FINE...
...WHERE IN THE HELL AM I?
YOU ARE IN YOUR HOME WITH YOUR WIVES.
WIVES WHO ALL ADORE YOU, AND WORRY ABOUT YOUR HEALTH.
YOU HAVEN'T SLEPT A FULL NIGHT IN WEEKS...
...SLEEP NOW, SAVE YOUR STRENGTH FOR MORE USEFUL THINGS.
NAPPIN' DOES SOUND PRETTY GOOD...
NO!
GET OFFA ME--!

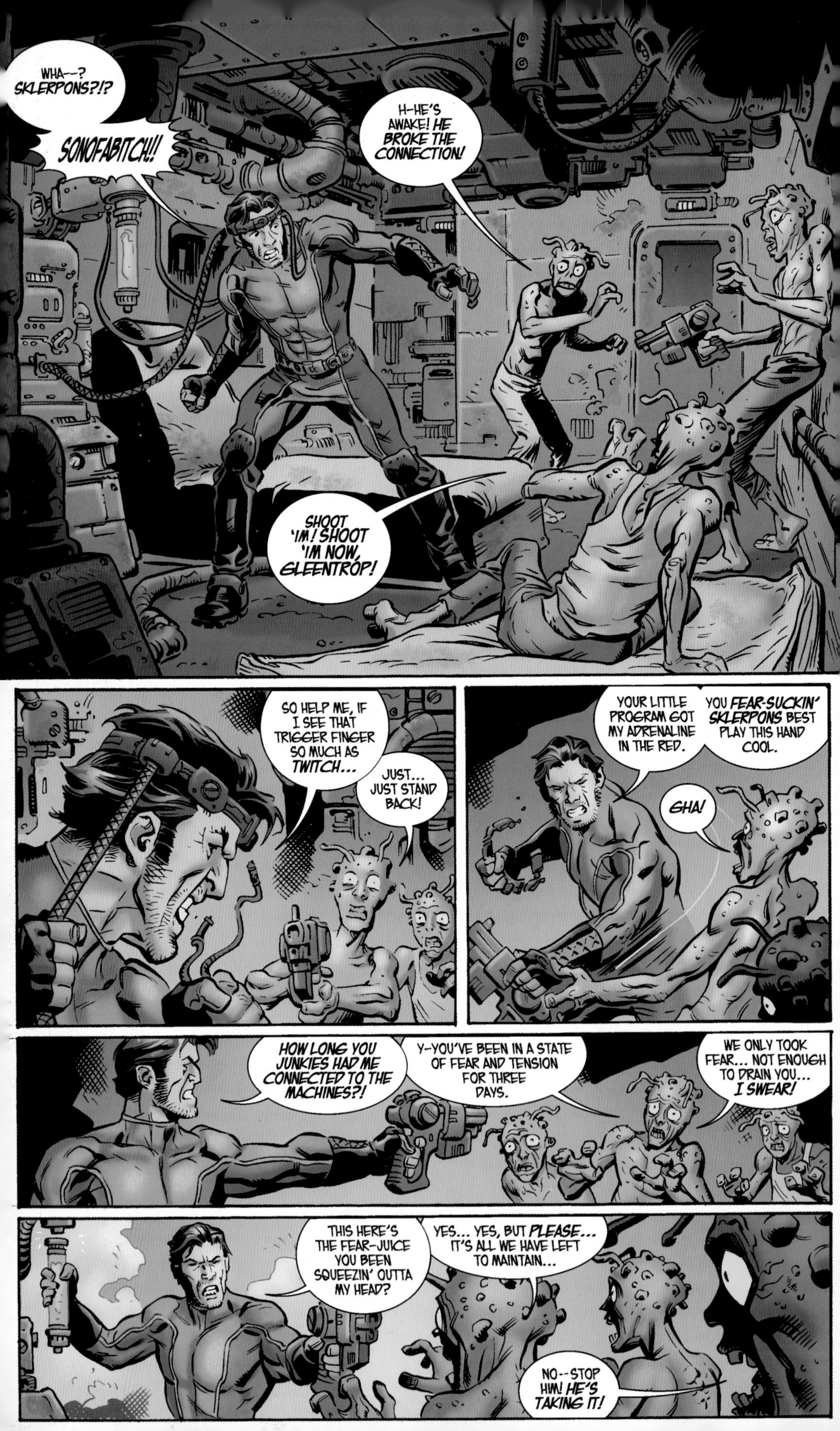
WHA--? SKLERPONS?!?
SONOFABITCH!!
H-HE'S AWAKE! HE BROKE THE CONNECTION!
SHOOT 'IM! SHOOT 'IM NOW, GLEENTROP!
SO HELP ME, IF I SEE THAT TRIGGER FINGER SO MUCH AS TWITCH...
JUST... JUST STAND BACK!
YOUR LITTLE PROGRAM GOT MY ADRENALINE IN THE RED.
YOU FEAR-SUCKIN' SKLERPONS BEST PLAY THIS HAND COOL.
GHA!
HOW LONG YOU JUNKIES HAD ME CONNECTED TO THE MACHINES?!
Y-YOU'VE BEEN IN A STATE OF FEAR AND TENSION FOR THREE DAYS.
WE ONLY TOOK FEAR... NOT ENOUGH TO DRAIN YOU... I SWEAR!
THIS HERE'S THE FEAR-JUICE YOU BEEN SQUEEZIN' OUTTA MY HEAD?
YES... YES, BUT PLEASE... IT'S ALL WE HAVE LEFT TO MAINTAIN...
NO--STOP HIM! HE'S TAKING IT!

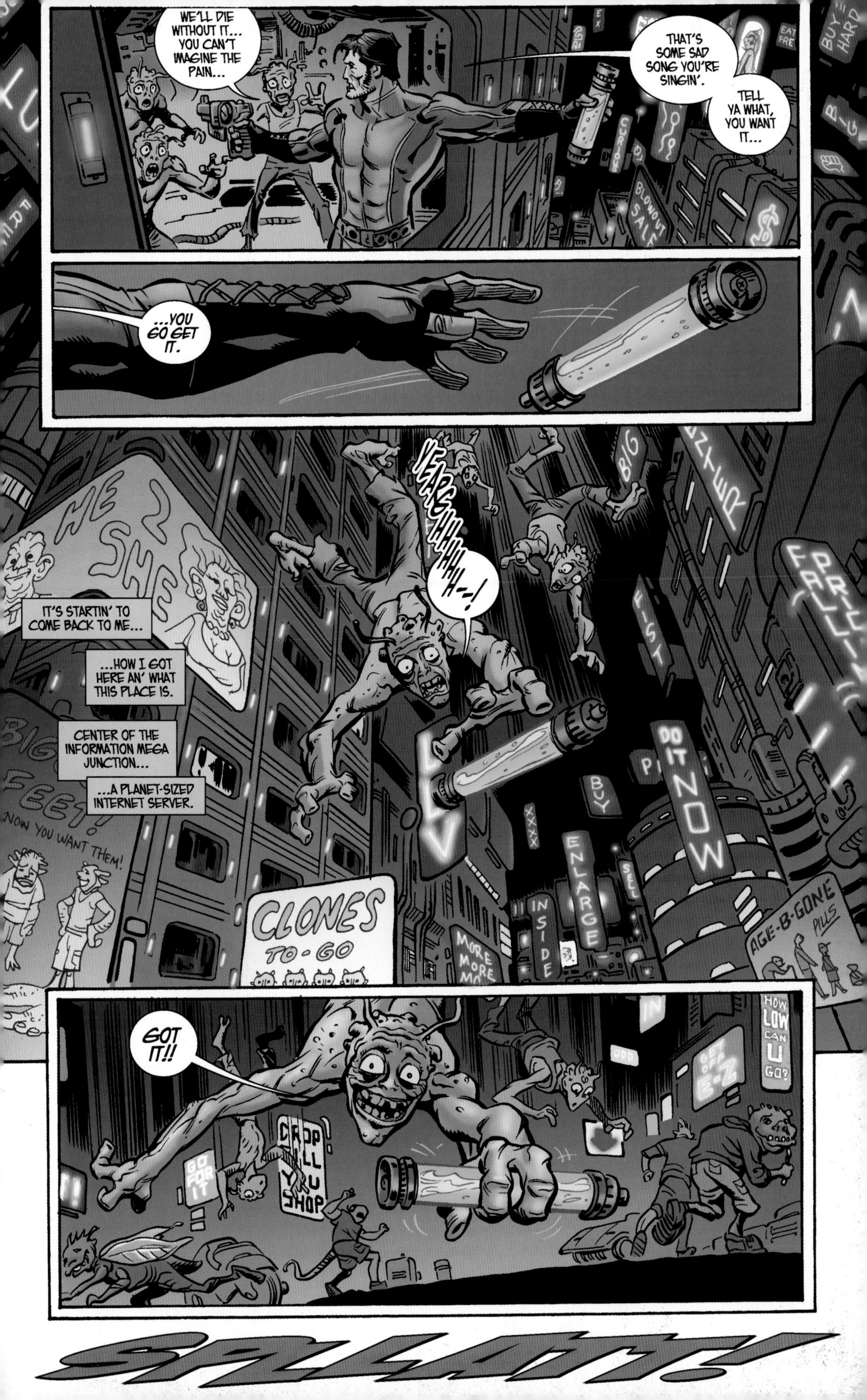
WE'LL DIE WITHOUT IT... YOU CAN'T IMAGINE THE PAIN...
THAT'S SOME SAD SONG YOU'RE SINGIN'.
TELL YA WHAT, YOU WANT IT...
...YOU GO GET IT.
YEARGHHHHH--!
IT'S STARTIN' TO COME BACK TO ME...
...HOW I GOT HERE AN' WHAT THIS PLACE IS.
CENTER OF THE INFORMATION MEGA JUNCTION...
...A PLANET-SIZED INTERNET SERVER.
CLONES TO-GO
BIG FEET! NOW YOU WANT THEM!
DO IT NOW
ENLARGE
INSIDE
AGE-B-GONE PILLS
HOW LOW CAN U GO?
GOT IT!!
SPLAT!!

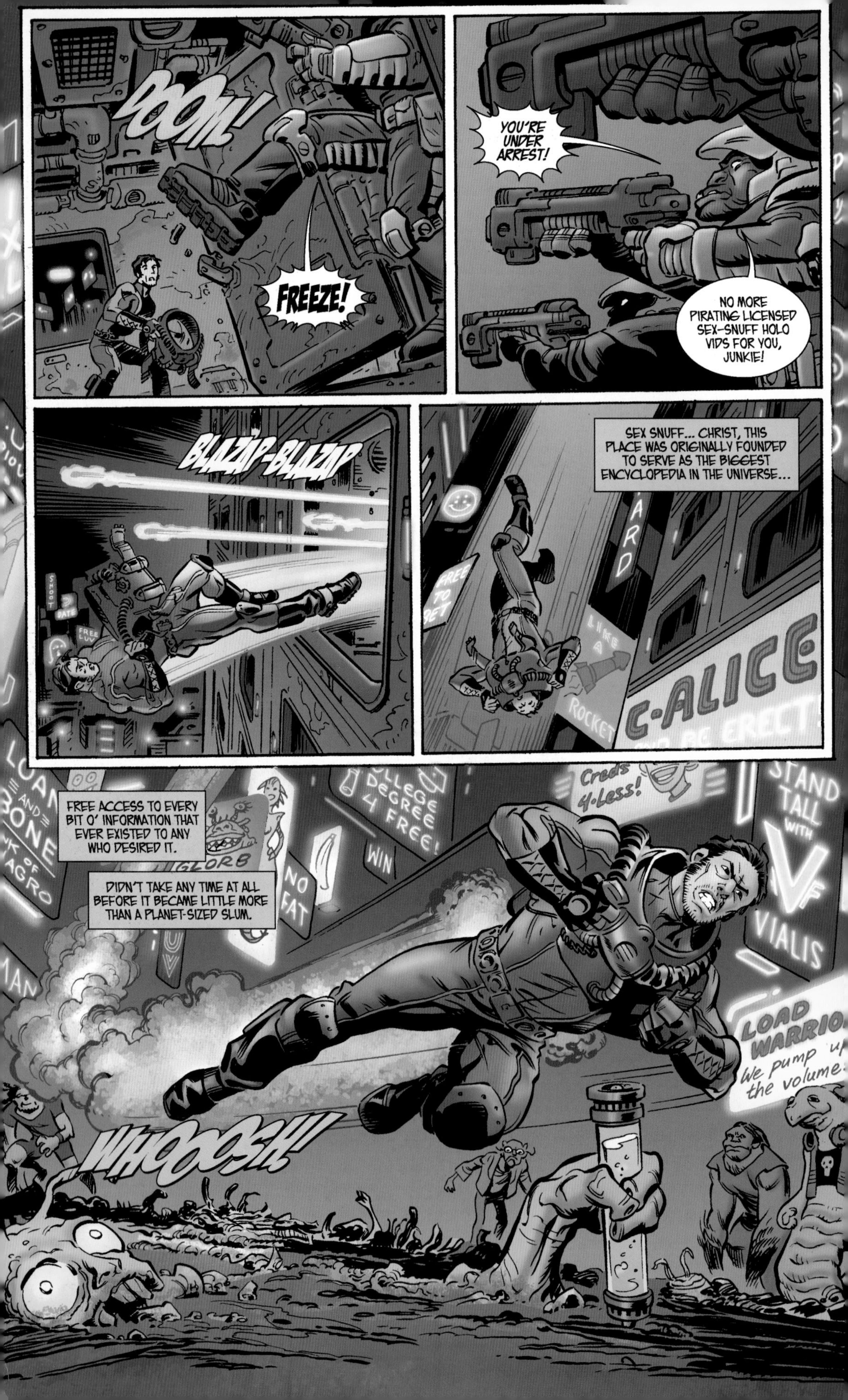
DOOM!
FREEZE!
YOU'RE UNDER ARREST!
NO MORE PIRATING LICENSED SEX-SNUFF HOLO VIDS FOR YOU, JUNKIE!
BLAZAP-BLAZAP
SEX SNUFF... CHRIST, THIS PLACE WAS ORIGINALLY FOUNDED TO SERVE AS THE BIGGEST ENCYCLOPEDIA IN THE UNIVERSE...
C-ALICE
FREE ACCESS TO EVERY BIT O' INFORMATION THAT EVER EXISTED TO ANY WHO DESIRED IT.
DIDN'T TAKE ANY TIME AT ALL BEFORE IT BECAME LITTLE MORE THAN A PLANET-SIZED SLUM.
Creds 4-Less!
COLLEGE DEGREE 4 FREE!
STAND TALL WITH
VIALIS
LOAD WARRIO
We pump u the volume
WHOOOSH!

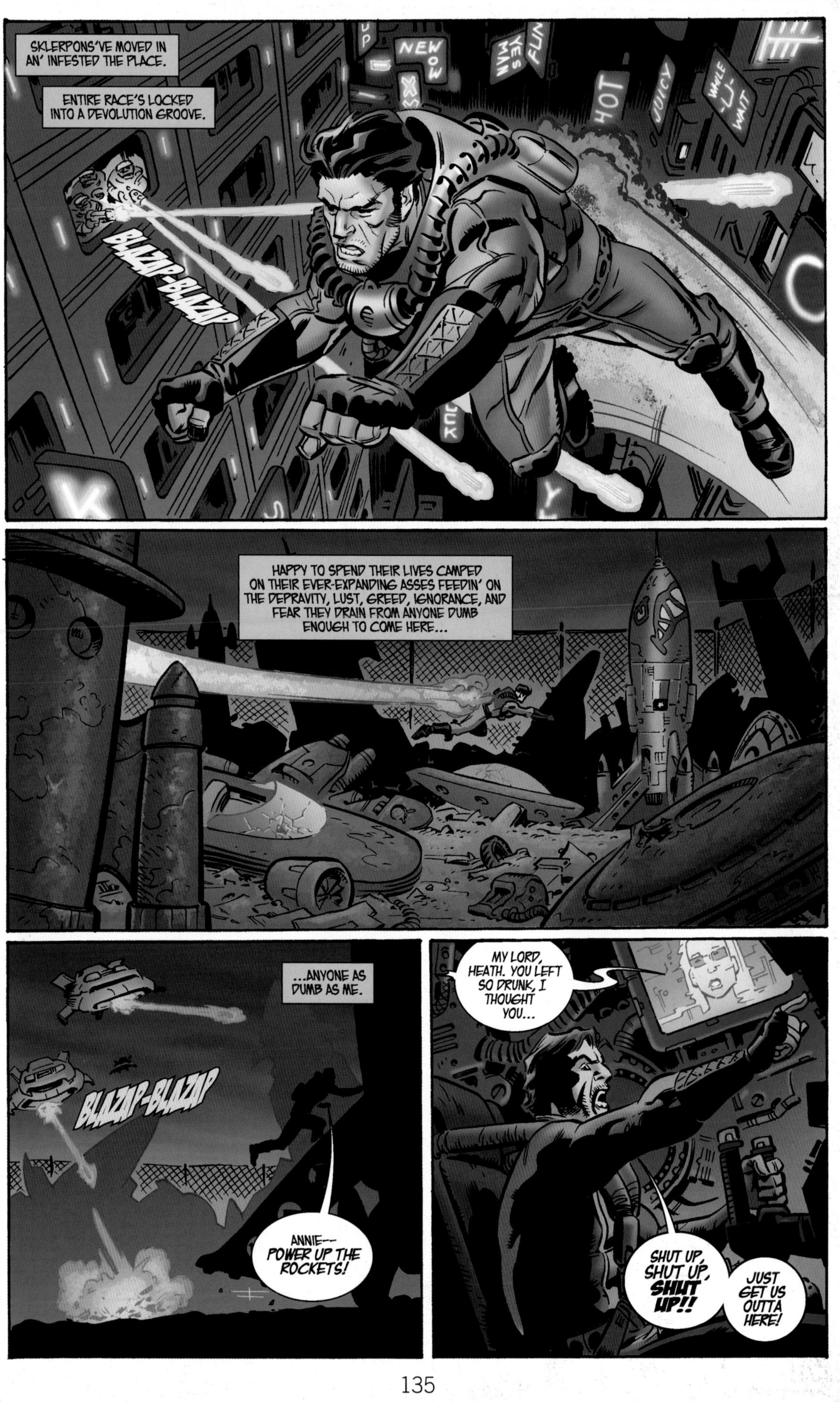

SKLERPONS'VE MOVED IN AN' INFESTED THE PLACE.
ENTIRE RACE'S LOCKED INTO A DEVOLUTION GROOVE.
NEW
YES MAN
FUN
HOT
JUICY
WHILE U WAIT
BLAZAP-BLAZAP
HAPPY TO SPEND THEIR LIVES CAMPED ON THEIR EVER-EXPANDING ASSES FEEDIN' ON THE DEPRAVITY, LUST, GREED, IGNORANCE, AND FEAR THEY DRAIN FROM ANYONE DUMB ENOUGH TO COME HERE...
...ANYONE AS DUMB AS ME.
BLAZAP-BLAZAP
ANNIE-- POWER UP THE ROCKETS!
MY LORD, HEATH. YOU LEFT SO DRUNK, I THOUGHT YOU...
SHUT UP, SHUT UP, SHUT UP!!
JUST GET US OUTTA HERE!

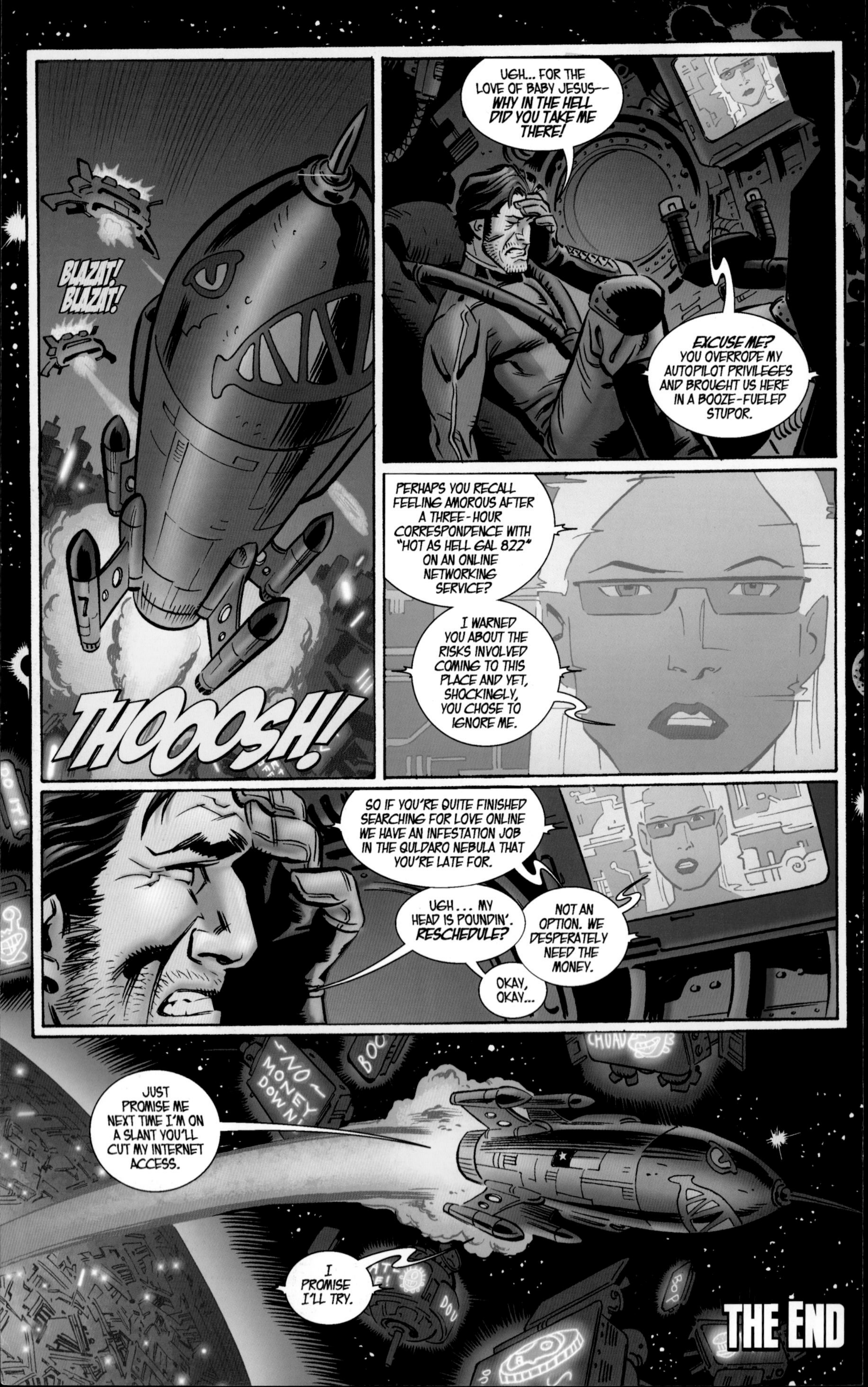
BLAZAT! BLAZAT!
THOOOSH!
UGH... FOR THE LOVE OF BABY JESUS-- WHY IN THE HELL DID YOU TAKE ME THERE!
EXCUSE ME? YOU OVERRODE MY AUTOPILOT PRIVILEGES AND BROUGHT US HERE IN A BOOZE-FUELED STUPOR.
PERHAPS YOU RECALL FEELING AMOROUS AFTER A THREE-HOUR CORRESPONDENCE WITH "HOT AS HELL GAL 822" ON AN ONLINE NETWORKING SERVICE?
I WARNED YOU ABOUT THE RISKS INVOLVED COMING TO THIS PLACE AND YET, SHOCKINGLY, YOU CHOSE TO IGNORE ME.
SO IF YOU'RE QUITE FINISHED SEARCHING FOR LOVE ONLINE WE HAVE AN INFESTATION JOB IN THE QULDARO NEBULA THAT YOU'RE LATE FOR.
UGH... MY HEAD IS POUNDIN'. RESCHEDULE?
NOT AN OPTION. WE DESPERATELY NEED THE MONEY.
OKAY, OKAY...
NO MONEY DOWN
JUST PROMISE ME NEXT TIME I'M ON A SLANT YOU'LL CUT MY INTERNET ACCESS.
I PROMISE I'LL TRY.
THE END

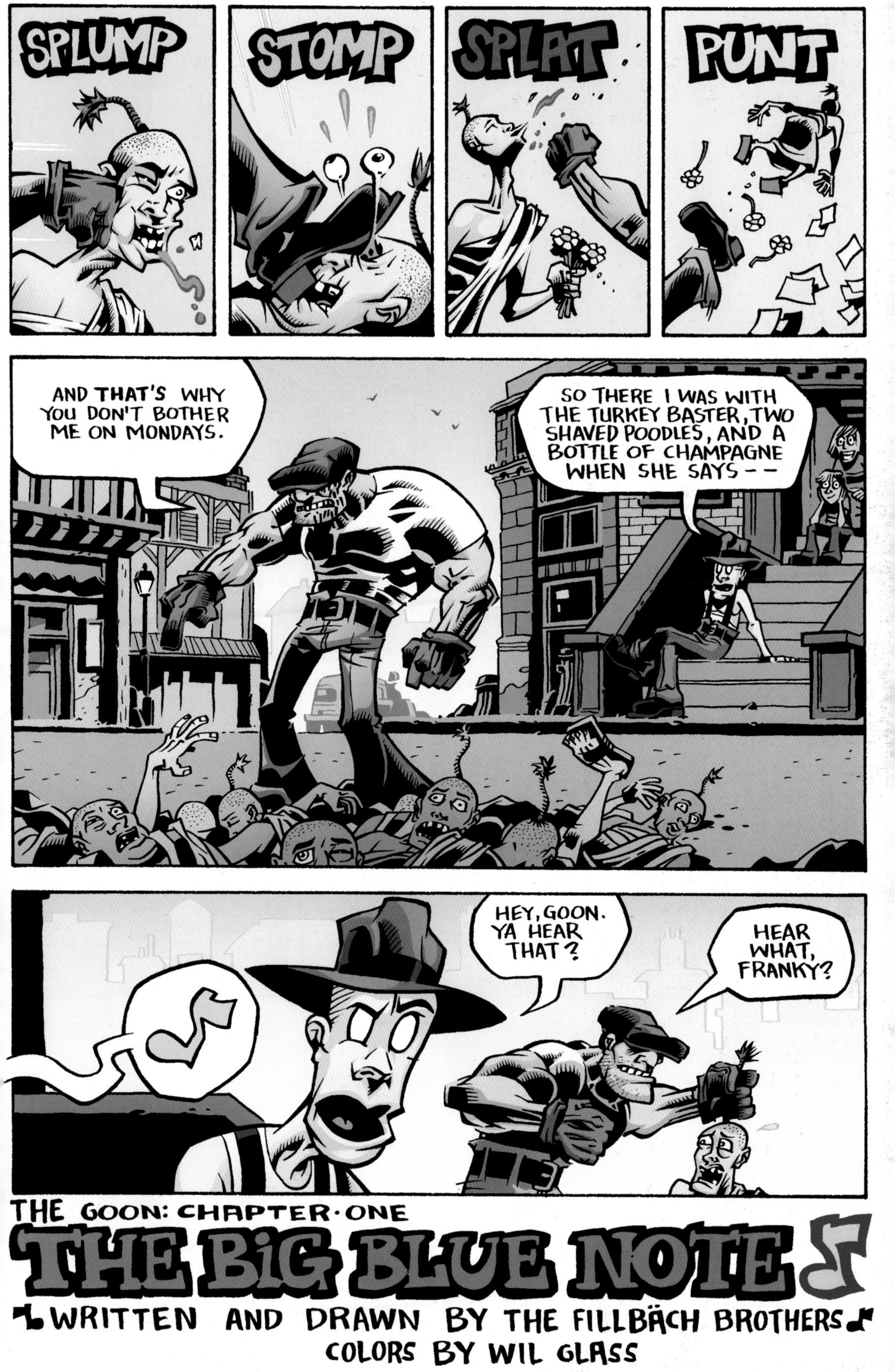
SPLUMP
STOMP
SPLAT
PUNT
AND THAT'S WHY YOU DON'T BOTHER ME ON MONDAYS.
SO THERE I WAS WITH THE TURKEY BASTER, TWO SHAVED POODLES, AND A BOTTLE OF CHAMPAGNE WHEN SHE SAYS--
HEY, GOON. YA HEAR THAT?
HEAR WHAT, FRANKY?

THE GOON: CHAPTER·ONE

THE BIG BLUE NOTE

WRITTEN AND DRAWN BY THE FILLBÄCH BROTHERS

COLORS BY WIL GLASS

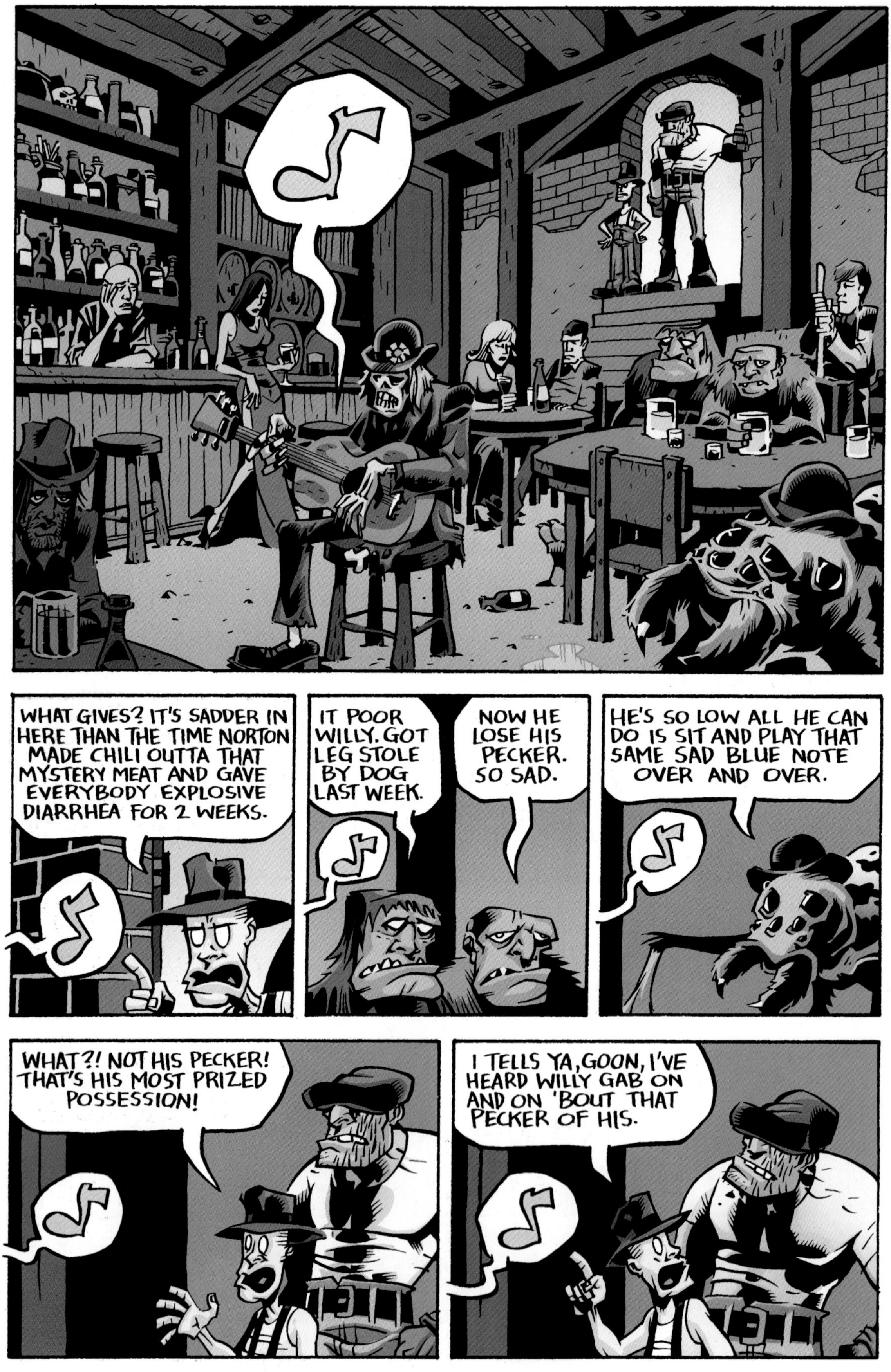
WHAT GIVES? IT'S SADDER IN HERE THAN THE TIME NORTON MADE CHILI OUTTA THAT MYSTERY MEAT AND GAVE EVERYBODY EXPLOSIVE DIARRHEA FOR 2 WEEKS.
IT POOR WILLY. GOT LEG STOLE BY DOG LAST WEEK.
NOW HE LOSE HIS PECKER. SO SAD.
HE'S SO LOW ALL HE CAN DO IS SIT AND PLAY THAT SAME SAD BLUE NOTE OVER AND OVER.
WHAT?! NOT HIS PECKER! THAT'S HIS MOST PRIZED POSSESSION!
I TELLS YA, GOON, I'VE HEARD WILLY GAB ON AND ON 'BOUT THAT PECKER OF HIS.

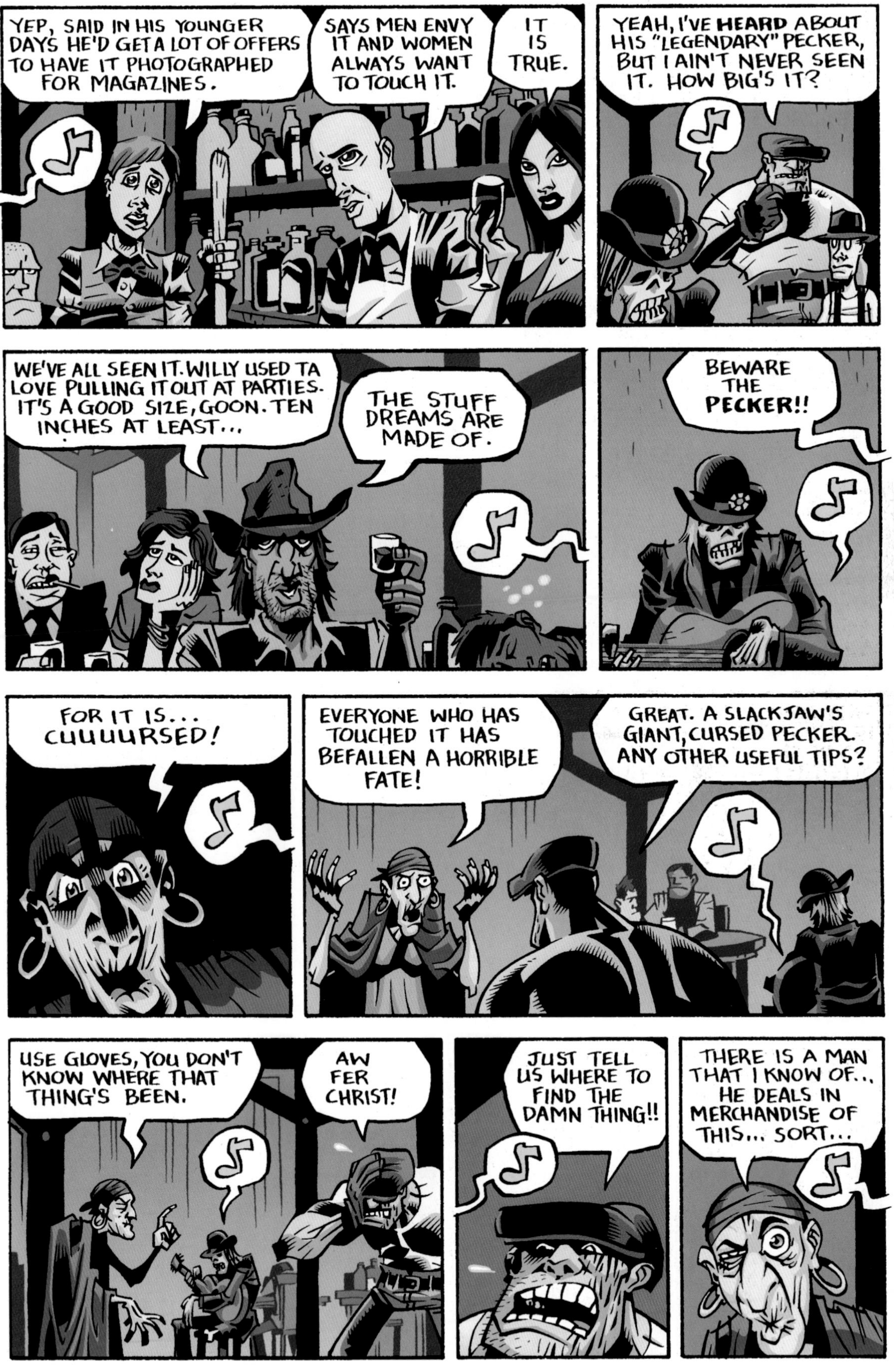
YEP, SAID IN HIS YOUNGER DAYS HE'D GET A LOT OF OFFERS TO HAVE IT PHOTOGRAPHED FOR MAGAZINES.
SAYS MEN ENVY IT AND WOMEN ALWAYS WANT TO TOUCH IT.
IT IS TRUE.
YEAH, I'VE HEARD ABOUT HIS "LEGENDARY" PECKER, BUT I AIN'T NEVER SEEN IT. HOW BIG'S IT?
WE'VE ALL SEEN IT. WILLY USED TA LOVE PULLING IT OUT AT PARTIES. IT'S A GOOD SIZE, GOON. TEN INCHES AT LEAST...
THE STUFF DREAMS ARE MADE OF.
BEWARE THE PECKER!!
FOR IT IS... CUUUURSED!
EVERYONE WHO HAS TOUCHED IT HAS BEFALLEN A HORRIBLE FATE!
GREAT. A SLACKJAW'S GIANT, CURSED PECKER. ANY OTHER USEFUL TIPS?
USE GLOVES, YOU DON'T KNOW WHERE THAT THING'S BEEN.
AW FER CHRIST!
JUST TELL US WHERE TO FIND THE DAMN THING!!
THERE IS A MAN THAT I KNOW OF... HE DEALS IN MERCHANDISE OF THIS... SORT...

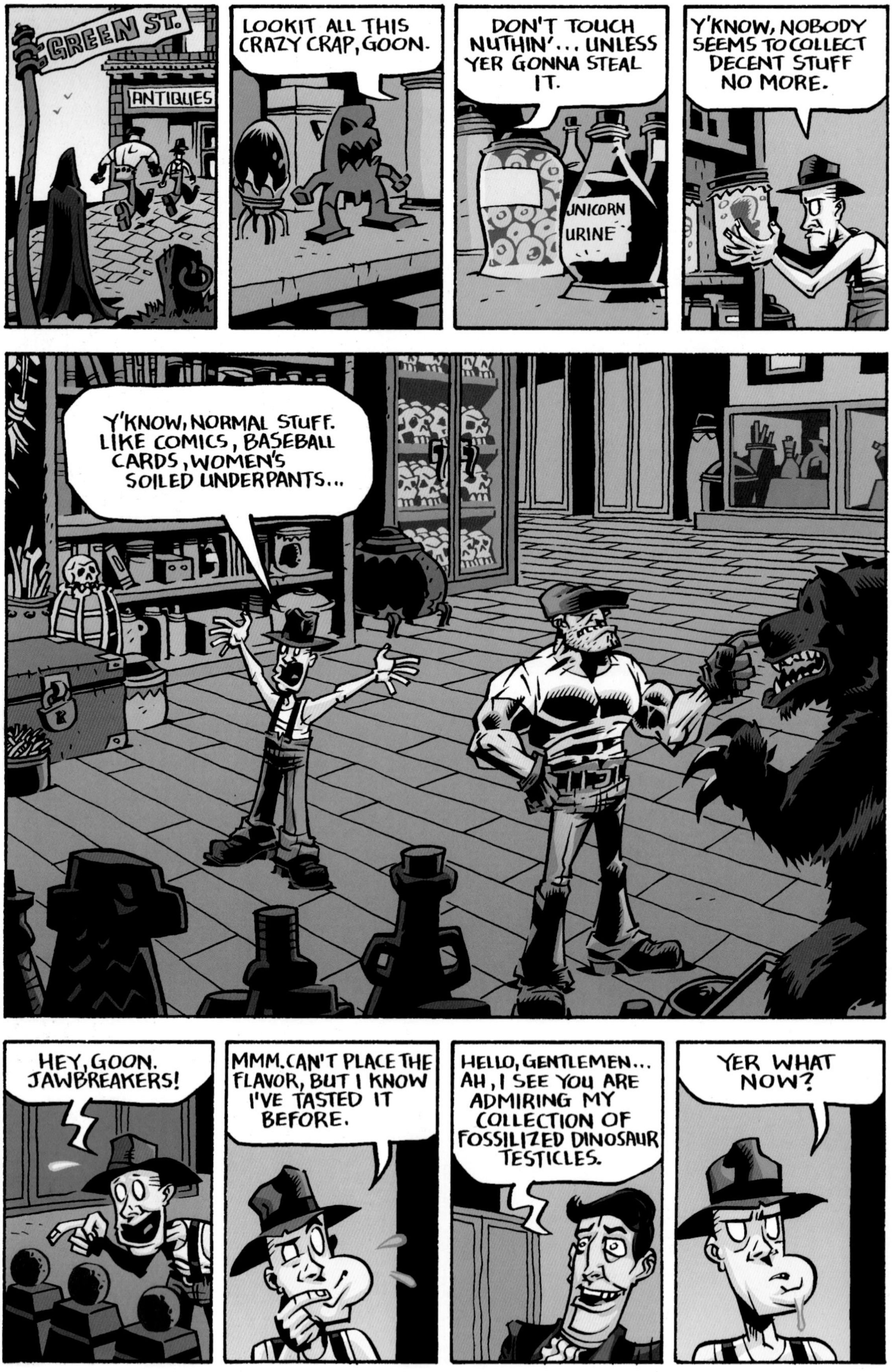
GREEN ST.
ANTIQUES
LOOKIT ALL THIS CRAZY CRAP, GOON.
DON'T TOUCH NUTHIN'... UNLESS YER GONNA STEAL IT.
UNICORN URINE
Y'KNOW, NOBODY SEEMS TO COLLECT DECENT STUFF NO MORE.
Y'KNOW, NORMAL STUFF. LIKE COMICS, BASEBALL CARDS, WOMEN'S SOILED UNDERPANTS...
HEY, GOON. JAWBREAKERS!
MMM. CAN'T PLACE THE FLAVOR, BUT I KNOW I'VE TASTED IT BEFORE.
HELLO, GENTLEMEN... AH, I SEE YOU ARE ADMIRING MY COLLECTION OF FOSSILIZED DINOSAUR TESTICLES.
YER WHAT NOW?

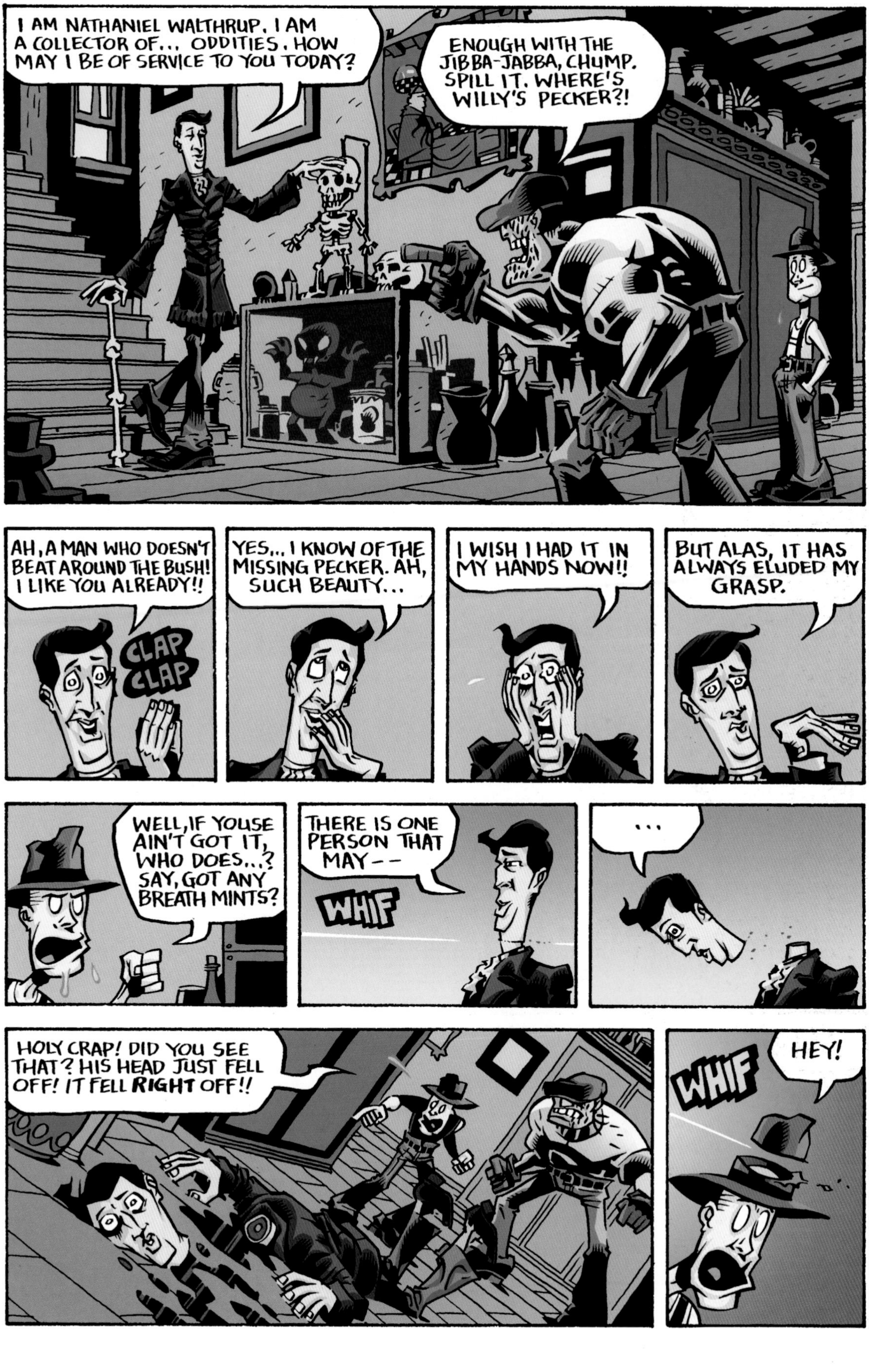
I AM NATHANIEL WALTHRUP. I AM A COLLECTOR OF... ODDITIES. HOW MAY I BE OF SERVICE TO YOU TODAY?
ENOUGH WITH THE JIBBA-JABBA, CHUMP. SPILL IT. WHERE'S WILLY'S PECKER?!
AH, A MAN WHO DOESN'T BEAT AROUND THE BUSH! I LIKE YOU ALREADY!!
CLAP CLAP
YES... I KNOW OF THE MISSING PECKER. AH, SUCH BEAUTY...
I WISH I HAD IT IN MY HANDS NOW!!
BUT ALAS, IT HAS ALWAYS ELUDED MY GRASP.
WELL, IF YOUSE AIN'T GOT IT, WHO DOES...? SAY, GOT ANY BREATH MINTS?
THERE IS ONE PERSON THAT MAY--
WHIF
...
HOLY CRAP! DID YOU SEE THAT? HIS HEAD JUST FELL OFF! IT FELL **RIGHT** OFF!!
WHIF
HEY!

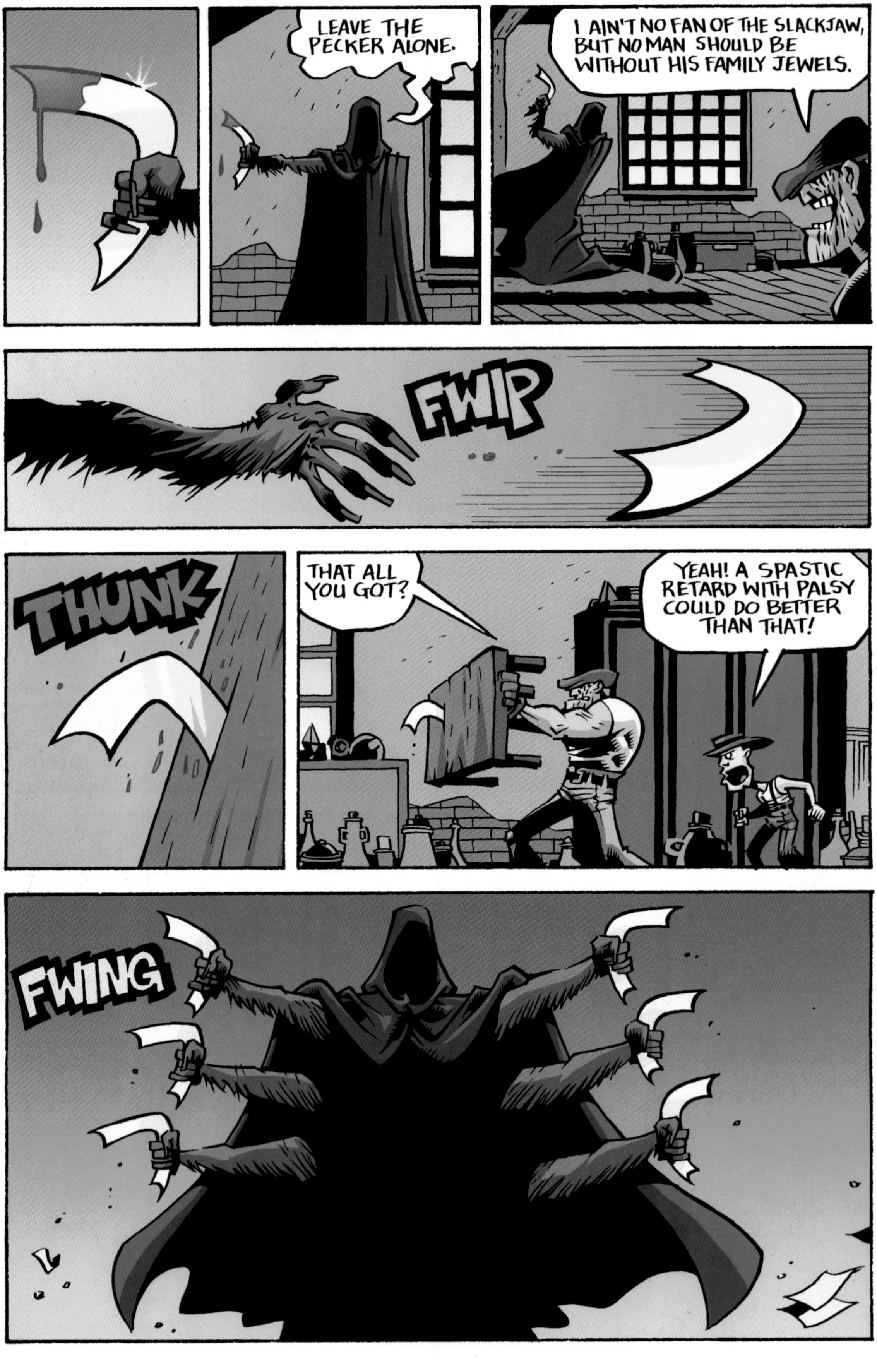
LEAVE THE PECKER ALONE.
I AIN'T NO FAN OF THE SLACKJAW, BUT NO MAN SHOULD BE WITHOUT HIS FAMILY JEWELS.
FWIP
THUNK
THAT ALL YOU GOT?
YEAH! A SPASTIC RETARD WITH PALSY COULD DO BETTER THAN THAT!
FWING

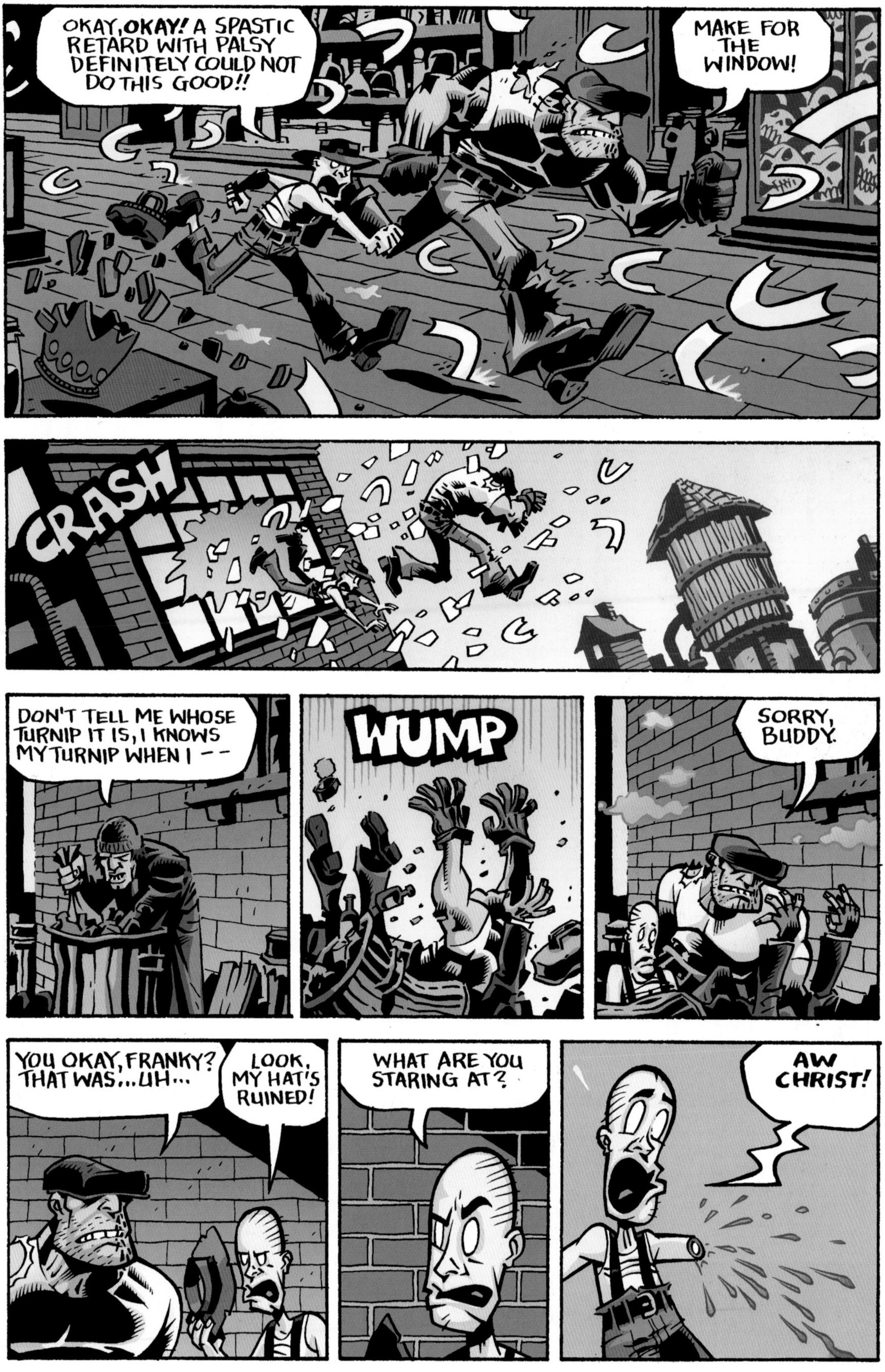
OKAY, OKAY! A SPASTIC RETARD WITH PALSY DEFINITELY COULD NOT DO THIS GOOD!!
MAKE FOR THE WINDOW!
CRASH
DON'T TELL ME WHOSE TURNIP IT IS, I KNOWS MY TURNIP WHEN I --
WUMP
SORRY, BUDDY.
YOU OKAY, FRANKY? THAT WAS...UH...
LOOK, MY HAT'S RUINED!
WHAT ARE YOU STARING AT?
AW CHRIST!

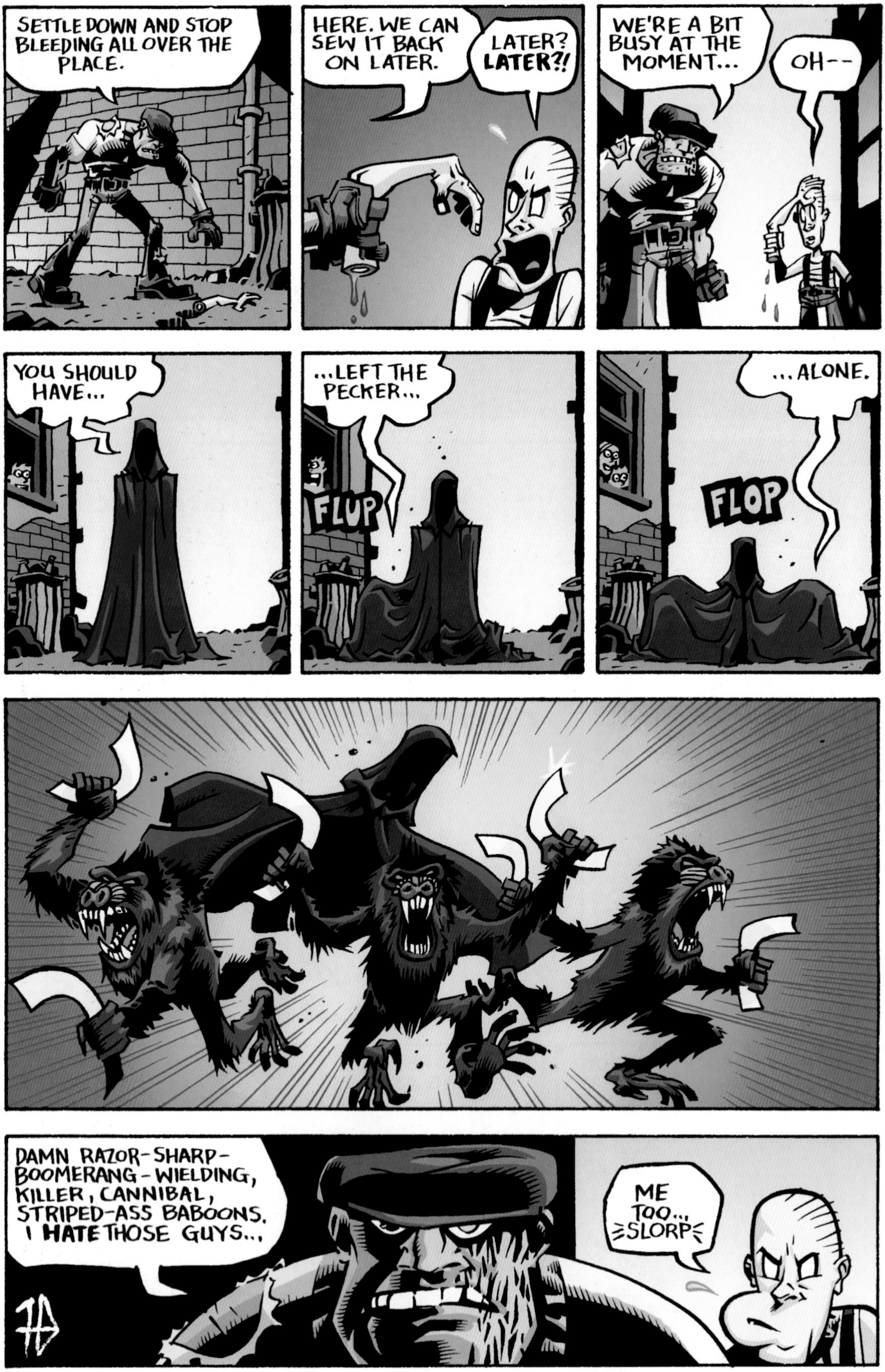
SETTLE DOWN AND STOP BLEEDING ALL OVER THE PLACE.
HERE. WE CAN SEW IT BACK ON LATER.
LATER? LATER?!
WE'RE A BIT BUSY AT THE MOMENT...
OH--
YOU SHOULD HAVE...
...LEFT THE PECKER...
FLUP
...ALONE.
FLOP
DAMN RAZOR-SHARP-BOOMERANG-WIELDING, KILLER, CANNIBAL, STRIPED-ASS BABOONS. I HATE THOSE GUYS...
ME TOO... SLORP

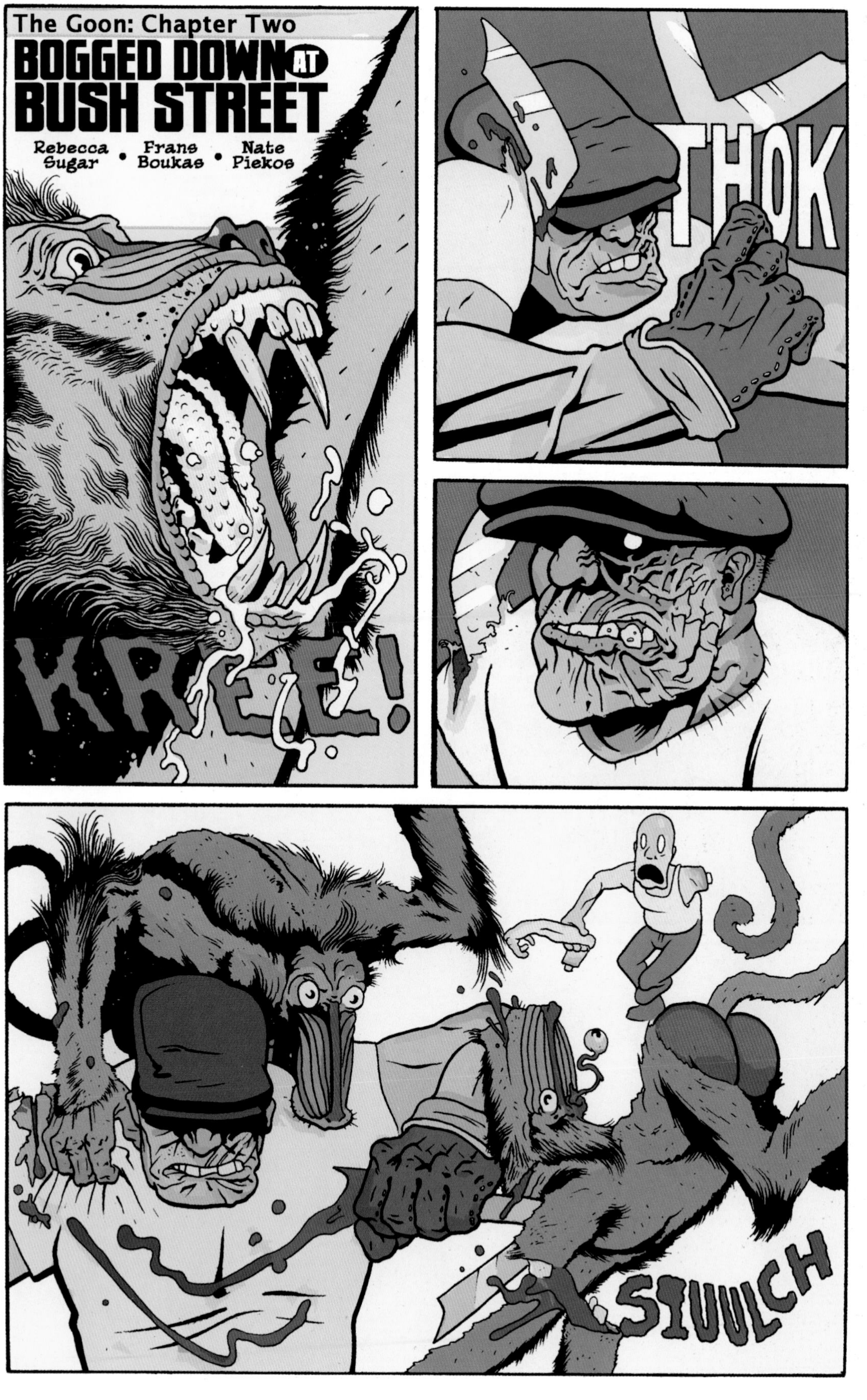
The Goon: Chapter Two
BOGGED DOWN AT BUSH STREET
Rebecca Sugar • Frans Boukas • Nate Piekos
KREEE!
THOK
SLUULCH

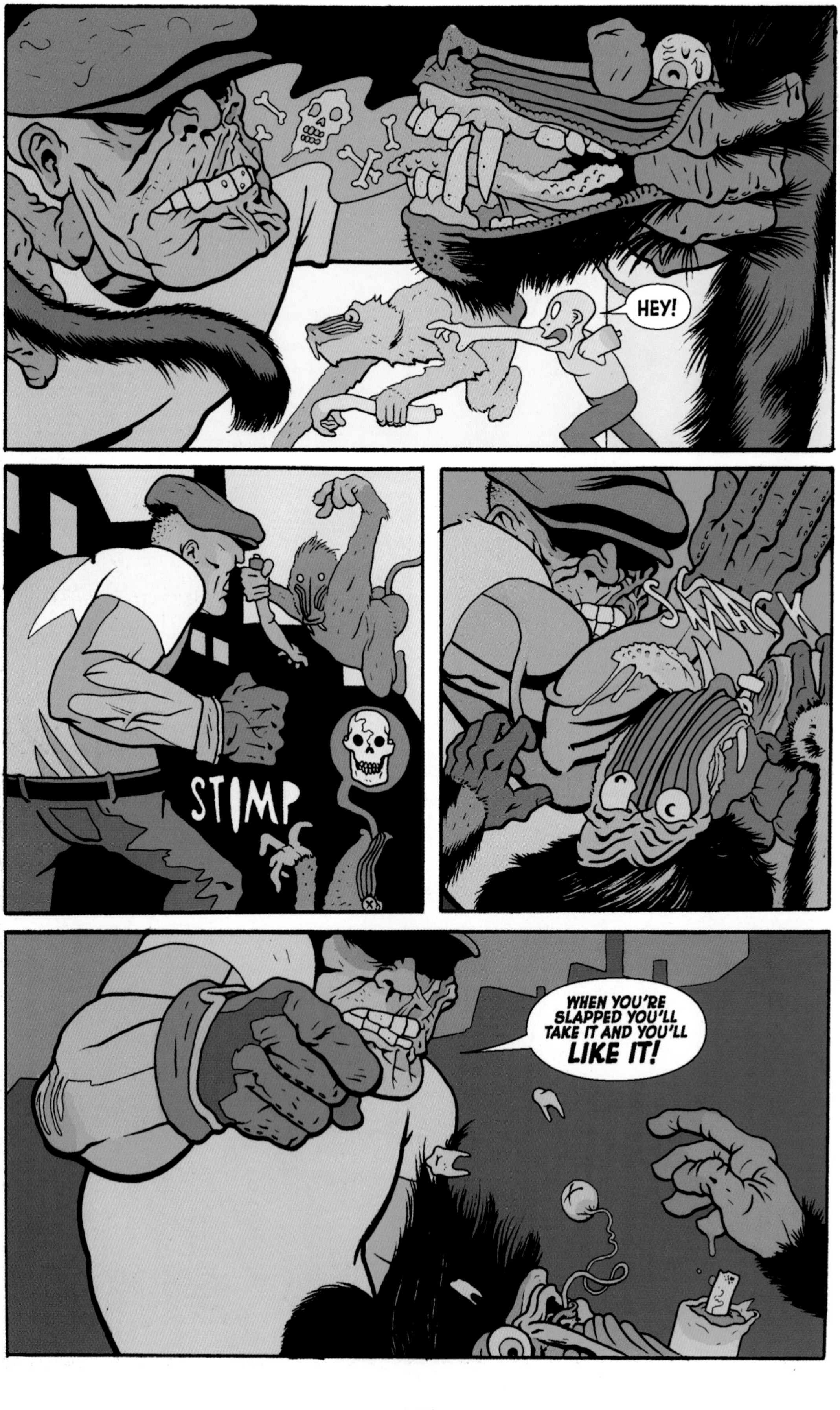
HEY!
STIMP
SMACK
WHEN YOU'RE SLAPPED YOU'LL TAKE IT AND YOU'LL LIKE IT!

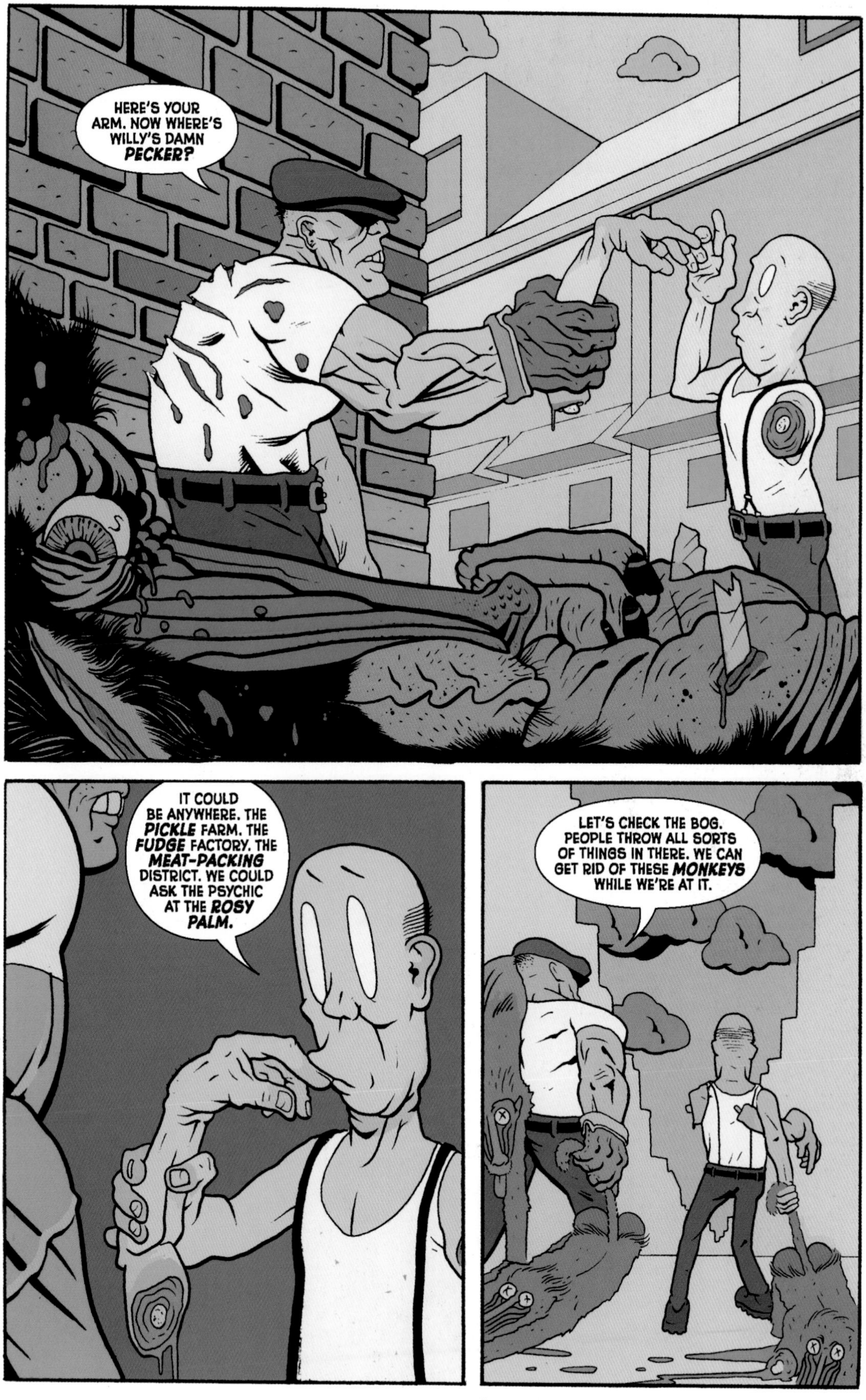
HERE'S YOUR ARM. NOW WHERE'S WILLY'S DAMN PECKER?
IT COULD BE ANYWHERE. THE PICKLE FARM. THE FUDGE FACTORY. THE MEAT-PACKING DISTRICT. WE COULD ASK THE PSYCHIC AT THE ROSY PALM.
LET'S CHECK THE BOG. PEOPLE THROW ALL SORTS OF THINGS IN THERE. WE CAN GET RID OF THESE MONKEYS WHILE WE'RE AT IT.

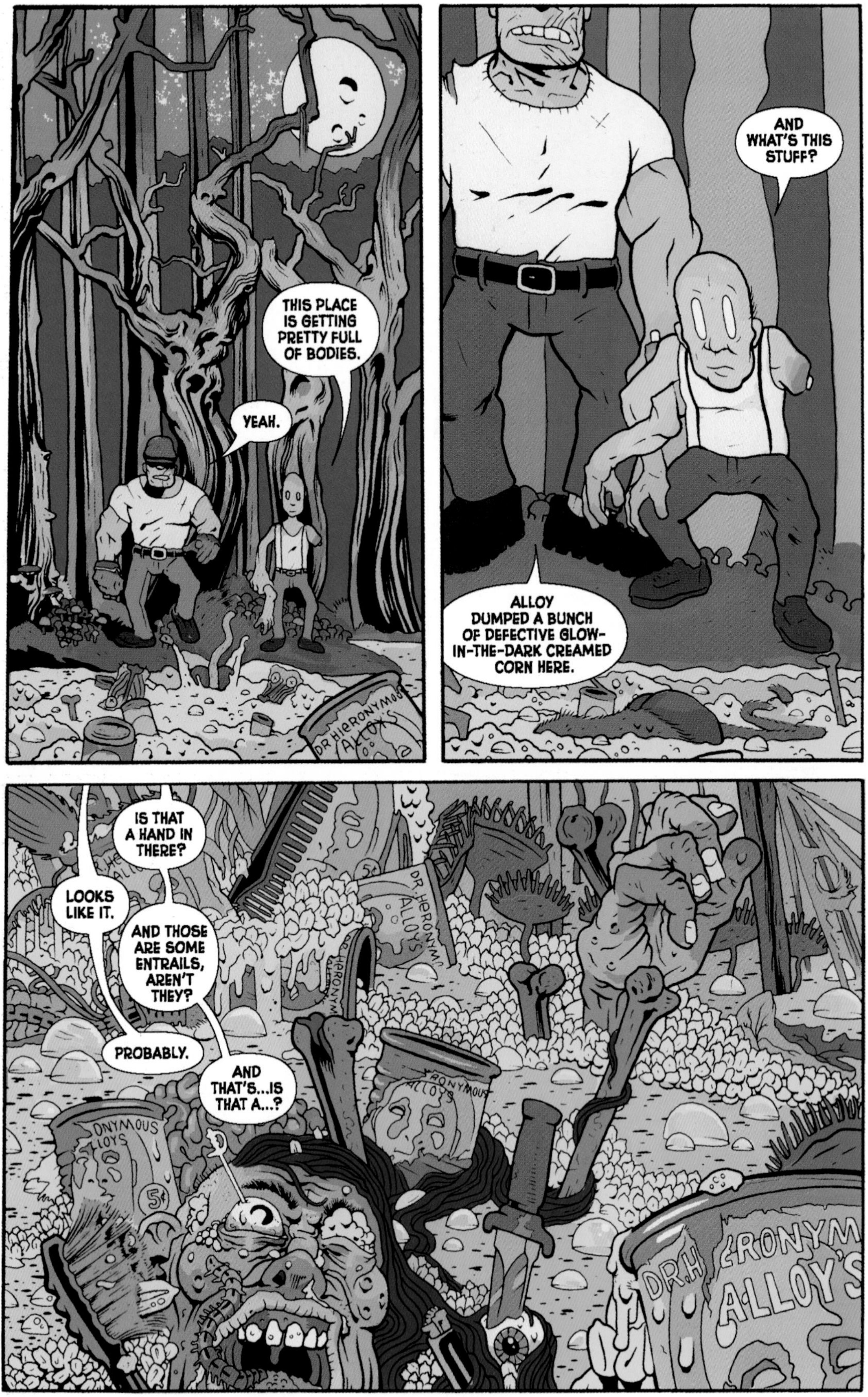
THIS PLACE IS GETTING PRETTY FULL OF BODIES.
YEAH.
AND WHAT'S THIS STUFF?
ALLOY DUMPED A BUNCH OF DEFECTIVE GLOW-IN-THE-DARK CREAMED CORN HERE.
IS THAT A HAND IN THERE?
LOOKS LIKE IT.
AND THOSE ARE SOME ENTRAILS, AREN'T THEY?
PROBABLY.
AND THAT'S...IS THAT A...?

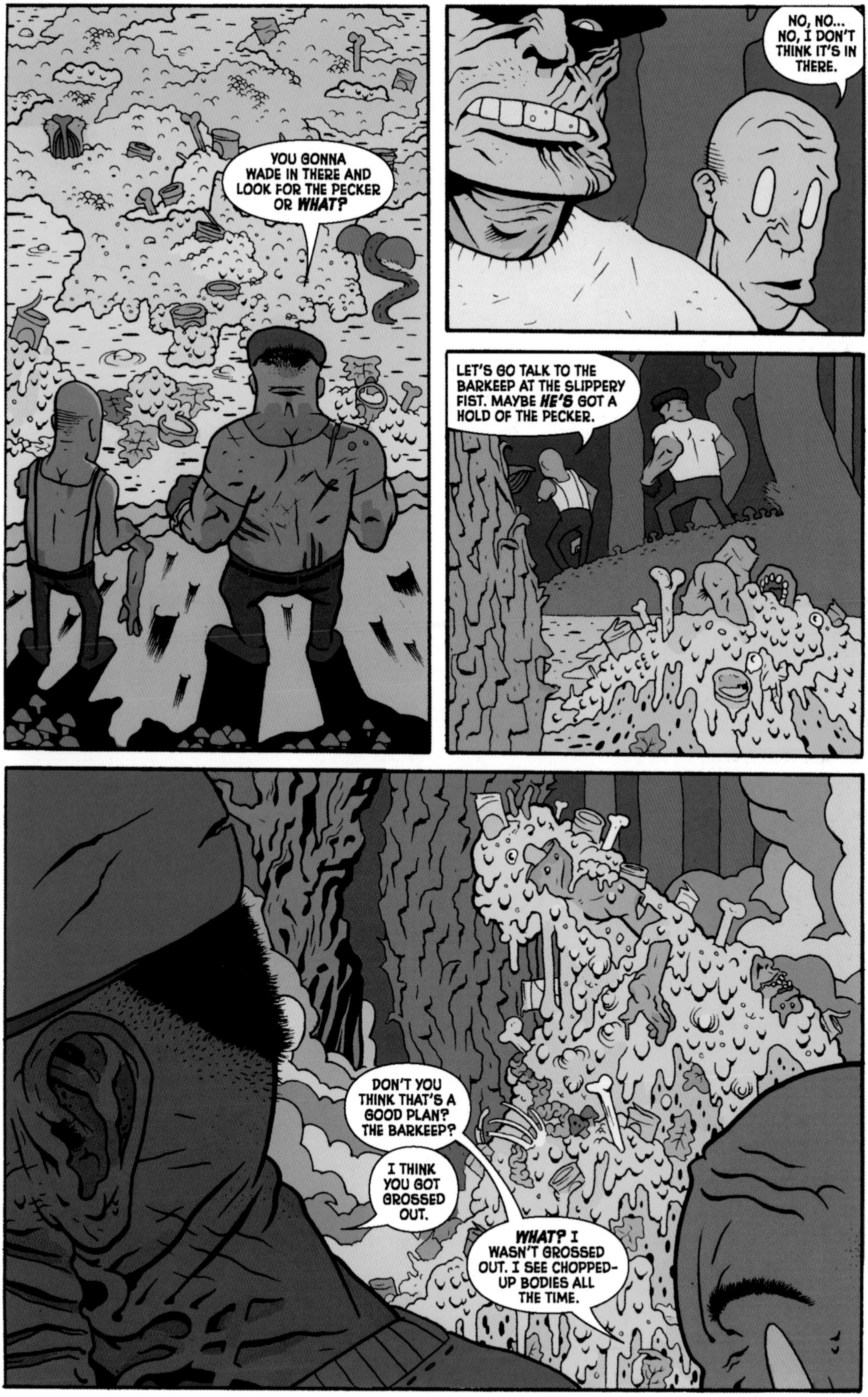
YOU GONNA WADE IN THERE AND LOOK FOR THE PECKER OR *WHAT?*
NO, NO... NO, I DON'T THINK IT'S IN THERE.
LET'S GO TALK TO THE BARKEEP AT THE SLIPPERY FIST. MAYBE *HE'S* GOT A HOLD OF THE PECKER.
DON'T YOU THINK THAT'S A GOOD PLAN? THE BARKEEP?
I THINK YOU GOT GROSSED OUT.
WHAT? I WASN'T GROSSED OUT. I SEE CHOPPED-UP BODIES ALL THE TIME.

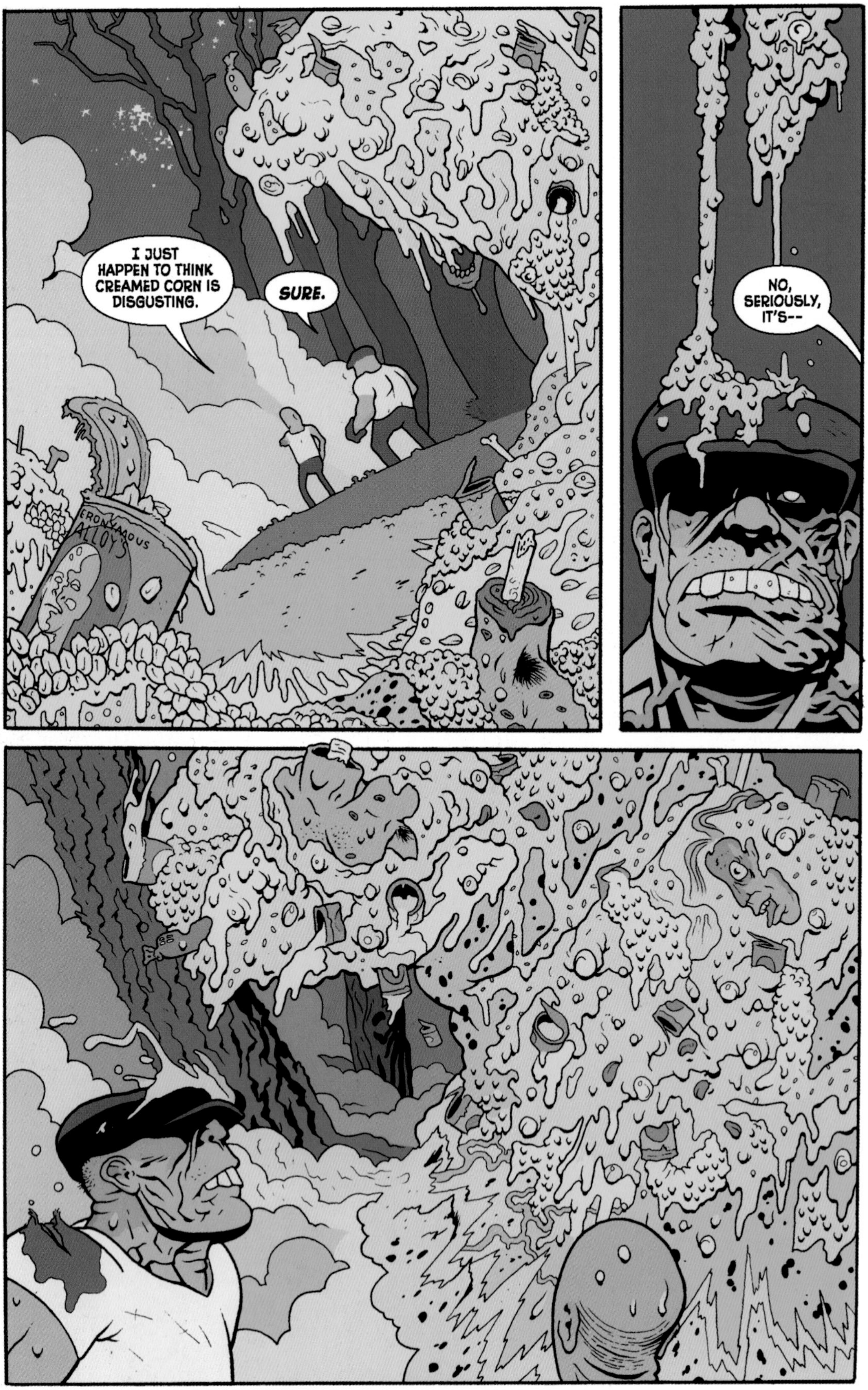

I JUST HAPPEN TO THINK CREAMED CORN IS DISGUSTING.
SURE.
NO, SERIOUSLY, IT'S--

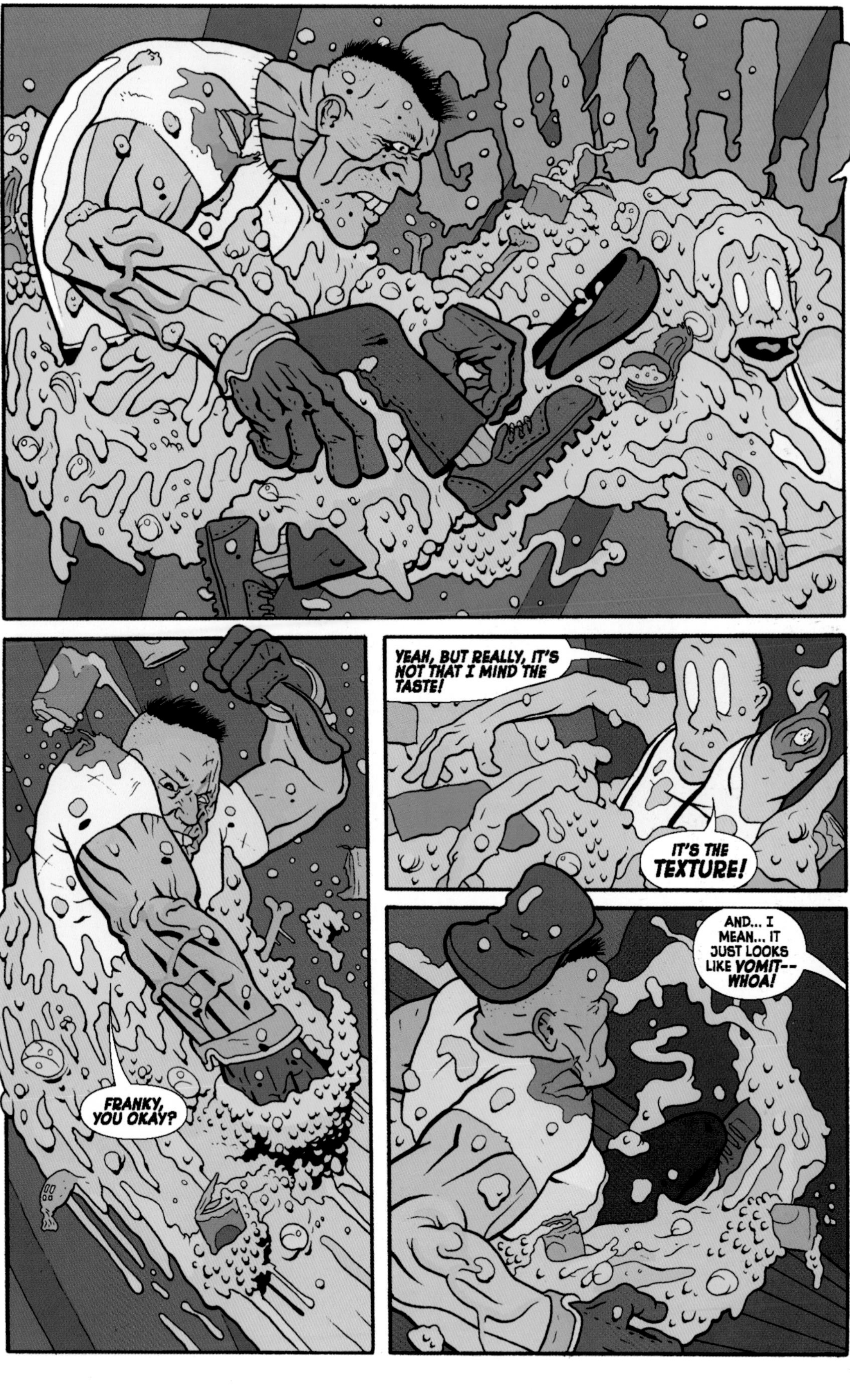
GOOJJ
YEAH, BUT REALLY, IT'S NOT THAT I MIND THE TASTE!
IT'S THE TEXTURE!
FRANKY, YOU OKAY?
AND... I MEAN... IT JUST LOOKS LIKE VOMIT-- WHOA!

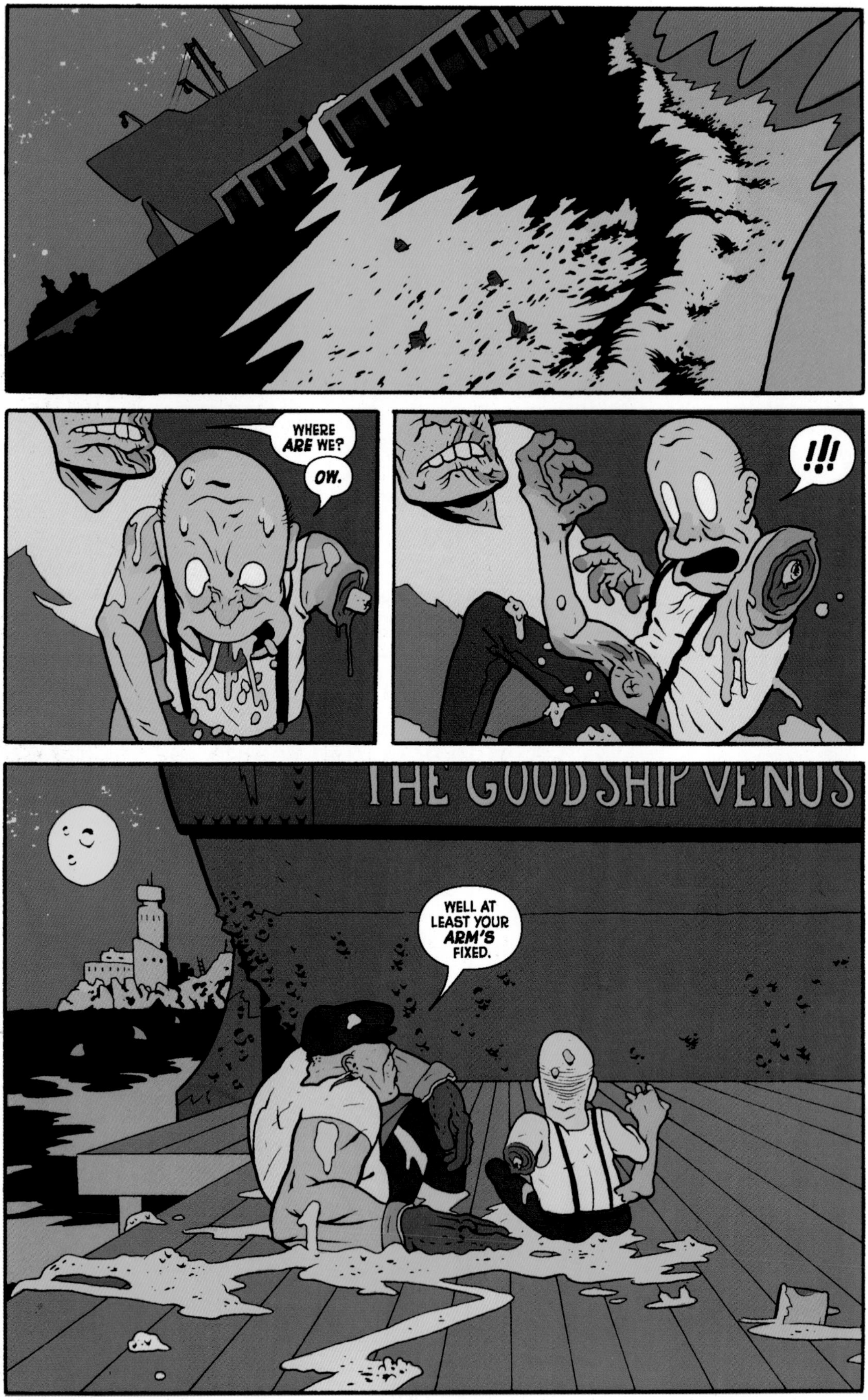
WHERE *ARE* WE?
OW.
!!!
THE GOOD SHIP VENUS
WELL AT LEAST YOUR *ARM'S* FIXED.

The Goon: Chapter Three

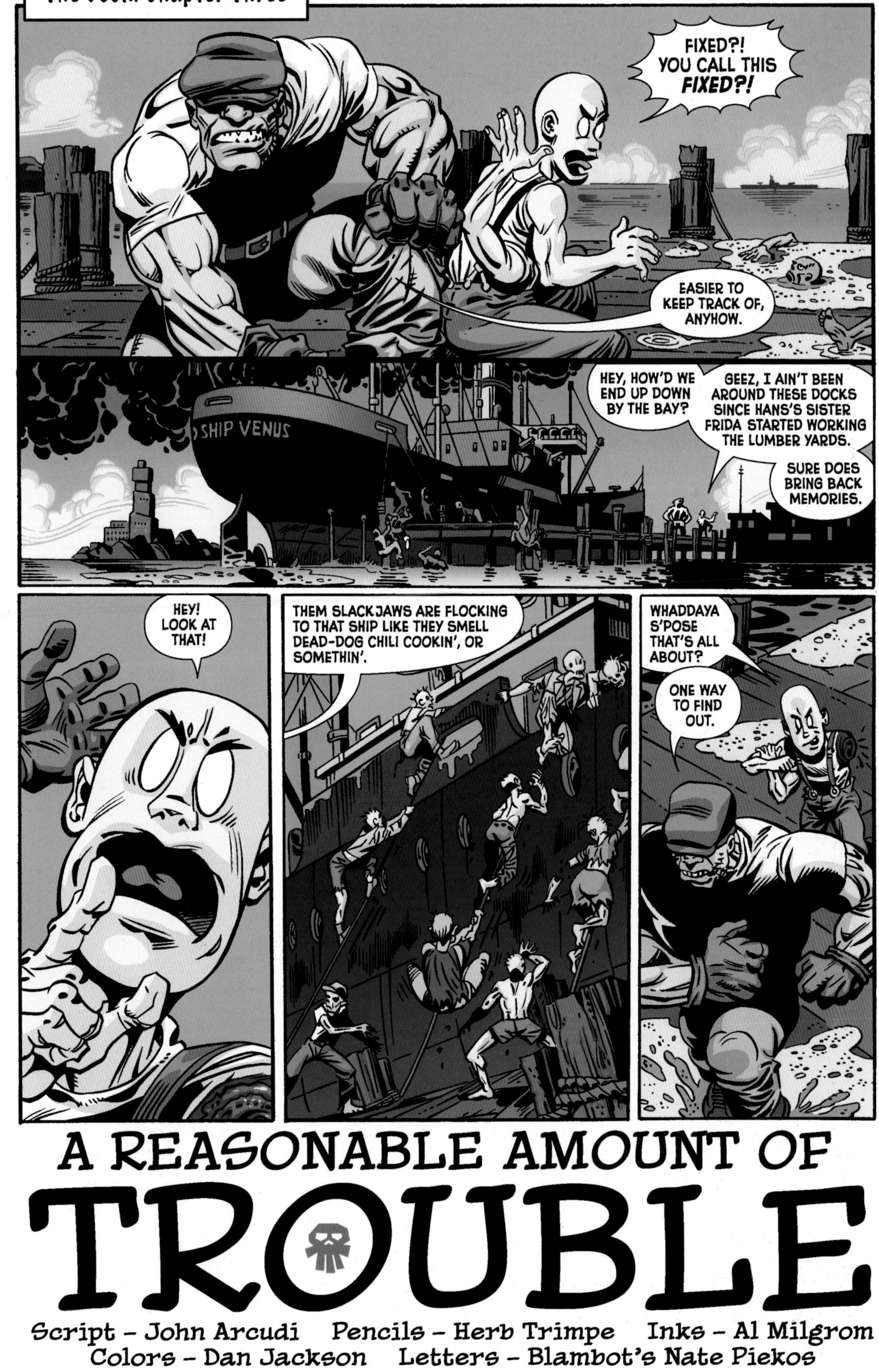
FIXED?! YOU CALL THIS *FIXED?!*
EASIER TO KEEP TRACK OF, ANYHOW.
SHIP VENUS
HEY, HOW'D WE END UP DOWN BY THE BAY?
GEEZ, I AIN'T BEEN AROUND THESE DOCKS SINCE HANS'S SISTER FRIDA STARTED WORKING THE LUMBER YARDS.
SURE DOES BRING BACK MEMORIES.
HEY! LOOK AT THAT!
THEM SLACKJAWS ARE FLOCKING TO THAT SHIP LIKE THEY SMELL DEAD-DOG CHILI COOKIN', OR SOMETHIN'.
WHADDAYA S'POSE THAT'S ALL ABOUT?
ONE WAY TO FIND OUT.

A REASONABLE AMOUNT OF TROUBLE

Script – John Arcudi Pencils – Herb Trimpe Inks – Al Milgrom
Colors – Dan Jackson Letters – Blambot's Nate Piekos

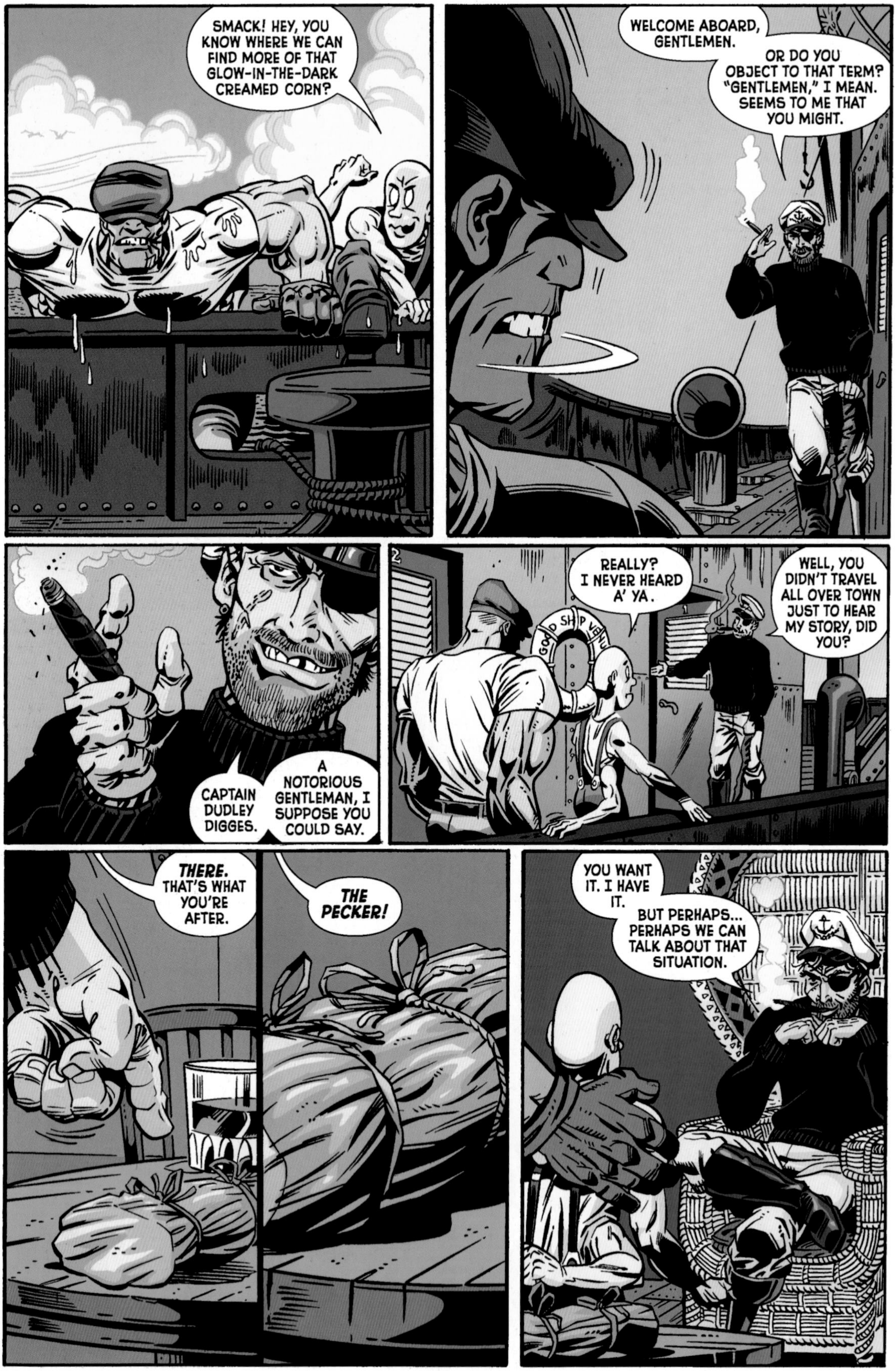
SMACK! HEY, YOU KNOW WHERE WE CAN FIND MORE OF THAT GLOW-IN-THE-DARK CREAMED CORN?
WELCOME ABOARD, GENTLEMEN.
OR DO YOU OBJECT TO THAT TERM? "GENTLEMEN," I MEAN. SEEMS TO ME THAT YOU MIGHT.
CAPTAIN DUDLEY DIGGES.
A NOTORIOUS GENTLEMAN, I SUPPOSE YOU COULD SAY.
REALLY? I NEVER HEARD A' YA.
WELL, YOU DIDN'T TRAVEL ALL OVER TOWN JUST TO HEAR MY STORY, DID YOU?
THERE. THAT'S WHAT YOU'RE AFTER.
THE PECKER!
YOU WANT IT. I HAVE IT.
BUT PERHAPS... PERHAPS WE CAN TALK ABOUT THAT SITUATION.

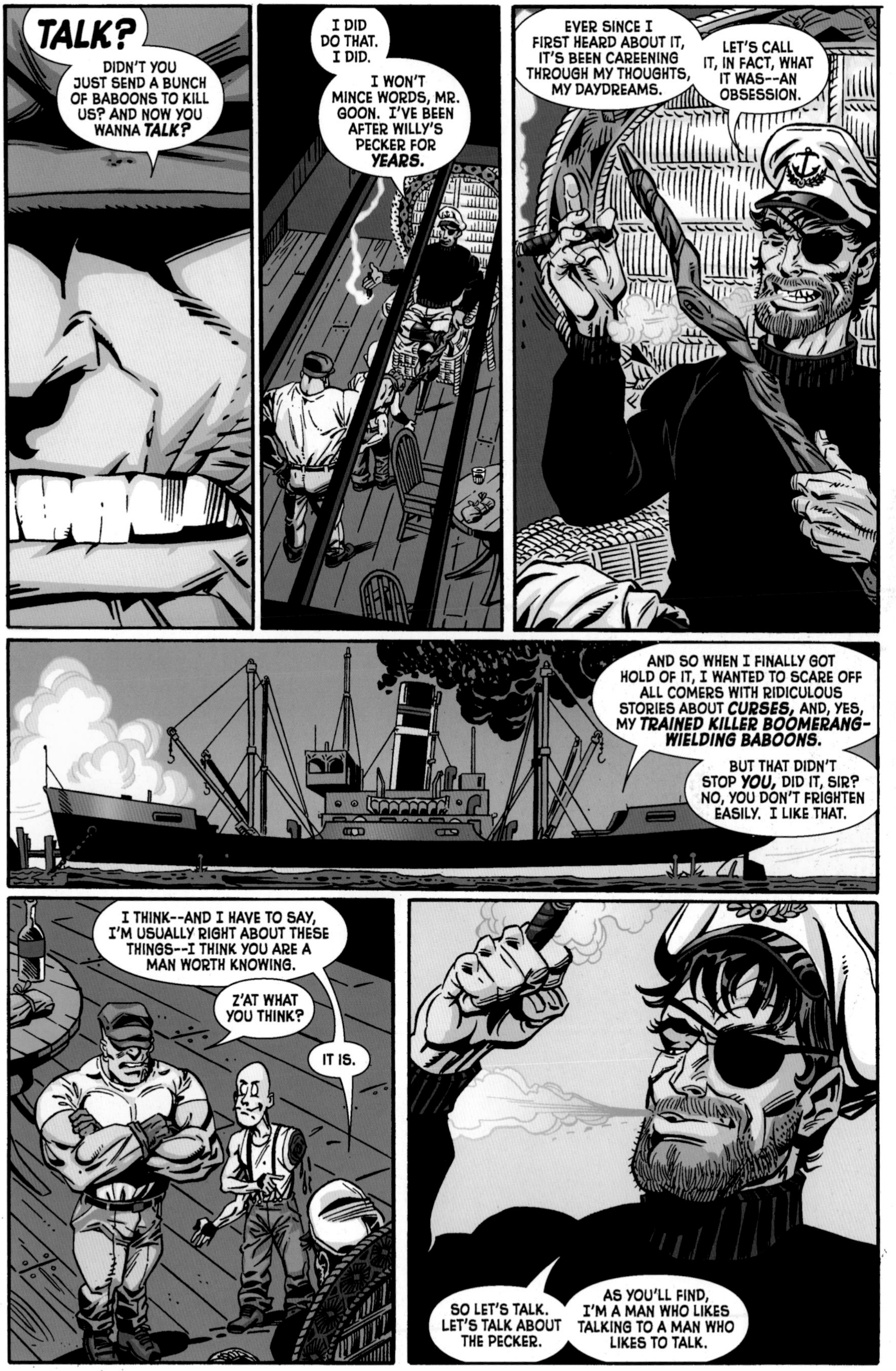
TALK?
DIDN'T YOU JUST SEND A BUNCH OF BABOONS TO KILL US? AND NOW YOU WANNA TALK?
I DID DO THAT. I DID.
I WON'T MINCE WORDS, MR. GOON. I'VE BEEN AFTER WILLY'S PECKER FOR YEARS.
EVER SINCE I FIRST HEARD ABOUT IT, IT'S BEEN CAREENING THROUGH MY THOUGHTS, MY DAYDREAMS.
LET'S CALL IT, IN FACT, WHAT IT WAS--AN OBSESSION.
AND SO WHEN I FINALLY GOT HOLD OF IT, I WANTED TO SCARE OFF ALL COMERS WITH RIDICULOUS STORIES ABOUT CURSES, AND, YES, MY TRAINED KILLER BOOMERANG-WIELDING BABOONS.
BUT THAT DIDN'T STOP YOU, DID IT, SIR? NO, YOU DON'T FRIGHTEN EASILY. I LIKE THAT.
I THINK--AND I HAVE TO SAY, I'M USUALLY RIGHT ABOUT THESE THINGS--I THINK YOU ARE A MAN WORTH KNOWING.
Z'AT WHAT YOU THINK?
IT IS.
AS YOU'LL FIND, I'M A MAN WHO LIKES TALKING TO A MAN WHO LIKES TO TALK.
SO LET'S TALK. LET'S TALK ABOUT THE PECKER.

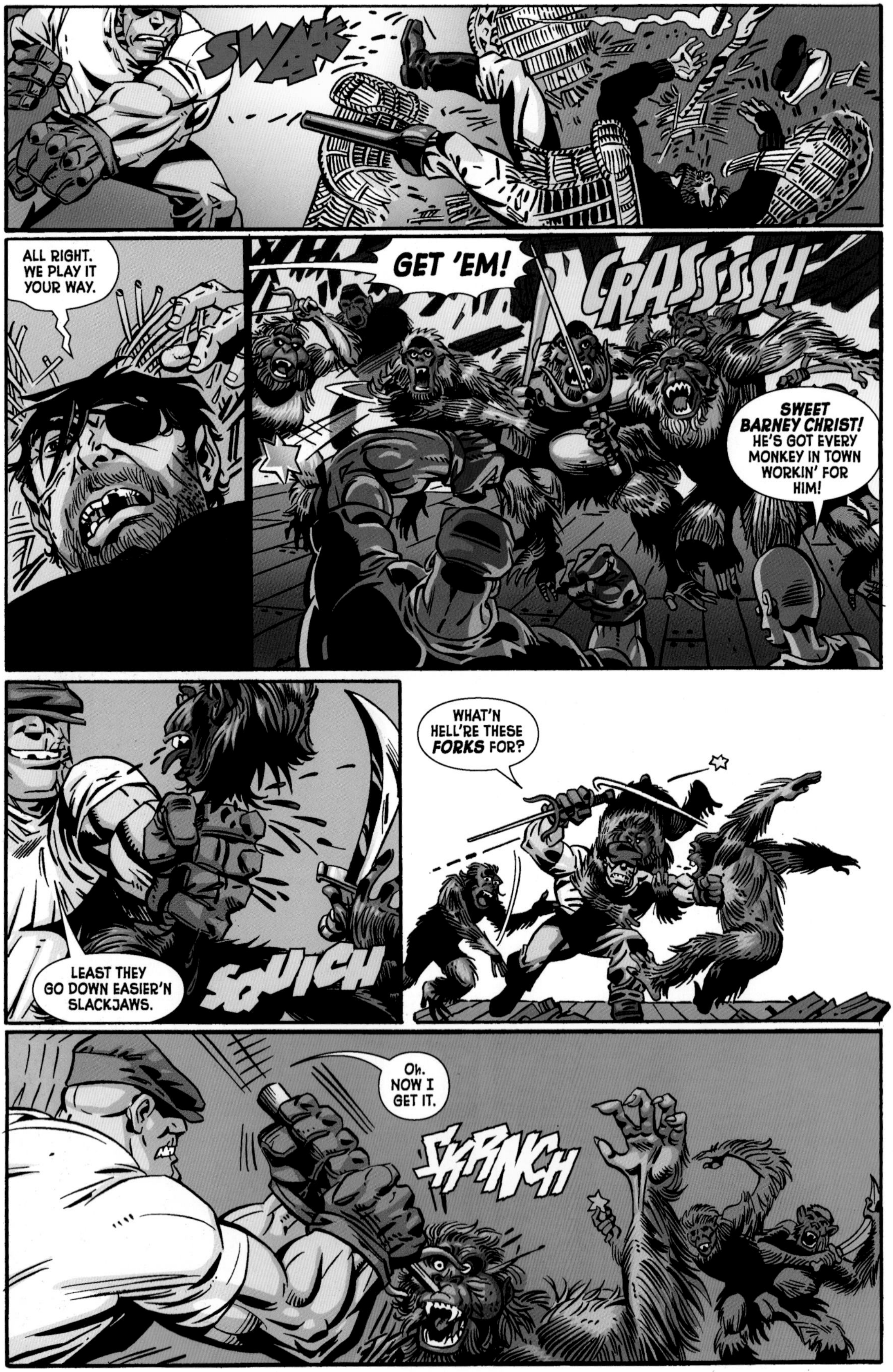

SWAK
ALL RIGHT. WE PLAY IT YOUR WAY.
GET 'EM!
CRASSSSH
SWEET BARNEY CHRIST! HE'S GOT EVERY MONKEY IN TOWN WORKIN' FOR HIM!
LEAST THEY GO DOWN EASIER'N SLACKJAWS.
SQUICH
WHAT'N HELL'RE THESE FORKS FOR?
Oh. NOW I GET IT.
SKRNCH

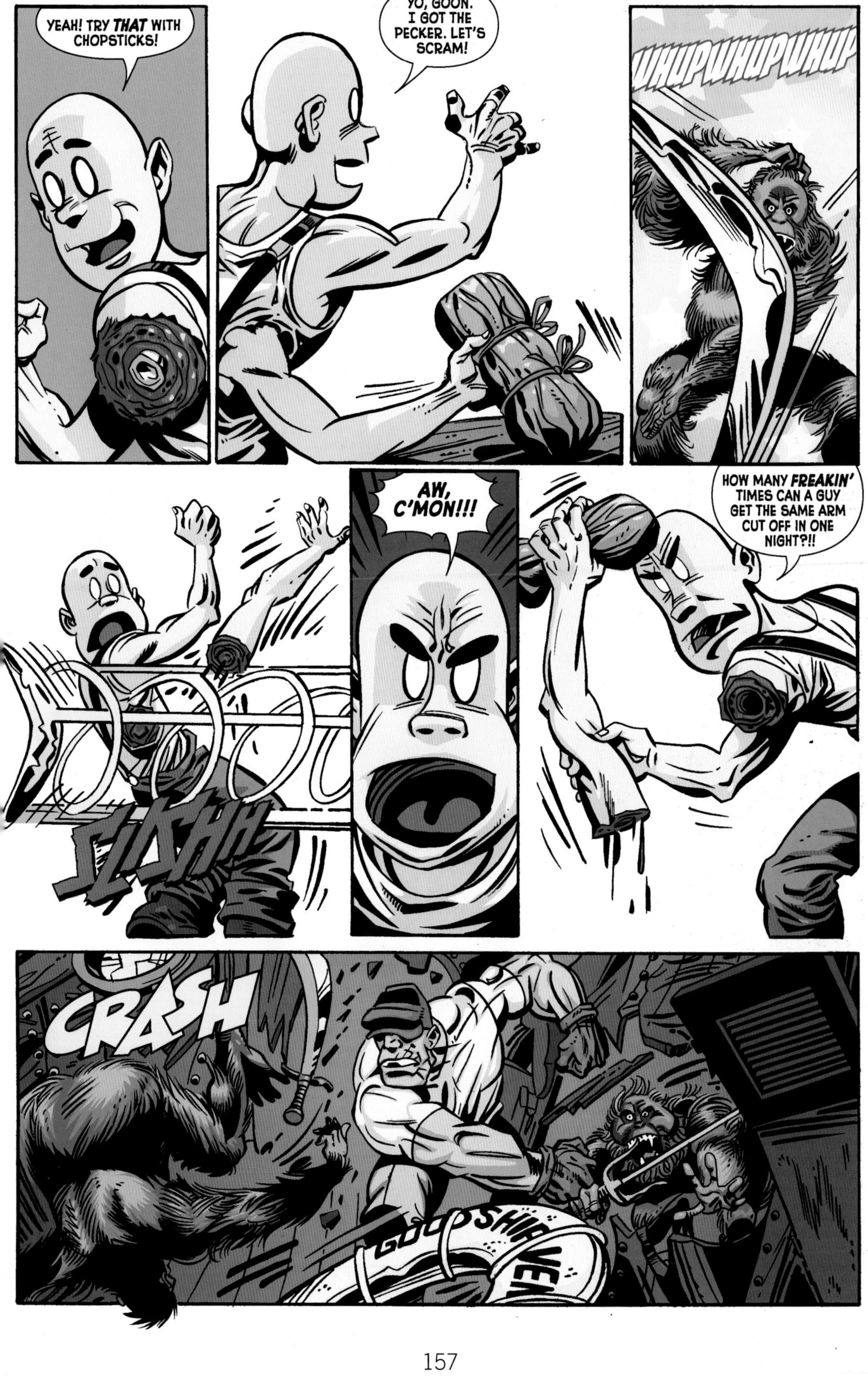
YEAH! TRY THAT WITH CHOPSTICKS!
YO, GOON. I GOT THE PECKER. LET'S SCRAM!
WHUPWHUPWHUP
AW, C'MON!!!
HOW MANY FREAKIN' TIMES CAN A GUY GET THE SAME ARM CUT OFF IN ONE NIGHT?!!
CRASH

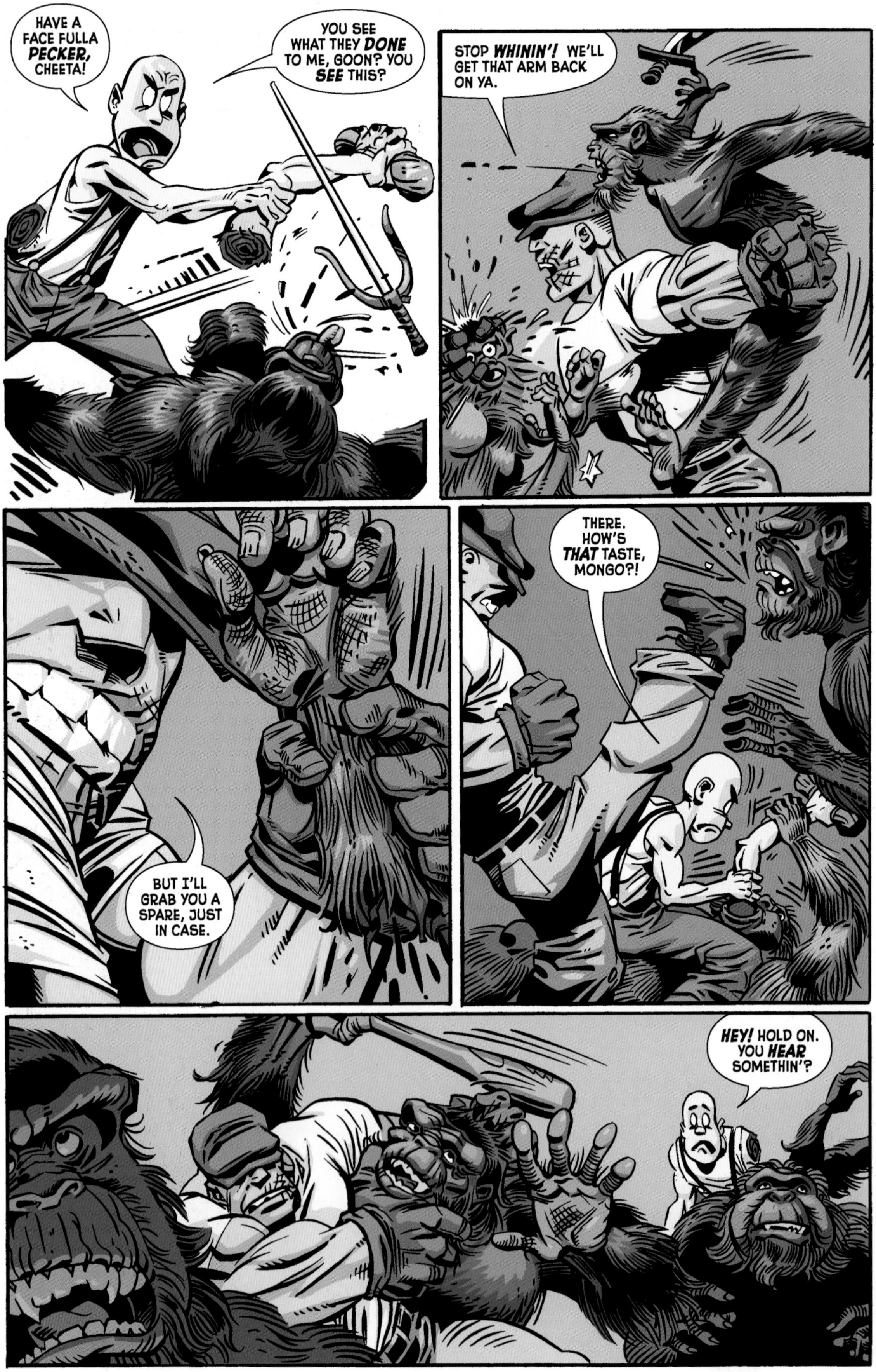

HAVE A FACE FULLA **PECKER,** CHEETA!
YOU SEE WHAT THEY **DONE** TO ME, GOON? YOU **SEE** THIS?
STOP **WHININ'!** WE'LL GET THAT ARM BACK ON YA.
BUT I'LL GRAB YOU A SPARE, JUST IN CASE.
THERE. HOW'S **THAT** TASTE, MONGO?!
HEY! HOLD ON. YOU **HEAR** SOMETHIN'?

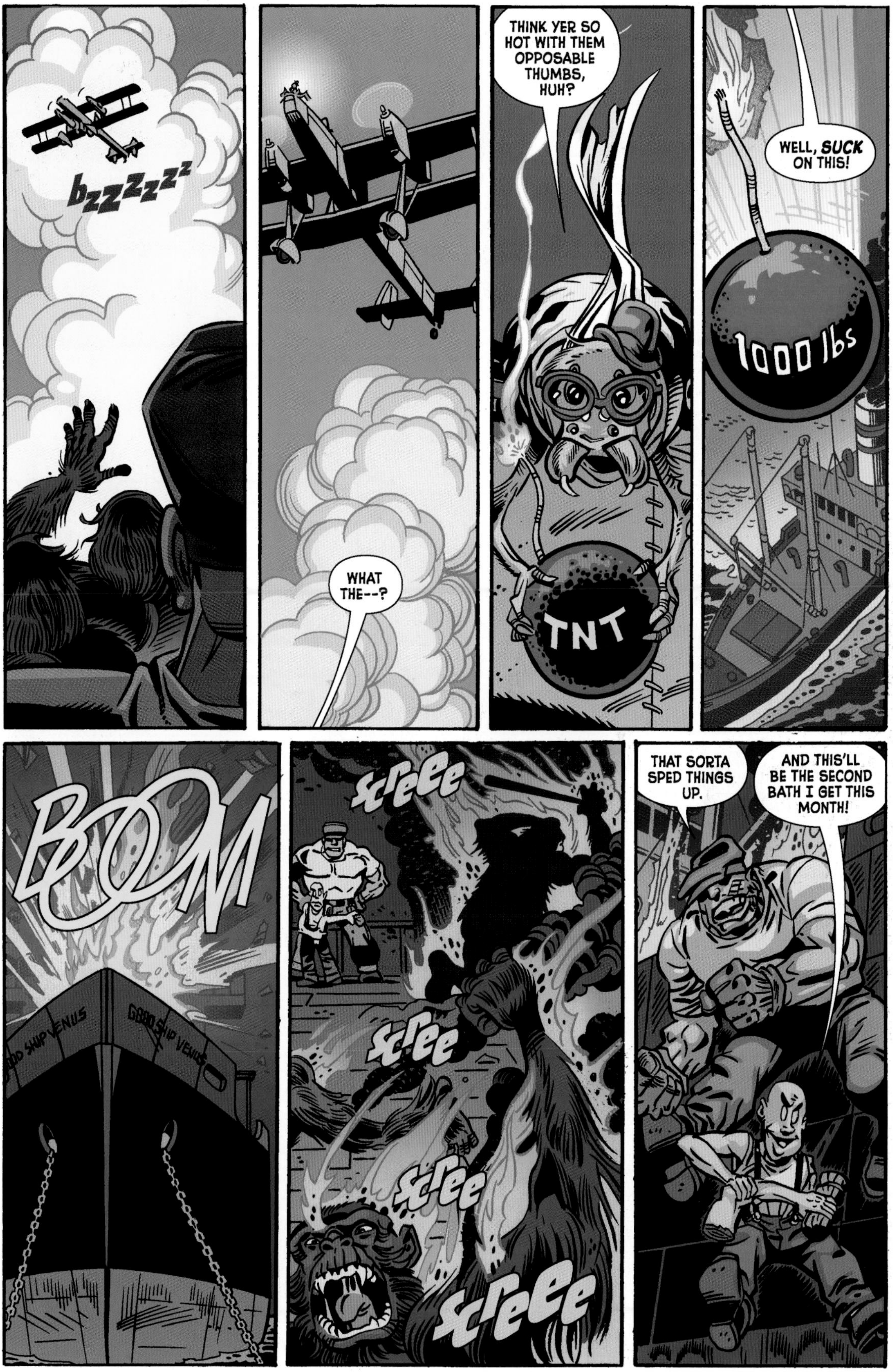
bzzzzzz
WHAT THE--?
THINK YER SO HOT WITH THEM OPPOSABLE THUMBS, HUH?
TNT
WELL, SUCK ON THIS!
1000 lbs
BOOM
GOOD SHIP VENUS
GOOD SHIP VENUS
Screee
Scree
Scree
Screee
THAT SORTA SPED THINGS UP.
AND THIS'LL BE THE SECOND BATH I GET THIS MONTH!

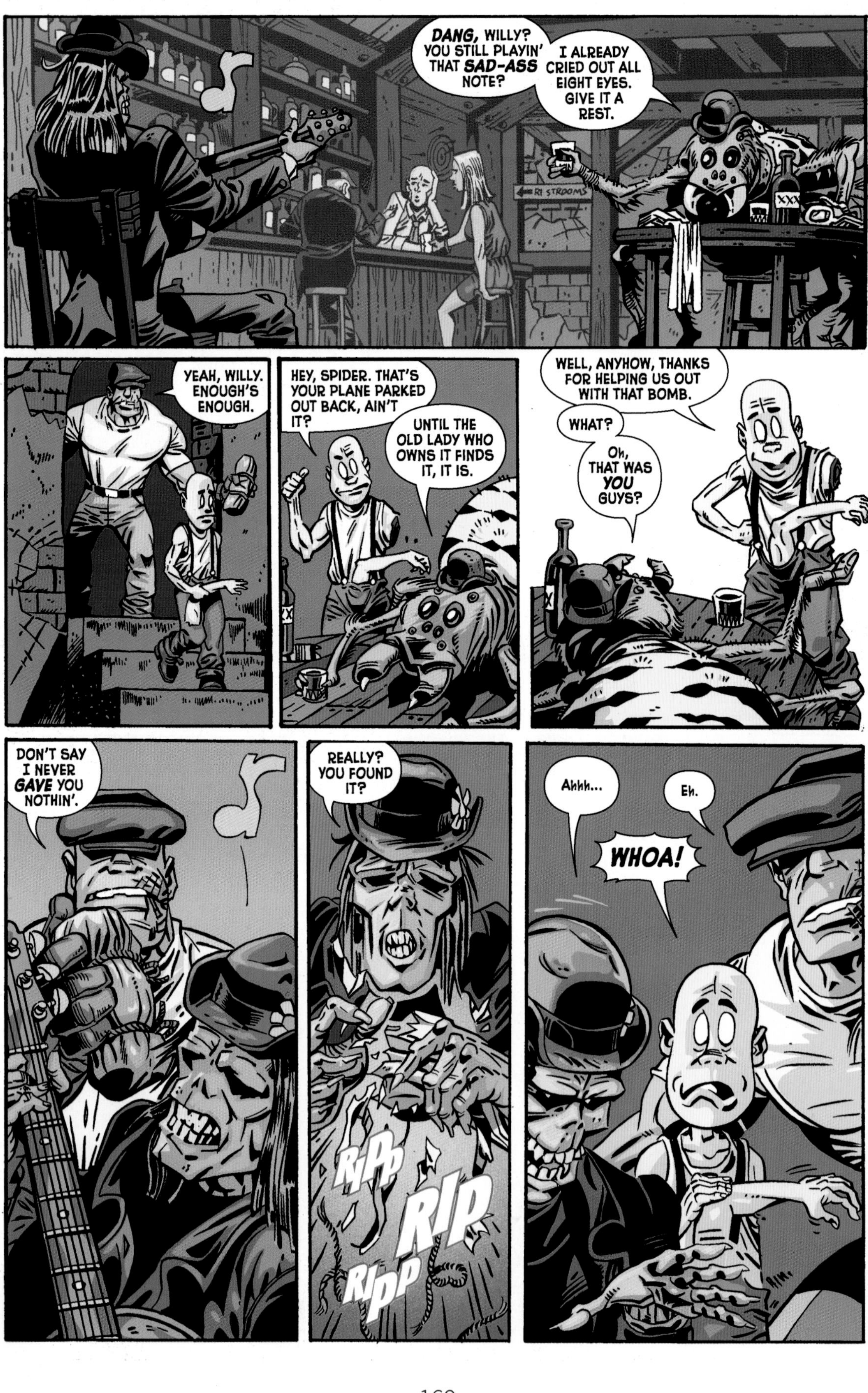

DANG, WILLY? YOU STILL PLAYIN' THAT SAD-ASS NOTE?
I ALREADY CRIED OUT ALL EIGHT EYES. GIVE IT A REST.
RESTROOMS
YEAH, WILLY. ENOUGH'S ENOUGH.
HEY, SPIDER. THAT'S YOUR PLANE PARKED OUT BACK, AIN'T IT?
UNTIL THE OLD LADY WHO OWNS IT FINDS IT, IT IS.
WELL, ANYHOW, THANKS FOR HELPING US OUT WITH THAT BOMB.
WHAT?
Oh, THAT WAS YOU GUYS?
DON'T SAY I NEVER GAVE YOU NOTHIN'.
REALLY? YOU FOUND IT?
RIPP
RIP
RIPP
Ahhh...
Eh.
WHOA!

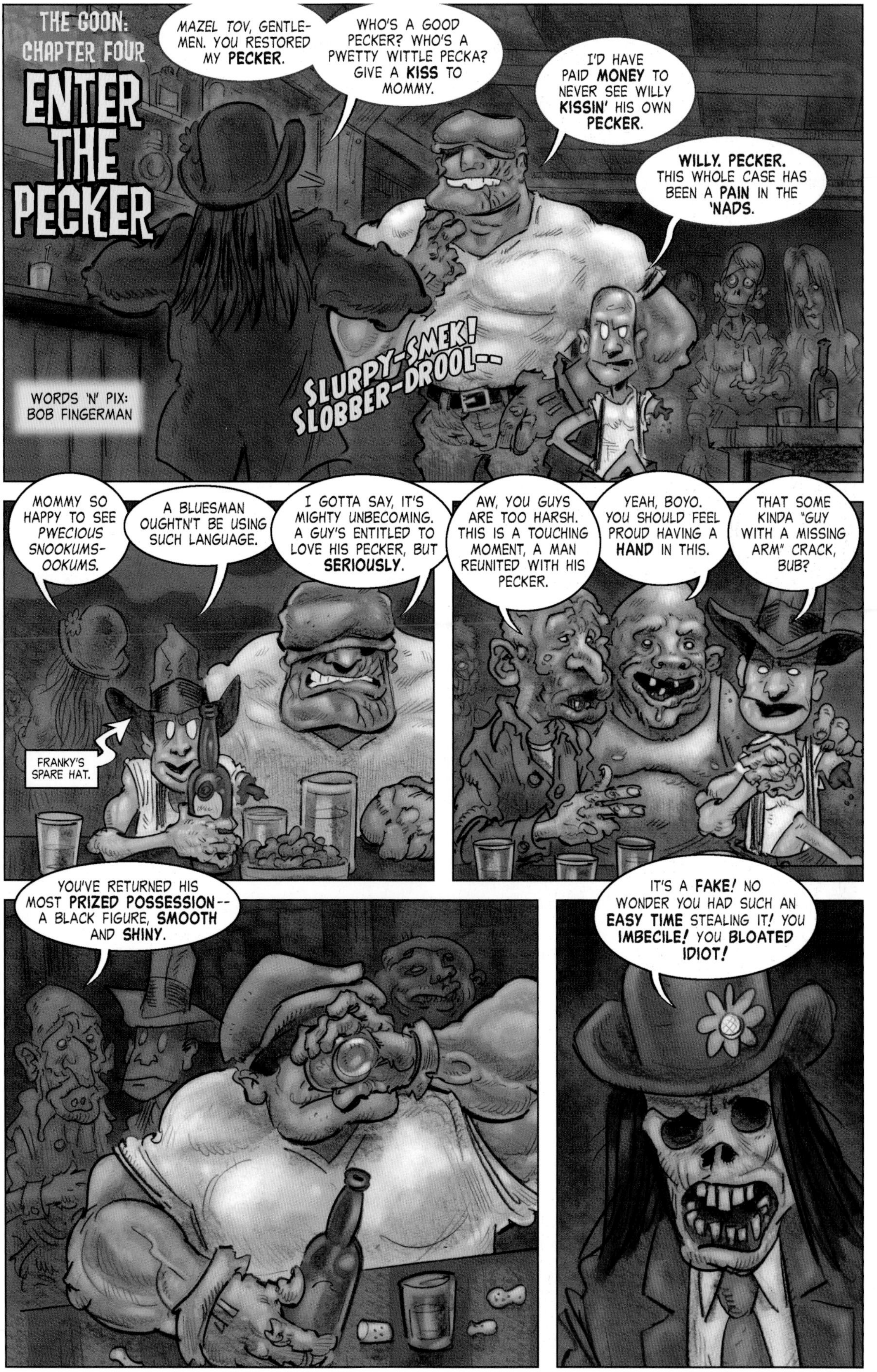
THE GOON: CHAPTER FOUR
ENTER THE PECKER
MAZEL TOV, GENTLE-MEN. YOU RESTORED MY PECKER.
WHO'S A GOOD PECKER? WHO'S A PWETTY WITTLE PECKA? GIVE A KISS TO MOMMY.
I'D HAVE PAID MONEY TO NEVER SEE WILLY KISSIN' HIS OWN PECKER.
WILLY. PECKER. THIS WHOLE CASE HAS BEEN A PAIN IN THE 'NADS.
SLURPY-SMEK! SLOBBER-DROOL--
WORDS 'N' PIX: BOB FINGERMAN
MOMMY SO HAPPY TO SEE PWECIOUS SNOOKUMS-OOKUMS.
A BLUESMAN OUGHTN'T BE USING SUCH LANGUAGE.
I GOTTA SAY, IT'S MIGHTY UNBECOMING. A GUY'S ENTITLED TO LOVE HIS PECKER, BUT SERIOUSLY.
FRANKY'S SPARE HAT.
AW, YOU GUYS ARE TOO HARSH. THIS IS A TOUCHING MOMENT, A MAN REUNITED WITH HIS PECKER.
YEAH, BOYO. YOU SHOULD FEEL PROUD HAVING A HAND IN THIS.
THAT SOME KINDA "GUY WITH A MISSING ARM" CRACK, BUB?
YOU'VE RETURNED HIS MOST PRIZED POSSESSION-- A BLACK FIGURE, SMOOTH AND SHINY.
IT'S A FAKE! NO WONDER YOU HAD SUCH AN EASY TIME STEALING IT! YOU IMBECILE! YOU BLOATED IDIOT!

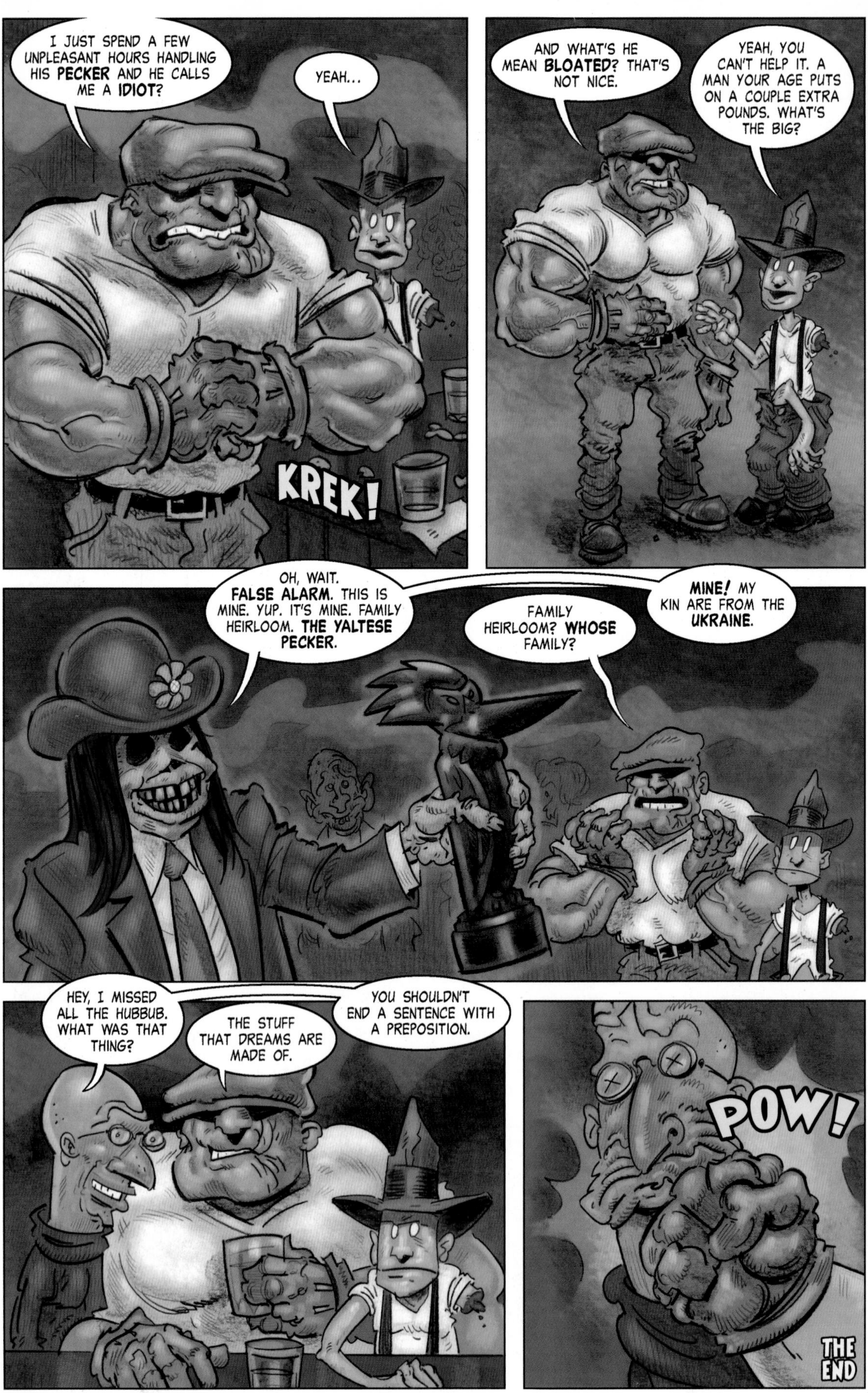
I JUST SPEND A FEW UNPLEASANT HOURS HANDLING HIS **PECKER** AND HE CALLS ME A **IDIOT**?
YEAH...
KREK!
AND WHAT'S HE MEAN **BLOATED**? THAT'S NOT NICE.
YEAH, YOU CAN'T HELP IT. A MAN YOUR AGE PUTS ON A COUPLE EXTRA POUNDS. WHAT'S THE BIG?
OH, WAIT. **FALSE ALARM**. THIS IS MINE. YUP. IT'S MINE. FAMILY HEIRLOOM. **THE YALTESE PECKER**.
FAMILY HEIRLOOM? **WHOSE** FAMILY?
MINE! MY KIN ARE FROM THE **UKRAINE**.
HEY, I MISSED ALL THE HUBBUB. WHAT WAS THAT THING?
THE STUFF THAT DREAMS ARE MADE OF.
YOU SHOULDN'T END A SENTENCE WITH A PREPOSITION.
POW!
THE END

MYSPACE DARK HORSE PRESENTS™

MISCELLANY

Fábio Moon's first completed group shot of what would become the best band in the galaxy—Sugarshock. As you can see, Robot Phil made some transformations from Fábio's earliest conception. Today Robot Phil struts bare chested and noseless.

The next two pages feature Fábio's final look for Sugarshock. This limited-edition *MySpace Dark Horse Presents* poster was handed out at San Diego Comic-Con in 2007, following the announcement and live debut of *MDHP* online. Poster design by Micah Smith.

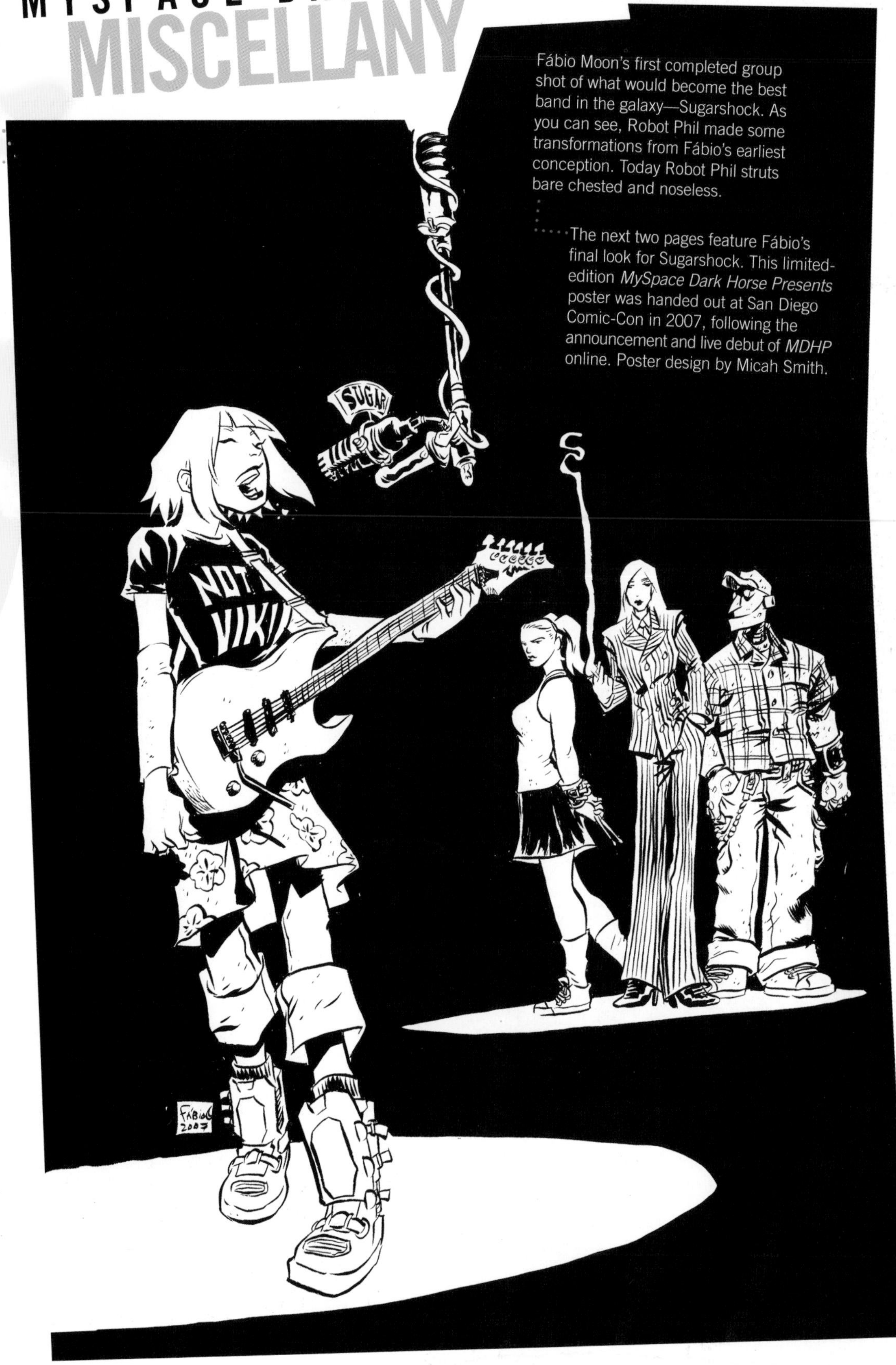
SUGAR
FÁBIO
2007

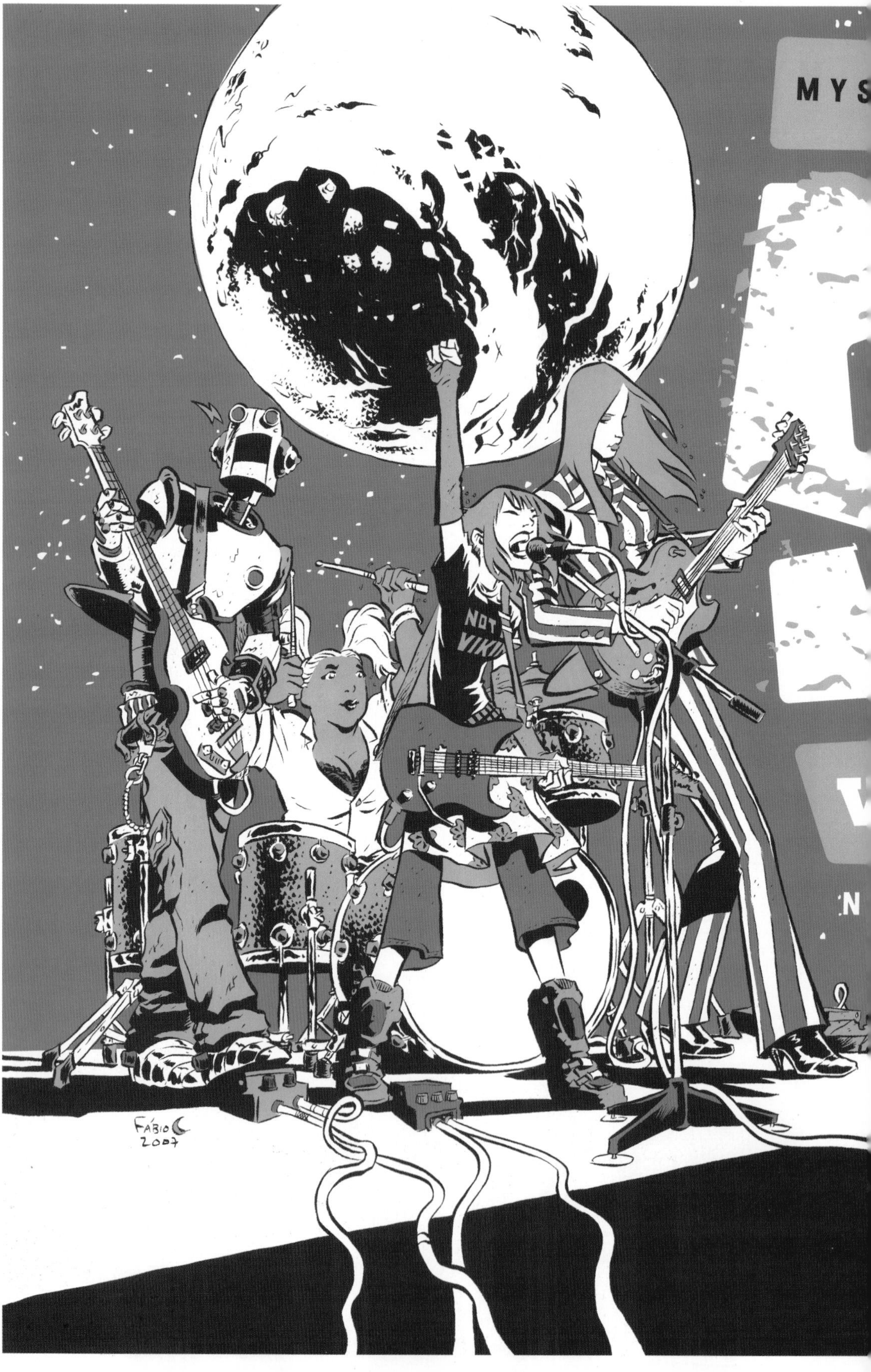
MYS
NOT
VIK
FÁBIO
2007

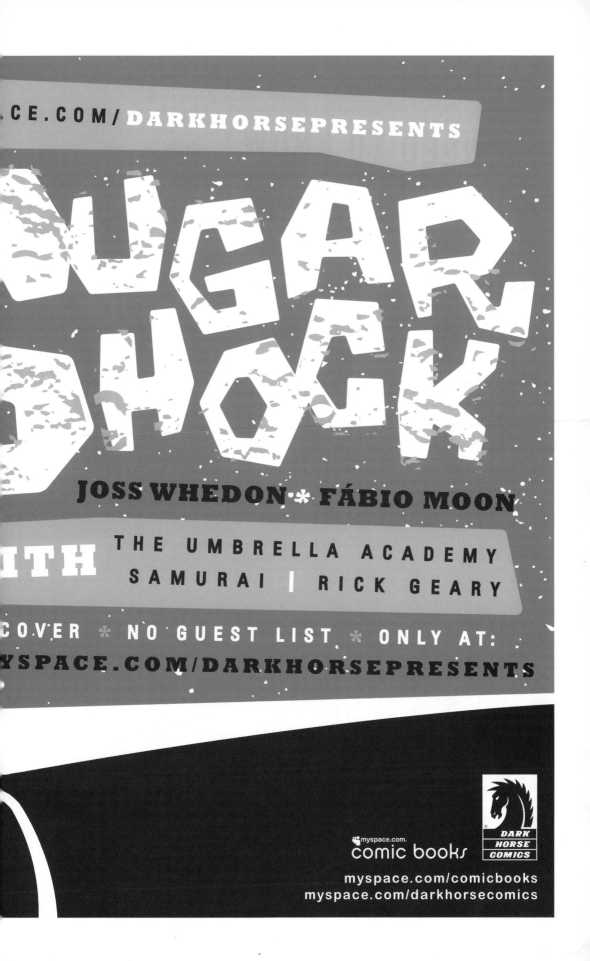

NEED TO KNOW

When we told *Goon* creator Eric Powell that we wanted to dedicate a month of *MDHP* to *The Goon*, he and writer Tom Sniegoski came up with the idea of having the Goon and his pal Frankie embark on the hunt for Willy's missing pecker, as an homage to *The Maltese Falcon*. As you well know by having reached this portion of the book, the story was broken up into four parts and written and drawn by a variety of talent. First on deck were the Fillbäch Brothers. We left it to them to decide how this absurd story would begin, and as soon as we could get their script, we'd pass it on to the next team, and so on. We requested a pitch from the brothers—you know, a quick paragraph or two about the direction they'd take the story.

What we received were eight penciled and lettered pages for the story "The Big Blue Note." It showed up on a Friday, and before we knew it, it was the weekend. So we didn't get back to the Fillbächs immediately, and on Monday (after they'd assumed that we didn't like the first "pitch"), they delivered *another* penciled and lettered eight-page story. We liked them both, and let the Fillbächs choose which strip to finish for the online feature. We've decided to include the unused story here.

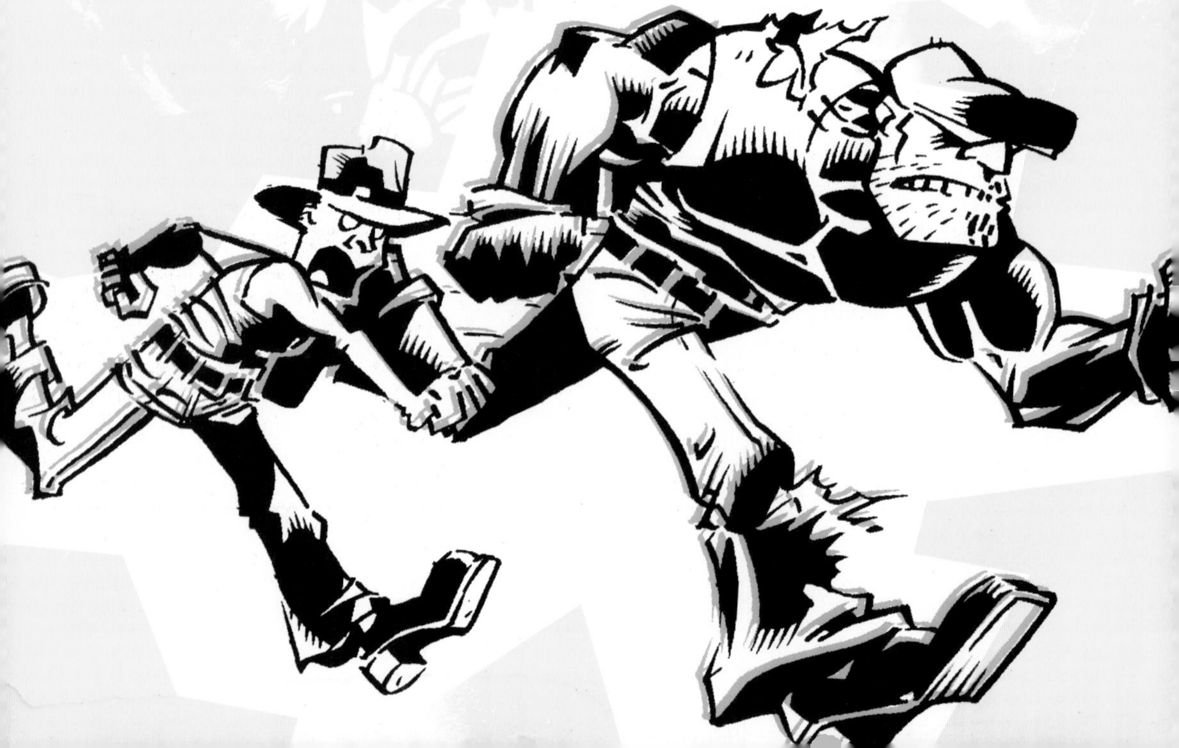

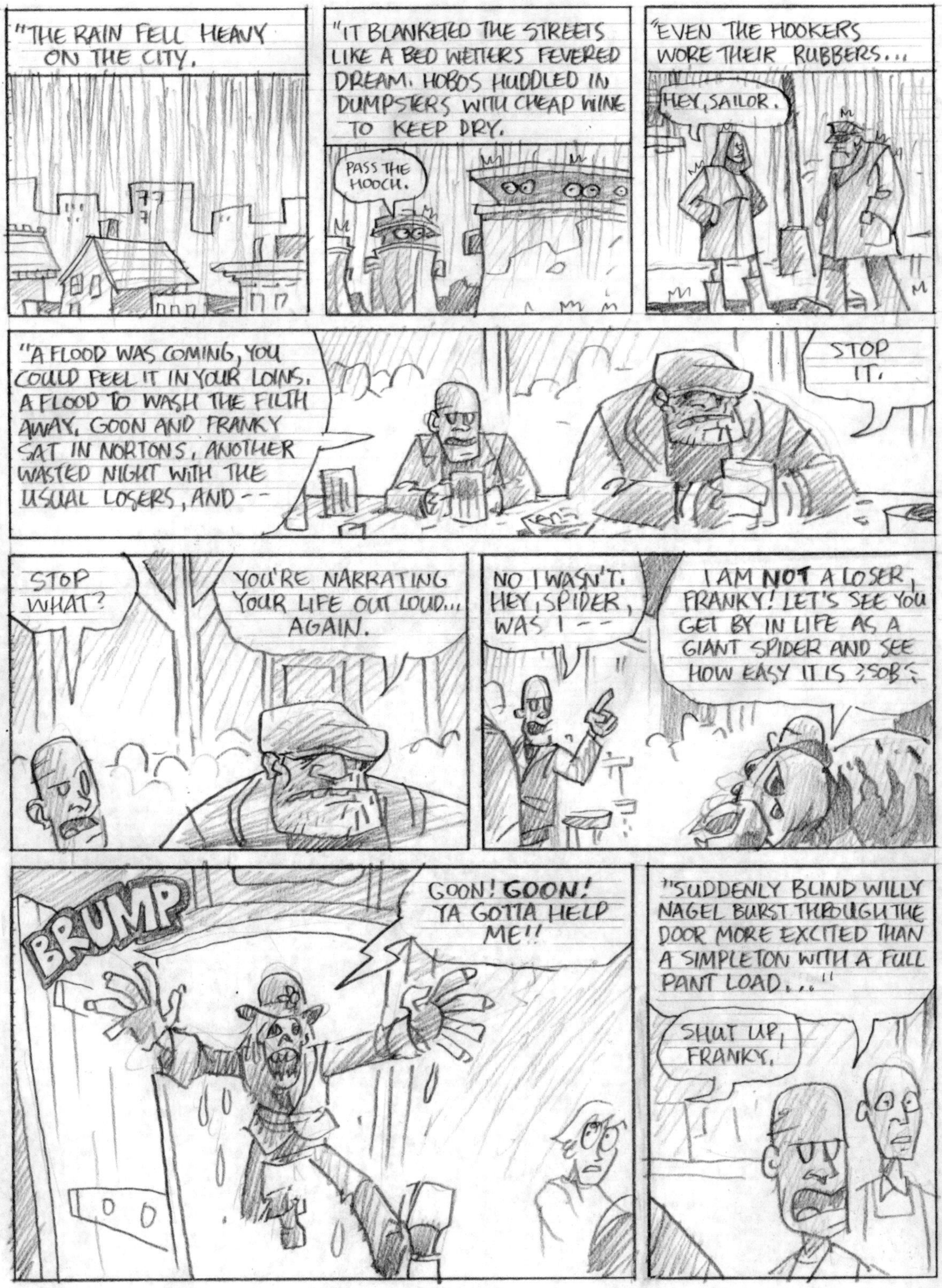
"THE RAIN FELL HEAVY ON THE CITY.
"IT BLANKETED THE STREETS LIKE A BED WETTERS FEVERED DREAM. HOBOS HUDDLED IN DUMPSTERS WITH CHEAP WINE TO KEEP DRY.
PASS THE HOOCH.
"EVEN THE HOOKERS WORE THEIR RUBBERS...
HEY, SAILOR.
"A FLOOD WAS COMING, YOU COULD FEEL IT IN YOUR LOINS. A FLOOD TO WASH THE FILTH AWAY. GOON AND FRANKY SAT IN NORTONS, ANOTHER WASTED NIGHT WITH THE USUAL LOSERS, AND--
STOP IT.
STOP WHAT?
YOU'RE NARRATING YOUR LIFE OUT LOUD... AGAIN.
NO I WASN'T. HEY, SPIDER, WAS I--
I AM NOT A LOSER, FRANKY! LET'S SEE YOU GET BY IN LIFE AS A GIANT SPIDER AND SEE HOW EASY IT IS ≷SOB≶
BRUMP
GOON! GOON! YA GOTTA HELP ME!!
"SUDDENLY BLIND WILLY NAGEL BURST THROUGH THE DOOR MORE EXCITED THAN A SIMPLETON WITH A FULL PANT LOAD..."
SHUT UP, FRANKY.

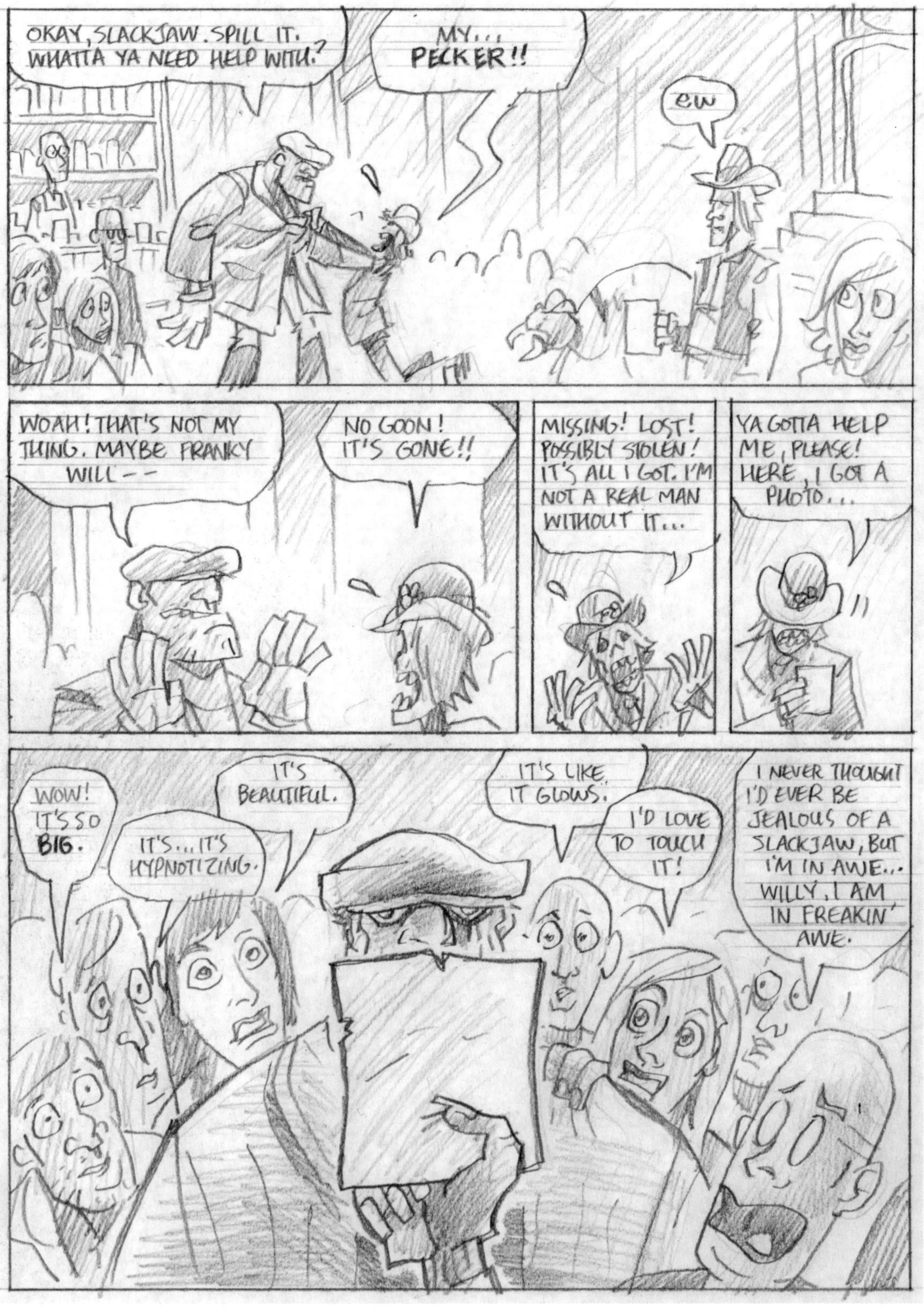
OKAY, SLACKJAW. SPILL IT. WHATTA YA NEED HELP WITH?
MY... PECKER!!
EW
WOAH! THAT'S NOT MY THING. MAYBE FRANKY WILL--
NO GOON! IT'S GONE!!
MISSING! LOST! POSSIBLY STOLEN! IT'S ALL I GOT. I'M NOT A REAL MAN WITHOUT IT...
YA GOTTA HELP ME, PLEASE! HERE, I GOT A PHOTO...
WOW! IT'S SO BIG.
IT'S... IT'S HYPNOTIZING.
IT'S BEAUTIFUL.
IT'S LIKE IT GLOWS.
I'D LOVE TO TOUCH IT!
I NEVER THOUGHT I'D EVER BE JEALOUS OF A SLACKJAW, BUT I'M IN AWE... WILLY, I AM IN FREAKIN' AWE.

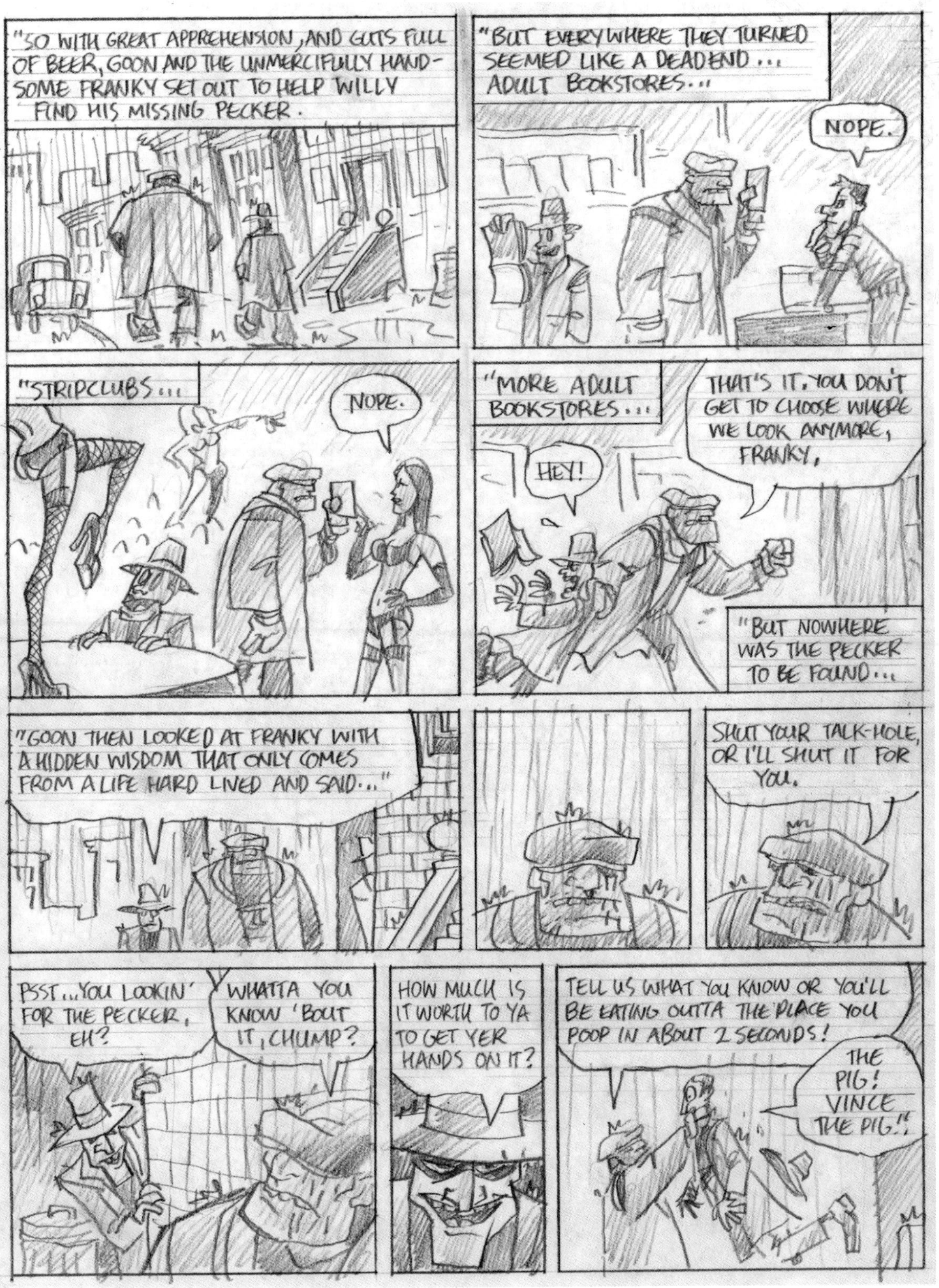
"SO WITH GREAT APPREHENSION, AND GUTS FULL OF BEER, GOON AND THE UNMERCIFULLY HANDSOME FRANKY SET OUT TO HELP WILLY FIND HIS MISSING PECKER.
"BUT EVERYWHERE THEY TURNED SEEMED LIKE A DEADEND... ADULT BOOKSTORES...
NOPE.
"STRIPCLUBS...
NOPE.
"MORE ADULT BOOKSTORES...
THAT'S IT. YOU DON'T GET TO CHOOSE WHERE WE LOOK ANYMORE, FRANKY.
HEY!
"BUT NOWHERE WAS THE PECKER TO BE FOUND...
"GOON THEN LOOKED AT FRANKY WITH A HIDDEN WISDOM THAT ONLY COMES FROM A LIFE HARD LIVED AND SAID..."
SHUT YOUR TALK-HOLE, OR I'LL SHUT IT FOR YOU.
PSST... YOU LOOKIN' FOR THE PECKER, EH?
WHATTA YOU KNOW 'BOUT IT, CHUMP?
HOW MUCH IS IT WORTH TO YA TO GET YER HANDS ON IT?
TELL US WHAT YOU KNOW OR YOU'LL BE EATING OUTTA THE PLACE YOU POOP IN ABOUT 2 SECONDS!
THE PIG! VINCE THE PIG!!

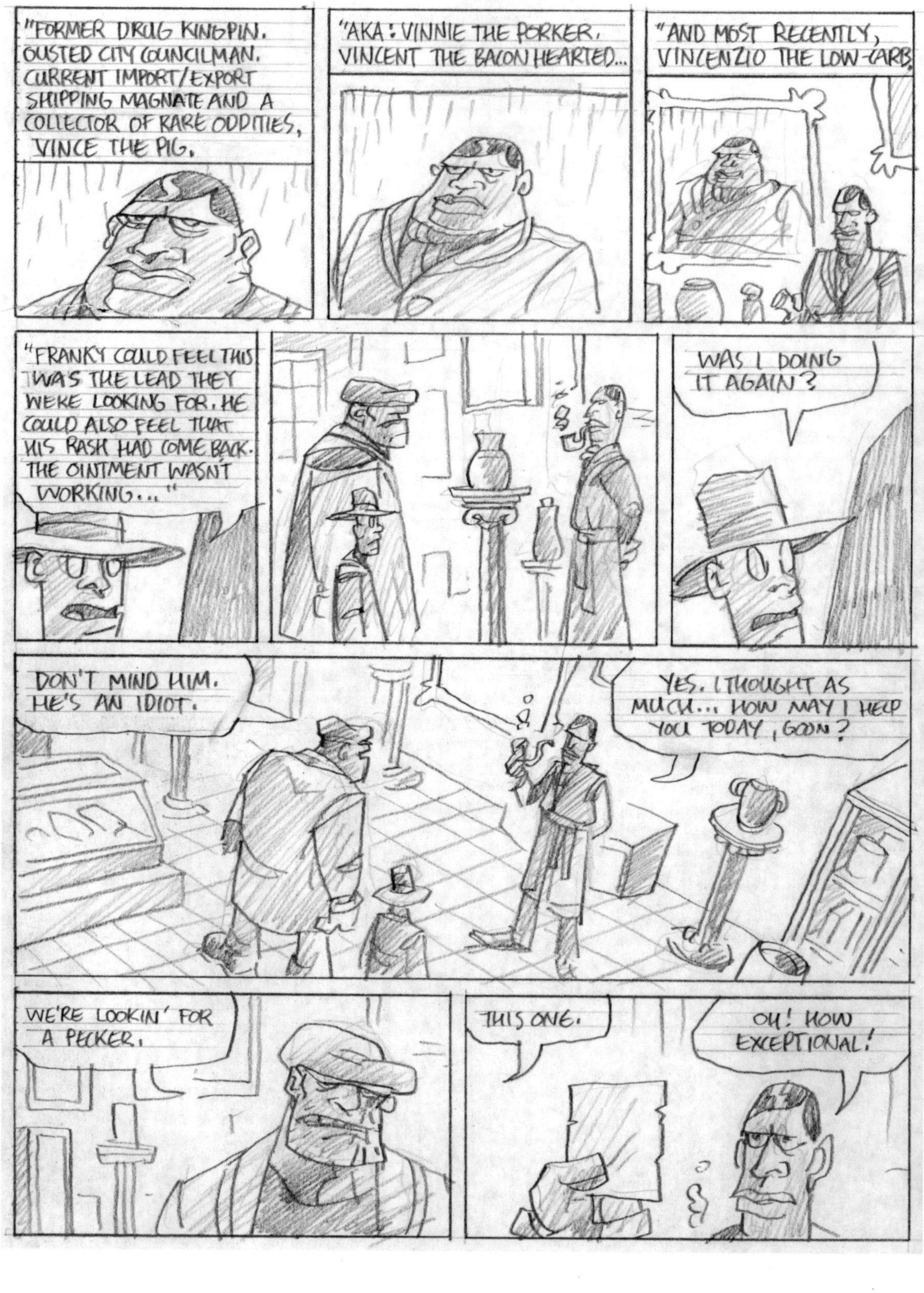
"FORMER DRUG KINGPIN. OUSTED CITY COUNCILMAN. CURRENT IMPORT/EXPORT SHIPPING MAGNATE AND A COLLECTOR OF RARE ODDITIES, VINCE THE PIG.
"AKA: VINNIE THE PORKER, VINCENT THE BACON HEARTED...
"AND MOST RECENTLY, VINCENZIO THE LOW-CARB.
"FRANKY COULD FEEL THIS WAS THE LEAD THEY WERE LOOKING FOR. HE COULD ALSO FEEL THAT HIS RASH HAD COME BACK. THE OINTMENT WASN'T WORKING..."
WAS I DOING IT AGAIN?
DON'T MIND HIM. HE'S AN IDIOT.
YES. I THOUGHT AS MUCH... HOW MAY I HELP YOU TODAY, GOON?
WE'RE LOOKIN' FOR A PECKER.
THIS ONE.
OH! HOW EXCEPTIONAL!

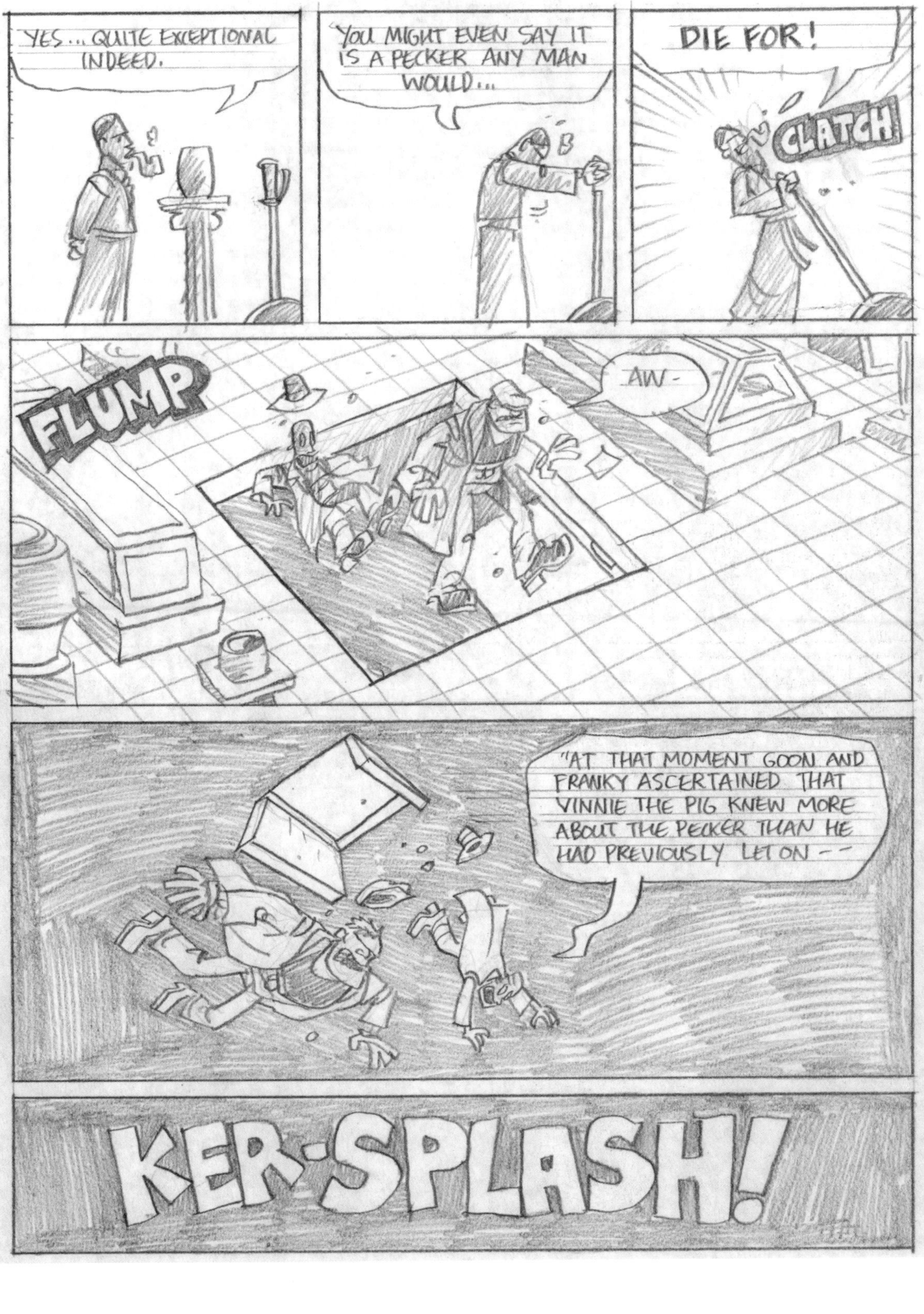
YES... QUITE EXCEPTIONAL INDEED.
YOU MIGHT EVEN SAY IT IS A PECKER ANY MAN WOULD...
DIE FOR!
CLATCH
FLUMP
AW-
"AT THAT MOMENT GOON AND FRANKY ASCERTAINED THAT VINNIE THE PIG KNEW MORE ABOUT THE PECKER THAN HE HAD PREVIOUSLY LET ON--
KER-SPLASH!

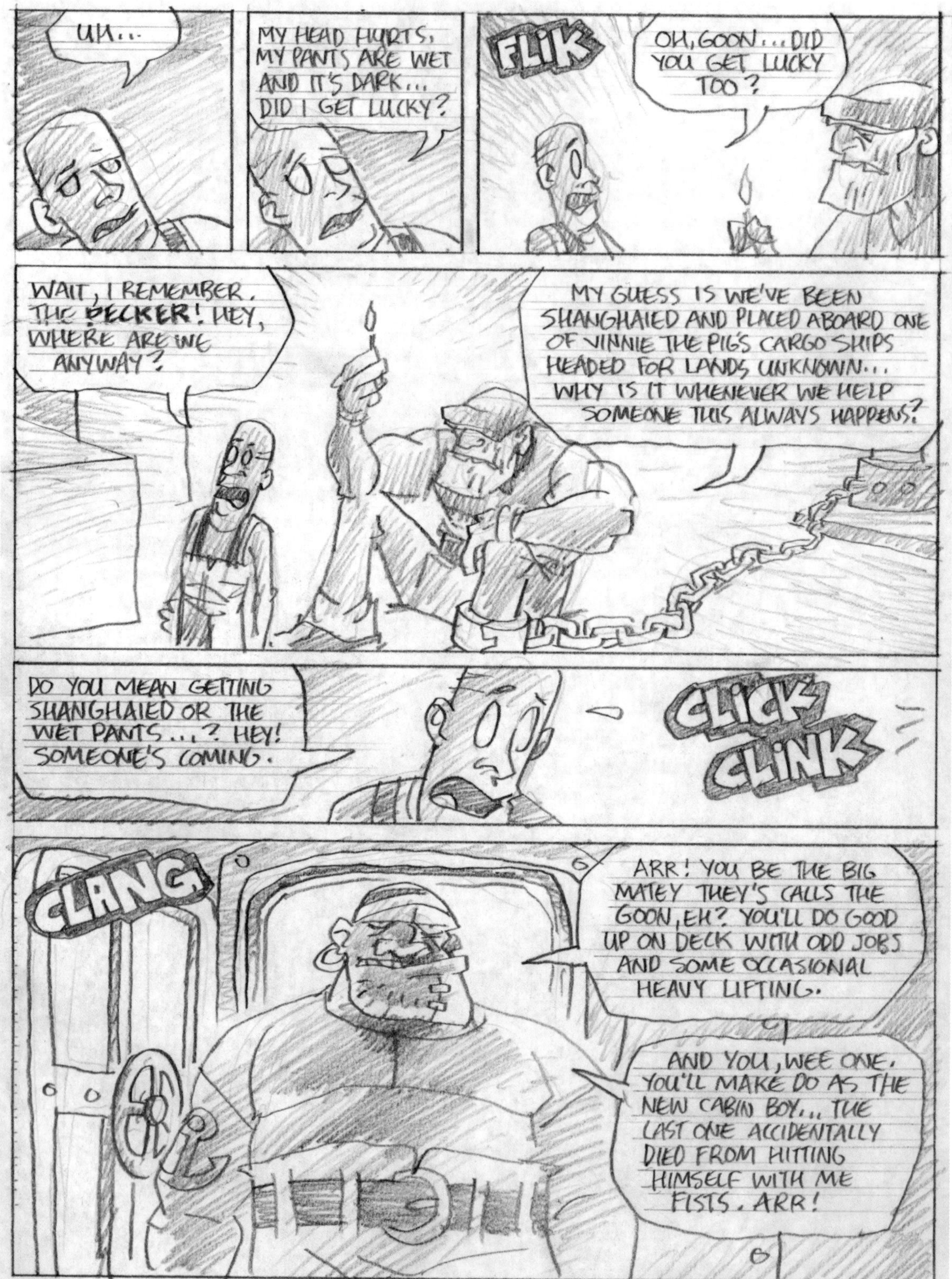
UH...
MY HEAD HURTS, MY PANTS ARE WET AND IT'S DARK... DID I GET LUCKY?
FLIK
OH, GOON... DID YOU GET LUCKY TOO?
WAIT, I REMEMBER. THE DECKER! HEY, WHERE ARE WE ANYWAY?
MY GUESS IS WE'VE BEEN SHANGHAIED AND PLACED ABOARD ONE OF VINNIE THE PIG'S CARGO SHIPS HEADED FOR LANDS UNKNOWN... WHY IS IT WHENEVER WE HELP SOMEONE THIS ALWAYS HAPPENS?
DO YOU MEAN GETTING SHANGHAIED OR THE WET PANTS...? HEY! SOMEONE'S COMING.
CLICK
CLINK
CLANG
ARR! YOU BE THE BIG MATEY THEY'S CALLS THE GOON, EH? YOU'LL DO GOOD UP ON DECK WITH ODD JOBS AND SOME OCCASIONAL HEAVY LIFTING.
AND YOU, WEE ONE. YOU'LL MAKE DO AS THE NEW CABIN BOY... THE LAST ONE ACCIDENTALLY DIED FROM HITTING HIMSELF WITH ME FISTS. ARR!

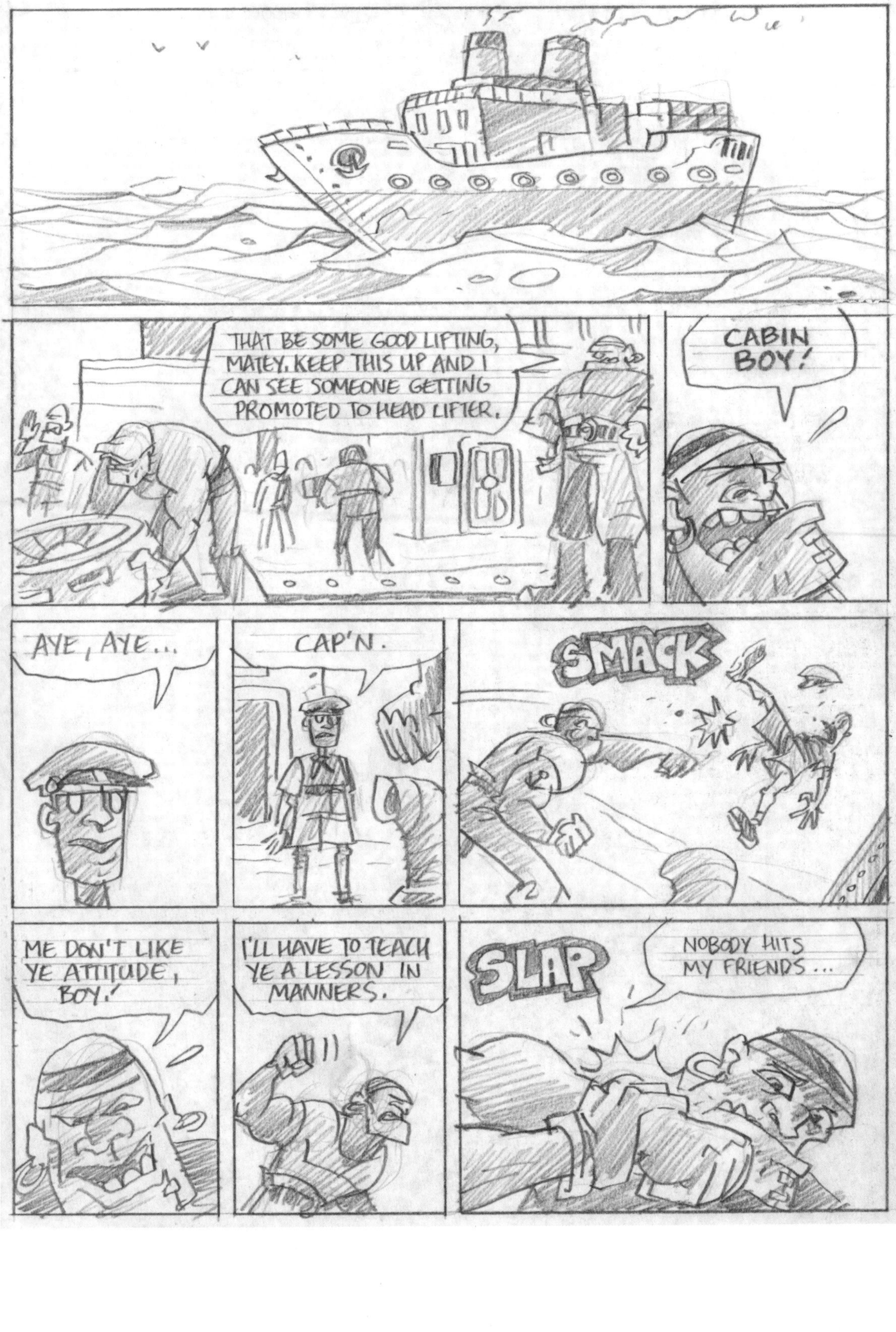
THAT BE SOME GOOD LIFTING, MATEY. KEEP THIS UP AND I CAN SEE SOMEONE GETTING PROMOTED TO HEAD LIFTER.
CABIN BOY!
AYE, AYE...
CAP'N.
SMACK
ME DON'T LIKE YE ATTITUDE, BOY!
I'LL HAVE TO TEACH YE A LESSON IN MANNERS.
SLAP
NOBODY HITS MY FRIENDS...

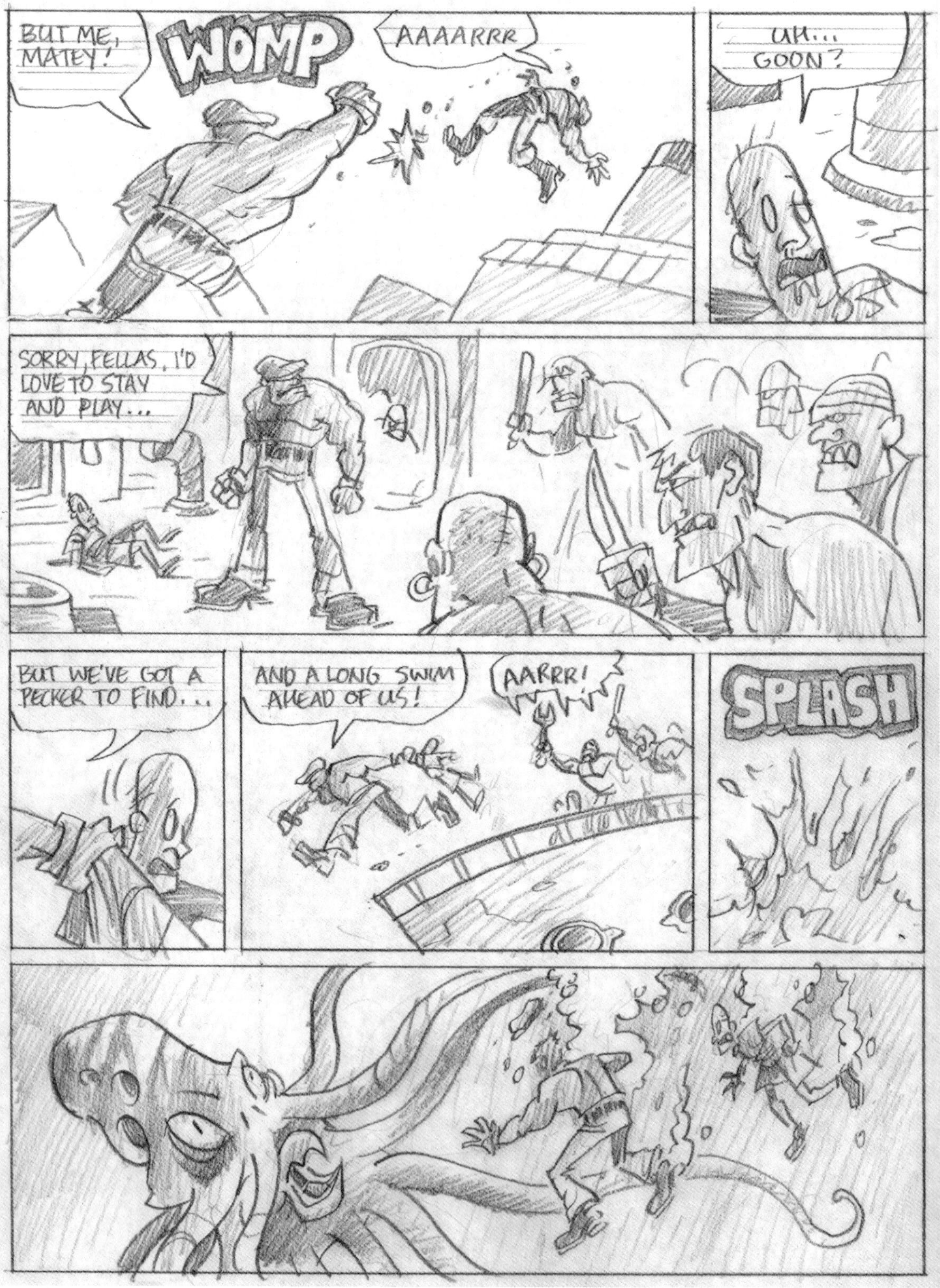
BUT ME, MATEY!
WOMP
AAAARRR
UH... GOON?
SORRY, FELLAS, I'D LOVE TO STAY AND PLAY...
BUT WE'VE GOT A PECKER TO FIND...
AND A LONG SWIM AHEAD OF US!
AARRR!
SPLASH

RECOMMENDED READING . . .

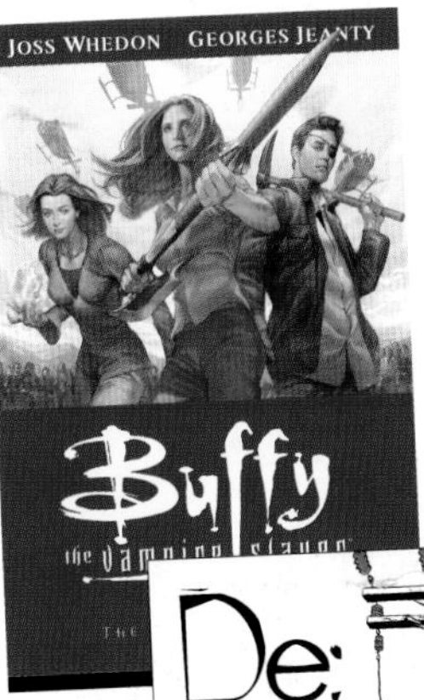
JOSS WHEDON GEORGES JEANTY
Buffy
the vampire slayer

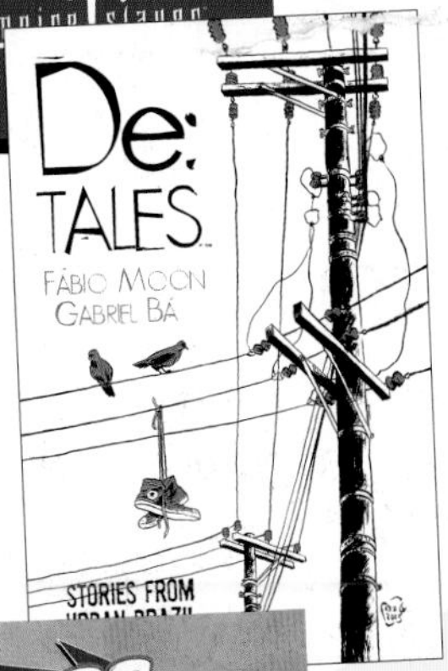
De:
TALES
FÁBIO MOON
GABRIEL BÁ
STORIES FROM

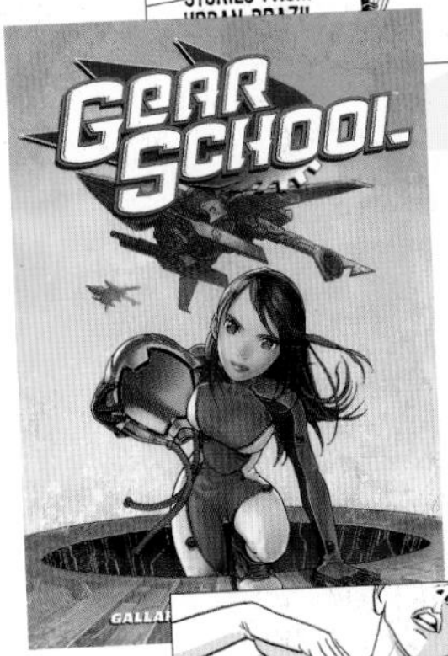
GEAR SCHOOL

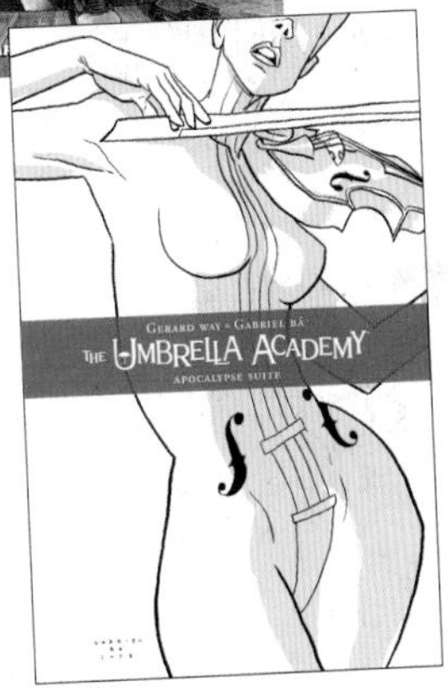
THE UMBRELLA ACADEMY

BUFFY SEASON EIGHT VOLUME ONE: THE LONG WAY HOME
Joss Whedon and Georges Jeanty
978-1-59307-822-5
$15.95

DE:TALES
Fábio Moon and Gabriel Bá
978-1-59307-485-2
$14.95

SOCK MONKEY: THE INCHES INCIDENT
Tony Millionaire
978-1-59307-842-3
$9.95

CRAVAN
Mike Richardson and Rick Geary
978-1-59307-291-9
$14.95

THE UMBRELLA ACADEMY VOLUME ONE: APOCALYPSE SUITE
Gerard Way and Gabriel Bá
978-1-59307-978-9
$17.95

APOCALYPSE NERD
Peter Bagge
978-1-59307-902-4
$13.95

GEAR SCHOOL
Adam Gallardo and Núria Peris
978-1-59307-854-6
$7.95

SAMURAI VOLUME ONE: HEAVEN AND EARTH
Ron Marz and Luke Ross
978-1-59307-388-6
$14.95

EMPOWERED VOLUME ONE
Adam Warren
978-1-59307-672-6
$14.95

AVAILABLE AT YOUR LOCAL COMICS SHOP OR BOOKSTORE
To find a comics shop in your area, call 1-888-266-4226.
For more information or to order direct visit darkhorse.com or call
1-800-862-0052 • Mon.–Sat. 9 A.M. to 5 P.M. Pacific Time. *Prices and availability subject to change without notice

CHICKENHARE VOLUME ONE: THE HOUSE OF KLAUS
Chris Grine
978-1-59307-574-3
$9.95

CRIMINAL MACABRE: A CAL MCDONALD MYSTERY
Steve Niles and Ben Templesmith
978-1-56971-935-0
$14.95

CONAN VOLUME ONE:
THE FROST-GIANT'S DAUGHTER AND OTHER STORIES
Kurt Busiek and Cary Nord
978-1-59307-301-5
$15.95

STAR WARS: CLONE WARS ADVENTURES VOLUME ONE
Haden Blackman, Ben Caldwell, and the Fillbäch Brothers
978-1-59307-243-8
$6.95

B.P.R.D. VOLUME EIGHT: KILLING GROUND
Mike Mignola, John Arcudi, Guy Davis, and Dave Stewart
978-1-59307-956-7
$17.95

FEAR AGENT VOLUME ONE: RE-IGNITION
Rick Remender and Tony Moore
978-1-59307-764-8
$14.95

MAXWELL STRANGEWELL
The Fillbäch Brothers
978-1-59307-794-5
$19.95

RECESS PIECES
Bob Fingerman
978-1-59307-450-0
$14.95

THE GOON: CHINATOWN
Eric Powell
978-1-59307-833-1
$19.95

YA ZONE

Dobbs Ferry Public Library
55 Main St.
Dobbs Ferry, NY 10522

AVAILABLE AT YOUR LOCAL COMICS SHOP OR BOOKSTORE
To find a comics shop in your area, call 1-888-266-4226.
For more information or to order direct visit darkhorse.com or call
1-800-862-0052 • Mon.–Sat. 9 A.M. to 5 P.M. Pacific Time. *Prices and availability subject to change without notice